THE ROMAN WORLD
IN THE TIME OF JESUS

OTHER BOOKS BY MERRILL C. TENNEY:

John: The Gospel of Belief
Galatians: The Charter of Christian Liberty
Interpreting Revelation
New Testament Times

NEW TESTAMENT SURVEY

Revised

by

Merrill C. Tenney

Formerly Dean of the Graduate School, Wheaton College

Revised by

Walter M. Dunnett

Professor of Bible, Northwestern College

WM. B. EERDMANS PUBLISHING COMPANY
INTER-VARSITY PRESS

NEW TESTAMENT SURVEY, *Revised*
© Copyright 1985 Wm. B. Eerdmans Publishing Company
a revision of
NEW TESTAMENT SURVEY
© Copyright 1961 Wm. B. Eerdmans Publishing Co.
which is a revision of
THE NEW TESTAMENT
An *Historical and Analytic Survey*
Copyright, 1953, by Wm. B. Eerdmans Publishing Company

Inter-Varsity Press
38 De Montfort Street, Leicester LE1 7GP, England
Wm. B. Eerdmans Publishing Company
255 Jefferson S.E., Grand Rapids, MI 49503

Printed in the United States of America

Library of Congress Cataloging-in-Publication Data
Tenney, Merrill Chapin, 1904-
New Testament survey, revised.

Rev. ed. of: New Testament survey. 1961.
Bibliography: p.
Includes indexes.
1. Bible. N.T. — Introductions. I. Dunnett,
Walter M. II. Tenney, Merrill Chapin, 1904-
New Testament survey. III. Title.
BS23302.2.T45   1985   225.6'1   85-16030

ISBN 0-8028-3611-9

IVP edition 0-85111-635-8

Inter-Varsity Press is the publishing division of the Universities and Colleges Christian Fellowship (formerly the Inter-Varsity Fellowship), a student movement linking Christian Unions in universities and colleges throughout the United Kingdom and the Republic of Ireland, and a member movement of the International Fellowship of Evangelical Students. For information about local and national activities write to UCCF, 38 De Montfort Street, Leicester LE1 7GP.

To
Beth and Wallace Paddon
whose fraternal interest has been a constant delight

CONTENTS

PART II:

THE GOSPELS: THE RECORDS OF THE LIFE OF CHRIST

The Period of Inception: 6 B.C. to A.D. 30

PART III:

THE RECORDS OF THE EARLY CHURCH

The Period of Expansion: A.D. 30 to 60

PART IV:

THE PROBLEMS OF THE EARLY CHURCH

The Period of Consolidation: A.D. 60 to 100

PREFACE TO THE FIRST EDITION

AMONG evangelical believers there has always been the profound conviction that a broad knowledge of the Bible is an integral part of basic education. The material which is learned in the home or in the Sunday school needs to be reinforced by academic study if the young believer is to become settled in his faith. To accomplish this end, many Christian educational institutions have established required courses in Bible for all their students.

Bible survey is fundamental to all Bible study. If a student expects to comprehend any part or doctrine of the Scriptures, he must know what they teach as a whole. Each book is a part of that whole, and can be fully understood only when it is seen in relation to the entire stream of divine revelation that begins with Genesis and that ends with the Apocalypse.

The message of the New Testament can be apprehended best when one has some comprehension of the world into which it first came. The literary, political, social, economic, and religious backgrounds of the first century are the context for the revelation of God in Christ. The terms which the apostles and their associates used for teaching were taken from the common life of their day and were familiar to the average man in the streets of Alexandria, Antioch, or Rome. As these terms become plain to the modern reader, their message will become increasingly clear.

The interpretation of the New Testament, nevertheless, does not depend solely upon antiquarian knowledge. Its precepts are binding not because modern civilization accidentally duplicates the culture of the Graeco-Roman world, but because man's relation to God is ever the same, and because the eternal God is unchanging in his attitude to man. The vitality of the word of God is not dependent upon the chance similarity of two eras. Its eternal quality transcends local conditions of space, time, and society. Once the meaning of the words of Scripture is correctly understood, the words are as true today as they ever were, and they cannot be discarded as the obsolete sentiments of a vanished civilization. They still convey the living gospel of the eternal God to the thirsty souls of sinning men.

In this book each writing of the New Testament has been placed in its setting and has been outlined for the reader in order that he may readily

discern its main line of thought. The aim of the textbook is not to substitute the opinions of the author for the discoveries of the student, but
rather to place at his disposal a compact guide to the essential facts that will
help him to interpret the Bible for himself. Like the Ethiopian eunuch who
asked that someone should direct him in his initial study of the written
word, the modern student needs a helper through the perplexities that
confront him.

Technical problems of introduction and of theology are not treated
here at any length because they do not belong properly in a survey course.
For investigation of these fields the student may have recourse to adequate
works, which are mentioned in the bibliography. Minute points of interpretation are omitted since this book does not pretend to be a commentary. Footnotes have been generally restricted to references to primary
sources of information. They have been kept at a minimum to avoid
confusing the reader who is not a professional scholar. Secondary sources
have been included in the final bibliography. The sole aim is to offer a
general integrated approach which will increase understanding of the New
Testament and a love for it. As the devout believer sees how the revelation
of God was pertinent to the world of the first century, he will discover how
it is applicable also to the surroundings of his own life.

In the use of this book in class, the teacher should supplement it with
his own lectures, developing in detail the phases of thought which are only
suggested here. The classified list of books at the end will provide ample
material for collateral reading and for research. Outlines are intended
chiefly as models by the aid of which the teacher or the student may
construct others that are original. Biblical references will facilitate the
independent study of the text to verify or enlarge the themes which it
presents.

The author acknowledges gratefully the kindness of the trustees and
administration of Wheaton College, who released him from all teaching
duties in the summer of 1952 in order that this manuscript might be
completed. Without this concession early publication would have been
impossible.

Permission to quote from George Foot Moore's *Judaism* has been generously granted by the Harvard University Press of Cambridge, Massachu-
setts, and the quotation has been identified by a footnote reference.

The author owes special thanks to his wife, Helen J. Tenney, for her
stimulating encouragement and keen criticism during the process of writing and revision; to Dr. A. Berkeley Mickelsen and to Professor Stefania
Evans of the Wheaton College faculty for reading the manuscript and for
offering helpful suggestions; to Miss Edna E. Smallwood for her professional assistance in preparing the manuscript for publication; and to the
many students of former years whose needs have become the directions in
shaping this book.

M. C. T.

PREFACE TO THE REVISED EDITION

Numerous changes have taken place in the field of New Testament study since the first edition of this book was published. New discoveries such as the Dead Sea Scrolls, with their wealth of information on Palestinian religion in the time of Christ, the shift of scholarly opinion on problems of the New Testament, and an enlarging bibliography have prompted this revision. The gratifying response of the public to this work has warranted some further changes in content to improve its breadth and usefulness.

New material has been included on the Gospels and the Dead Sea Scrolls, a chapter on text and transmission has been added, and the bibliography has been brought up to date. A change in typography and the inclusion of pictures should make the book more useful for class work and generally more attractive. A few inaccuracies have been corrected.

The author expresses gratitude to his friends for the suggestions that have given direction to the new edition of this work.

M. C. T.

PREFACE TO
NEW TESTAMENT SURVEY, REVISED

THE continued usefulness of this book as a basic text is eloquent testimony to the expertise with which the author has crafted his work. It has been with a sense of retaining the quality of the text that this second revision has been undertaken at the request of Dr. Merrill C. Tenney and Mr. William B. Eerdmans, Jr. I gratefully express my appreciation to them for their invitation; it has been a personal pleasure for me.

This 1985 revision includes two major features: a new chapter on the Jewish background of the New Testament (now Chapter 5), and an enlarged and updated bibliography. The bibliographies to the individual chapters have been made into sections for further reading and placed at the ends of their respective chapters. Many other new sections have been added, including materials on the Gospels and the Canon of the New Testament.

Thanks also goes to Mr. Charles Van Hof of Eerdmans Publishing Company for his cooperation and encouragement in seeing the task through.

W. M. D.

LIST OF ILLUSTRATIONS

LIST OF MAPS

LIST OF CHARTS

xix

PART I

THE WORLD OF THE NEW TESTAMENT

CHAPTER 1

THE POLITICAL WORLD

THE EMPIRE OF ROME

At the time when the New Testament was written the entire civilized world, with the exception of the little-known kingdoms of the Far East, was under the domination of Rome. From the Atlantic Ocean on the west to the Euphrates River and the Red Sea on the east, and from the Rhone, the Danube, the Black Sea, and the Caucasus mountains on the north to the Sahara on the south, stretched one vast empire under the headship and virtual dictatorship of the emperor, called both "king" (I Pet. 2:17) and "Augustus" (Luke 2:1) in the New Testament.

Rome took its name from the capital city in Italy, the original settlement from which the Roman state grew. Founded in 753 B.C., it was at first a community comprising a union of small villages in its vicinity and ruled by a king. About the beginning of the fifth century B.C. it had achieved a degree of solid political organization under a republican form of government. By alliances with surrounding communities and through a long succession of wars against the Etruscans in the north and other tribes in the south, Rome became mistress of the Italian Peninsula by 265 B.C. The conquered peoples were bound by treaty to keep the peace and were absorbed gradually into the Roman domain.

During the years 265–146 B.C. Rome was engaged in a great struggle with Carthage, the chief maritime power of the western Mediterranean. Carthage was originally a colony of Phoenicia; but with the overthrow of the mother country by Alexander, the colony had been compelled to act independently. By following the pattern of the Phoenicians, it had become a wealthy and powerful nation. Its ships carried the commerce of the Mediterranean. Its civilization was oriental in character, its society was an oligarchy maintained by a mercenary army, and it was governed by autocratic rule. As Rome expanded it came into conflict with the outposts of the Carthaginian empire. Aside from the fact that the two civilizations were alien to each other in racial origin and in political theory, there was not enough room for both of them in the same territory; one had to succumb. The wars between them ended in 146 B.C. when the Roman general Scipio Aemilianus captured the city of Carthage and razed it to the ground. Rome thus established dominion over Spain and North Africa. At the same time Macedonia was made a Roman province, and with the sack of Corinth in the same year (146 B.C.) Achaia came under Roman control. In 133 B.C. Attalus III, king of Pergamum, died, and bequeathed his realm to the Romans. Out of it they organized the province of Asia. Wars in the eastern part of Asia Minor continued until Pompey completed the conquest of Pontus and the Caucasus. In 63 B.C. he organized Syria into a province and annexed Judea. From 58 to 57 B.C. Caesar conducted his famous campaigns in Gaul and made it a Roman country. Thus through five hundred years of almost uninterrupted war Rome grew from an obscure village on the banks of the Tiber to become the ruling empire of the world.

The rapid territorial expansion, however, brought great changes in the life of the Roman people. As the military leaders gained a taste of power, they began to use their armies not only for foreign conquest, but also for enforcing their supremacy at home. The century between the conquest of Carthage and Greece and the death of Julius Caesar was marked by a constant succession of civil wars. Marius, Sulla, Caesar, Antony, and Octavian—one after the other strove to make himself master of the Roman state, until finally Octavian, or Augustus as he was called by the Senate, succeeded in exterminating his opponents in 30 B.C., and became the first emperor.

Augustus, 27 B.C. to A.D. 14

Under his rule the Roman *imperium,* or power of the imperial state, was thoroughly established. The people, tired of war, longed for peace. Augustus became the *princeps,* or first citizen of the land. He ruled wisely and well. Politically, the new principate was a compromise between the old republicanism and the dictatorship that Julius Caesar had advocated. The Senate was retained as the theoretical ruling body. In 27 B.C. it conferred on Augustus the office of commander-in-chief of the armed forces of the empire. In 23 B.C. he was given the tribunitial power for life, which meant that he had control over the popular assemblies and was appointed the permanent representative of the people. He was given the prerogative of introducing the first topic of discussion in the Senate and the right to call its meetings. All of his rights were founded on a constitutional basis rather than on any arbitrary seizure of power.

During the reign of Augustus many reforms were effected. The Senate was purged of unworthy members. A large part of the army was demobilized, and the discharged veterans were settled in colonies or on land supplied by purchase. A regular professional army was created; it became a school for citizens. On retirement from the ranks the veterans were given a bonus and were settled in colonies in the provinces, where they could make a good living and at the same time be community leaders loyal to Rome.

Augustus also sought to improve the morale of the people. He revived the state religion and rebuilt many temples. The imperial cult, a worship of Rome as a state, was introduced to the provinces. In many places the emperor himself was worshiped as *Dominus et Deus* (Lord and God), although he did not demand such worship. The Julian laws of 19 and 18 B.C. attempted to restore family life by encouraging marriage and the establishment of homes.

Statue of Augustus Gaius Julius Caesar Octavianus addressing his troops; in Vatican Museum, Rome.

To consolidate the empire at large, Augustus took a census of the population and of all property as a basis for recruiting the army and for taxation. Spain, Gaul, and the Alpine districts were subjugated. He strengthened the defense of the frontiers, though his armies suffered a crushing defeat at the hands of the Germans in the Teutoberg forest. Augustus organized the police and fire departments of Rome and appointed a supervisor for the grain supply.

Augustus' boast was that he had found Rome brick and had left it marble. During the forty-one years of his administration he brought order out of chaos. He restored confidence in the government, replenished the treasury, introduced an efficient public works department, and promoted peace and prosperity.

Tiberius, A.D. 14 to 37

At the death of Augustus his adopted son Tiberius was chosen to succeed him. The *imperium* or power that Augustus had received under constitutional regulations and for a limited period was conferred on Tiberius for life. He was fifty-six years old at the time of his succession and had been engaged during most of his life in the service of the state, so that he was no novice in politics. Unfortunately, Augustus insisted that he divorce the wife whom he loved and that he marry Julia, Augustus' daughter, a woman of openly profligate life. The bitterness of this experience soured his temper permanently. He was distant, haughty, suspicious, and irascible. Although he was impartial and wise in his policies, he was never popular and was generally feared and disliked. During his reign the Roman armies suffered reverses in Germany,

Statue of Tiberius Claudius Nero; in Vatican Museum, Rome.

with the result that he withdrew the frontier to the Rhine. Domestic troubles clouded his later years. In A.D. 26 he retired to Capri, leaving the government in the hands of the city prefect. The absence of Tiberius gave opportunity to Aelius Sejanus, the captain of the praetorian guard, to carry out a conspiracy to seize the principate. By A.D. 31 he had almost perfected his plans when Tiberius discovered them. Sejanus was executed and the plot was overthrown, but its effect on Tiberius was disastrous. He became even more suspicious and cruel, so that the merest whisper against a man would bring calamity down on him. When he died in A.D. 37, the Senate could once more breathe freely.

Caligula, A.D. 37 to 41

Gaius Caligula, or "Little Boots," as he was affectionately called by the soldiery, was made Tiberius' successor by the Senate. At the outset of his career he was as popular as Tiberius had been unpopular. He pardoned political prisoners, reduced taxes, gave public entertainments, and endeared himself generally to the populace. Before long, however, he began to show signs of mental weakness. He demanded to be worshiped as a god, which alienated the Jews in his realm. When Herod Agrippa visited Alexandria the citizens insulted him publicly by lampooning him and his followers, and then tried to compel the Jews to worship the images of Gaius. The Jews appealed to the emperor, who not only paid no heed to them, but ordered his Syrian legate to erect his statue in the temple at Jerusalem. The legate was wise enough to delay action rather than to risk an armed rebellion, and the death of Caligula in A.D. 41 prevented the issue from coming to a crisis. Some think that Mark's reference to the "abomination of desolation" (Mark 13:14) reflects the threatened erection of the emperor's statue in the temple at Jerusalem.

Caligula's reckless expenditure of the funds that Augustus and Tiberius had so carefully gathered quickly exhausted the public treasury. In order to replenish it he resorted to violent means: confiscation of property, compulsory legacies, and extortion of every kind. His tyranny finally became so unbearable that he was assassinated by a tribune of the imperial guards.

Claudius, A.D. 41 to 54

At the death of Caligula the Senate debated the idea of restoring the republic, but the question was quickly decided for them when the praetorian guard selected Tiberius Claudius Germanicus as emperor. He had been living in comparative obscurity during the reigns of Tiberius and Caligula, and had not taken part in the political activities of Rome. An early illness, possibly some form of infantile paralysis, had left him so weakened that his public appearance was almost ludicrous, for his shambling form and drooling mouth made him look idiotic. He was not, however, of inferior mentality, for he was a good scholar, and proved to be an abler ruler than his contemporaries expected.

Bust of Tiberius Claudius Drusus Nero Germanicus; in Uffizi Gallery, Florence.

The rapidly expanding empire needed a new type of government to make it efficient. Under Claudius Rome became a bureaucracy, governed by committees and secretaries. He extended the privilege of citizenship to provincials. His generals succeeded in gaining a foothold in Britain and conquered it as far north as the Thames River. At this time Thrace, on the death of its prince, who had been an ally of Rome, was made a province.

Claudius made a determined attempt to restore the ancient Roman religion to its former prominence in society. He possessed a strong antipathy for foreign cults. Suetonius states that under Claudius the Jews were expelled from Rome because of some riots that had taken place "at the instigation of one Chrestus."[1] It is uncertain whether Suetonius misunderstood Chrestus for Christus, and was referring to a disturbance among the Jews occasioned by the preaching of Jesus as the Christ, or whether Chrestus was the actual name of some insurgent. In any case, the order of expulsion is probably the one that caused the removal of Aquila and Priscilla from Rome (Acts 18:2).

Through the influence of one of his freedmen, Pallas, Claudius was persuaded to take his niece, Agrippina, as his fourth wife. She was determined to obtain the succession for Domitius, her son by a previous husband. Domitius was formally adopted by Claudius under the name of Nero Claudius Caesar. In A.D. 53 Nero married Octavia, Claudius' daughter. A year later Claudius died, leaving to Nero the succession of the imperial throne.

Nero, A.D. 54 to 68

The first five years of Nero's reign were peaceful and successful. With Afranius Burrus, the prefect of the praetorian guard, and L. Annaeus Seneca, the philosopher and writer, as his advisors, Nero managed his realm very well. Agrippina, however, sought to maintain an ascendancy over him which both he and his advisors resented. In A.D. 59 he had his mother murdered and took full charge of the government himself.

Nero was by temperament an artist rather than an executive. He was more eager to enter upon a stage career than to excel in political administration. His carelessness and extravagance emptied the public treasury, and he, like Caligula, resorted to oppression and violence in order to replenish it. By so doing he incurred the hatred of the Senate, whose members feared that at any time he might give orders for their death and for confiscation of their property.

In A.D. 64 a great fire broke out in Rome that destroyed a large part of the city. Nero was suspected of having deliberately set it in order to make room for his new Golden House, a splendid palace that he had built on the

---

1. Suetonius *Claudius* XXV.4.

Esquiline hill. This massive complex, which housed the great palace, covered a total of 125 acres, including a colonnade with three rows of columns one mile long, dining rooms with ivory ceilings, walls covered with decorations of fantastic decor, and in the vestibule a colossus of Nero himself 120 feet in height. There were parks, groves, and a lake, all (it was said) for the pleasure of one man. In order to divert the blame from himself, he accused the Christians of having caused the disaster. Their attitude of aloofness from the heathen and their talk of the ultimate destruction of the world by fire lent plausibility to the charge. Many of them were brought to trial and were tortured to death. Tradition says that Peter and Paul perished in this persecution, the first one conducted by the state.

There is little evidence to show how extensive this persecution was. Probably it did not affect any territory outside of Rome and its immediate environs, although the provinces

Bust of Nero Claudius Caesar Drusus Germanicus; in Vatican Museum, Rome.

may have been threatened with it. (Cf. I Pet. 4:12–19.)

In the meantime the excesses of Nero had rendered him increasingly unpopular. Several conspiracies against him had failed and were suppressed by the execution of his enemies. Finally a revolt of the troops and provincials in Gaul and Spain proved successful. Nero fled from Rome and was killed by one of his own freedmen at his command in order to avoid capture.

Galba, A.D. 68

The revolt of the legions had shown that the empire was really commanded by the army, since it could nominate and enthrone its candidate without reference to the Senate. Galba, Nero's successor, was not the unanimous choice of the legions. When he adopted as his successor Lucius

Calpurnius Piso, Otho, who had once supported him in hope of being emperor himself, persuaded the praetorian guards to kill Galba and to make him emperor.

Otho, A.D. 69

Otho's rule was short-lived. The Senate concurred in his appointment, but Vitellius, the legate of Germany, marched on Rome with his troops. Otho was killed in battle and Vitellius took his place.

Vitellius, A.D. 69

Vitellius was recognized by the Senate, but he was unable to control the soldiery, nor could he establish any stable government. The army of the east intervened in the affairs of state and made its general, Vespasian, emperor. At that time Vespasian was engaged in the siege of Jerusalem. Leaving it in charge of his son Titus, he proceeded to Egypt, where he gained control of the country and cut off the food supply of Rome. His lieutenant, Mucianus, set out for Italy. In spite of the spirited resistance of the troops of Vitellius, Vespasian's partisans captured and sacked Rome. Vitellius was killed, and Vespasian was proclaimed ruler.

Vespasian, A.D. 69 to 79

Vespasian was a plain old soldier who was frugal in his habits and vigorous in his administration. He suppressed revolts among the Bataviae and among the Gauls, while Titus completed the reduction of Jerusalem. The city was completely destroyed and the province was put under a military legate. He strengthened the frontiers by reducing dependent principalities to the status of provinces. The treasury was made solvent by strict economy and by the imposition of new taxes. He built the now famous Colosseum. He died in A.D. 79, leaving his office to Titus, whom he had made his coregent. He was the first of the Flavian dynasty, which included his sons Titus and Domitian.

Bust of Titus Flavius Vespasianus.

Titus, A.D. 79 to 81

The brevity of Titus' reign did not allow much time for the accomplishment of any remarkable deeds. In spite of the handicap, however, he was one of the most popular emperors that Rome ever had. The magnificence of the public entertainments that he sponsored and his personal generosity disarmed the potential antagonism of the Senate, who feared that he would be a dictator like his father.

The catastrophic overthrow of Pompeii and Herculaneum, villages on the Bay of Naples, in the eruption of Vesuvius, occurred during his reign. Titus appointed a commission and did his utmost to rescue as many of the victims as

Bust of Titus Flavius Sabinus Vespasianus.

possible. A few months later Rome suffered a severe fire that destroyed the new Capitol, the Pantheon, and Agrippa's Baths. Titus even sold some of his private furniture to contribute to the general need. He erected new buildings, including a large amphitheater.

Domitian, A.D. 81 to 96

Titus died in A.D. 81, leaving no son, and the Senate conferred the imperial power on his younger brother Domitian. Domitian was a thorough autocrat. He tried to raise the moral level of Roman society by restraining the corruptions of the Roman stage and by checking public prostitution. The temples of the older gods were rebuilt and foreign religions were suppressed, especially those which sought to make converts. He was thought to have instigated a persecution of Christians, though evidence for any extensive legislation or action against them in his reign is lacking. He demanded worship for himself and insisted on being hailed as *Dominus et Deus*. As an economist, he was a good manager. The business affairs of the empire were conducted efficiently by his subordinates.

Both Jews and Christians refused to accord worship to Domitian (namely, his "godhead"). In A.D. 93 he executed some Christians for refusing to offer sacrifice before his image. According to tradition, this included his own nephew, Flavius Clemens.

Domitian was hard by nature and suspicious of rivals. Lacking the geniality of his brother Titus, he made numerous enemies. When their plots were discovered he was pitiless in his vengeance. The last years of his reign were a nightmare to the senatorial order, who were kept in constant terror of spies and informers. Even his own family did not feel safe, and finally, in self-defense, they procured his assassination.

Statue of Titus Flavius Domitianus; in Vatican Museum, Rome.

Nerva, A.D. 96 to 98

Nerva, Domitian's successor, was selected by the Senate. He was a man of advanced years and of mild demeanor, and was probably regarded as a "safe" candidate by the senatorial order. His general administration was kindly and was relatively free from internal tensions. The army had resented Domitian's assassination, for the Flavians were popular in military circles. Nerva, however, was astute enough to provide as his successor Trajan, who was capable of holding the troops in subjection and of administering government with a strong hand.

Trajan, A.D. 98 to 117

Nerva died in A.D. 98, and Trajan succeeded him. He was a Spaniard by birth, a soldier by profession, energetic and aggressive in temperament. He annexed Dacia, north of the Danube, and began the enlargement of the eastern frontiers by the conquest of Armenia, Assyria, and Mesopotamia. A revolt of the Jews in the Near East was suppressed in A.D. 115; but new insurrections in Africa, Britain, and on the Danubian border occasioned his recall to Rome. He died en route to the capital in Cilicia in A.D. 117.

In this environment of imperial expansion Christianity grew from an obscure Jewish sect to a world religion. Jesus was born in the reign of Augustus (Luke 2:1); his public ministry and death occurred in the time of Tiberius (3:1); the great period of missionary expansion came in the reigns of Claudius (Acts 18:2) and Nero (25:1–12). According to tradition, the Apocalypse was written in the reign of Domitian,[2] and its allusion to imperial power and governmental tyranny may have been reflections of conditions prevalent at that time.

The relative scarcity of allusions in the New Testament to contemporary events in the Roman world is not surprising. The national interest of the Gospels and of much of the Acts, which are the principal historical works, lies in Judaism rather than in Rome. Furthermore, the message of the New Testament was directed to the inner lives of its readers rather than to their outward circumstances. The spiritual rather than the political, and the eternal rather than the temporal were stressed. Nevertheless, at numerous points the New Testament does connect with the political surroundings of the first century, and its historical importance must be interpreted in that connection.

THE PROVINCIAL GOVERNMENT

Unlike the United States of America, in which the federal authority presides over fifty states that are generally uniform in government and organization, the Roman empire was a miscellany of independent cities, states, and territories—all of which were subject to the central government. Some of them had become part of the empire by voluntary alliance; others had been annexed by conquest. As Rome extended its sovereignty over these allied or subject peoples, its governmental machinery also grew into the Roman provincial system.

The word *provincia*, from which "province" is derived, meant originally the office of carrying on war, or a post of command. As applied to the authority of a general it was extended to the sphere of his authority, and hence to the territory that he conquered, which became his *provincia*. When Rome conquered new domains, they were organized into provinces that became part of the general imperial system.

Rome's acquisition of provinces began with Sicily, which was taken from Carthage in the first Punic War (264–241 B.C.). In succession she added Sardinia (237 B.C.), two provinces in Spain (197 B.C.), Macedonia (146 B.C.), and Africa (146 B.C.). Asia was not taken by force of

---

2. Irenaeus *Against Heresies* V.xxx.3.

arms, but was bequeathed to the Roman people by its king in 133 B.C., and was organized as a province in 129 B.C. Transalpine and Cisalpine Gaul were added about 118 B.C. Cyrene was bequeathed to Rome in 96 B.C., and Bithynia was also presented to Rome in 75 B.C. In 67 B.C. Pompey annexed Cilicia and Crete, and in 63 B.C. he took over Palestine and made it into the province of Syria. Except for Italy itself, the bulk of the Roman world consisted of territory under provincial government.

This government was of two kinds. The provinces that were relatively peaceful and loyal to Rome were under proconsuls (Acts 13:7) who were responsible to the Roman Senate. The more turbulent provinces were under the authority of the emperor, who often stationed armies in them, and they were governed by prefects, procurators, or propraetors who were appointed by the emperor and answerable directly to him. To the former class belonged Achaia, of which Gallio was proconsul at the time of Paul's visit (18:12). Palestine in the time of Christ was under the supervision of the emperor, whose agent was the prefect Pontius Pilate (Matt. 27:11; translated "governor"). Proconsuls held their office by annual appointment and were generally changed every year. Procurators and propraetors held office as long as the emperor wanted them at a given post.

Under the administration of these officers the provinces enjoyed considerable liberty. The individual city-states were permitted to retain their own local sovereignty and even to mint coins. The Romans never interfered with the religious freedom of the subject peoples, so that the indigenous worship was customarily retained in each place. The Roman rulers usually took the advice of the provincial councils in their administration. Officials who plundered their subjects were liable to prosecution and recall. Although some of the proconsuls and procurators did indulge in the time-honored pastime of graft, the majority probably gave more to the provinces in administrative wisdom than they took out in money. Roads were constructed, public edifices were erected, and commerce was developed rapidly.

In order to unite the provinces more closely with the mother city of Rome, little settlements of Romans were begun at strategic centers in the provinces. Gradually the Roman civilization spread, so that in time the provinces became more Roman than Rome. In the second century when Rome still used Greek as its predominant language, Gaul, Spain, and Africa were predominantly Latin.

The imperial cult had its widest following in the provinces. The worship of the Roman state and of the reigning emperor began with Augustus. He ordered that temples be erected to the honor of Julius Caesar at Ephesus and at Nicaea by the citizens of Rome who resided there, and he permitted the nationals of the country to establish shrines in his own honor. The worship of the state was fostered by the local councils, who assumed the responsibility of directing the provincial worship.

A good illustration of a provincial council appears in Acts 19:31, where the "Asiarchs" are mentioned. They were magistrates who were regarded as the responsible leaders of the province and who may have served as high priests of the state worship. In Acts they were represented as friendly to Paul, since they warned him against exposing himself to the violence of the multitude in the theater.

The Roman provinces that appear in the New Testament are Spain (Rom. 15:24), Gaul (II Tim. 4:10, variant reading), Illyricum (Rom. 15:19), Macedonia (Acts 16:9), Achaia (Rom. 15:26), Asia (Acts 20:4), Pontus (I Pet. 1:1), Bithynia (Acts 16:7), Galatia (Gal. 1:2), Cappadocia (I Pet. 1:1), Cilicia (Gal. 1:21; Acts 6:9), Syria (Gal. 1:21), Judea (Gal. 1:22), Cyprus (Acts 13:4), Pamphylia (Acts 13:13), and Lycia (Acts 27:5). Some of these are mentioned more than once; and in the case of Illyricum, its later name, Dalmatia, appears in the Pastoral Epistles (II Tim. 4:10). Paul usually employed provincial names in alluding to divisions of the empire, while Luke also used national divisions. Provinces often included more than one ethnic group, such as the Lycaonians of Lystra and Derbe (Acts 14:6, 11), who were under the province of Galatia.

Governorship of the provinces was sought by public officials because they found it a fruitful source of income. So rapacious were some of these rulers that the provinces were rapidly impoverished by heavy taxation. Others who were more public-spirited made wise use of the taxes by building roads and harbors, so that commerce thrived and the general economic level of life improved. Rome regarded the provinces as her rightful field of exploitation. Until the time of Constantine they were tributary to the central government and never were treated as equal states within a common federation.

THE HELLENISTIC KINGDOMS

The cultural atmosphere of the first century owed its origin not only to the political organization of Rome but also to the diffusion of the Hellenic spirit that had permeated both the West and the East. Rome's conquests had absorbed the Greek colonies that had been established along the seacoasts of Gaul and Spain, in the island of Sicily, and on the mainland of the lower Italian peninsula. The conquest of Achaia, ending in the sack of Corinth, 146 B.C., had made available to the Romans vast treasures of art that they deported to grace their own villas. Greek slaves, many of whom were more learned than their masters, became part of Roman households. Often they were not only employed in the more menial tasks of the house, but were teachers, physicians, accountants, and overseers of farms or of businesses. Furthermore, the Greek universities of Athens, Rhodes, Tarsus, and other cities were attended by aristocratic young Romans who learned to speak Greek in much the same way that the nineteenth-century Englishman learned French as the language of diplomacy and culture. So thoroughly did the vanquished Greeks conquer their victors culturally that Rome itself became a Greek-speaking city. Juvenal, one of the famous satirists of his day, complained: "I cannot, fellow Romans, bear a city wholly Greek."[3]

The Conquests of Alexander

In the eastern half of the Roman world where most of the action of the New Testament took place, the spread of Greek civilization began with the Greek traders who carried the commerce of the Peloponnesus far and wide. As early as 600 B.C. Greek musical instruments and weapons were known in Babylonia, and Greek mercenaries fought in the armies of Cyrus, as Xenophon's well-known *Anabasis, The March of the Ten Thousand,* attests. The Hellenizing of the East was greatly accelerated by the campaigns of Alexander the Great. Philip his father, the king of Macedonia, had forged the Macedonians into a unified military state. From the sturdy peasants and shepherds of his mountainous country he had organized an army of unusual mobility and endurance. In twenty years' time Philip succeeded in making the Greek city-states subservient to Macedonia. When Philip died in 337 B.C. he had completed an alliance with the Greeks by which he hoped to undertake the conquest of Asia.

Alexander possessed his father's aggressiveness and military genius overlaid with a thicker veneer of Greek culture. He had been brought up on Homer's *Iliad* under the tutelage of Aristotle, so that he had profound admiration for Hellenic traditions and ideals. In 334 B.C. he crossed the Hellespont into Asia Minor and defeated the Persian forces at the battle of the Granicus River. He liberated the Hellenic cities of the coast and then penetrated the hinterland. He routed the Persians again at the battle of Issus, which gave him command of all Asia Minor, and then he turned southward down the Syrian coast into Egypt, where he founded the city of Alexandria.

Having subdued Syria and Egypt, he moved eastward and inflicted a final defeat on the Persian army at Arbela. In rapid succession he occupied Babylon and the capitals of Persia, Susa, and Persepolis.

The next three years were spent in consolidating the new empire. Alexander encouraged the marriage of his soldiers to oriental women. He

---

3. Juvenal *Satire* III.60–61.

began the education of thirty thousand of the Persians in the Greek language. Through further campaigns in India he extended the borders of his domain to the Indus River. He established numerous colonies and he explored country that had not up to that time been seen by Europeans.

Upon his return to Babylon Alexander began preparations for the invasion of Arabia, but he was not destined to complete them. If he had succeeded in partially Hellenizing the East, the East had also partly orientalized him. He took on more and more of the attitude of the oriental despot and became increasingly arbitrary and suspicious. The luxury and the revels of Babylon weakened his constitution so that he contracted fever and died in 324 B.C. at the age of thirty-two.

Bust of Alexander the Great; in the Capitoline Museum, Rome.

Alexander's empire did not long survive his death. He left no heirs who were capable of managing it and finally it was partitioned among his generals. Ptolemy took Egypt and southern Syria; Antigonus claimed most of the territory in northern Syria and west Babylonia; Lysimachus held Thrace and western Asia Minor; and Cassander ruled Macedonia and Greece. Antigonus' territory was taken by Seleucus I after the battle of Ipsus in 301 B.C., and the kingdom of Lysimachus was also absorbed into the realm of the Seleucidae.

The constant hostility between the Seleucidae of Syria and the Ptolemies of Egypt kept Palestine between the hammer and the anvil. The coastal plain of Sharon was the corridor along which the armies of these two powers marched to war. The varying fortunes of conflict put Palestine sometimes under the dominion of one and sometimes under the dominion of the other.

The Seleucidae in Syria

The Seleucid dominion in Asia Minor gradually diminished as the local people asserted their independence and founded kingdoms of their own. In Syria, however, the rule of the Seleucidae was maintained and their influence was potent in the political affairs of Palestine. In the year 201–200 B.C. Antiochus III of Syria, called the Great, defeated the Egyptian army under a general named Scopas at the battle of Panias, near the springs of the Jordan in northern Palestine. In two years Antiochus III gained control of all of Palestine and became the new overlord of the Jews. His attempt to Hellenize the Jews provoked the Maccabean revolt that resulted in the revival of the Jewish commonwealth. Their rule ended when Pompey made Syria a Roman province in 63 B.C.

The effect of the Seleucid dominion was tremendous. Antioch, the capital of their country, became the third largest city of the Roman empire and was the meeting place of the East and West. Greek language and literature were widely disseminated through the Near East and afforded a common medium of culture for oriental and western peoples. Many of the cities of Palestine, especially in Galilee, were bilingual and their religions savored of both eastern and western deities.

The Ptolemies of Egypt

Similar to the career of the Seleucidae was the reign of the Ptolemies in Egypt. The rivalry between the two kingdoms was bitter and caused numerous wars of varying fortunes. With the death of Cleopatra in 30 B.C. the last of the Ptolemies perished, and Rome annexed Egypt to serve as her granary. The city of Alexandria grew in importance and became an outstanding mart of commerce and a center of education. Under the patronage of the Ptolemies a great library was founded in which the chief literary treasures of antiquity were preserved. Its librarians were noted scholars and initiated the study of Greek grammar and of textual criticism.

The Jewish influence in Alexandria was strong from the founding of the city. Alexander himself assigned a place to Jewish colonists and admitted them to full citizenship. Under Ptolemy Philadelphus (285–246 B.C.) the Jewish Scriptures were translated into Greek. This version, known as the Septuagint, became the popular Bible of the Jews of the Dispersion and was generally used by the writers of the New Testament.

The constant wars of the Seleucidae and the Ptolemies brought radical increase in taxation of their lands. So severe was the drain on the public treasury that the peasants, on whom the burden rested most heavily, were reduced to abject poverty. The Punic wars of Rome destroyed Egypt's western markets and consequently trade languished. Popular unrest culminated in revolt against the government, or in the abandonment of property that could no longer be utilized profitably because of the excessive taxation. The marked decline in the fortunes of both kingdoms in the first century before Christ perhaps accounts for the ease with which Rome overcame them.

Cultural Effects

The political effects of the Hellenistic conquest of the East were not lasting. The Seleucidae and the Ptolemies were regarded as foreign dynasties who did not belong to the people; and while they were supported by the ruling class, they never succeeded in making their realms wholly Greek in character. On the contrary, these kings assumed the absolutism of the oriental monarch who demanded obeisance from his courtiers. The free camaraderie of the Greek democracy, or even the more formal organization of the Macedonian court, was eclipsed by the capricious despotism of the kings who claimed to be deity. Jesus alluded to the Seleucidae and the Ptolemies when he said that the kings of the Gentiles call themselves "benefactors" (Luke 22:25), for the Greek word *euergetēs* ("benefactor") was one of their titles. The masses over which they ruled paid taxes to them and prostrated themselves before them, but they would have done the same for any other master.

Culturally, the Seleucidae and the Ptolemies introduced Greek customs and manners in the East. Greek architecture prevailed in the urban centers where they lived. Greek was the language of the court and became the common speech of the people, as the papyri show. Love letters, bills, receipts, amulets, essays, poetry, biographies, and business communications were all written in Greek. In Egypt the titles of the popular officials were Greek, even into the time of the Roman occupation. The rulers sought to unite the Hellenistic culture with the life of the people. Greek names were given to the local gods, and gymnasiums and amphitheaters were built in the major cities. The veneer of western civilization was spread over the Near East.

Through the medium of this culture the gospel of Christ was disseminated in the earliest of its missionary endeavors. With a Greek Bible from which to preach and with the Greek language as its universal medium of communication, it soon reached the outposts of civilization.

THE JEWISH STATE

The Exile, 597 to 322 B.C.

When Nebuchadnezzar, king of Babylon, overran Judea and captured Jerusalem in 597 B.C., the independence of the Jewish state came to an end. Jehoiachin, the king, was taken prisoner to Babylon, together with all the court. The ruling classes of the people, including the skilled artisans, were also deported. Jehoiachin's uncle, Mattaniah, was renamed Zedekiah, and was placed on the throne as a puppet king (II Kings 24:10–17).

From 597 to 586 B.C. Judea enjoyed a twilight existence as a tributary kingdom. Zedekiah was obligated by oath to serve the king of Babylon; but the temptation to intrigue with Egypt was strong, especially when the stake was independence. There was a division of opinion, even in the prophetic circles. Hananiah, the son of Azzur, declared repeatedly that God would break the yoke of Babylon and that in two years' time from his prediction the golden vessels that Nebuchadnezzar had taken away from the temple would be restored (Jer. 28:1–4). Jeremiah, on the other hand, charged Hananiah with lying, and predicted that Babylon's grip would not be relaxed. The radical party expected that Egypt would come to their aid; the conservative group, represented by Jeremiah, cherished no such illusions (28:12–17).

In 590 B.C. Zedekiah thought that his opportunity to rebel had come. Psammetichus II of Egypt was pushing northward along the Palestinian coast and was steadily encroaching on the domains of Babylon. Feeling that at last he had a champion, Zedekiah cast in his lot with Egypt.

Nebuchadnezzar did not overlook the challenge. He marched to the defense of Tyre and in 588 B.C. laid siege to Jerusalem. The siege was lifted temporarily at the advance of the Egyptian army, but the latter soon beat a retreat into Egypt and the Babylonian army resumed operations. In 586 B.C. the walls were breached and the Babylonians took the city. Zedekiah was captured in an attempted escape, and, after being blinded, was taken in chains to Babylon. The sacred vessels of the temple were plundered; the building itself, together with the royal palace and the mansions of the nobles, was burned. The walls of the city were leveled and the population was deported to Babylon (39:4–10).

In order to preserve a semblance of organization, Nebuzaradan, the Babylonian general in charge of the campaign, appointed Gedaliah as governor. The dissident factions within the land still persisted, however. Baalis, the king of the Ammonites, instigated a rebellion in which Gedaliah was assassinated. General civil strife followed in which the insurgent party was finally beaten. The remnant of them escaped to Egypt, taking the prophet Jeremiah with them into involuntary exile (Jer. 41 to 43).

The end of the Jewish state did not mean the end of Judaism; in fact, the practice of "orthodox Judaism" had its beginning in these events. Many of those who went into captivity took with them the law and the prophets, which they cherished as their Scriptures. Although the sacrifices of the temple had ceased, the worship of God continued. Some of the most devout and best educated of the Jews had been taken to Babylon, and with their settlement in that land there sprang up a community that took the place of Jerusalem in religious leadership.

In no small measure the religious development of this community was promoted by Ezekiel, who had been carried away in the first deportation under Jehoiachin. He was a combination of visionary and Puritan. The imagery of his preaching is grotesque, but his ethics were stern and his

The Cyrus Cylinder records Cyrus' capture of Babylon and his policy of religious toleration, including the release of the Jewish exiles and the restoration of the temple.

spiritual standards were lofty. He predicted the restoration of the people to their own land and expected revival that would purify them from the abominations that they had committed during the years of their captivity (Ezek. 36:22–31).

The seventy years of the Babylonian captivity witnessed the rise of synagogue worship among the Jews. Groups of the faithful banded themselves together in the name of Jehovah and formed congregations in which the law was taught and revered. Teachers were appointed who took the place of the temple priesthood as religious leaders of the people. The study of the law became a substitute for animal sacrifices, and ethical observances took the place of ritual.

The fall of Babylon occurred in 539 B.C. Cyrus, king of Persia, captured Babylon by the stratagem of diverting the waters of the Euphrates from their usual channel, so that they no longer flowed through the city. His armies marched through the dry bed of the river under the gates into the city and so captured it almost without a battle. The sovereignty of the Middle East passed to the Medo-Persians.

Cyrus proved to be a benevolent despot. From the first he treated the conquered peoples with consideration. In the initial year of his reign he issued a decree that the Jews should be permitted to return home and that the spoils of their temple should be restored to them. The rebuilding of the temple was to be financed by the royal treasury (Ezra 6:1–5).

Not all of the Jews in Babylonia returned to Palestine under the decree of Cyrus. The majority preferred to remain with their businesses and with their homes. About forty-two thousand, mostly from the tribes of Judah, Benjamin, and Levi, set out for Jerusalem. Under the leadership of

Sheshbazzar, a prince of royal blood whom Cyrus appointed governor, they reached the city about 537 B.C. (1:3, 5–11). They commenced to rebuild the temple (3:1–13), but the construction was not completed at that time. There was opposition to the project from the people who had stayed in the land (4:1–5). For seventeen years nothing further was done, though the returning exiles prospered and built homes for themselves (Hag. 1:4). Under the urgent preaching of the prophets Haggai and Zechariah the work was resumed about 520 B.C. (Ezra 5:1–2). The provincial officials, apparently ignorant of the original decree of Cyrus, ordered the Jews to desist. The Jews appealed to Darius, who searched the records and re-affirmed by special decree the privileges that Cyrus had granted. The work then went forward rapidly and the building was completed in 516 B.C. (6:1–15). Worship was resumed at the time of the Passover and the priestly ministry was reestablished.

For another period of about sixty years between 516 B.C. and 458 B.C. the records are silent concerning the state of the Jews in Palestine. In 458 B.C., "the seventh year of Artaxerxes the king" (7:7), another migration set out from Babylon under the leadership of Ezra the scribe, a descendant of Hilkiah, who had been high priest in the reign of Josiah. He was accompanied by a number of priests and singers and possessed a letter from Artaxerxes that gave him authority to renew the temple services and provided for financial aid by the magistrates for such worship under penalty of punishment.

The new settlement was absorbed into the population of the land and seemingly effected no change in general conditions. "In the twentieth year of Artaxerxes the king" (Neh. 2:1; 446 B.C.) a messenger from Jerusalem approached Nehemiah, the Jewish cupbearer of the Persian king, and informed him that the wall of Jerusalem had been broken down and that its gates had been burned with fire. In all probability the devastation of the city was fairly recent at the time of Nehemiah, for there would have been no point in taking a long journey to announce to him the results of the siege occurring nearly a century and a half previously. From the hints given in the book of Nehemiah, one may conclude that the revival of Jewish political activities provoked hostility from the other inhabitants of Palestine, especially the Samaritans. Perhaps the calamity that Hanani announced was the result of some guerrilla raid on Jerusalem that the Jews were not well organized enough to resist.

The appeal of Hanani brought direct results. Nehemiah obtained leave of absence from his royal master, who also gave him a requisition on Asaph, the keeper of the royal forest, for lumber with which to rebuild the gates. Nehemiah promptly proceeded to Jerusalem. On the third night after his arrival he inspected the fortifications of the city and resolved to rebuild immediately. Various sections of the wall were assigned to different men, making the work proceed rapidly. So bitter was the enmity of Sanballat, the governor of Samaria, that he threatened violence, and the construction had to be done under an armed guard. Under Nehemiah's energetic administration the repairs were completed in less than two months (Neh. 6:15–16) and the ramparts of the city were again intact.

Nehemiah also promoted economic and social reforms. In the time of destitution the people had mortgaged their lands and chattels for money with which to buy food. The ruinous interest exacted by the moneylenders had made recovery impossible. Nehemiah abolished interest on loans between brethren and required restitution of property. He brought the public records up to date (7:5) so that the descendants of those who had returned from captivity might be known.

The knowledge of the law was renewed under Ezra the scribe, who read and interpreted it. Apparently he read in Hebrew, which was translated into Aramaic by his assistants (8:2, 7–8). The law had doubtless been forgotten in the strenuous years of conflict and rebuilding and its reading produced a profound effect on the Jews: "All the people wept, when they heard the words of the law" (8:9). The Feast of Tabernacles was celebrated (8:13–18) and a moral reform was effected.

Nehemiah's application of the principles of the law was strict. Temple worship was renewed and contributions were exacted for its support. Mixed marriages with the people of the land were forbidden (10:30), Sabbath-breaking was proscribed (10:31), and regular administration of tithes was established (12:44). By the close of Nehemiah's administration twelve years later the chief elements of Jewish orthodoxy had been well planted among the remnant in Jerusalem.

During Nehemiah's regime Manasseh, a grandson of the high priest, who had married the daughter of Sanballat the governor, was expelled from the country. According to Josephus he fled to Samaria where he built a temple on Mt. Gerizim, and established a rival cult that became the center for the worship of the Samaritans.

The reforms of Nehemiah left a permanent effect. Throughout the rest of the Persian period and down to the times of the Maccabees a stalwart group remained who were tenaciously loyal to the law of God, in spite of the strong influences of paganism to which many of the people and even of the priesthood succumbed.

While few details have survived regarding Jewish history from the time of Nehemiah until the second century B.C., certain movements of great significance took place. The Jews and Samaritans became ethnically separated; Aramaic began to replace Hebrew as the vernacular of Palestine; and Hellenism threatened Judaism. During this period the "Three Pillars of

Judaism" developed: (1) the sacred writings (=the Old Testament); (2) the synagogue (with new liturgical and nonsacrificial worship); and (3) Rabbinism (culminating in Talmud and Midrash).

The priesthood persisted as the central political power in the land. Josephus says that Alexander the Great, pushing through Palestine on his way to Egypt from the conquest of Tyre, was greeted by Jaddua the high priest, and offered worship to the true God.[4] Most modern historians reject the story as pure fiction.[5] Whether it be fiction or legend, it reflects the concept that the priesthood was dominant in Judaism during these comparatively silent centuries. The royal house of David had disappeared, and the reference to it in the New Testament shows that it was represented by commonplace artisans, such as Joseph of Nazareth.

Two aspects of Jewish life disappeared during the Persian and Greek periods: the monarchy, and the prophetic office. All pretensions to independence seem to have centered in the priesthood. Prophecy, after Malachi, vanished completely. No trace of the reforming and predictive message of the prophets is present in the Dispersion of this time.

The priesthood retained some of its ancient power and became much more political in its influence than it had been under the monarchy. One or two new religious emphases appeared. The intensive study of the law that began in the exile produced a new class of leaders, the scribes. The wide dispersion of the people into congregations created a demand for copies of the law, since each congregation wanted to own one. The professional copyists had to make a study of the text in order to transcribe it correctly, and consequently became expert at it. When Herod wished to learn about the prophecies of the Messiah, he called together the chief priests and the scribes of the people (Matt. 2:4). The scribes were regarded as on a plane of equality with the priesthood in religious matters.

Another development that perhaps began in Ezra's time was the rise of the "Great Synagogue," a council of one hundred and twenty members that was formed for the purpose of administering the law and that was the forerunner of the Sanhedrin of Jesus' day. Simon the Just, who is probably to be identified with the high priest Simon I, living at the beginning of the third century B.C., is reputed to have been the last surviving member of the body. Since the references to this Great Synagogue all come from late Talmudic literature, which is notoriously inexact in historical allusions, the very existence of this body has been challenged. Some sort of govern-

---

4. Josephus *Antiquities* XI.vii.4–5.
5. See R. H. Pfeiffer, *History of New Testament Times* (New York: Harper and Brothers, Publishers, 1949), p. 9, n. 2.

ment by eldership may very well have existed, but the formal establishment of this particular organization seems unlikely.[6]

Under the Ptolemies, 322 to 198 B.C.

With the death of Alexander the Great came the collapse and the inevitable partition of his empire. He left no heirs old enough or strong enough to be his successors, and his four generals divided the realm among themselves. Ptolemy took Egypt, and Antigonus became ruler of Syria. Palestine became the battleground and the prey of both. In 320 B.C. Ptolemy invaded the land and captured Jerusalem. In 315 B.C. Antigonus recovered it, but lost it again three years later at the battle of Gaza. In 301 B.C. Antigonus was killed in the battle of Ipsus and so Ptolemy reasserted his claim. Antigonus was succeeded by Seleucus I in the rule of Syria.

Comparatively little is known of the state of the Jews in Palestine during this period. Palestine lay between the two hostile powers of Syria and Egypt and suffered equally from both. One aspect of this strife was favorable for the Jews. Both the Egyptian and Syrian rulers desired their favor, since they held the balance of power in the land. The result was that whenever one king came into possession of Palestine the Jews who had favored the other migrated to his domain. Under the first Ptolemy a group of Jews were deported to Egypt and were settled in Alexandria. Commercial opportunities and working conditions there were so good that others followed them so that within a few years a large colony had become established. Apparently Jews were quite acceptable as colonists in the new Hellenistic cities that were being founded in this era, for they were sober, energetic, and industrious.

Under the Ptolemies the Jews in Palestine enjoyed many of the privileges of a free community. The high priest was the governing officer by whom the law was administered. He was aided by the council of priests and elders. The temple was the center of national life. The Feasts of the Passover, of Weeks, and of Tabernacles were regularly observed and were attended by devout pilgrims from the whole world. The study of the law was zealously maintained, and during this period its interpretation was developed in detail.

The economic status of the people under the Ptolemaic regime seems to have been poor. They paid a very low tax, which, in consideration of the prevalent avarice of the kings and of the tax collectors of that day, probably means that they were unable to pay much. Constant warfare and emigra-

---

6. See H. L. Strack, "Synagogue, the Great," *The New Schaff-Herzog Encyclopedia of Religious Knowledge*, XI, 217.

tion had impoverished the land. In the latter part of the Ptolemaic rule Joseph, a nephew of the high priest Onias, persuaded Ptolemy III Euergetes to delegate to him the commission of collecting the taxes. So successful was his diplomacy that Ptolemy also gave him two thousand troops to assist in enforcing the collections. Those who refused to pay suffered confiscation of their entire property. Ptolemy was satisfied and Joseph grew wealthy, but the land was drained of its few remaining resources.[7] Perhaps the financial oppression of the last few years of the third century caused the people to turn their allegiance more readily from Ptolemy V to Antiochus III of Syria.

The Ptolemies, for the most part, treated the Jews very well. Under Ptolemy Philadelphus (285–246 B.C.), the successor of Ptolemy Lagus, thousands of the Jewish slaves were liberated at royal expense. Some of these were given posts of responsibility to fill. The younger generation took on Greek customs and spoke the Greek language so that they began to lose their distinctively Semitic habits of thought.

As noted earlier, during the reign of Ptolemy Philadelphus the Greek version of the Old Testament, known as the Septuagint, was created. According to the story current in Josephus' time, Ptolemy's librarian, Demetrius, was collecting copies of all known books for the great library that he was assembling in Alexandria. Hearing that the Jews had written records of their nation, Demetrius petitioned Ptolemy to secure them for him in accurate translation. Ptolemy sent to Eleazar, the Jewish high priest, asking that he send delegates, six elders from each tribe, who should be able to perform the work of translation. Eleazar reciprocated by sending the men and a copy of the law. The legend says that the seventy-two elders completed their work in seventy-two days and that when the resulting translation was read to the Jews, they all approved it.[8] The accuracy of some of the details in the story is questionable; but there can be no doubt that the Septuagint arose in Alexandria, and that it was translated to meet the demand for the Scriptures by a Greek-speaking Jewish population. By the time of Christ it was widely circulated throughout the Dispersion in the Mediterranean world and became the Bible of the early Christian church.

Under the Seleucidae, 198 to 168 B.C.

Parallel with the development of the Ptolemaic empire in Egypt was the dominion of the Seleucidae in Syria, whose capital was Antioch on the Orontes River. The rivalry between the two kingdoms involved them in constant strife. Antiochus I of Syria (280–261 B.C.) attempted to conquer

---

7. Josephus Antiquities XII.iv.2–6, 10.
8. Ibid. XII.ii.4–7, 13.

Palestine, but failed to do so. His son, Antiochus II, agreed to marry Berenice, the daughter of Ptolemy (249 B.C.), if he could secure with her the rights to the land. On the death of Ptolemy he divorced Berenice, to take back his former wife, Laodice. She, however, had him poisoned and had Berenice and her child murdered. Ptolemy III Euergetes (246–222 B.C.), thirsting for revenge, invaded Syria and plundered it. The war went on with varying fortunes until Ptolemy IV defeated Antiochus III at Raphia in 217 B.C. The Syrians were driven from Jerusalem and the country was claimed by Egypt. In 198 B.C. the tide of war turned again. The Egyptian army was severely beaten and Palestine again came under the rule of the Seleucidae.

As might be expected, the advent of the Syrians was not unanimously welcomed. A large party of the Jews, led by the priesthood under Onias III, persisted in their allegiance to Egypt. Their opponents, the house of Tobias, were more liberal in their interpretation of the law and favored Syria. In a conflict that arose between them, the house of Onias prevailed and expelled the followers of Tobias. The disgruntled Tobiads promptly reported their woes to Seleucus IV with the hint that he might be able to replenish his empty treasury with funds from the temple. Legend says that he sent his treasurer, Heliodorus, to Jerusalem for the purpose of confiscating the temple treasure, and that he was prevented from doing so by a vision that terrified him.

Seleucus died in 175 B.C., and was succeeded by his brother Antiochus IV, who was a thorough Hellenist. He was a vigorous ruler, but was so erratic that many called him Epimanes, "the madman," rather than Epiphanes, "the manifest god," which was his official title. Antiochus interfered in the affairs of Palestine by replacing Onias III with his brother Jason, who promised to pay large sums into the royal treasury and to introduce Greek customs into Jerusalem if the Jews would be registered as citizens of Antioch. The appointment of Jason was followed by the establishment of a gymnasium in Jerusalem almost under the shadow of the temple. The priests left the service of the temple for the games. Jason actually stooped to sharing in the games in honor of the Tyrian god Melkarth and sent gifts for offerings. Even his messengers refused to participate in this sacrilege, and so the gifts were applied to the building of the Syrian navy.

Antiochus became embroiled in a contest with Egypt. Fearing that Jason would not be loyal to him, he replaced him with Menelaus, another Hellenizing Jew, who favored Syria's program. Antiochus' invasion of Egypt was a failure, for the Roman envoy compelled him to withdraw. Enraged by this defeat he returned to Jerusalem in a bad mood and proceeded to vent his anger on the Jews. A large number of the inhabitants of the city were sold as slaves. The walls of the city were destroyed. The temple was plundered of its treasures and was converted into a shrine of Olympian Zeus. On December 15, 168 B.C., an image of the god was set up on its altar, and ten days later a sow was sacrificed in its honor. Heathen altars were erected everywhere throughout the country, and the observance of heathen festivals was made compulsory. Judaism was proscribed completely. The death penalty was inflicted on those who possessed or read the Torah. Sabbath observance and circumcision were forbidden.[9]

The situation became intolerable for all devout adherents of the law, and conflict was inevitable. The spark that touched off the conflagration of war was the revolt of Mattathias, an old priest in the village of Modin. When the royal agent came to Modin to compel heathen sacrifices, he offered rewards to Mattathias if he, as the oldest and most respected citizen of the village, would be the first to comply. Mattathias protested vehemently against the request, and when some less conscientious Jew approached to offer his sacrifice, Mattathias killed him at the altar. Aroused by the profanation of God's law, he also killed the king's agent and demolished the altar.

Mattathias and his sons fled into the wilderness with their families, where they were joined by others. In the war that followed, the Jews were worsted at first. Mattathias died shortly after and was buried at Modin. The contest was carried on by his son Judas, nicknamed Maccabeus ("The Hammer"). The Syrians regarded the Maccabees as guerrilla fighters of negligible importance, but after a strong Syrian detachment was routed at Beth-horon, Antiochus began to take the revolt more seriously. He raised a large army, paid it for a year in advance, and left it in charge of his general Lysias while he himself went on an eastern expedition. In a short but decisive campaign Judas twice defeated the Syrians and expelled them from Jerusalem. The temple was cleansed and a new altar was erected. A rededication service was held, and a new feast (variously called the Feast of Lights, the Feast of Dedication [cf. Jn. 10:22], or, currently, Hanukkah) was established to commemorate the occasion. He completed his success by the conquest of the lands east of the Jordan and had Palestine within his grasp.

When the news of his army's defeat reached Antiochus IV he was so shocked that he died soon thereafter. The contest was maintained by his successor. Judas Maccabeus appealed to Rome for help, but though the reply was friendly, he received no material aid. He was killed in battle and was succeeded by his brother Jonathan. The war dragged on until 143 B.C., when Simon, another brother, was recognized as an ally by Demetrius II, contestant for the crown of Syria. In 142 B.C. Demetrius gave

---

9. I Maccabees 1:21–50.

Simon political freedom and release from all taxes present and future. The independence of Judea was won and the struggles of the Maccabees had ended.

The victory of the Maccabees really terminated the influence of the Seleucidae in Palestine and gave virtual autonomy to the Jewish state until the advent of the Romans. Nevertheless, the effect of the Seleucid dominion was tremendous. Its Hellenizing pressure consolidated the Jews into a resistance group jealous of its national life and practically indissoluble among the nations through whom it was scattered.

Under the Hasmoneans, 142 to 37 B.C.

With the attainment of Jewish freedom, Simon was made high priest for life. His reign, though brief, was prosperous. A treaty was negotiated with Rome and confirmed in 139 B.C., recognizing the independence of the Jewish state and commending it to the friendship of Rome's subjects and allies. Economic conditions improved, justice was ably administered in the courts, and Jewish religious life was revived.

THE MACCABEES AND THE HASMONEANS (166 B.C.-A.D. 100)

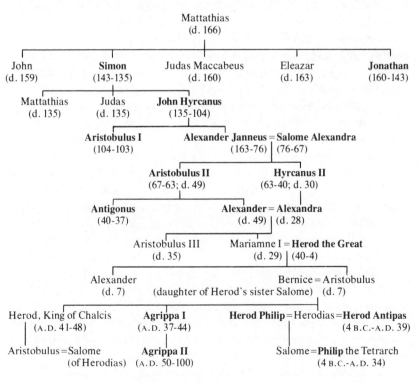

Rulers' names are in boldface.

The happy interval, however, was all too short. Demetrius II of Syria was dethroned and captured by the Parthians (139 B.C.). His brother who succeeded him, Antiochus VII, broke the pact of friendship with Simon and demanded heavy tribute in the place of free aid. Under Simon's sons, Judah and Jonathan, the Syrians were defeated, and so the external danger was averted.

The real peril to Judea was internal strife. Simon and two of his sons were treacherously murdered by Ptolemy, his son-in-law, in 135 B.C. His surviving son, John Hyrcanus (135–104 B.C.), took possession of Jerusalem before Ptolemy could capture it and then besieged Ptolemy in his castle. Ptolemy finally fled to Egypt.

In the meantime Antiochus VII of Syria had besieged Jerusalem. The Jews were forced to capitulate and to pay tribute to the king of Syria. At his death the claimants for the throne plunged Syria into civil war. Hyrcanus immediately made the most of his opportunity by conquering Idumea on the south and the Samaritans on the north, as well as Medeba and the neighboring cities on the east of the Jordan. Hyrcanus became high priest and head of the state and the founder of the Hasmonean dynasty.

When he died he committed the government of the state to his wife and to his oldest son, Judah Aristobulus. Aristobulus imprisoned his mother and his brothers and seized the government for himself. In a year's time he died, and his widow, Salome Alexandra, married the next surviving brother, Alexander Jannaeus, who was king from 103 to 76 B.C. Alexander continued the conquest of Palestine. His reign was filled with civil turmoil, in which he nearly lost his throne.

Aristobulus II, son of Salome Alexandra, became king after her death. He removed his older brother, Hyrcanus II, from the priesthood. By this time the general chaos in the affairs of Palestine and Syria had attracted the attention of Rome. Pompey detached his lieutenant Scaurus to investigate and to settle the political fracas. Scaurus decided for Aristobulus, who suddenly revolted. The Romans attacked Jerusalem, and the following of Aristobulus would have fought to the death, had not Hyrcanus surrendered the city. The Romans reappointed him as king and took Aristobulus with his family and many other captives to Rome to grace the triumphal procession.

Alexander, Aristobulus' son, escaped while en route to Rome, and attempted a revolt against Hyrcanus. He was overcome by the Roman proconsul of Syria, who placed all of Palestine under the governor of Syria.

In the civil war between Pompey and Caesar in 49 B.C., Hyrcanus aided Caesar, who rewarded him by recognizing him as the responsible head of the Jewish nation, and by restoring the coastal cities to his rule. His minister Antipater was granted Roman citizenship. Antipater was the real power behind the throne. He appointed his own son Phasael prefect of Jerusalem, and his other son, Herod, as prefect of Galilee.

Through the changing fortunes of the civil wars of Rome, Herod succeeded in keeping himself in favor with the ruling party. Hyrcanus gave Herod his support. Antony appointed Herod and Phasael corulers of Judea. While Antony was in Egypt, the Parthians attacked Jerusalem and captured Hyrcanus and Phasael. Herod escaped from the city in time to save his life. Antigonus (40–37 B.C.), another son of Aristobulus II, backed by the Sadducean party, and viewed by the Jews as an enemy of Rome, marched against Herod. With the support of the Parthians, he claimed the kingship, but was defeated by the Roman general Sosius in Jerusalem in 37 B.C. At the instigation of Herod, Antony ordered Antigonus beheaded— the first case in which a captured king had been executed by the Romans. With the death of Antigonus came the end of the Hasmonean dynasty.

Under the Herods, 37 B.C. to A.D. 6

The Herodian dynasty began with Antipater. His son Herod, called the Great, inherited all of his father's ability in diplomacy and government, in addition to the throne of Judea, which had been vacated by the death of Hyrcanus. Farrar says that "Antipater built the superstructure; Herod put on it the coping-stone; and turned the tent of his Idumean ancestors into a royal palace, which was regarded during his lifetime as one of the most splendid of all the world."[10]

Herod the Great, 37 to 4 B.C.   Herod began his reign in 37 B.C. at the age of twenty-two. Driven from Palestine by the invasion of the Parthians who supported Antigonus as the successor of Hyrcanus, he succeeded in making his escape. In his company were his mother Kypros, his sister Salome, and Mariamne, the daughter of Hyrcanus, who was engaged to him. Leaving them under the care of his brother Joseph at the fortress of Masada on the Dead Sea, he fought his way to Alexandria and thence sailed to Rome.

By persuasive speech or by secret intrigue he obtained the favor of Antony and Octavian and was duly inaugurated as king of the Jews. He returned to Palestine, rescued his family from the siege, and proceeded to make himself master of the country. He exterminated the brigands who infested Galilee. He contested with Antigonus for the possession of Jerusalem and finally captured it with the aid of Roman forces. Antigonus was sent in chains to Antioch, where he was executed by the Romans.

---

10. F. W. Farrar, *The Herods* (London: Service & Paton, 1898), p. 61.

Among Herod's first acts was the appointment of a high priest. Inasmuch as he could not hold the office himself because of his Idumean blood, and because he did not want to take a member of the Hasmonean family who might cherish political ambitions, he selected Hananiel of Babylon, probably identifiable with Annas who is mentioned in the Gospels. Alexandra, the mother of Mariamne, sought the post for her son Aristobulus III, and by her intrigues with Antony through Cleopatra of Egypt forced Herod to appoint him, though he was underage. Hananiel was deposed and Aristobulus took his place. So great was the esteem in which the populace held Aristobulus that Herod was jealous. At a banquet given in his honor at Jericho Herod's servants did away with Aristobulus by drowning him while bathing.

Herod was summoned to Egypt to answer for his crime. He entrusted Mariamne to her uncle Joseph, giving orders that if he were condemned, Joseph should slay both Mariamne and her mother. Herod returned safely, having made peace with Antony, only to find that Mariamne had discovered his order. He interpreted Joseph's failure to keep his secret as proof that Mariamne had been unfaithful, and so he executed Joseph at once.

In 29 B.C. the Roman Senate declared war on Antony and Cleopatra. Herod was forced to make the choice of deserting his friend or fighting a hopeless battle with Rome. This disastrous dilemma was resolved by Cleopatra, who, fearing Herod as an enemy, persuaded Antony to send him on a minor campaign in Arabia. Herod won the campaign. When Antony and Cleopatra lost the naval battle of Actium, Herod realized that he could no longer support them, and so he withdrew from his embarrassing alliance.

Herod made peace with Octavian, the victor of Actium, and was confirmed in his position as king of Judea and ally of the Roman people. The death of Cleopatra removed one of his chief dangers, for her constant plots to acquire the kingdom of Judea had been the source of many of his troubles.

The victorious return from the conference with Octavian was spoiled for Herod by the coldness of Mariamne, the one woman whom he really loved. She had learned that when he left for Rhodes to meet Octavian, he had repeated the instructions of the former occasion that she should be killed if he failed to return. She accused him of the murder of her grandfather Hyrcanus, who had been executed for complicity in a plot of her uncle and her brother. The tension between them was made more acute by the lies of Herod's sister and mother, who were intensely jealous of her. Mariamne was imprisoned and was ultimately executed.

Remorse so gripped Herod that he became physically and mentally ill. Alexandra, thinking that his end had come, plotted to put his sons and her

Ruins of the Herodium, one of Herod the Great's fortresses, near Bethlehem.

grandsons, Alexander and Aristobulus, on the throne. Enraged by this conspiracy, Herod ordered that she should be destroyed.

Herod conferred many benefits on the people through subsidies in time of famine and by erecting public works. The military installations and fortifications that he built made Palestine free from foreign invasion. Because of the greatly stimulated building program the trades flourished and economic conditions improved greatly. Peace brought prosperity, and in spite of the incessant intrigues that went on in his court, Herod's reign was in some measure successful.

Herod did not succeed in winning the friendship of the Jews. His Idumean blood made him a foreigner in their eyes, and his willingness to support heathen cults by his gifts aroused suspicion concerning his loyalty to Judaism. In spite of the fact that he built a new temple of great magnificence at which he gave occasional perfunctory attendance, he was never a truly godly Jew. His cynical use of the priesthood as a political tool and the looseness of his personal life made him generally hated by the devout men of Judaism.

In 23 B.C. Herod married another wife named Mariamne, the

daughter of Simon, son of Boethus, a priest. In order to please her he removed the high priest and gave his office to Simon. The new priest soon became the target of universal hatred. Four years later when the two sons of Mariamne I were recalled from Rome, where Herod had sent them to be educated, the populace acclaimed them with undisguised enthusiasm. The people recognized them as scions of the Hasmoneans through their mother, and evidently hoped that they might someday relieve the miseries that the oppressive policies of their father had created. The young princes, who had learned at Rome to speak their minds, were a little too free with their sentiments. They incurred the enmity of their half-brother Antipater, who accused them to Herod; and after a long and tortuous series of accusations and reconciliations, they too met death.

The last days of Herod were filled with violence and hatred. Antipater, who had tried to accelerate his father's death in order that he might succeed to the throne, suffered the same fate as his brothers. Augustus, to whom Herod appealed for permission to execute Antipater, remarked in a biting witticism that he would rather be Herod's hog than his son.[11] Smitten with dropsy and cancer of the intestines, and haunted by the memory of his murders, Herod died on April 1, 4 B.C.

The jealous and unscrupulous character of this man explains the duplicity of his dealing with the Magi from the East and his brutality in ordering the massacre of the children in Bethlehem (Matt. 2:1–18). The silence of history concerning the massacre at Bethlehem can be explained easily, for the slaughter of a dozen infants in an obscure Judean village would not arouse much comment in comparison with the enormity of Herod's greater crimes.

Herod's Successors.   By Herod's last will the kingdom was bequeathed to Archelaus. In order to secure confirmation of the appointment, Archelaus resolved to go to Rome as speedily as possible. The resentment against the cruelties of the Herodian family was so strong in Judea that he felt the necessity of pacifying the country before he left. A rebellion broke out at the Passover that was quelled only by the use of troops.

Archelaus went to Rome, leaving his brother Philip in charge. Antipas, a third brother, who had been appointed as Herod's successor in his second will, also went there to press his claims. Augustus did not render an immediate decision at the first hearing, because of the conflicting parties that were represented.

Before the case was continued, a second revolt broke out in Judea. Sabinus, the procurator whom Augustus had sent out to administer affairs after Herod's death until some settlement could be made with the heirs,

---

11. Greek *hys*=hog; *huios*=son.

seized Jerusalem and plundered the temple. He was besieged in turn by the rebels and was rescued only by the arrival of Varus, the governor of Syria, and his legions. The Jews sent an embassy to Rome asking that none of the Herods be appointed king, but that they should be given autonomy. Philip also appeared at the tribunal to support the claims of Archelaus.

At the second hearing, Augustus confirmed Herod's will. Archelaus obtained Judea, Samaria, and Idumea, with the title of ethnarch. Antipas became tetrarch of Galilee and Perea. Philip was made tetrarch of Batanea, Trachonitis, and Auranitis, north of the Sea of Galilee on the east side of the Jordan.

Archelaus, 4 B.C. to A.D. 6. Archelaus married Glaphyra, daughter of the Cappadocian king Archelaus, who had been the wife of his half-brother Alexander, and, after his death, the wife of Juba of Mauretania. This marriage brought Archelaus into further disfavor with the Jews, because he had divorced his own wife to marry her, and because she already had children by Alexander.

Like his father, Archelaus promoted the building of public works. His rule was so distasteful to his people that after nine years a delegation of the Jewish and Samaritan leaders went to Rome to file complaint against him. Augustus, after listening to their petition, deposed Archelaus from his office and banished him to Vienne in Gaul in A.D. 6.

The character of Archelaus' reign receives a curious confirmation in an incidental reference in the Gospels. Matthew, in telling of the return of Joseph and Mary from Egypt, says:

> But when he [Joseph] heard that Archelaus was reigning over Judea in the room of his father Herod, he was afraid to go thither; and being warned of God in a dream, he withdrew into the parts of Galilee.
>
> (Matt. 2:22)

Evidently Archelaus' reputation for jealousy of possible rivals and for general vindictiveness was equal to his father's.

Philip the Tetrarch, 4 B.C. to A.D. 34. The territory assigned to Philip included the northeast corner of Palestine bounded on the west by the Sea of Galilee, the upper Jordan River, the Lake of Merom, and the southern Lebanon range. On the north it extended to the borders of Abilene near Damascus. On the east and southeast it projected into the desert, and on the south it bordered on the Decapolis. Its population was largely Syrian and Greek, with a much smaller Jewish element than lived in Archelaus' domain.

Philip was a happy exception to the Herods in general. He followed their precedent as a builder; but in his dealings with his people he was just and fair. Caesarea Philippi, mentioned in the Gospels (Matt. 16:13; Mark 8:27), was built on the site of the ancient Panias, at the springs of the Jordan, and was named for the emperor and for him. Bethsaida Julias, on the northwest side of the Lake of Galilee, was also one of his cities.

He married Salome, the daughter of Herodias. Josephus had only good to say of him.[12] He died peacefully in A.D. 34. His tetrarchy was placed under the Roman administration of Syria until, in A.D. 37, it was given by Caligula to his nephew, Agrippa I.

Philip is mentioned by Luke (3:1) as being tetrarch of Iturea and Trachonitis. He is not mentioned elsewhere in the narrative of the New Testament.

Herod Antipas, 4 B.C. to A.D. 39. The Herod who is most prominent in the Gospels is Herod Antipas, the tetrarch of Galilee and Perea. Jesus alluded to him as "that fox" (Luke 13:32), or, more exactly, "that vixen." The epithet was a characterization not only of his slyness, but of his craftiness and vindictiveness as well.

During his reign of forty-three years he built a new capital on the shores of the Lake of Galilee named Tiberias. Because the city was erected on the site of an ancient graveyard, the strict Jews would not live in it, and so he had to colonize it by force. Its government was modeled on the Greek system.

By religion, Herod Antipas was a Jew. He took the side of the Jewish populace in protesting against Pilate's setting up a pagan votive shield in Jerusalem, and he attended the Feast of the Passover when it was held in that city (23:7).

Herod Antipas appears in the Gospels as the murderer of John the Baptist, and as the one before whom Jesus was tried (23:7–12). His wife Herodias was the daughter of his half-brother Aristobulus, and had been originally the wife of another half-brother, Herod Philip I (Matt. 14:3; Mark 6:17; Luke 3:19), mentioned only in the Gospels and not to be confused with Philip the Tetrarch. When Antipas went to Rome he stayed with Herod Philip, who was living there as a private citizen, and he became enamored of Herodias. Antipas promptly divorced his own wife, who was a daughter of the Arabian king Aretas. Aretas' daughter, learning of Antipas' intentions, fled to her father, who made war on Herod.

Herod carried through his marriage with Herodias, who, with her daughter Salome, joined him at Tiberias. Perhaps at this time Herod went down to the fortress of Machaerus in Perea in order that he might watch more closely the ministry of John the Baptist. Although Herod seems to have respected the blunt honesty of the prophet who rebuked him boldly

---

12. Josephus *Antiquities* XVIII.v.4.

for his misdeeds, Herodias was infuriated and finally succeeded in securing his death. Antipas was too weak or too indifferent to justice to save the life of the man who had told him the truth (Matt. 14:1–12; Mark 6:14–29; Luke 3:19).

The marriage with Herodias finally cost Antipas his kingdom. When Caligula became emperor at Rome after the death of Tiberius in A.D. 37, one of his first acts was to make Agrippa I, brother of Herodias and son of Aristobulus, king of the territory that had formerly been the tetrarchy of Philip. Agrippa's good fortune incited Herodias to urge her husband to petition Caligula for a royal title. When he arrived at Rome and presented himself to Caligula, Fortunatus, the representative of Agrippa, accused him of treasonable negotiations against Rome. Caligula promptly deposed Antipas and banished him to Lyons in Gaul, where he died. Agrippa succeeded to his rival's tetrarchy.

Herod Agrippa I, A.D. 37 to 44. Herod Agrippa I was the son of Aristobulus and his cousin Berenice, daughter of Salome, sister of Herod the Great. After completing his education at Rome, he returned to Palestine in A.D. 23 and secured an appointment from Herod Antipas, his brother-in-law, as overseer of markets in Tiberias. He quarreled with Her-

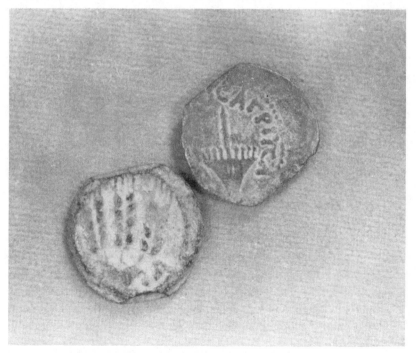

Coins from the time of Herod Agrippa (A.D. 41–44).

od and later with the Roman governor in Antioch to whom he had fled for refuge. On returning to Italy, he became tutor of Tiberius' grandson and was an intimate friend of Caligula, to whom, on one occasion, Agrippa suggested that he should be the next emperor. When Tiberius learned of this remark, he threw Agrippa into prison, but the death of Tiberius occurred soon afterward, and Agrippa was released.

Immediately on his accession Caligula gave Agrippa his appointment. Agrippa had enough sympathy for the Jews and enough influence with Caligula to keep the latter from erecting an image of himself in the temple at Jerusalem. By so doing he averted what would have been a violent uprising of the Jews.

When Caligula was murdered in A.D. 41 Agrippa was still in Rome. He supported Claudius' succession, and Claudius in return confirmed not only the realm Caligula had given to him, but also Judea and Samaria. Agrippa I, then, held under his own power the reunited domain of Herod the Great.

On his return to Palestine he took up residence in Jerusalem and worshiped regularly at the temple. He lived in accord with the strict Jewish law and suppressed all attempts to bring pagan ceremonies or images into the synagogues. Agrippa's devotion to Judaism made him one of the first persecutors of Christianity. During his rule the tension between the Pharisaic party and the new sect of believers in Jesus had been mounting until finally the king intervened. He arrested and executed James, the son of Zebedee, and imprisoned Peter. The latter was released by divine interposition. Agrippa ordered that the guards should be punished by death, and he went down to Caesarea (Acts 12:11–19).

Herod's death occurred suddenly in A.D. 44. Josephus and Luke agree[13] in the general details of the account. The former says that he attended games in honor of the emperor at Caesarea, dressed in a silver robe. The resplendent appearance of his garments as they glistened in the sun caused his flatterers to avow that he was a god. Shortly afterward he was stricken with severe intestinal distress, and he died within five days.

Herod Agrippa II, A.D. 50 to 100.   Herod Agrippa I left four children, three daughters and a son. Drusilla, one of the daughters, married Felix, the Roman procurator of Judea. Agrippa II, the son, was in Rome at the time of his father's death. In A.D. 50, after the death of his uncle, Herod of Chalcis, he was given the kingdom, which included the right to appoint the high priest of the temple in Jerusalem. In A.D. 53 he relinquished the kingdom of Chalcis and was given the former tetrarchies of Philip and

---

13. Cf. Acts 12:20–23 with Josephus *Antiquities* XVIII.vi.7.

Lysanias. After the death of Claudius in A.D. 54, Nero added to his realm some parts of Galilee and Perea.

When Festus became procurator of Judea, Agrippa, in company with his sister Bernice who had become his consort, went down to Caesarea to welcome him to his new office. At this time he acted as the religious adviser for Festus in the case of Paul, whose status was a puzzle to the pagan Roman (Acts 25:13–26:32). Though Agrippa had a good knowledge of Judaism, he was indifferent to its deeper claims; and while he observed its ceremonial requirements, he never exhibited any sincere convictions of its truth.

In the revolution of A.D. 66 he openly sided with the Romans. He gave his allegiance to Vespasian, and joined with Titus in the triumph over his own people. His kingdom was enlarged by the new emperor. In A.D. 75 he and Bernice moved to Rome, where Bernice and Titus became involved in a scandal. Titus had planned to marry her, but he desisted when he realized the intensity of the popular feeling against them. Agrippa died in A.D. 100.

Under the Priests to the Fall of Jerusalem, A.D. 70

The various foreign rulers that dominated Palestine—the Ptolemies, the Seleucidae, the Herods, and later the Romans—were generally regarded by the Jewish people as usurpers whose rule had to be tolerated but who were never the rightful sovereigns. The people may have had to submit to their political yoke, but they never gave them hearty allegiance. The real controlling power of the Jewish mind was the priesthood.

During the history of Israel various types of civil government had prevailed at different times. Under Moses elders represented the tribes and counseled with the leader concerning his action. In the period of the judges there was no central government, but as need arose from time to time aggressive leaders appeared who gained a popular following but established no permanent order. In the eras of the united and divided kingdoms the king was the head of the state. In all of these regimes, however, the word of the priest was final because he was a spokesman for God and in the Jewish state religious authority was regarded as supreme. If the priesthood was corrupt, political life was also debased; and if there was a revival, the worship of Jehovah was restored and the civil authority was strengthened.

During the exile the functioning of the priesthood as a class was temporarily suspended by the destruction of the temple. The priests, however, did not disappear; for when the captives returned in 536 B.C. a large company of priests and Levites were among them (Ezra 2:36–54). When the temple was rebuilt these resumed their duties, and with a few interruptions the worship continued until the final destruction of Jerusalem by the Romans.

Throughout this long period the priesthood served as the central control in Judaism. The high priest took office by hereditary right and retained it for life. He exercised supreme authority in the state under the overlord who happened to possess the country at the time. To what extent the conquerors of Judea gave a free hand to the high priest cannot be ascertained positively. Probably he was independent as long as he did not interfere with tribute or with foreign policies. Both the Greeks and the Romans gave considerable latitude to the subject peoples in administering their national affairs.

Associated with the high priest was a council of elders comprised of the wisest and most experienced men of the nation. Some of them were priests; some, like Ezra, were scribes and professional students of the law; others were drawn from the wealthy and better educated landholders and businessmen. The government was really in the hands of a religious aristocracy, of which the Sanhedrin, as this body was later called, was representative.

The succession of the priesthood through the Persian period is given without comment in Nehemiah 12:1–11. Josephus adds that John, the high priest (evidently identical with Jonathan in Neh. 12:11), had a brother, Jesus, whose friend Bagosus, a general of the Persian army, had promised to procure him the priesthood. The two brothers quarreled in the temple, and so John killed Jesus, to the general scandal of the people and the Persian authorities.[14]

The place of the high priest as the leader of that nation was clearly demonstrated in the negotiations with Alexander as reported by Josephus. When Alexander invaded Palestine and laid siege to Tyre, he demanded of the high priest that all support which the Jews had formerly given to Persia should be transferred to him. The high priest refused, because he had given his oath to Darius and would not go back on it. Alexander replied with a threat that when he had finished his conquest, he would teach the priest to whom he should give his oaths.

Josephus' account states that when Alexander approached Jerusalem, Jaddua, the high priest, went out to meet him with a procession. Alexander was deeply impressed and gave reverence to the priest, who showed him predictions of his conquest in the Jewish Scriptures. The negotiations proceeded peacefully and the Greek army departed from Palestine, leaving the Jews to govern themselves.[15]

In the Ptolemaic period the priesthood remained powerful and provided good government. Onias I, son of Jaddua, and his son Simon I, the Just, received favorable mention in Josephus. With the passing of time, however, the high priesthood became a political prize that was generally

---

14. Josephus *Antiquities* XI.vii.1.
15. *Ibid.* XI.viii.4, 5. See above, nn. 4 and 5.

sold to the highest bidder. The successful candidate had to comply with the wishes of his political lord if he wished to hold his position. Consequently the high priesthood lost much of its independent influence and was, until the time of the Maccabees, largely subservient to the state.

With the Maccabean revolt came a change in the priesthood. The older line of priests who had held office under the Seleucidae was displaced by the Hasmonean dynasty whose progenitor was John Hyrcanus, himself a descendant of the Maccabees. Under the last of the Seleucidae and under the Herods the priesthood maintained its ascendancy in Judaism, except for a few lapses when Herod changed the priestly appointment.

From the death of Herod the Great until the fall of Jerusalem the priesthood was again the chief political power of Judea. The high priest acted as adviser to the Roman procurator and not infrequently his political pressure caused the governor to change his policy. Through his influence over the populace the high priest was able to mold public opinion and thus he could bend stubborn officials to his will or else compel them to risk the emperor's displeasure for failing to keep on good terms with their subjects. The cry of the populace at Jesus' hearing before Pilate, "If thou release this man, thou art not Caesar's friend" (John 19:12), was a good example of such machinations; for Mark says that "the chief priests stirred up the multitude" (Mark 15:11).

The rule of the priests was concurrent with the three periods previously mentioned and it continued until the fall of Jerusalem, at which time the temple was destroyed and the priesthood was dispersed.

Under the Romans Until Bar-Cochba, A.D. 135

Clear-cut chronological divisions between the successive national sovereignties over Judea are impossible to establish. Just as the priesthood was concomitant with the sovereignty of the Ptolemies, the Seleucidae, and the Herods, so the Herods and the priesthood held sway simultaneously with Rome. From the conquest of Pompey in 63 B.C. Rome had assumed a protectorate over Judea, and had regarded both Herod and the priesthood as vassal kings. When on the death of Herod the Great his less capable son Archelaus followed him as king, he proved to be so unpopular a ruler that Rome deposed him, and appointed Coponius as prefect of Judea. From that time, with some local exceptions, Rome ruled the country directly until the last futile revolt in A.D. 135.

These governors were not generally popular, and many of them did not remain in office longer than three years. Valerius Gratus (A.D. 15–26) was disliked because he had interfered with the succession of the priesthood by appointing one of his own candidates. His successor, Pontius Pilate (A.D. 26–36), is perhaps the best known of the prefects because of his connection with the trial and death of Jesus. At the very beginning of his term he offended the Jews needlessly by insisting that his troops should carry into Jerusalem banners bearing on them the image of the emperor. The Jews protested violently against such a profanation of the city. Pilate yielded only when he saw that nothing but useless bloodshed could follow his course of action. Later he became embroiled in a dispute with the Samaritans and was replaced in A.D. 36 by Marcellus.

The accession of the emperor Caligula in A.D. 37 brought a new crisis. Under the delusion that he was a god, Caligula issued orders that his statue should be set up in the temple at Jerusalem. Petronius, the legate of Syria, was delegated to carry out the command. He was thus faced with the dilemma of disobeying the emperor's command by refusing to erect the image or of plunging the whole country into a religious war. He succeeded in postponing action, and fortunately for him the dilemma was solved by the death of Caligula in A.D. 41.

Throughout the entire period up to the opening of the Jewish war in A.D. 66 there was constant tension between the Roman officials and the people. Local outbursts of armed resistance were not infrequent. The party of the Zealots, who were stronger in the rural sections and in the highlands of Galilee, openly advocated a holy war on Rome. The procurators had to maintain vigilance to the point of oppressiveness to maintain order. The popular hatred of Rome was only increased by the occasional skirmishes between the Jewish outlaws and the Roman legionaries, and the appearance of a leader with Messianic ambitions was enough to draw after him a numerous and fanatical crowd of followers.

Among the later procurators M. Antonius Felix and Porcius Festus are mentioned in Acts in connection with Paul (Acts 23:24–24:27; 25:1–26:32). Under Felix' regime the latent hostility of Jews against Romans began to crystallize into a definite attempt to break the Roman yoke. Josephus records an incident of an Egyptian Jew who gathered a group of supporters by promising to make the walls of Jerusalem fall at his word, but Felix' soldiers dispersed them and compelled their leader to flee.[16] Evidently the centurion who took Paul into protective custody had this episode in mind when he asked him if he were not "the Egyptian, who before these days stirred up to sedition and led out into the wilderness the four thousand men of the Assassins" (21:38).

Whether because of malice or mismanagement Felix' procuratorship was characterized by constant turmoil. The contrast between the opening words of Tertullus and of Paul at the latter's hearing before Felix is significant. Whereas Tertullus flattered Felix by saying,

---

16. *Ibid.* XX.vii.6. Cf. Acts 21:38.

Seeing that by thee we enjoy much peace, and that by thy providence evils are corrected for this nation . . .

(Acts 24:2),

Paul introduced his defense by stating that Felix had "been of many years a judge unto this nation" (24:10), a statement that was strictly true. The stern measures Felix took to repress the riots that recurred in Caesarea and the general miseries Judea suffered under his rule prompted his recall to Rome, where he would certainly have been punished for malfeasance had not his brother Pallas, a favorite of Nero, interceded for him.

Porcius Festus, his successor, seems to have been an honest man and a conscientious administrator. He died in office after two years, but his successors undid whatever small good he had been able to accomplish.

Between the death of Festus and the opening of the Jewish war political conditions in Judea deteriorated rapidly. The high priests were avaricious and cruel and the Roman governors were rapacious and oppressive. The Gentile inhabitants of Caesarea went out of their way to provoke the ire of the Jewish population, and Florus plundered the temple treasury. Finally the Jews, infuriated by constant abuse, rebelled.

The conflict began in A.D. 66 with a series of local uprisings in various cities, in which the Roman garrisons were massacred by the Jewish rebels; or, if the Gentiles proved the stronger, the Jewish population suffered frightfully. Cestius Gallus, the legate of Syria, marched on Jerusalem and laid siege to the city, but for some unaccountable reason he lifted the siege suddenly and retreated in disorder. This unexpected good fortune convinced the Jews that divine aid was on their side and they united their forces for war.

Nero appointed Vespasian as commander of the Roman forces in Judea. Early in A.D. 67 he mustered an army of sixty thousand men and proceeded to Jerusalem. In the meantime John of Gischala, a leader of the Zealots, had entered Jerusalem and had plunged the city into civil war. Vespasian, realizing that Jerusalem was torn by internal strife, used the opportunity to conquer Perea, Judea, and Idumea, and was about to resume the siege of the city when he received news of Nero's death. In July of A.D. 69 the legions of the East proclaimed him emperor. Leaving his son Titus in charge of the operations in Judea, he went to Alexandria and thence to Rome, where he arrived in A.D. 70.

Within Jerusalem John of Gischala had been joined by another Zealot, Simon Bar-Giora, and by Eleazer, son of Simon. The three leaders quarreled among themselves, and so their followers fought each other with utter savagery. In the spring of A.D. 70 Titus tightened the siege. Weakened by famine and internecine strife, the city fell to the Romans in August, when the walls were breached and the gates were burned. Contrary to Titus'

Aerial view of Masada, showing the fortress on top and Herod's three-tiered palace.

orders, the temple was set on fire, the population was either massacred or sold into slavery, and the city was razed to the ground.

Three more years were required to complete the conquest of the remaining fortresses of Herodium, Machaerus, and Masada. The contest was hopeless, however. For all practical purposes it may be said that the Jewish commonwealth ended with the destruction of the temple.

During the reign of Trajan insurrections of the Jews in Egypt and Cyrene were crushed relentlessly. The last spark of Jewish independence was extinguished with the revolt of Bar-Cochba in A.D. 135 under Hadrian. Bar-Cochba, "son of the star," was so named because he was regarded by the rabbinate as the "star out of Jacob" (Num. 24:17) prophesied by Balaam. The revolt was caused by Hadrian's law that forbade circumcision and by his order to build a temple of Jupiter on the site of the former temple in Jerusalem. Bar-Cochba was driven from the city and was captured, Jerusalem was made a Roman city that no Jew could enter under pain of death, and the temple of Jupiter was built where formerly sacrifices to Jehovah were offered by his worshipers.

The nation perished politically, but Judaism had not died. In A.D. 90, Jonathan Ben Zakkai, a Jewish teacher, opened at Jamnia a school for the study of the law. With him were associated other teachers, Pharisean by creed, who kept alive the observances of their faith. Although the priesthood disappeared and the sacrifices were ended, the teachers of the law persisted, substituting good works and study for the offerings that no longer had an altar.

FOR FURTHER READING*

Angus, Samuel, "Roman Empire, and Christianity," in *International Standard Bible Encyclopedia*, IV, 2598–2611. Broad general article, covering whole period.

Boak, A. E. R. *A History of Rome to 565 A.D.* New York: The Macmillan Company, 1921. Pp. xvi, 444. A college textbook on Roman history.

Busch, Fritz-Otto. *The Five Herods.* Translated from the German by E. W. Dickes. London: Robert Hale, Ltd., 1958. Pp. 192.

Cambridge Ancient History. Editors S. A. Cook, F. E. Adcock, and M. P. Charlesworth. Vol. X: *The Augustan Empire 44 B.C.–A.D. 70.* New York: The Macmillan Company, 1934. Pp. xxxii, 1058. An exhaustive discussion of the period.

Duckworth, H. T. F. "The Roman Provincial System," in *Beginnings of Christianity*, Part I, Vol. I, pp. 171–207. Editors F. J. Foakes-Jackson and Kirsopp Lake. London: Macmillan & Company, Ltd., 1920. A thorough discussion of the Roman provincial system.

Durant, Will. *Caesar and Christ.* New York: Simon and Schuster, 1944.

Grant, Michael. *Nero: Emperor in Conflict.* New York: American Heritage Press, 1970.

Hammond, Mason. *The Augustan Principate.* Cambridge, Mass.: Harvard University Press, 1933. Pp. 341. Very full bibliography. Deals with aspects of the Principate, such as the Senate, the army, etc.

Lissner, Ivar. *The Caesars: Might and Madness.* New York: G. P. Putnam's Sons, 1958.

Marsh, Frank Burr. *The Reign of Tiberius.* Oxford: University Press, 1931. Pp. vii, 335. For the last days of Tiberius, see pp. 160–229.

Mattingly, Harold. *Roman Imperial Civilization.* London: Edwin Arnold (Publishers) Ltd., 1957. Historical and cultural background of Rome.

Perowne, Stewart. *The Life and Times of Herod the Great.* London: Hodder & Stoughton, 1956. Pp. 186.

_____. *The Later Herods.* London: Hodder & Stoughton, Ltd., 1958. Pp. xiv, 216.

Ramsay, W. M. *The Church in the Roman Empire Before A.D. 170.* New York and London: G. P. Putnam's Sons, n.d. Pp. xv, 494.

Rostovtzeff, M. *A History of the Ancient World.* Vol. II: *Rome.* Translated from the Russian by J. D. Duff. Oxford: Clarendon Press, 1928. Pp. 387. Thorough and well illustrated.

_____. *The Social and Economic History of the Hellenistic World.* Three volumes. Oxford: Clarendon Press, 1941. Pp. 602, 1312, 1779. See esp. Vol. I, Chap.

---

*For a list of General Tools (The Text, Commentaries, Concordances, Dictionaries, Handbooks, Archaeology, Introduction, and Geography) see the General Bibliography on pp. 435–440.

III, pp. 126–187 for economic and social conditions; Vol. II, Chap. VIII, pp. 1032–1098 for a good general estimate of Hellenism.

Salmon, Edward T. *A History of the Roman World from 30 B.C. to A.D. 138.* New York: The Macmillan Company, 1944. Pp. 363. Brief, clear, comprehensive.

Sherwin-White, A. N. *Roman Society & Roman Law in the New Testament.* Oxford: Clarendon Press, 1963.

Stauffer, Ethelbert. *Christ and the Caesars.* London: SCM Press, 1955.

Tarn, W. W. *Alexander the Great.* Vol. I: *Narrative.* Cambridge: University Press, 1948. Pp. xi, 161. A condensed account of Alexander's campaigns. See pp. 121–148 for discussion of his personality and aims.

Waddy, Lawrence. *Pax Romana and World Peace.* New York: W. W. Norton & Company, n.d.

HISTORY OF THE JEWS

Finkelstein, Louis, ed. *The Jews: Their History, Culture, and Religion.* Two volumes. New York: Harper & Brothers, Publishers, 1949. Pp. xxxiii, 744, vi, 1431. For Post-Biblical Literature and the Talmud, see pp. 70–114, 115–215. See also "Hellenistic Jewish Literature" by Ralph Marcus, pp. 745–783.

Graetz, H. *Popular History of the Jews.* Translated by Rabbi A. B. Rhine. Six volumes. Fifth Edition. New York: Hebrew Publishing Company, 1937. See Vol. II, pp. 1–232. Contains Jewish estimate of John the Baptist and Jesus.

Josephus, Flavius. *Antiquities of the Jews* and *Wars of the Jews.* English translation by H. St. John Thackeray and Ralph Marcus. *Loeb Library Translation.* Eight volumes. London: William Heinemann, 1926–.

Kent, Charles Foster. *A History of the Jewish People During the Babylonian, Persian, and Greek Periods.* Fifth Edition. New York: Charles Scribner's Sons, 1902. Pp. xxii, 380. For the Greek period, see pp. 271–340. Useful maps and charts. Written on basis of liberal critical view.

Latimer, Elizabeth W. *Judea from Cyrus to Titus, 537 B.C.–70 A.D.* Chicago: A. C. McClurg & Company, 1899. Pp. 382. Elementary, but full and helpful.

Oesterley, W. O. E. *A History of Israel.* Vol. II: *From the Fall of Jerusalem to the Bar-Kokhba Revolt, A.D. 135.* Oxford: The Clarendon Press, 1939.

Riggs, James Stevenson. *A History of the Jewish People During the Maccabean and Roman Periods.* New York: Charles Scribner's Sons, 1908. Pp. xxi, 320. Contains maps and numerous charts.

Sachar, Abram Leon. *A History of the Jews.* Second Edition, revised to 1940. New York: Alfred A. Knopf, 1940. Pp. xv, 397, xvi.

Schurer, E., Vermes, G., and Millar, F. *The History of the Jewish People in the Age of Jesus Christ.* Edinburgh: T. & T. Clark, 1973–. To be issued in three volumes.

Ruins of the Propylaea at the entrance to the Acropolis at Athens. They were erected in 437 B.C. by Pericles under the direction of the architect Mnesicles.

CHAPTER 2

THE SOCIAL WORLD AND THE ECONOMIC WORLD

THE SOCIAL WORLD

THE world of the first century was not unlike the modern world of the twentieth century. Rich and poor, virtuous men and criminals, freemen and slaves lived side by side, and the social and economic conditions that prevailed were similar to those of the present day in many respects.

JEWISH SOCIETY

Both in Judaism and in the pagan world there was a wealthy aristocracy. In Judaism it was a religious group, consisting chiefly of the families of the priesthood and of the leading rabbis. The clan of the Hasmoneans had dominated Palestinian society from the days of the Maccabees until the time of Herod the Great. During his reign and during the reigns of his sons the Hasmonean priesthood was in control, and the glimpses of the hierarchy that appear in the Gospels show that they were the virtual rulers of Judea. They controlled the business traffic that was connected with the temple, and they participated in the revenues that were derived from the sale of animals for sacrifice and from the exchange of money involved in the temple taxes.

Among the members of the Sanhedrin, which was the high council of Judaism, were well-to-do men like Nicodemus and Joseph of Arimathea. Probably they were landowners who rented out their farms and profited from a share of the crops.

48

The majority of the Palestinian people were poor. Some were farmers, some were artisans, and a few were businessmen. Slavery was not widely practiced in Judaism, and probably the vast majority of the Palestinian Jews were freemen. Some, like the fishermen who became disciples, owned small independent enterprises that supported them fairly well.

Social divisions among the Jews were somewhat restrained by the common obligation that the law imposed on its followers. If they were all equally responsible to God for obedience to it, they were consequently morally equal in his sight. Although the Jew regarded the wealthy man as especially blessed by God's favor, and therefore as righteous, there was no reason why any man should not by good works merit equal favor. While an aristocracy tends to be self-perpetuating, at least the inherent moral equality kept the Jewish oligarchy from becoming too oppressive.

PAGAN SOCIETY

The Aristocracy

In the pagan world of the first century of the strata of society were more sharply contrasted. The civil wars of Rome, which had preceded the rise of the principate, had disrupted the entire social life of the empire. The old free landholding populace of Italy had disappeared. Many of the earlier senatorial families had perished in the party struggles, though some had survived. In their places had risen a new aristocracy, the landholders, who controlled public lands by their influence and who bought cheaply the private lands of those whose families were impoverished by war or by the impossibility of making a living from a small farm. The exploitation of the newly conquered provinces opened another avenue of profit, and the businessmen who acted as government contractors and as speculators reaped an enormous harvest. The consequent luxury enervated the aristocracy and discouraged the lower classes, who found that for all their toil they seemed to prosper less as the years rolled along.

The Middle Class

Largely because of the rise of slavery, which was built on the use of military captives, the middle class was almost crushed out of the empire. Many had been killed in the wars and proscriptions. Many others had been unable to meet the competition of slave labor and had slowly been starved out of their small farms and estates. Gradually they swelled the homeless and foodless mobs that filled the great cities, especially Rome, and they became dependent for their sustenance on the state. The hungry, idle crowds, who would vote for any candidate whose promises sounded better than those of his competitor, were a dangerous and unpredictable factor in the social life of the empire.

The Plebs

The plebs, or poor people, were numerous and their condition was pitiful. Many lacked steady employment and were worse off than slaves, who at least had assurance of food and clothing. The unemployed proletariat were ready to follow any man who would give them a dole to feed their stomachs and amusements to wile away their idle hours. They were easy prey for demagoguery of every description.

The Slaves and the Criminals

Slaves made up a large proportion of the population of the Roman empire. No exact figures are obtainable, but probably less than half of the inhabitants of the Roman world were free men, and only relatively few of them were citizens with full rights. War, debt, and birth recruited the ranks of the slave population at a rapid rate. Not all of them were ignorant. Many, in fact, were physicians, accountants, teachers, and skilled artisans of every kind. Epictetus, the renowned Stoic philosopher, was one of them. They performed most of the work in the great agricultural estates, they acted as household servants and as clerks in business houses, and publishers employed them as copyists. Where modern enterprises operate by machinery, the ancients used cheap labor.

The effect of slavery was debasing. The ownership of slaves made the masters dependent on the labor and skill of their servitors to the extent that they lost their own ingenuity and ambition. Morality and self-respect were impossible among those whose only law was the will of an arbitrary master. Trickery, flattery, fraud, and fawning obedience were the slave's best tools to obtain what he wanted from his superiors. In many households the children were entrusted to the care of these menials, who taught them all of the vices and sly tricks that they knew. Thus the corruption that prevailed among the oppressed classes spread to their overlords.

Undoubtedly many masters and mistresses treated their servitors kindly, just as many slaves labored in the bond of friendship rather than in the bond of fear. Some of them were able to amass a bit of property from tips and gifts, with which they purchased their freedom, and some were manumitted by their masters either during the lifetime of the latter or at death. Consequently a steady stream of freedmen poured into the life of the empire, filling with trained workers the ranks of the lower and middle classes that had been depleted by the wars. Many of these freedmen, like Pallas under Claudius, became prominent in the government, and were important in the growth of the bureaucracy.

The institution of slavery is reflected in the New Testament by the frequent use of the term "slave" and by occasional references to the ownership of them. Nowhere in its pages is the institution attacked, nor is it defended. According to Paul's letters to the Asian churches, there were

Christians among both slaves and slaveholders. The slaves were enjoined to obey their masters and the masters were commanded not to be cruel to them. Such was the power of Christian fellowship, however, that the institution of slavery gradually weakened under its impact and finally disappeared.

The restless hordes of the unemployed, the sharpers who made their way to the great cities for the purpose of preying on society, the despairing and the disinherited—all made a fertile ground for the breeding of criminals. To say that crime prevailed in the empire might be unfair, for there were a large number of decent citizens; but in consideration of the unscrupulous and immoral character of so many of the emperors and higher officials, it is not surprising that society at large was permeated with all kinds of evils. The ghastly picture of the heathen world that appears in Romans 1:18–32 was not overdrawn. There was no inherent standard in paganism to check the downward moral drift.

CULTURAL ATTAINMENTS

Literature

Under Augustus came a literary revival in Rome. Vergil, the poet, became the prophet of the new era. His *Aeneid* was an attempt to glorify the Rome of Augustus by showing through the epic adventure of his hero the divine origin and destiny of the empire. In his writings the hope of a golden age to come was also reflected, and at least one of the Eclogues (the Fourth) seems to show that he had some knowledge of the Old Testament. The Augustan age was the golden period of Roman poetry, graced by Horace, who cast Latin poetry in Greek molds, and by Ovid, whose stories of Greek and Roman mythology reveal the contemporary moral attitudes of the Roman people.

Nothing of note was produced between the periods of Augustus and Nero. Seneca, the Stoic moralist and Nero's tutor, wrote philosophic essays and dramatic tragedy. Petronius, the wealthy social arbiter of Nero's court, composed a novel that is still one of the best sources for understanding the common life of his day.

In the latter third of the first century Pliny the Elder wrote his *Natural History*, one of the first attempts at a scientific account of the natural world. It was encyclopedic in scope and showed a vast amount of research, although it was quite uncritical and inadequate when judged by modern standards. Grammar and rhetoric were treated extensively by Quintilian. Martial, whose spicy epigrams still make pungent reading, was the newspaper columnist of his day.

Under the governments of Nero, Trajan, and Hadrian, literature took the turn of self-criticism. Tacitus and Suetonius, the historians, narrated

Aerial view of the Colosseum, completed by Emperor Titus in A.D. 80. It seated forty to fifty thousand spectators. The Arch of Constantine is lower left.

the history of the Caesars in unvarnished language. Tacitus in particular, since he was connected with the old republican aristocracy, was not very friendly toward the emperors. The content of his *Annals* and *Histories* shows the feeling against the principate that smoldered under the surface of public opinion. The satirist Juvenal also wrote in the early second century. Like Martial, he was a bitter critic of the manners and morals of his day. Even if it be granted that some of his caricatures are overdrawn, they reveal the prevalent corruption of high Roman society and generally confirm the impression left by his predecessor, Martial.

Art and Architecture

Under the emperors of the first century Rome expanded materially, and new construction was continually going on. Although the Romans were not singularly original in their decorative art, they excelled in producing enduring monuments of utilitarian character. Many of their bridges, aqueducts, theaters, and baths still remain as a witness to Roman thoroughness in construction. They knew how to use the principle of the arch to good effect and were skilled in building with brick and cement.

In ornamental and memorial art they created a great deal of statuary; it

Interior view of the Colosseum. The absence of the main floor gives a fine view of the subcellars and dens in which wild beasts and human victims were kept until the hour of "performance."

generally represented persons rather than abstract ideas. Funerary carving on tombs and sarcophagi, busts and equestrian statues of the reigning emperors, and historical sculpture such as the Arch of Titus in Rome were common.

Music and Drama

Music and the stage were committed to entertainment of the mob rather than to stimulating the thought of intellectuals. The Roman stage degenerated rapidly and contributed directly to the moral degradation of the people. The farces and mimes of the early empire were coarse and cheap; their plots dealt with the lowest kind of life and their presentation was shameless. The theatrical representations of the first century A.D. were far different from those of the great Greek tragedians such as Aeschylus and Euripides, who were almost as much philosophers and theologians as they were playwrights.

Music of all kinds was familiar in the empire. Stringed instruments and flutes were used chiefly, but brass, wind instruments, and drums and cymbals were employed occasionally. The lyre and the harp were the most popular instruments. Religious rites and processions were generally accompanied by music, and the aristocracy entertained guests with dinner music that their slaves provided.

The Arena

The amphitheater was a more pernicious influence on the Roman public than the stage. The bloody contests between men and beasts or between men and men were promoted by the emperor, or occasionally by aspirants for political office who wished to gain the favor of the crowds. The participants were usually trained gladiators who were slaves, captives of war, condemned criminals, or volunteers who sought fame in the arena as a modern pugilist does. Some of them succeeded in winning favor and fortune for themselves so that they were able to retire to peaceful private life. The majority probably died in the arena. The gladiatorial shows accustomed the audience to the sight of bloodshed, and even whetted their appetite for it. In order to please their patrons, the spectacles became increasingly elaborate and increasingly shocking. If the stage with its coarse mimes and farces schooled the populace in obscenity and lust, the gladiatorial shows glorified brutality.

Languages

The chief languages of the Roman world were Latin, Greek, Aramaic, and Hebrew. Latin was the language of the law courts and of the literature of Rome. As a popular tongue it was spoken mostly in the western Roman world, particularly in North Africa, Spain, Gaul, and Britain, as well as in Italy itself. It was the language of the conquerors and was learned by the subject peoples, who quickly adapted its pronunciation and vocabulary to their own dialects. Greek was the cultural language of the empire, familiar to all educated persons, and was the *lingua franca* of the majority of the populace from Rome eastward. Even in Palestine Greek was currently spoken, and was probably used by Jesus and his disciples whenever they had to deal with Gentiles. Aramaic was the predominant tongue of the Near East. Paul addressed the people of Jerusalem in Aramaic (Acts 22:2) when he made his impromptu defense from the steps of the Castle of Antonia, and some recorded quotations of Jesus indicate that he used it customarily (John 1:42; Mark 7:34; Matt. 27:46). It also appears in the religious phraseology of the early church, such as *Abba* (Rom. 8:15) and *Maranatha* (I Cor. 16:22), showing that the earliest believers spoke Aramaic. Classical Hebrew, to which Aramaic was closely related, had been a dead language since the times of Ezra, except among the learned rabbis who made it a medium for theological thought. It was not understood by the rank and file of the people.

The wide use of the first three of these languages is shown by the statement that the inscription on the cross over the head of Jesus was written "in Hebrew [Aramaic], *and* in Latin, *and* in Greek" (John 19:20). Even in Palestine all three were current and were recognized.

Such interchange of language in the center where Christianity originated brought to bear on it the influence of the civilization and literature that these languages represented and gave to Christianity a means for universal expression. Neither Latin nor Hebrew played a large part in the history of the church during the first century, but Aramaic and Greek did. Tradition says that some of the earliest accounts of the words of Jesus were composed in Aramaic, and the fact that the New Testament as a whole was circulated in Greek almost from the time of its origin is too patent to need comment. All of the epistles were composed in Greek, and the Gospels and Acts have survived only in Greek form, even if it should be granted that some Aramaic accounts of the words of Jesus were extant in the middle of the first century.

Science

The Romans, who dominated the world of the first century, were not interested primarily in mathematical and scientific pursuits. They were largely content to confine themselves to such elementary processes as were necessary in the measurement of land or in the calculation of finance. The appliances that they possessed, such as ships for navigation and engines of war, had all been invented by the Greeks, from whom they borrowed.

Certain fields of learning had already been explored by the time of Christ. Geometry, literally the science of measuring land, had begun with the Babylonians and Egyptians, and was brought to the Greek world by Thales of Miletus, if tradition is correct. Euclid of Alexandria (c. 300 B.C.) developed plane geometry so completely that his propositions have been studied with little change to the modern day.

Mechanics and physics had been investigated by Archimedes of Syracuse (287–212 B.C.), who developed the theory of the lever and discovered the principle of estimating the composition of bodies by the relation of their weight to the weight of the volume of water they displaced. He found the formula for the ratio of the circumference of a circle to its diameter, and in doing so he discovered the basic approach to calculus. Several of his numerous mechanical devices were used in the wars of Syracuse against Rome.

Astronomy made great advances in the pre-Christian world. The sphericity of the earth and its revolution on its own axis were known to some Greek scientists in the fourth century B.C. Hipparchus (c. 160 B.C.)

invented both plane and spherical trigonometry and calculated the size of the moon and its distance from the earth. The predominant theory of the motion of the earth and of the planets was not that all revolved about the sun, but that the planets revolved around the earth. Eratosthenes of Alexandria (273–192 B.C.) calculated the circumference of the earth to a surprising degree of accuracy in spite of his crude instruments.

The science that owed its greatest advance to the period including the first century was geography. Ptolemy of Alexandria (A.D. 127–151) wrote a work on astronomy that remained the standard until the rise of the Copernican theory in modern times. He created maps of the world that included all regions known at that time.

Medicine flourished in various centers of the world. The university of Tarsus had an affiliated hospital in the temple of Aesculapius, where the sick went to be healed. A school of Greek medicine was begun in Rome during the reign of Augustus. Celsus, a physician, who lived in the reign of Tiberius, wrote a treatise on surgery that showed extensive knowledge of the technique of operating. Another doctor, Dioscorides, wrote a description of some six hundred plants and their medical uses. Galen (A.D. 129–200) reduced Greek medical knowledge to a system. He carried on biological experiments and made notes of his discoveries. Although many of his conclusions were erroneous, he exercised a powerful influence on medical science down to the close of the Middle Ages.

Such scientific knowledge as the Romans did possess showed little originality or intellectual curiosity. Pliny's *Naturalis Historia* was an encyclopedia of the learning of his day in thirty-seven volumes. It covered every subject from agriculture to zoology. Pliny drew heavily on other writers as well as on his own observations. He may be regarded as an honest witness to the culture of his times, but he failed to distinguish between fact and fable, so that his conclusions were not always reliable.

The Hebrews were not particularly interested in speculative science. In the first century none of them was renowned for proficiency in mathematics or the natural sciences. The church, which sprang from the matrix of Judaism, did not concern itself with science as such, for its main interests were in the ethical and religious fields. On the other hand, the revelation on which the church based its teaching was not inherently opposed to science. Paul, speaking of God, says that "the invisible things of him since the creation of the world are clearly seen, being perceived through the things that are made, *even* his everlasting power and divinity . . ." (Rom. 1:20). There is no conflict between the theological investigation of God's revelation through his Spirit and the scientific investigation of his revelation through creation. The New Testament is not primarily a book of science, nor was it written by men whose training could be called scientific in the full modern sense of the term, but it is not antiscientific either in its statements or in its spirit.

Schools

The modern system of free compulsory education by the state for all children under the age of sixteen was unknown in the Roman empire. Not until the time of Vespasian did the rulers take any active interest in supporting public education. The training of the child in the average Roman household began with the *paidagōgos*, a slave who was charged with the responsibility of teaching the child his first lessons and of conducting him to and from one of the private schools in the city where he lived. Up to the time of his acknowledgment as a young man with adult responsibilities, the Roman boy was under the superintendence of his tutor.

The schools themselves were rather dreary affairs, held in the public alcoves or halls where the markets and the shops were located. Schoolmasters knew and practiced little educational psychology, but taught by endless repetition, punctuated with corporal punishment. With rare exceptions these schoolrooms were bare, chilly, unattractive halls, devoid of the blackboards, charts, decorations, and other equipment regarded as essential to the modern school.

The curriculum was essentially practical. Reading, writing, and arithmetic were the basic subjects of the elementary curriculum. As the pupil progressed, he studied the Greek and Latin poets, and memorized long passages that he had to recite with the proper expression. Later he might learn the elements of oratory: how to compose a speech, and how to deliver it convincingly. Sometimes the wealthier youths went abroad to study in the Greek universities of Athens, Rhodes, Tarsus, or Alexandria, or they might attend the lectures of traveling philosophers.

The education of the Jewish boy followed somewhat the same pattern, except that his curriculum was more restricted. He learned to read and write from the Old Testament. Among the Jews of the Dispersion the synagogue schools doubtless used both Greek and Hebrew. He also learned the traditions of the fathers and was schooled in the ritual of Judaism. In some instances he was permitted to read Gentile literature. If he aspired to become a scholar, he usually went to study with some great rabbi, as Paul received instruction at the feet of Gamaliel according to the strict manner of the law of his fathers (Acts 22:3).

No adequate data exist for drawing conclusions concerning the state of education in every corner of the empire. Apparently each municipality of people within its bounds was responsible for its own educational program. The prevalence of writing, however, even in the poorest parts of Egypt as attested by the papyri, shows that a fair degree of literacy was attained by the people of the first century and that reading and writing were practiced by the lower classes. Probably the average attainment of the early empire would compare very favorably with that of the Middle Ages, or even with some parts of Europe in the eighteenth century of the present era.

MORAL STANDARDS

The moral condition of the Roman empire as a whole may not have been as black as some historians have painted it. As usual the virtuous people went unnoticed because of their virtue and the criminals were singled out for attention. Only crime was "news." Nevertheless, all indications in the history, literature, drama, and art that have survived point to a standard of morality generally lower than our own. The tremendous indictment of mankind in Romans 1:18 to 3:20 was originally directed against the empire, and all available witness supports its accuracy.

Moral declension does not mean that no comparatively decent people existed, or that virtue was completely stifled. It does mean that the prevailing trend in society verged downward to indulgence and lawlessness. Human life was cheap and murder was frequent. Divorce was easy to obtain and was generally accepted in "society." The exposure of unwanted infants was a common practice, as illustrated in the well-known letter of Hilarion to his wife Alis: "Should you bear a child, if it is a boy, let it live; if it is a girl, expose it."[1] Superstition and trickery of every kind flourished.

There were moralists like Seneca, Nero's tutor, who in their writings advocated lofty ideals and spoke words of wisdom; but their protestations made little impact on the entrenched evils of their day. They imparted to their readers no spiritual dynamic that could make their precepts effective, and, as in the case of Seneca, they did not exemplify their own counsel. Paganism was devoid of any power to lift it above itself, and the growing consciousness of its own impotence brought on it a pessimism and a depression that it could not escape. Corruption in politics, debauchery in pleasure, fraud in business, and deceit and superstition in religion made life in Rome depressing for the many and unendurable for the few.

THE ECONOMIC WORLD

The Christians of the first century, like the Christians of today, had to earn their living in a workaday world. The propagation and practice of their faith were affected by prevailing economic conditions much as Chris-

---

1. *Papyrus Oxyrhynchus* 744, dated 1 B.C. "Expose" meant to abandon the child to die.

tianity is affected today. Agriculture, industry, finance, and transportation and travel—all had a bearing on the spread of the gospel.

AGRICULTURE

During the time of Christ and the early church the Roman empire occupied the lands surrounding the Mediterranean basin. Judging from the ruins of towns that are still extant, the coastal territories were more fertile than they are today. North Africa, which is now semiarid or else largely desert, contained immense farms on which cattle grazed or which grew fruits and vegetables. In Italy were large estates, which the owners rented out to tenant farmers and sharecroppers, where almost all kinds of fruits and grains could be grown. In the western provinces of Britain, Gaul, and Germany, agriculture flourished, and some of the farms were irrigated by government projects established by Augustus.

INDUSTRY

Manufacturing never was so important in ancient times as it is today, for machine tools were practically unknown, and goods had to be produced by human labor. In many cases the factories were private enterprises employing slaves. Small shops were the rule rather than the exception. Certain types of goods were produced in particular localities: copper vessels were manufactured in Campania; linens and paper came from Egypt; the best quality of earthenware originated in north Italy. Small wares, furniture, and household goods were generally produced locally, in the same way that similar commodities were supplied in the early American colonies by the skill and ingenuity of the town craftsmen such as the blacksmith and the carpenter. Probably every small village in the empire had its workmen who provided for the needs of their fellow townsmen.

Luxury goods were imported. Gold, ivory, and rare woods came from Africa and from the East; pearls and jewels were found in India; furs came from central Asia and Russia, and amber came from the far north. Caravans were cumbersome and were subject to attack by robbers. Although the empire had a large number of good roads, vehicles were drawn by animals, so that traffic was costly and slow. Shipping was done on navigable rivers and on the ocean only during the summer months. Mass production of cheap goods was practically impossible, for neither machinery nor transportation was available.

FINANCE

The standard coins in the empire were the *denarius* and the gold *aureus*, or pound. One pound was worth forty *denarii*. The *denarius* is mentioned several times in the New Testament, where it is variously translated "penny" or "shilling." It was the ordinary day's wage for a laboring man in the East (Matt. 20:2). Many of the cities of the empire had the right to mint their own coinage, and the coins of the conquered nations were not retired from circulation, so that various kinds of money were used concurrently within the realm. Money changers did a thriving business in dealing with travelers, as the episode of Jesus' cleansing of the temple showed (21:12).

Banking was generally practiced, although it was not like the intricate system of finance that is known to the modern world. The banks were not subsidized by the state, but consisted usually of private companies. Sometimes mercantile firms with foreign connections carried on negotiations for their customers. Borrowing, lending, discounting of notes, and foreign exchange were undertaken, and letters of credit were issued. Funds were often supplied to the banks by private individuals, whereas the bank acted only as agent. The normal rate of interest varied from four to twelve percent, though individual brokers often charged more. Brutus on one occasion paid as high as forty-eight percent on a loan. The parables of the talents (25:15) and of the pounds (Luke 19:13) show that moneylending was a common means of enlarging one's fortune.

View of the Via Appia Nuova and the Claudian aqueduct.

TRANSPORTATION AND TRAVEL

The rule of Rome over the provinces was greatly facilitated by its excellent system of roads, which, until the recent era of the automobile, were the best that the world had ever seen. The Romans built their roads as straight as possible, making cuts through hills and using viaducts to bridge valleys and streams. In building their highways they excavated the topsoil and filled the roadbed with three different layers of road material, crowning the center to throw off water, and then paving the top with stone. The roads were seldom more than fifteen feet wide, but they were smooth and durable. Some of them are in use to the present day.

Along these roads, which stretched in every direction from Rome to the frontiers, moved the armies and the caravans of commerce. The imperial post carried the government dispatches, whereas private businesses had their own couriers.

Several of these roads were famous in antiquity. The Appian Way was the main line of communication between Rome and the south of Italy. It ran from Rome through Capua to Brundisium. From Brundisium a traveler could sail eastward to Dyrrhachium on the western side of Illyricum, from which the Egnatian highway crossed Illyricum and Macedonia to Thessalonica, and from there to Byzantium, now Istanbul. Another route led from Troas down to Ephesus on the western coast of Asia Minor, then eastward through Laodicea and Colosse to Antioch of Pisidia, and from there southward through Iconium and Derbe to the pass of the Cilician Gates, through which it went on to Tarsus and to Syrian Antioch. From Antioch roads led eastward to the Euphrates, where they tapped the trade routes to India.

The Via Flaminia ran northward from Rome to Ariminum and thence to Mediolanum. From Mediolanum several roads branched out westward to Gaul, Germany, Rhaetia, and Noricum. The Via Claudia Augusta, begun in 15 B.C. and completed by Claudius, connected Verona with the Danube. Roads along the Danube connected Verona with Byzantium.

To the west, the Via Aurelia ran from Rome to Genoa, from which the Via Domitia communicated with Massilia (Marseilles). From Massilia the Via Augusta crossed the Pyrenees to Tarraco, from there southward to the Sucro River, and through Corduba and Hispalis to Gades in Spain.

In Gaul and Britain numerous shorter roads connected the chief towns with each other.

The vehicles on these roads varied according to the wealth of their owners. Some people trudged the weary miles on foot. Some rode on donkeys. The more well-to-do afforded horses or mules, and officials or magnates might travel in light carriages. Inns were located at convenient intervals, so that the travelers could stop for meals and shelter. Few of the inns were luxurious, and probably still fewer were really clean. Middle- and upper-class travelers usually counted on the hospitality of their friends, so that they were not at the mercy of avaricious landlords and their conscienceless servants.

Most of the commercial transportation was by water rather than by land. The Mediterranean Sea abounded in good ports; these were busy all through the season for navigation. Alexandria was the chief port, since it was the outlet for the grain crop of Egypt.

The Alexandrian merchant ships were the largest and finest of the day. Some of them were more than two hundred feet in length. They were propelled by sails and carried enough oars so that the crew could maneuver the ship in an emergency. One of the largest ships of which there is any record carried twelve hundred passengers in addition to its cargo. Most of the Alexandrian ships were engaged in the corn trade that supplied Rome with grain. Under Claudius, their upkeep was subsidized by the government in order to insure a regular delivery of grain for the needs of the populace. Paul, at the time of his shipwreck, was aboard an Alexandrian ship (Acts 27:6), and after his rescue at Malta sailed for Italy in another (28:11) named "The Two Brothers."

Warships were lighter and faster than merchantmen, and were generally propelled by oars pulled by galley slaves. Ships with two, three, and five banks of oars were not at all uncommon, while some had even ten banks. Sails were sometimes used in cruising. In battle, where the outcome depended on the action of the ships, propulsion by hand became necessary for safe and accurate control.

On the inland rivers and canals barges were used, chiefly for carrying cargoes of freight. Apparently they were not greatly patronized by passenger trade. No mention of such travel appears in the New Testament.

FOR FURTHER READING

Angus, Samuel. *The Environment of Early Christianity.* New York: Charles Scribner's Sons, 1920. Pp. xi, 240. See esp. pp. 30–67.

Bailey, Cyril, ed. *The Legacy of Rome.* Oxford: The Clarendon Press, 1924. Pp. xii, 512. Science, pp. 265–325; Agriculture, pp. 475–512.

Couch, Herbert N. and Geer, Russell M. *Classical Civilization: Rome.* Russell M. Geer. Second Edition. New York: Prentice-Hall, Inc., 1950. Pp. xxiv, 482. Treats cultural and social life of Rome very satisfactorily.

Dampier-Whetham, William C. D. *A History of Science.* New York: The Macmillan Company, 1929. Pp. xxi, 514.

Frank, Tenney. *Rome and Italy of the Republic.* Vol. I: *An Economic Survey of Ancient Rome.* Baltimore: Johns Hopkins Press, 1933. See Chap. VII, "Agriculture," pp. 358–368, and Chap. V, "Money and Banking," pp. 347–352.

McGregor, G. H. C. *Jew and Greek: Tutors unto Christ. The Jewish and Hellenistic Background of the New Testament.* New York: Charles Scribner's Sons, 1936. Pp. x, 11–366.

Meeks, W. A. *The First Urban Christians: The Social World of the Apostle Paul.* New Haven: Yale University Press, 1983.

Metzger, Bruce M. "The Language of the New Testament," in *The Interpreter's Bible.* Vol. VII, pp. 43–59. New York: Abingdon-Cokesbury Press, 1951.

Moulton, James H. *A Grammar of New Testament Greek.* Vol. I: *Prolegomena.* Third Edition. Edinburgh: T. & T. Clark, 1908. Pp. xxiv, 293. See Chap. I, "General Characteristics," pp. 1–21.

Reymond, Arnold. *History of the Sciences in Greco-Roman Antiquity.* Translated by Ruth Gheury DeBray. London: Methuen & Co., Ltd., 1927. Pp. x, 245. Bibliography in French. See esp. pp. 92–112.

Skeel, C. A. J. *Travel in the First Century.* Cambridge: University Press, 1901. Pp. x, 159. Excellent essay on transportation and travel in the time of Christ.

Tucker, T. G. *Life in the Roman World of Nero and St. Paul.* New York: The Macmillan Company, 1924. Pp. xix, 453.

CHAPTER 3

THE RELIGIOUS WORLD

Christianity did not begin its growth in a religious vacuum in which it found people blankly waiting for something to believe. On the contrary, the new faith in Christ had to fight its way against entrenched religious beliefs that had been in existence for centuries. Many had degenerated into feeble superstitions and meaningless rituals; others were relatively new and vigorous. In general there were five distinct types.

THE GRAECO-ROMAN PANTHEON

The primitive religion of Rome in the early days of the republic was animism. Each small farmer worshiped the gods of his own farm and fireside, which personified for him the forces with which he had to deal in living his daily life. Gods of the forest and field, gods of the sky and stream, gods of the sowing and of the harvest—all received his worship in their proper places and at their proper seasons. Some vestiges of local feasts and rites survive to this present day among the peasants of Italy and Greece. It is possible that the festivities of the Roman Saturnalia that celebrated the turning of the year at the winter solstice are still echoed in the Christian observance of Christmas.

With the growth of the military state and the consequent contacts with Greek civilization came a fusion of deities under the dominating influence of the Greek pantheon. Jupiter, the god of the sky, was identified with the Greek Zeus; Juno, his wife, with Hera; Neptune, the god of the sea, with Poseidon; Pluto, the god of the underworld, with Hades; and so on. The entire list of Homeric deities was assimilated to their Roman

Remains of the temple of Olympian Zeus, the largest in ancient Greece.

Interior view of the Pantheon, Rome; it is one of the best preserved buildings from the imperial period.

counterparts. Under Augustus new temples were erected and new priest-hoods were founded. Many worshipers followed the old gods, whether Roman or Greek, and paid them homage.

The worship of the Greek pantheon, however, had begun to decline by the time of Christ. The gross immoralities and the petty squabbles of these deities, who were only magnified men and women, exposed them to the ridicule of the satirists and to the scorn of the philosophers. Plato, more than three centuries before Christ, had said that the tales of the gods should be excluded from the ideal state, since they would tend to corrupt youth by their evil example.[1] The philosophic cults had no place for the gods in their scheme of things and openly made fun of them. Undoubtedly there were many devout worshipers of the gods, but their numbers were diminishing rather than increasing.

Another factor tended to destroy the older attitude of reverence to-ward the gods. Up to this time they had not been uniformly worshiped in all cities, but each city or city-state had one of them as a patron. Worship was

---

1. Plato *Republic* II.376; III.390.

semipolitical; a man was a worshiper of Zeus or Hera or Artemis because he happened to live in a town over which that particular deity presided. When the city-states capitulated to the military might of Rome, the question would naturally be asked, "Why did not the local deity protect his people?" The vanquished peoples tended to abandon faith in gods who were either too weak or too fickle to aid them.

The public observance of religious rites survived well beyond the first century. An outstanding example in the New Testament of such a cult is the worship of Artemis of Ephesus, the image that reputedly had fallen from heaven (Acts 19:27, 35). The fanatical devotion given to a local goddess is well illustrated by the shrieking mob who crowded the amphitheater and shouted aloud, "Great *is* Diana [Artemis] of the Ephesians" (19:34).

EMPEROR WORSHIP

Although the worship of local deities persisted, the growing cosmopolitan consciousness in the empire prepared the way for a new type of religion, the worship of the state. For many years the Hellenistic kingdoms of the Seleucidae and the Ptolemies had exalted their kings to the position of deity and had applied to them such titles as Lord (*Kyrios*), Savior (*Sōtēr*), or Manifest Deity (*Epiphanēs*). The concentration of the executive functions of the Roman state in the person of one man had vested him with powers unprecedented in the history of the world. The fact that he was able to utilize those powers for the good of the empire created the feeling that there must be something divine in him.

The imperial cult was not established arbitrarily. It grew gradually out of the increasing ascription of superhuman honors to the emperor and out of the desire to centralize the allegiance of the people in him. After his death Julius Caesar was called *Divus Julius.* From Augustus' time each of the emperors was deified at his death by vote of the Senate, although some of them did not take the honor very seriously. Caligula ordered that his statue should be set up in the temple at Jerusalem, but since he was generally considered to be insane, his action cannot be regarded as representative of the general imperial policy. Not until the time of Domitian at the close of the first century did a reigning emperor attempt to compel his subjects to worship him.

The refusal of all Christians to participate in such worship precipitated violent persecution, for the Christians consistently objected to worshiping a human being. The polytheistic Romans, who could always add one more god to their list of deities, looked on their refusal as a lack of proper recognition for the emperor and as a distinctly unpatriotic attitude. Between these two viewpoints there could be no reconciliation. The Christian attitude on this question of the worship of the state, or of its head, is reflected in the Apocalypse, which reveals unmistakably the hostility between the claims of Christ and the claims of the emperor.

There can be no doubt, however, that emperor worship had great value for the state. It unified patriotism and worship and made the support of the state a religious duty. It was the totalitarianism of the first century.

THE MYSTERY RELIGIONS

Neither the state religion nor emperor worship proved completely satisfying. Both were observed by ritual sacrifices; both were maintained collectively rather than individually; both sought protection by deity rather than fellowship with deity; and neither offered any personal solace or strength for times of stress and trouble. People were seeking a more personal faith that would bring them into immediate contact with deity, and they were ready for any sort of experience that would promise them that contact.

The mystery religions fulfilled that desire. They were mostly of Eastern origin, though the Eleusinian mysteries had been celebrated in Greece for a long time. The cult of Cybele, the Great Mother, came from Asia; that of Isis and Osiris or Serapis, from Egypt; Mithraism originated in Persia. While all of them differed from each other in origin and in detail, all were alike in certain broad characteristics. Each was centered about a god who had died and who was resuscitated. Each had a ritual of formulas and lustrations, of symbol and of secret dramatic representations of the experience of the god, by which the initiate was inducted into that experience, and so was presumably rendered a candidate for immortality. The procedure of these initiations was somewhat similar to that of modern secret societies. Each religion maintained a brotherhood in which slave and master, rich and poor, high and low met on the same footing.

The mystery religions satisfied the desire for personal immortality and for social equality. They offered an outlet for emotion in religion as the state religion seldom did and they made religious experience emphatically personal. Nothing is said of them directly in the New Testament, but it is thought that Paul used their vocabulary on occasion, and that the "worship of angels" mentioned in Colossians (2:18–19) is a reflection of an attempted fusion of some eclectic philosophic cult with Christianity at Colosse.

THE WORSHIP OF THE OCCULT

Akin in many ways to the mystery religions was the occultism of the day, the superstitious observances and regard of the masses for the powers of the universe, which they could not understand but which they could vaguely

Incantation bowl with spiral inscription in Jewish Aramaic for protection of the household of Babai.

feel. For them the entire world was inhabited by spirits and demons who could be invoked or commanded to do one's bidding if only one knew the correct rite or formula to use. Allusions in contemporary literature and fragments from the papyri bear witness to the widespread belief in magic that prevailed throughout the Roman domain. Jew and Gentile alike shared these superstitious beliefs; in fact, the Jews were often more interested in magic than were the Gentiles.

Reliance on magic began in early times. The Romans had practiced augury or foretelling the future by the examination of the entrails of slaughtered animals or by observing the flight of birds since the founding of Rome. The Greeks were familiar with the oracles, where the gods were supposed to communicate their will to men through priests or priestesses whom they possessed. The Babylonian captivity brought many Jews into contact with the mystic lore of the East, and they became professional exorcists and necromancers. The conquests of Alexander established contacts with the Persians, from whom the mysticism of the East flowed back into the West. Under Tiberius the mania for horoscopes reached its peak, but magic was popular down through the succeeding centuries, as the papyri show.

Jewish interest in magic appears in the New Testament. The Pharisees cast out demons, and sorcerers are mentioned in Acts as rivals of preachers of the gospel (Acts 8:9–24; 13:6–11). Pagan magic was recognized as hostile to Christianity by the Ephesian Christians, who burned their books of spells in a bonfire that cost fifty thousand pieces of silver (19:19), an amount possibly equivalent to 50,000 day's wages (if one assumes a refer-ence to the Greek *drachma*, or the Roman *denarius*, a day's wage for a laborer). The biblical attitude toward occult worship, however, was invari-ably hostile. Although the reality of demonic forces was recognized, com-merce with them was strictly forbidden both in the Old and New Testa-ments (Deut. 18:10–12, 20; Mic. 5:12; I Cor. 10:20–21).

Specimens of magical formulas that were used to control the spirits or to bring good luck appear in the papyri. One of these, an excerpt from the great Paris magical papyrus of the third century, will show the curious combination of pagan, Jewish, and Christian phraseology that was used as a charm for exorcising a demon:

> A notable spell for driving out demons. Invocation to be uttered over the head [of the possessed one]. Place before him branches of olive, and standing behind him say: Hail, spirit of Abraham; hail, spirit of Isaac; hail, spirit of Jacob. Jesus the Christ, the holy one, the spirit [here follow a series of apparently meaningless words] drive forth the demon from the man, until the unclean demon of Satan shall flee before thee. I adjure thee, O demon, whoever thou art, by the God Sabarbarbathioth Sabarbarbathiuth Sabarbarbathoneth Sabarbar-baphai. Come forth, O demon, whoever thou art, and depart from so and so at once, at once, now! Come forth, O demon, for I shall chain thee with adamantine chains not to be loosed, and I shall give you over to black chaos in utter destruction.[2]

The foregoing formula illustrates both the respect of the pagan world for the power of the gospel of Christ and also its misconception of that gospel. Had there been no real power in Christianity against the demonic influences of paganism, the names of Abraham, Isaac, Jacob, and Jesus would never have been used at all. This misconception lay in taking for granted that these terms made just one more magical charm to be used at the convenience of the exorcist. The user of this formula was repeating the error of Simon Magus, who thought that the power of God could be bought with money. Such a mixture of faith and superstition was by no means

---

2. George Milligan, *Selections from the Greek Papyri* (Cambridge: The University Press, 1910), pp. 112–114.

uncommon among a people who were intensely religious in nature, but who had no access to regular teaching or to a written copy of the Scriptures.

Astrology was also popular in the empire during the first century. It had originated in Babylonia, where the clear night skies afforded full opportunity for unobstructed vision of the stars and of the planets. Because the Babylonian priests had regarded the planets as emblematic of their gods, they had kept a careful record of their movements. The order of the universe impressed them and they sought to connect it with the course of human life. Through the conquests of Alexander, which made contacts between the eastern and western worlds, astrological lore became known to the Greeks. Through them and through the eastern soothsayers who went westward to seek their fortunes, astrology was introduced into the Roman empire.

The theory of astrology was based on the assumption that the sovereign powers of the world who controlled the planets and human life worked simultaneously in both, and so often presaged the careers of men by the courses of the planets under which they were born. In order to find what the celestial bodies had to say, the path of the sun and the planets through the heavens was divided into the twelve signs of the zodiac, each of which was marked by a special constellation. By knowing the exact time of birth of a person, one could ascertain under which sign he was born, and one could calculate the positions of the various planets at that moment. From their positions, their potential influence on his career could be determined, and his future could be predicted, or he could be warned what to expect and what to avoid. The tabulation of these data was called a horoscope.

With the rise of the Copernican system of astronomy, which made the sun the center of the solar system rather than the earth, astrology waned in importance. In the time of Christ, however, it commanded considerable attention not only from the lower classes, but also from the aristocracy. Augustus employed it on occasion and Tiberius resorted to it regularly. Never did it penetrate Christianity, for the Christians repudiated it utterly.

THE PHILOSOPHIES

When religion degenerates into empty ritualism or ignorant superstition, thoughtful people may abandon it altogether because they feel that it has no real satisfaction to offer them. They cannot, however, ignore the necessity of finding some rational answer to the problems the world poses for them. The mysteries of the universe call for explanation unless one is content to be such a dolt that he is never disturbed by them.

Philosophy is the attempt to correlate all existing knowledge about the universe into systematic form and to integrate human experience with it. Philosophies have been crude, or naive, or subtle, or profound. Some of them have acknowledged the existence of a supreme power or a personal deity. Others have been frankly materialistic and have dismissed the concept of gods as either ridiculous or unnecessary. In any case, philosophy has never depended on a revelation from God. It has always assumed the potential adequacy of humans to understand their world and decide their fate. The knowledge by which decisions are to be determined will be derived from individual or communal experience. The formulation of knowledge into a coherent system should be governed by the rules of logic that man has devised. Through the increasing scope of his observation and through the advancing perfection of his logic man should be able at last to attain full comprehension of the mysteries of which he is a part.

To achieve this end various systems of philosophy were created. Insofar as they reflect basic attitudes toward life, they persist to the present day, though perhaps not under their original titles. All of these were founded on premises different from basic Christian principles. Although many of them possessed features that resembled those of Christianity, and although the vocabulary and even some usages of these competing faiths later were absorbed into the thought of the church, they can generally be regarded as

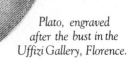

*Plato, engraved
after the bust in the
Uffizi Gallery, Florence.*

opposing forces rather than as the material out of which Christianity was formed. An elementary understanding of them is essential to a clear comprehension of the intellectual and religious environment of the first century.

Platonism

Platonism derived its name from Plato, the great Athenian philosopher and founder of the Academy, who lived in the fourth century before Christ. He was a friend and pupil of Socrates. From his master he inherited an inquiring mind and a habit of thinking in abstract concepts. The world, he taught, consisted of an infinite number of particular things, each of which is a more or less imperfect copy of a real idea. For instance, there are many kinds of chairs, but none of them could be the chair from which all other chairs are derived. The real chair, then, is not the one made of wood, but is the ideal chair of which the wooden one is a copy.

The real world, then, is the world of ideas of which the material world is only a shadow. These ideas are organized into a system, at the head of which is the idea of the Good. Plato never seemed to personalize the idea of the Good, nor did he identify it with the Demiurge, or Creator, who produced the material world. He did regard the ideas as having objective existence; in fact, they were the only real existence, of which the present world is a feeble and garbled reflection.

Such a concept of the world led inevitably to dualism. If the real world is the unseen realm of ideas, and if the changing cosmos in which man lives is only transitory, his quest will be to escape from the unreal to the real. Reflection, meditation, and even asceticism will open the way to deliverance. Knowledge is salvation; sin is ignorance. By seeking the Highest Good, the End, the Supreme Idea, man may liberate himself from the enslaving material world and may rise to a comprehension of the real world.

Platonism was too abstract to gain the attention and thought of the common man. It is not mentioned directly in the New Testament as one of the philosophies that Christianity encountered. Its dualism, however, was reflected by Gnosticism, which may have taken its rise in the first century, and by Neo-Platonism, which was sponsored by Plotinus in the third century.

Gnosticism

Gnosticism, as its name implies (derived from the Greek *gnōsis*, "knowledge"), was a system that promised salvation by knowledge. God, said the Gnostics, was too great and too holy to have created the material world with all of its baseness and corruption. The Gnostics held that from the supreme Deity had proceeded a series of successive emanations, each one a little inferior to the one from which it sprang, until finally the last of these emanations, or "aeons," as they were called, created the world. Matter was thus equated with evil. If man wished to obtain salvation, he could do so by renouncing the material world and seeking the invisible world. Two contradictory ethical conclusions arose from the argument. The first was asceticism, which contended that since the body was material, it was evil, and should therefore be kept under strict control. Its appetites should be curbed and its impulses should be disregarded and suppressed. The other conclusion was drawn from the assumption that the spirit was real and the body was unreal. If the body were only temporary, its acts were inconsequential. Full gratification of its desires would thus have no effect on the ultimate salvation of the spirit, which alone would survive.

There is a possibility that this teaching promoted the heresy to which Paul alludes in Colossians, where he warns his readers to "take heed lest there shall be any one that maketh spoil of you through his philosophy and vain deceit, after the tradition of men, after the rudiments of the world, and not after Christ" (Col. 2:8). Apparently this heresy denied the fullness of the Godhead in Christ and perhaps made him one of the lesser emanations or manifestations of God. Furthermore, the asceticism that certain forms of Gnosticism promoted may be echoed in the attitude of "Handle not, nor taste, nor touch" (2:21) that Paul so roundly condemned. Absolute identification of this error with Gnosticism is not possible, but there are similarities.

Neo-Platonism

The principles of Plato were adopted by Plotinus (A.D. 204–269) of Lycopolis in Egypt, who taught philosophy in Rome for twenty-five years. Plotinus was indebted for his training to Ammonius Saccas of Alexandria, who had been a Christian but who had returned to heathenism. He was also strongly influenced by Persian ideas of dualism that he had encountered while serving in a Roman military expedition.

Neo-Platonism was distinctly a religious philosophy based on the Platonic dualism of the universal ideal and the particular thing, and on the Persian dualism of light and darkness. In Neo-Platonism the spirit was considered to be inevitably good and the body was inherently evil. Salvation consisted in eliminating completely all bodily desires as one gradually retreated from the life dependent on sensation and moved toward the life of the spirit, which would finally be achieved at death. Then the body's evil influence would cease and the true spiritual life would blossom forth.

Neo-Platonism went beyond Platonism in teaching that the attainment of spiritual life would not be reached by intellectual effort but by a mystical absorption into the Infinite. Since no reasoning can compass God, only feeling can establish communication with him.

In the dualistic thinking of Gnosticism and Neo-Platonism a great gulf is fixed between reality and matter, not only in the metaphysical sense that the two are irreconcilable in essence, but also in the ethical sense that the one is good and the other is evil. There is consequently no room in either for the Christian doctrine of the incarnation. Consistent Neo-Platonists would regard the union of God and man, deity and flesh, as simply unthinkable. The atonement would be unnecessary, since no act that took place in the material world could leave any effect on the real world of spirit. The resurrection of the body would be a hideous mistake, since it would only perpetuate the evil of material existence. Julian, "the Apostate," Christianity's last imperial opponent, was a Neo-Platonist.

Epicureanism

Epicureanism was named for Epicurus, the son of an Athenian, who studied at Athens and founded his own school about 306 B.C. His teaching was best represented in the works of his pupil Lucretius, the materialistic Roman philosopher and poet of the pre-Christian century. The world, he taught, began in a shower of atoms, some of which, by pure chance, moved a trifle obliquely and collided with others. These collisions produced other collisions, until the ensuing movement brought into being the present universe. The cosmology of Epicureanism is similar to that of modern materialistic evolution.

In such a world of chance there could be neither purpose nor design. There could not, therefore, be any final or absolute good. The highest possible good, Epicurus said, was pleasure, which he defined as the absence of pain. Contrary to the popular conception of Epicureanism, both then and now, it did not advocate sensuality, but rather it urged the choice of those enjoyments which would give the longest and fullest satisfaction to the individual. If abstinence from some indulgences would bring greater ultimate satisfaction than the indulgences themselves, abstinence was recommended. Epicureanism did not advocate dissipation, but it offered no check to selfishness.

Epicureanism was essentially antireligious. If the world originated with matter and chance, no creative power was necessary. If chance dominates the outcome of cosmic affairs, there is no room for a directive, purposeful Mind. The Epicureans, to be sure, did speak of the gods, and did not categorically deny their existence; but the gods as they pictured them were confined to a distant haven of bliss where they enjoyed their own society and had no interest in the trivial affairs of men. Epicureanism at best was deistic and in effect atheistic, for a god who is inaccessible or uninterested in human affairs might as well not exist at all.

As a philosophy Epicureanism was quite popular because it did not indulge in much abstract reasoning. It appealed to emotional considerations, for it supplied a philosophic justification for doing what most people do anyway—make pleasure the chief goal of life. It brushed aside all thought of sin or of accountability at a final judgment, because it predicated neither purpose nor terminus for the present world-process. There was no recognition of immortality, for a body composed only of atoms did not survive the present life. In consideration of the main tenets of Epicureanism, it is small wonder that the Athenians laughed at Paul's address at the Areopagus when he preached "Jesus and the resurrection" (Acts 17:18, 32).

Stoicism

Coupled with Epicureanism in the foregoing New Testament passage was Stoicism. Stoicism was founded by Zeno (340–265 B.C.), a native of Cyprus and possibly of Semitic descent. Zeno did not recognize a personal God, but he taught that the universe is controlled by an Absolute Reason, or divine will immanent in it and pervading it thoroughly. The world process is thus governed not by chance but by a progressive purpose.

Conformity to reason, then, becomes the highest good. Personal feeling is immaterial or even harmful since it tends to unbalance the rational solution of human problems. Perfect self-control, unmoved by sentimental considerations, was the goal of the Stoic. The resulting attitude has given the chief meaning to the modern use of the term.

Because the Stoics believed that nature was as it should be and that whatever came to pass was regulated by Providence, there was no room for altering the process or for staying its inexorable course. The universe was to be accepted, not to be changed. This fatalistic attitude inculcated self-restraint and consequently fostered a fairly high type of morality. It appealed to the rigid, legal Roman mind, and many of the better Roman statesmen, such as Cicero, adhered to its tenets.

The Stoic creed, however virtuous, was not Christianity. In it was no allowance for free will or for the real existence of evil. All apparent evils were for the Stoic only parts of a larger good. Such an attitude would exclude any idea of reform or of change in the existing order of things. The individual was obligated to act virtuously himself and conform to the highest reason he knew, but he was under no obligation to seek to change the common lot of men nor to shield them from adversities.

No personal dealing with God was possible to the Stoic. If nature dealt impartially with all people, it would not play favorites with any. Furthermore, the idea of personal relation with universal reason or with the cosmic process would seem about as incongruous as showing affection for the law of gravitation. God, according to the Stoic, took no personal interest in the affairs of men because he was not personal. The entire concept of the

Christian gospel, in which God had countered evil by sending his Son into the world to die for sinners, would be utterly ridiculous to the Stoic. Although much of the Stoic ethic was commendable, and although in some points it resembled the highest standards of Christian ethics, the two systems were leagues apart in their presuppositions and their practice.

Two other systems deserve notice, although they were less popular and influential than those heretofore mentioned.

Cynicism

Cynicism, like Platonism, grew out of Socratic teaching. Since Socrates taught that the person with simple needs can usually survive under conditions that would frustrate completely one with elaborate wants, the Cynics contended that the height of virtue would be to have no wants at all. In order to be independent of all desire they sought to abolish desire. They abandoned all standards and conventions and became complete individualists. Often the Cynics were purposely scurrilous and indecent in language and behavior simply for the purpose of demonstrating that they were "different." Socrates' criticism of Antisthenes, the founder of the Cynic sect, was probably the most penetrating analysis of the whole movement that has ever been given. "I can see your pride," he said, "through the holes in your cloak."

Scepticism

Pyrrho of Elis (365–295 B.C.) was the first of the Sceptics. Briefly, their argument was as follows: If knowledge rests on experience, there can be no final standard, since the experience of each person differs from that of all his fellows. Customs acceptable in one country are regarded as reprehensible in another. Impressions of the same objects will vary with the time and conditions where they are observed. All terms of judgment are relative: a weight that is light to one man may be heavy for the next man. Unless one final starting-point for reasoning can be found, no criterion of judgment is valid, and no such thing as truth can exist. The Sceptics, if they proceeded by their own logic, would be unable to make any statement whatsoever, since they could prove nothing by any acceptable premises. Scepticism would logically end in complete intellectual paralysis.

Cynicism and Scepticism arose from the abandonment of standards. The former dealt with ethics; the latter, with intellect. Christianity differed from both in its assertion that God is the ultimate standard for man. It insisted that man is necessarily dependent on God, which fact set a limit to Cynic independence; and that God is the beginning of all thinking, so that his personal revelation serves as the regulating factor in the acquisition of knowledge by experience.

Evaluation of Philosophies

However popular these and other variant philosophies may have been, they were unsatisfactory because they were too abstract for the ordinary person to grasp in their entirety, and because they lacked finality. Their reasonings always ended in a peradventure. Plato expressed this failure exactly when he put into the mouth of Simias the following statement:

> For I dare say that you, Socrates, feel as I do, how very hard or almost impossible is the attainment of any certainty about questions such as these [immortality] in the present life. And yet I should deem him a coward who did not prove what is said about them to the uttermost, or whose heart failed before he had examined them on every side. For he should persevere until he has attained one of two things: either he should discover or learn the truth about them, or, if this is impossible, I would have him take the best and most irrefragable of human notions, and let this be the raft upon which he sails through life—not without risk, as I admit, if he cannot find some word of God which will more surely and safely carry him.[3]

Thus philosophy, according to its own acknowledgment, had not been successful in the quest of truth. To Simmias' dilemma Christianity has the answer: "The Word became flesh, and dwelt among us (and we beheld his glory, glory as of the only begotten from the Father), full of grace and truth" (John 1:14).

FOR FURTHER READING

Angus, S. *The Environment of Early Christianity.* New York: Charles Scribner's Sons, 1920. See Chap. IV, "Religious Conditions of the Graeco-Roman Period," pp. 68–139.

Bailey, Cyril. "Religion and Philosophy," in *The Legacy of Rome,* pp. 237–264.

Barrett, C. K., ed. *The New Testament Background: Selected Documents.* New York: Harper & Row, 1961.

Bruce, F. F. *Israel and the Nations.* Grand Rapids: Wm. B. Eerdmans Publishing Company, 1969. Pp. 254.

David, M. and Van Groningen, B. A. *Papyrological Primer.* Second (English) Edition. Leiden: E. J. Brill, 1946. Pp. IX, 167. See No. 72, pp. 138–146, "Two Magical Texts."

Davies, W. D. and Daube, D., eds. *The Background of the New Testament and Its Eschatology.* Cambridge: University Press, 1956.

Ellis, E. Earle. *Prophecy and Hermeneutic in Early Christianity: New Testament Essays.* Grand Rapids: Wm. B. Eerdmans Publishing Company, 1978.

---

3. Plato *Phaedo* 85. See Benjamin Jowett, *The Dialogues of Plato* (New York: Scribner, Armstrong, & Company, 1873), I, 414.

Friedlander, L. *Roman Life and Manners Under the Early Empire.* Four volumes. Authorized Translation of the 7th enlarged and revised edition of the *Sittengeschichte Roms* by L. A. Magnus. Second Edition. New York: Dutton, n.d. See Vols. I, II.

Glover, Terriot Reavely. *The Conflict of Religions Within the Roman Empire.* Seventh Edition. London: Methuen & Company, Ltd., 1918. Humanistic view of Jesus. Good sketch of Roman religion.

Gundry, R. H. *Soma in Biblical Theology.* Cambridge: University Press, 1975.

Guthrie, Donald. *New Testament Theology.* Downers Grove, Ill.: Inter-Varsity, 1981.

Hyde, Walter Woodburn. *Paganism to Christianity in the Roman Empire.* Philadelphia: University of Pennsylvania Press, 1946. Pp. 296. For a lucid account of pagan religions, see pp. 9–76. The book is strongly anti-Christian in its bias.

Hyde, William DeWitt. *The Five Great Philosophies of Life.* New York: The Macmillan Company, 1923. Pp. x, 296. Read pp. 1–106 for material on Epicureans and Stoics.

Kennedy, H. A. A. *St. Paul and the Mystery Religions.* London: Hodder & Stoughton, 1913. Pp. 311.

Machen, J. Gresham. *The Origin of Paul's Religion.* Grand Rapids: Wm. B. Eerdmans Publishing Company, 1947. Pp. 329.

Rogers, Arthur Kenyon. *A Student's History of Philosophy.* New Edition, Revised. New York: The Macmillan Company, 1907. See pp. 174–184.

Rose, Herbert J. *Ancient Roman Religion.* London: Hutchinson's University Library, n.d. Pp. 164.

Rose, H. J. *Religion in Greece and Rome.* New York: Harper & Brothers, 1959.

Uhlhorn, Gerhard. *The Conflict of Christianity and Heathenism.* Edited and translated from the Third German Edition by Egbert C. Smyth and C. J. H. Ropes, Revised Edition. New York: Charles Scribner's Sons, 1901. Pp. 508. Unusually good bibliography.

CHAPTER 4

JUDAISM

Among the religions of the Roman empire in the first century, Judaism held a unique place. It was national, having originated with the Jewish people, and yet it was not confined to them, for its proselytes were numbered by the hundreds. It was not the only cult that emphasized the worship of one God, but unlike the others it was exclusively monotheistic in the sense that its adherents were not allowed to worship or even to admit the existence of any other god or gods. Other religions had temples and sacrificial worship, but in no other faith did the temple with its imageless sanctuary play so great a part or hold the single allegiance of so large a company of people. Many of the philosophies had well-articulated ethical systems, but the ethics of Judaism were inherent in the nature of its worship and were rigidly enforced on all of its adherents. Most of the ethnic religions of the day were founded on tradition or on mystic intuition. Judaism was based on a revelation from God recounted in the sacred Scriptures of the law and the prophets, which claimed to be the reproduction of the words of God himself as he spoke to his chosen servants.

Some understanding of Judaism is indispensable to the student of the New Testament, for Christianity is the child of Judaism. The books of the New Testament, with two exceptions, were written by Jews. The teachings of the New Testament concerning God, man, sin, salvation, law, grace, prayer, and many other subjects fundamental to the Christian life strike their roots back into Old Testament soil. Even the arguments of the New Testament against legalism are drawn from statements in the Old Testament, and the text of the writings of the apostolic age is filled with Old Testament quotations. The Christians were first known as "the sect of the

Nazarenes" (Acts 24:5, 14), which was regarded as a rivulet from the mainstream of Judaism. Jesus himself was a Jew born of a Jewish family (Matt. 1:16), and was circumcised as all Jewish male infants were (Luke 2:21). He was taken to Jerusalem as a boy that he might participate in the Passover feast (2:41), and throughout his life he observed Jewish customs and moved in Jewish society. The present rift between Christianity and Judaism is not the result of a wide difference in historical and theological origins. It is rather the outcome of the repudiation of the Lord Jesus by the Jewish people, as John said: "He came unto his own [home], and they that were his own [people] received him not" (John 1:11).

ORIGIN

Judaism as it existed in the first century was largely the product of the exile. Prior to the captivity the people of Israel and Judah had given only spasmodic loyalty to the law. The worship of Jehovah had been their rightful and official faith, but it had frequently been "more honored in the breach than in the observance." In the ninth century B.C. the entire northern kingdom had been alienated to the worship of Baal under the influence of Jezebel, Ahab's Phoenician queen, and had been brought back to the worship of Jehovah only by the heroic ministry of Elijah. Similarly the temple worship of the southern kingdom fell into neglect and disuse during the reigns of Manasseh and Amon in the eighth century, who sponsored the introduction of foreign deities. Under Josiah's vigorous administration, the temple was cleansed, the worship of Jehovah was restored, and the book of the law that was brought to light during the reconstruction of the temple was put back in its rightful place of authority (II Chron. 34:1–33). As long as the people lived in Palestine, surrounded by prosperous and powerful heathen neighbors and subjected to their influence, they were tempted to experiment with alien worship and to desert the God of their fathers. The prophets protested in vain against this tendency which had appeared during the wilderness wanderings of the people (Num. 25:1–3), and which had persisted even to the period of the captivity and exile (Ezek. 14:1–5; Jer. 7:16–20).

The captivity confronted the Jewish people with a demanding alternative. Either they must commit themselves utterly to the worship of Jehovah, the one true God, by which allegiance they would retain the genius and purpose of their national existence, or they would be absorbed both religiously and politically by the nations among whom they were driven into exile. If they were to choose the former alternative, they would have to pay closer attention to the requirements of the law, and they would have to devise some means of worship to take the place of the temple ritual that had ceased with the destruction of the central building and the subsequent dispersion of the priesthood. The book of the law could be carried with them to their new resting place, but the cult of the temple, as far as they could see, was gone forever.

While the captives of the southern kingdom were in Babylonia in the sixth century B.C. the new Judaism began to take form. Idolatry was first banned. Whereas the worship of Baal and other Canaanite deities had been madly espoused prior to the capture of Jerusalem, the bitter discipline of the captivity schooled the survivors to look toward Jehovah. The whole spirit of the book of Daniel, in which all participation in heathen worship is scorned and in which Daniel and his friends avowed their will to worship Jehovah alone at any cost, is a witness to the salutary change in spiritual temper that came over the exiles.

With the enforced cessation of sacrifice, the study of the law, or Torah, began to take its place. In the kingdoms, the individual worshiper may have relied largely on participation in public worship as an expression of his faith. That expression may have been sincere, but it could hardly have been as vital as the personal study of God's precepts could become. In the reform of Josiah the law was read to the people (II Chron. 34:29–30) as a special feature of a reforming movement, but in the exile there was an increasing tendency for each person to study the law for himself. The scribe, like Ezra, who studied and interpreted the law became as important a personage among the people as the priest had been while the first temple was standing (Ezra 7:1–6). In the days of Jesus the scribes were potent figures in the religion of Judaism.

A new center of worship was established with the rise of the synagogue. The wide dispersion of the people in the captivity and their wanderings in the years that followed made some local form of gathering necessary. Even when the temple was reestablished, together with the sacrifices, many people could not attend its ceremonies. In order to hold them together around the study of the law, wherever ten men could be found to form a regular congregation, synagogues were created in the various communities where they lived. In these the people gathered for prayer and worship on the seventh day of the week. So firmly established was the synagogue as an institution that it continued even after the rebuilding of the temple, and in the first century in Jerusalem some synagogues carried on their activities concurrently with those of the temple (Acts 6:9). Although no mention of the synagogue as such occurs in the Old Testament, there can be little doubt that it grew up in the years between the captivity and the advent of Christ, for in his lifetime it was flourishing in Palestine.

The religious life that grew up around the synagogue was an adaptation of the older rites and observances of Judaism to the new conditions under which the people had to live. Many of them had been moved from the pastoral and agricultural life of Palestine to the busy commercial activity of great cities. Feasts could not be observed with all the features that might be utilized in village worship. Problems and queries prompted by the new life called for new answers. New influences from the Gentile world surrounding them pressed in on them with great force. Some changes were inevitable, but in the main Judaism retained the essential principles of the older worship prescribed by the law and preached by the prophets.

THEOLOGY

Central to the whole faith of Judaism was its tenacious belief in the unity and transcendence of Jehovah. In contrast to the multiplicity of deities that the heathen world acknowledged, the Jew guarded jealously his short, sharp creed of Deuteronomy 6:4: "Hear, O Israel: Jehovah our God is one Jehovah." Jewish exclusivism in worship is amply attested by the attitude that the Gentiles took toward them. They were generally accused of atheism, not because they denied the existence of any god at all, but because they consistently refused to recognize the reality of any deity except their own.

Among the rabbinic teachers considerable emphasis was placed on the fatherhood of God. The introductory phrase of the Lord's Prayer, "Our Father who art in heaven," was no novelty. Isaiah had addressed God with this title:

> For thou art our Father, though Abraham knoweth us not, and Israel doth not acknowledge us: thou, O Jehovah, art our Father; our Redeemer from everlasting is thy name.
>
> (Isa. 63:16)

Rabbi Akiba taught that the Israelites were sons of God:

> Beloved (of God) are the Israelites, in that they shall be called sons of God; still more beloved in that it is made known to them that they are called sons of God.[1]
>
> (Cf. Deut. 14:1.)

This personal relation of God to Israel as expressed by the figure of fatherhood was emphasized chiefly by Palestinian teachers.

Philo, who belonged to the Hellenistic wing of Judaism, had a more philosophic conception of God. God is eternal, unchangeable, holy, free, and perfect. Because he is superior to all other beings, he is not definable by comparison with them, since definition would thus be equivalent to limitation. This concept illustrates a trend toward depersonalizing God that is still extant in modern Judaism. God thus becomes an actual but a vague

---

1. See G. F. Moore, *Judaism* (Cambridge: Harvard University Press, 1927), Vol. II, p. 203, n. 2.

and shadowy being concerning whose character and attitudes no definite assertions can be made. Perhaps this uncertainty about the nature of God, which sprang originally from a hesitation to limit him, was the reason for the indefiniteness expressed in John 1:18: "No man hath seen God at any time. . . ." At this point Christianity went beyond Judaism by presenting a God who was not only sole God and real, but who was also personal and knowable.

Man, according to Jewish theology, was the creation of God, endowed with the ability to choose between obedience and disobedience to God's revealed law, and by so doing to choose the consequences of life and of death (Deut. 30:11–20). Man's chief end in life was to keep the commandments of God and to maintain all of the forms that were prescribed for the people as a whole: namely, circumcision, the observance of the Sabbath, the various annual feasts, and worship in the synagogue. The law summarized the whole duty of man and established his relation to God.

Sin for the Jew consisted chiefly in a wrong relationship to the revealed law of God. The failure to obey one of its proscriptions, whether "weighty," such as the command "Thou shalt not kill," or "light," such as the prohibition of taking a bird from the nest with her fledglings or with the eggs (22:6–7), was regarded as a sin. This Jewish attitude is reflected in the New Testament in James 2:10: "For whosoever shall keep the whole law, and yet stumble in one *point*, he is become guilty of all." Judaism drew no distinction between the moral and ceremonial law, for both were inextricably connected with the life of the people as a whole. Severance from the elect people, which was the penalty for sin, was meted out to all offenders, not only on those who had committed some outrageous crime or who neglected some fundamental ordinance such as circumcision, but also on those who ate flesh with blood remaining in it (Lev. 17:14).

In the period before the exile, rewards and punishments were connected with the fate of the nation as a whole. If the nation observed God's law and worshiped him alone, it prospered. If the nation lapsed into idolatry and into neglect of the law, it suffered political and economic reverses. Sin was thus evaluated and judged on a communal scale rather than individually. There was, of course, personal consciousness of sin, as Psalm 51 shows, but the social and national implications of the individual's conduct were more marked in Judaism than they are in modern Protestant Christianity.

The uprooting of the nation in the captivity tended to destroy the connection of reward and punishment with ebb and flow of national prosperity in the land. The captivity itself was a discipline that the nation must endure until such time as God should see fit to restore them, but in the interim the generations that should be born and die must face the issues of life and death for themselves. This was the problem that confronted Ezekiel. When he was told by the fatalists of his day that "the fathers have eaten sour grapes, and the children's teeth are set on edge," he replied that one's relation to God is not determined by the sins or by the virtues of one's ancestors but by his own.

> As I live, saith the Lord Jehovah, ye shall not have occasion any more to use this proverb in Israel. Behold, all souls are mine; as the soul of the father, so also the soul of the son is mine: the soul that sinneth, it shall die.
> (Ezek. 18:3–4)

This reaffirmation of individual responsibility accords with the position of Judaism as it is reflected in the New Testament. The rich young ruler showed deep concern for his individual relation to God in spite of the fact that he felt that he had kept completely all the precepts of the moral law (Matt. 19:16–22). Communal responsibility was transferred from the people as inhabitants of a land to the people as the elect of God, whose manifestation of that election lay in their social solidarity rather than in their location.

The theology of punishment and of reward, when applied to the individual life, opened the question of immortality and the life hereafter. Little is given in the Old Testament concerning these subjects. Jacob and David both alluded to Sheol, a dim and shadowy region of the dead, where they might be reunited with their children who had suffered an untimely death (Gen. 37:35; II Sam. 12:23). Nowhere in the earlier records is there any direct statement concerning the resurrection of the body, although Jesus interpreted God's declaration to Moses, "I am the God of Abraham, the God of Isaac, and the God of Jacob" (Exod. 3:6), to mean that he was not the God of the dead but of the living (Matt. 22:32). The suggestion of resurrection emerges first in the poetical books and later in the prophets. The sixteenth Psalm, attributed to David, says:

> For thou wilt not leave my soul to Sheol;
> Neither wilt thou suffer thy holy one to see corruption.
> Thou wilt show me the path of life:
> In thy presence is fulness of joy;
> In thy right hand there are pleasures for evermore.
> (Ps. 16:10–11)

Isaiah, in predicting the future judgments of God and the salvation of Israel, says:

> Thy dead shall live; my dead bodies shall arise. Awake and sing, ye that dwell in the dust; for thy dew is as the dew of herbs, and the earth shall cast forth the dead.
> (Isa. 26:19)

In Daniel a prediction of resurrection also occurs:

*And many of them that sleep in the dust of the earth shall awake, some to
everlasting life, and some to shame and everlasting contempt.*

(Dan. 12:2)

The relative scarcity of references to the life hereafter or to a resurrection may seem strange when one contemplates the fact that Judaism was a part of the divine revelation to men. The revelation, however, carried with it an educative process that was closely connected with Israel's development in the land of Palestine. Their tenure of the land was conditioned on their behavior in this life, and their reward as a group was confined to this world, for common reward and common punishment would scarcely be meted out in another life where individual destiny was the determining factor. The emphasis under law for the Jewish nation was on collective salvation here, rather than on individual salvation hereafter.

The apocryphal and apocalyptic writings are more explicit. The unknown author of the Wisdom of Solomon, who probably wrote at Alexandria in the middle of the second century B.C., says: "The souls of the righteous are in the hands of God, and no torment shall touch them . . . and although they are chastened for a little time, they shall receive great blessings, for God tested them and found them worthy of himself" (Wis. of Sol. 3:1,5). In Second Maccabees, a work drawn from the original of Jason of Cyrene, the concept of a resurrection emerged clearly. Judas Maccabeus, according to the acount given in II Maccabees 12:42–44, had, by a surprise attack on Gorgias, governor of Idumea, retrieved the bodies of some Jews who had been killed in a previous skirmish with the Idumeans. When the bodies were removed for burial, under the coats of the dead were found things consecrated to idols. Judas, to expiate the sin that the deceased had committed, acted as follows:

*And when he had made a gathering throughout the company to the sum of
two thousand drachmas of silver, he sent it to Jerusalem to offer a sin-
offering, doing therein very well and honestly in that he was mindful of the
resurrection: for if he had not hoped that they that were slain should have
risen again, it had been superfluous and vain to pray for the dead.*

(II Macc. 12:43–44)

Sheol was regarded as an intermediate state preceding the resurrection and the final rewards and punishments. In II Maccabees 6:23 Eleazar, a martyr, speaks of going to Hades; and since he as a righteous man must be destined for the resurrection mentioned above, his stay in Hades would be only temporary.

A day of judgment in which the wicked should be sent to well-deserved doom and in which the righteous would be vindicated also appears in the apocryphal writings. The just "having been a little chastised . . . shall be greatly rewarded" (Wis. of Sol. 3:5), while the wicked "have no hope, neither comfort in the day of trial" (3:18). In II Esdras and in Enoch there are numerous allusions to a future day of doom, although the statements are not always coherent.

The Messianic expectation of the advent of a political deliverer for Israel was strong in the intertestamental period. In the Apocrypha, II Esdras is outstanding as a Messianic apocalypse. Oesterley thinks that it is the compilation of the work of several authors who wrote between A.D. 100 and 270.[2] The book, even at this late date, may still be independent of Christian influence, since it is unmistakably Jewish and contains no allusion to the person of Christ. It bears some traces of being a translation from a Hebrew original. It predicts that the divine kingdom shall succeed the rule of Rome; that the Messiah shall rule by law; and that after he has completed his work, he shall die and the judgment will follow. The Psalms of Solomon, written in the first century before Christ, depicts the coming of a righteous ruler for Israel who shall be sinless and who shall rule over the Gentiles (Ps. of Sol. 17). In all of this literature the Messiah is nowhere represented as suffering for men or as redeeming them by his personal sacrifice. The Messianic hope and the apocalyptic concept of it that is apparent in Daniel and that is treated at length in later books formed the background for the apostles' questioning of Jesus that evoked his well-known Olivet discourse (Matt. 24-25).

THE TEMPLE

The original temple of Solomon was destroyed when Jerusalem was sacked and burned by the troops of Nebuchadnezzar in 586 B.C. The second temple, built in the restoration and mentioned by Haggai and Zechariah, prophets of that period, was begun about 537 B.C., and was completed after many delays in 516 B.C. (Ezra 6:13-15).

Little is known of the history of this temple. In 168 B.C. Antiochus Epiphanes plundered it and desecrated it by introducing into it an altar to Olympian Zeus on which he offered sacrifice. Three years later Judas Maccabeus cleansed and repaired it. It was standing in 63 B.C. when Pompey conquered Jerusalem, and was robbed of its treasures by Crassus in 54 B.C. When Herod the Great took the city in 37 B.C. some of the temple structures were burned, but the main building was probably not greatly damaged.

Herod, however, in the eighteenth year of his reign (20-19 B.C.)

---

2. W. O. E. Oesterley, *An Introduction to the Books of the Apocrypha* (New York: The Macmillan Company, n.d.), pp. 147, 155-156. See W. M. Dunnett, "Esdras, Second (2)," in *The Zondervan Pictorial Encyclopedia of the Bible*, ed. M. C. Tenney (Grand Rapids: Zondervan Publishing House, 1975), II, 362-364.

Cameo portrait of Antiochus
Epiphanes, carved on an onyx,
apparently from a coin or medallion
of his period.

undertook the rebuilding of the temple. He collected the material before
he began the actual process of demolition and reconstruction, and proceeded slowly in order that the worship might be disturbed as little as
possible. The work was done by the priests. The sanctuary itself was completed in a year and a half, but the outer buildings and porticoes were not
finished until A.D. 62 or 64. When Jesus' enemies said that the temple had
been forty-six years in building, they implied that the work was still going
on (John 2:20).

The building itself was made of white marble, a large part of which was
covered with gold, which reflected the sunlight and made it an object of
dazzling splendor. The temple court occupied a rectangular space about
585 feet east to west and about 610 feet north to south. Inside the wall of
this court was a set of cloisters with a double row of columns on the south
side. The eastern cloister was known as Solomon's porch (John 10:23; Acts
3:11; 5:12) because it was traditionally a survival from Solomon's temple.
Offices were located along the walls or between the porticoes.

The outer court was known as the court of the Gentiles. No restrictions were placed on access to it, and it was at times used as a marketplace. At the northern end of the court and transverse to it was the
temple proper, consisting of the inner court with its buildings. At the
eastern end was the women's court, and at the western end was the court of
the Israelites from which women were excluded. Centered within the court
of the Israelites was the court of the priests, in the middle of which was the
sanctuary. The inner court stood on higher ground than the outer court.
Between the two, on the edge of the inner court, was a stone parapet, on

M. Avi-Yonah's model of the Herodian temple in Jerusalem.

which were inscriptions warning all Gentiles to stay out of the second enclosure under penalty of death. The wall was pierced by nine gates, four on the north, four on the south, and one on the end that may have been the Beautiful Gate mentioned in Acts 3.

The sanctuary itself was elevated above the inner court and was reached by a flight of twelve steps. Its divisions were similar to those of the Tabernacle: the Holy Place, on the east, which was about sixty feet long, and the Most Holy Place, which was about thirty feet long. The former contained the table of shewbread on the north, the seven-branched lamp-stand on the south, and the altar of incense between them. Only the priests were allowed to enter the Holy Place. The Most Holy Place was empty, for the ark of the covenant had been lost when the temple of Solomon was destroyed. The high priest entered the Most Holy Place once a year on the Day of Atonement, when he made propitiation with blood for the sins of the people. The division between the Holy Place and the Most Holy Place was a thick double veil, which shut off the inner sanctuary from prying eyes. On the outside of the sanctuary were built small rooms, arranged in three stories and accessible by a staircase, in which priests lived, or which could be used for storage.

Within the court of the priests, east of the sanctuary, was the great altar of burnt offering, about eighteen feet square and fifteen feet high. On this altar perpetual fire burned and animal sacrifices were consumed in the daily ritual. Just north of the altar was a space for slaughtering the victims and preparing them for sacrifice.

Only the priests could remain within the court of the priests, except for those who brought animals to be offered as sacrifices, since they had to lay their hands on the victim before it was slaughtered.

The Jews were allowed by the Romans to maintain a police corps to keep order within the temple precincts. Its chief officer was called a *stratēgos*, or "captain of the temple" (Acts 4:1; 5:24–26). It is possible that a detachment from these men took Jesus at the betrayal, rather than a cohort of Roman soldiers. They were charged with the apprehension and safekeeping of Peter and John when the latter were arrested for preaching, probably within the temple enclosure. The guard watched the temple day by day to see that no unauthorized person entered forbidden enclosures. At night the gates were shut and a watch was stationed to prevent the entrance of marauders.

The temple was the main center of worship in Jerusalem. Jesus himself and later his apostles taught and preached within its courts. As late as A.D. 56 the church in Jerusalem still had in its ranks men who made vows in the temple (21:23–26) and who adhered closely to its legal observance. Only with the development of the Gentile church did its connection with Christianity cease.

THE SYNAGOGUE

The synagogue played a large part in the growth and persistence of Judaism, as previously noted.[3] The Jews of the Dispersion founded synagogues in every city of the empire where there were enough Jews to maintain one, and foreign synagogues flourished in Jerusalem. Galilee, which in the days of the Maccabees was largely Gentile (I Macc. 5:21–23), was filled with synagogues in the time of Christ. The synagogue was the social center where the Jewish inhabitants of a city gathered weekly to meet each other. It was the educational medium for keeping the law before the people and for providing instruction for their children in the ancestral faith. It was the substitute for temple worship, which was precluded by distance or by poverty. In the synagogue the study of the law took the place of ritual sacrifice, the rabbi supplanted the priest, and the communal faith was applied to individual life.

Each synagogue had as its leader the "head of synagogue" (Mark 5:22), who was probably selected from among the elders by vote. The leader

---

3. Cf. above, p. 82.

presided over the services in the synagogue, acted as instructor in case of any dispute (Luke 13:14), and introduced visitors to the assembly (Acts 13:15). The syngagogue attendant, or *hazzan*, acted as custodian of the property and had the responsibility of caring for the building and its contents. His duties included warning the village people of the beginning of the Sabbath on Friday afternoon and notifying them as well of its close. Probably he was the official mentioned in Luke 4:20 who brought forth the roll of Scripture from which Jesus preached in the synagogue at Nazareth and who replaced the roll in its proper niche when Jesus had finished reading from it. On occasion the *hazzan* served as the master of the local synagogue school.

The synagogue buildings were usually substantial structures of stone, sometimes richly furnished if the congregation or sponsor was wealthy. Every synagogue had a chest in which the roll of the law was kept, a platform with a reading desk from which the Scripture of the day was read, lamps for lighting the building, and benches or seats for the congregation. Most of the equipment in use in the ancient synagogues still appears in its modern counterparts.

The synagogue service consisted of recitation of the Jewish creed or *Shema*, "Hear, O Israel: Jehovah our God is one Jehovah: and thou shalt love Jehovah thy God with all thy heart, and with all thy soul, and with all thy might" (Deut. 6:4–5), accompanied by sentences of praise to God called *Berakot* because they began with the word "Blessed." Following the *Shema* was a ritual prayer, concluding with an opportunity for individual silent prayer on the part of the members of the congregation. The reading of the Scriptures, which came next, began with special sections of the law that were assigned to holy days; but as time went on, the entire Pentateuch was divided into sections that gave a fixed cycle of one hundred fifty-four lessons to be read in a definite period of time. The Palestinian Jews read through the Pentateuch every three years, whereas the Babylonian Jews completed the reading in one year. The Prophets were also used, as Jesus' reading in the synagogue shows (Luke 4:16ff.). Probably on that occasion Jesus himself selected the reading. A sermon followed the reading of the Scripture, explaining the portion that had been read. The sermon in the synagogue at Nazareth was in full keeping with the regular procedure of the day. The service was closed with a blessing, pronounced by some priestly member of the congregation. If no person with priestly qualifications was present, a prayer was substituted for the blessing.

The influence of the nature and order of synagogue worship on the procedure followed by the church of the first century is fairly obvious. Jesus himself attended the service of the synagogue regularly and took part in it. His disciples also had been accustomed to its ritual. Paul in his travels made the synagogues of the Dispersion his first points of contact whenever he

entered strange cities, and he preached and debated with the Jews and
proselytes who gathered to hear him (Acts 13:5, 15–43; 14:1; 17:1–3, 10,
17; 18:4, 8; 19:8). The many close resemblances between the usages of the
synagogue and those of the church may doubtless be accounted for by the
fact that the latter absorbed or followed to some degree the procedure of the
former. It is possible that some early Christian worship may have been
carried on within the synagogue, even as early Christians continued to
frequent the temple, as "at the hour of prayer" (Acts 3:1). A possible
reference to this practice occurs in James 2:1–2 (although the Greek term
synagōgē may have been transferred to meetings of Christian congregations, as in Hebrews 10:25, where *episynagōgē* has basically the same sense).
Because of the summary and persistent rejection of the gospel of Christ by
the Jewish people, the church and the synagogue parted company. Today
they are far apart and are in many respects antithetical. Nevertheless, in
the prominence given to the written Scriptures and in the use of homily
and sermon, the synagogue and the church still show a close relationship.

THE SACRED YEAR

The Jewish year consisted of twelve lunar months, with an intercalary
month added to the calendar whenever it was needed to equate the lunar
year with the solar year. The civil year commenced with the seventh
month, corresponding roughly to October on the modern calendar. The
religious year began with the first month, in which occurred the Passover,
the first great feast of the Jewish cycle. The sequence of the months is as
follows, using the religious year as the standard:

	MONTH	SPECIAL DAYS
Nisan	(April)	14—Passover
		15—Unleavened Bread
		21—Close of Passover
Iyra	(May)	
Sivan	(June)	6—Feast of Pentecost—seven
		weeks from the Passover
		(Anniversary of the giving of
		the law on Mt. Sinai)
Tammuz	(July)	
Ab	(August)	
Elul	(September)	
Tishri	(October)	1 & 2—The Feast of Trumpets
		Rosh Hashanah, the beginning of
		the civil year
		10—Day of Atonement
		15–21—Feast of Tabernacles

MONTH		SPECIAL DAYS
Marchesvan	(November)	
Kislev	(December)	25—Feast of Lights, or Dedication *Hanukkah*
Tebeth	(January)	
Shebet	(February)	
Adar	(March)	14—The Feast of Purim

The festivals, or feasts, were seven in number: Passover, the Feast of Unleavened Bread, the Feast of Pentecost, the New Year and Day of Atonement, the Feast of Tabernacles, the Feast of Dedication, and the Feast of Purim. Of these, the first five were prescribed by the Mosaic law; the last two were postexilic in origin.

The Passover

The Passover was the most important of all the feasts, historically and religiously. It marked the anniversary of the deliverance of the Jews from Egypt and their establishment as an independent people by the redemptive act of God. Jewish usage distinguished between the "Egyptian Passover" and the "permanent Passover." The former was to be observed on the tenth of Nisan, when the blood was sprinkled on the doorposts and the lamb was eaten in haste. The permanent Passover was observed for seven days with the use of unleavened bread. Both were closely connected in time and constituted one festal season.

The public celebrations of the Passover were intended to be annual, but the Old Testament mentions only a few of them during the span of its recorded history (II Chron. 8:13; 30:15; II Kings 23:21; Ezra 6:19). Doubtless it was kept rather regularly, although there were probably occasional lapses during periods of religious declension. The feast seems to have been held regularly during the New Testament period, for Mary and Joseph took the boy Jesus up to Jerusalem at the time of the Passover (Luke 2:41) as was their regular custom, and he himself kept the feast during his ministry.

On the day of the feast every male Jew who was physically fit for travel and who was not disqualified by ceremonial uncleanness was requested to appear in Jerusalem if he lived within fifteen miles of the city. Women also participated in the worship, though they were not obligated to do so. Pilgrims came from the outlying sections of Palestine and even from foreign provinces to bring their offerings and join in the festive worship. Josephus states that at the Passover season the total population of Jerusalem may have reached three million.[4] Many of these people camped outside the city at night, since all accommodations within the walls were filled.

---

4. Josephus *Jewish Wars* II.ix.3; II.xiv.3.

During the Feast of Unleavened Bread sacrifices of two bullocks, one ram, and seven lambs of the first year were offered daily together with a goat as a sin offering (Num. 28:19–25). On the second day a sheaf of new grain was offered as a wave offering with a lamb of the first year for a burnt offering (Lev. 23:10–14).

Pentecost, or the Feast of Weeks

The Feast of Weeks, or the Day of the Firstfruits, was celebrated in the month Sivan, seven weeks after the offering of the wave sheaf after the Passover. The name *Pentecost* originated from the interval of fifty days that separated the two. According to Jewish tradition, it took place on the anniversary of the giving of the law at Mt. Sinai. The special feature of the day was the offering of two wave loaves of leavened bread, made from the ripe grain that had been harvested. Although the feast is not mentioned in the history of the Old Testament, it is of great importance in the New Testament as the time at which the Holy Spirit was poured out on the disciples of the Lord Jesus, who, in obedience to his command, were waiting in Jerusalem. It became the birthday of the church.

The Feast of Trumpets, or the New Year (Rosh Hashanah)

The civil year of the Jews began on the first day of Tishri. During the entire New Year's Day horns and trumpets were blown in the temple from morning to evening. Unlike the Passover and Pentecost, the feast did not attract many pilgrims to Jerusalem, for it was celebrated in the synagogue as well as in the temple. The book of Nehemiah (Neh. 8:2–12) states that those who returned from the exile observed the feast by the public reading of the law and by general rejoicing.

The Day of Atonement

The Day of Atonement was more properly a fast than a feast and is so called in the New Testament (Acts 27:9). The special feature of the day, apart from the ordinary daily sacrifices, was the presentation of the annual atonement by the high priest. Laying aside his ceremonial robes and dressed in plain white linen, he entered the Holy of Holies with a censer full of coals taken from the altar and with a basin full of blood from the bullock that had been killed as a sin offering. As the incense rose like a veil between the priest and the mercy seat, the priest sprinkled the mercy seat with the blood. The same process was repeated with the blood of the goat that had been made a sin offering. The altar of incense and the brazen altar outside of the sanctuary were also sprinkled with blood. A live goat was presented by the priest, who placed his hands on its head and confessed the sins of the people. The live goat was then taken out into the wilderness and released, apparently as a sign that the people's sins had been carried away forever (Lev. 16:23, 27–32; Num. 29:7–11).

When these ceremonies were completed, the high priest took off his linen clothes, bathed, and resumed his official robes, after which the usual routine sacrifices were offered. Much of the symbolism of the Day of Atonement is applied to Christ by the book of Hebrews. Many of the functions of his priesthood are described in terms of the ritual of the Old Testament.

In modern Judaism the New Year and the Day of Atonement are united in the days of penitence, during which the devout worshiper searches his heart and seeks forgiveness for the sins of the past year in order that he may enter forgiven into the year to come.

The Feast of Tabernacles

Five days after the Day of Atonement was the Feast of Tabernacles (Lev. 23:34; Deut. 16:13). The feast included the fifteenth to the twenty-second days of the month. It commemorated the wandering in the wilderness and was a thanksgiving at the close of the harvest. It was celebrated by the construction of booths or huts made of branches, in which the people lived temporarily as a reminder of the sojourning of their forefathers in the wilderness. Many sacrifices were offered on the successive days of the feast, and at the close there was one great day of convocation, called in John "the last day, the great day of the feast" (John 7:37), which marked the conclusion of the ecclesiastical year. Among the observances of this day that came into existence later than the giving of the law were the pouring out of water at the altar from a golden pitcher, the singing of the Hallel (Pss. 113–118), the lighting of the four great candelabra in the court of the women, and the singing of selected Psalms. The Feast of Tabernacles was popular and joyous in nature.

Two other feasts were added later in postexilic times: the Feast of Lights and the Feast of Purim.

The Feast of Lights

The Feast of Lights or the Feast of Dedication was observed for eight days beginning with the twenty-fifth of Kislev. It is mentioned in John 10:22. It was first established in 164 B.C. when Judas Maccabeus cleansed the temple, which had been profaned by Antiochus Epiphanes, and rededicated it to the service of God. Every Jewish home was brilliantly lighted in its honor and the stories of the Maccabees were repeated for the benefit of the children. It corresponds almost exactly in time to the Christian Christmas.

The Feast of Purim

Purim, or "lots," as the word signifies, was kept on the fourteenth and fifteenth days of Adar. On the evening of the thirteenth day the whole of the book of Esther was read publicly in the synagogue. It contained a minimum of religious observances and was rather a national holiday, corresponding somewhat to the Fourth of July as Americans used to celebrate it. It is not mentioned in the New Testament, unless John 5:1 is an allusion to it.

A few other minor fasts and feasts were current in the Judaism of the first century, but they were of no great importance and do not appear in the records of the New Testament.

THE EDUCATIONAL SYSTEM

Among the Jews of the Dispersion, education must have taken on an important place at an early date, for they were dependent solely on the perpetuation of their national convictions for their survival. Uprooted from their land, with no military defense of their own, they could keep their national identity only as they maintained themselves as a separate group with their own culture and spiritual life. As far back as the time of Ezra, there was public reading of the law and instruction in its meaning—a kind of adult education that was consistently maintained by the synagogue.

Along with the synagogue developed the school. Judaism never had the general compulsory education that prevails in America at the present day; but the Jewish community usually provided some sort of instruction for children so that they might read the Torah, write, and do simple arithmetic.

The schools of Palestine in the time of Christ were traditionally the result of the influence of a famous Pharisee and scribe, Simon ben Shatach, who lived about 75 B.C. According to the Talmud, he decreed that all children should attend an elementary school. His words as quoted are ambiguous. They may imply that all children should be put in schools already established, or that schools should be organized for them. In either case, Simon is credited with a reform by which the state provided teachers for boys from the provinces, and by which it also founded schools in the country towns. Joshua ben Gamla instituted public schools for boys of six or seven years of age in all the cities of Palestine. One teacher was provided for every twenty-five boys. If there were forty in the school the teacher was given an assistant.

The instruction was limited but it was thorough. Before the child went to school at all he would have learned at home the *Shema*, or Jewish creed (Deut. 6:4), to which Jesus referred when he was asked what was the great commandment of the law (Matt. 22:35–38). He would also have memo-

rized passages from the Torah, certain common proverbs, and some selected Psalms. In the school itself he would repeat the words of the Torah as
he was drilled by the teacher. Usually the teacher sat on a low platform
with his pupils seated in a semicircle on the ground before him, as Paul sat
"at the feet of Gamaliel" (Acts 22:3). As the pupil advanced he would be
instructed in the Oral Tradition (later assuming written form in the Mishna and the Talmud), and if he proved to be bright and alert he might
ultimately be sent to one of the training schools for scribes.

Jewish education was narrow but precise. The student was trained to
make fine distinctions of definition and to remember exactly what he had
learned. What he studied he mastered, and he could interpret the law from
every possible approach. Original thinking and scientific research were not
encouraged, however. The rabbis of Jesus' time were astute in interpreting
minute points of the law and in unraveling casuistic questions, but they laid
little emphasis on the knowledge of the natural world that has so large a
place in the curricula of modern schools.

Jewish education was thoroughly integrated, for every branch of Jewish
knowledge merged with theology. The law was the core of the curriculum.
Some knowledge of Greek and perhaps a little Latin were permitted in the
most advanced schools, but many of the rabbis frowned on Gentile learning, and would not permit their pupils to indulge in it.

The Jews favored vocational education. The rabbis had a saying,
"Whosoever does not teach his son a trade makes him a thief." Almost
every Jewish boy learned how to work with his hands and thus to support
himself. According to the Gospel records, the Lord Jesus was a carpenter
(Mark 6:3), or possibly a stone mason, since the Greek word translated
carpenter may mean *masterbuilder* or *mason*. [5] Paul worked at the tent
makers' trade (Acts 18:3). This healthy emphasis on manual training made
the Jewish male citizen independent. It balanced his intellectual pursuits
with physical skills and it enabled him to find gainful employment.

Girls were not generally educated in the synagogue schools. They were
trained at home in household arts in preparation for marriage.

With the fall of the Jewish state, Judaism succumbed to Hellenism in
the Diaspora. In Palestine the Jewish schools expelled the Greek learning
and laid the foundation for the strict system that has characterized Jewish
orthodoxy to the present day.

Enthusiasm for education was a marked characteristic of Jewish life.
The study of the Torah was a sign of piety, and the devout Jew spent much
time with the law. Since educational culture was regarded as an aspect of

---

5. Homes in Palestine were built of stone, not wood. Jesus uses numerous figures of
speech drawn from masonry, but almost none from the carpenter's trade. See Fritz-Otto
Busch, *The Five Herods* (London: Robert Hale, Ltd., 1958), pp. 56–57.

Page from the Septuagint, Codex B *(Codex Vaticanus), assigned to the fourth century; in the Vatican Library.*

religion, the Jewish people preserved an intellectual standard that many Gentiles did not have. As Moore says:

> . . . the endeavor to educate the whole people in its religion created a unique system of universal education, whose very elements comprised not only reading and writing, but an ancient language and its classic literature. The high intellectual and religious value thus set on education was indelibly impressed on the mind, and one may say on the character of the Jew, and the institutions created for it have perpetuated themselves to the present day.[6]

THE LITERATURE

More than any other nation of antiquity the Jews were the people of a book. Others may have possessed a larger and more varied literature or even a more ancient one, but none, not even the Greeks in the heyday of the Periclean Age, showed such an absorbing interest in their national writings

---

6. G. F. Moore, *Judaism,* 322. Quoted by permission.

Page from the Codex Sinaiticus, assigned to the fourth century; in the British Museum.

as the Jew showed in his law. For him the Torah was not simply representative of a cherished national culture, it was the voice of God. Its precepts were to be obeyed unquestioningly, and its most remote implications were to be regarded as sacred mandates. The ordinances were woven into the very fabric of his life and the underlying theism of the law colored all his thinking.

The influence of the canonical Jewish Scriptures on the New Testament is so obvious that it scarcely needs comment. The Lord Jesus Christ and his disciples were familiar with them from their earliest years. Jesus quoted with equal readiness from the Law, the Psalms, and the Prophets (Luke 24:44), the three divisions of the Hebrew Bible, and argued from them as the basis of revelational authority (John 10:34–36) concerning his own person. Throughout the Acts and Epistles the apostolic writers show by their frequent quotations their familiarity with the Old Testament, whether they used the Hebrew text or the Greek Septuagint. Paul asserted that the Old Testament was "God-breathed" (inspired of God, II Tim.

3:16) and declared to Timothy that the Scriptures of the Old Testament were "able to make . . . wise unto salvation through faith which is in Christ Jesus" (3:15). So thoroughly did the early church take over the Jewish Scriptures that a new Jewish version of the Old Testament in Greek was made, because the Septuagint had become to all intents and purposes a Christian book. About A.D. 130 Aquila, a Jew of Pontus, produced a very literal Greek translation of the Hebrew text. This was followed by the translation of Theodotion, like Aquila a proselyte to Judaism. The translation of Aquila became the official version for Greek-speaking Jews.

Following the era of the Old Testament, which closed with Malachi, the last of the prophets, at 450 B.C. or thereabouts, there grew up in Palestinian Judaism a body of works later called the *Apocrypha*. The term *Apocrypha*, which is of Greek derivation, means "hidden," "recondite," or "secret," as applied to matters that are not to be disclosed to common people, but are to be revealed only to the initiated few. As time went on, the name was applied to those works which had biblical or religious flavor, but which were not generally accepted as authoritative. They might be read for educational and moral purposes, but would not be regarded as on a par with the authoritative text. The Old Testament Apocrypha appear as an integral part of the Septuagint, being distributed throughout its text rather than being grouped in one place, as they appear in the Latin Vulgate and later in certain of the English versions, such as the Great Bible of 1539 and the original King James Version of 1611.

The apocryphal books are given as follows in their usual order: I Esdras, II Esdras, Tobit, Judith, The Rest of Esther, The Wisdom of Solomon, Ecclesiasticus, Baruch, The Song of the Three Holy Children, The History of Susanna, Bel and the Dragon, The Prayer of Manasses, I Maccabees, and II Maccabees. This order is not chronological. Exact dating is impossible, but an approximate location of these books with respect to their time of writing is given here, after the sequences proposed by Oesterley:[7]

PRE-MACCABEAN

I Esdras	c. 300 B.C.
Tobit	c. 250 B.C.
The Hymn in the Song of the Three Holy Children	c. 200 B.C.
Ecclesiasticus	c. 200 B.C.

MACCABEAN

The Prayer in the Song of the Three Holy Children	c. 160 B.C.

---

7. W. O. E. Oesterley, *An Introduction to the Books of the Apocrypha*, pp. 24–25.

Page containing Acts 28:8–30 from Codex Alexandrinus (Codex A), assigned to the fifth century. It was presented to Charles I by the Patriarch of Constantinople in 1628 and is now in the British Museum.

Judith	c. 150 B.C.
The Rest of Esther	c. 140–130 B.C.
Bel and the Dragon	c. 150 B.C.

POST-MACCABEAN

I Maccabees	90–70 B.C.
II Maccabees	50 B.C.
The History of Susanna	?
The Wisdom of Solomon	A.D. 40
Baruch	A.D. 70 or after
II Esdras	A.D. 100
Prayer of Manasses	?

Most of these books were written in the period of unsettled national life and struggle between the return from the exile and the destruction of Jerusalem. They reflect the restlessness and the dissatisfied spirit of the Jews, who were still dreaming of an independent commonwealth. Their themes indicate the Jewish reaction to the oppression, uncertainty, and hope that characterized the entire period.

Of the list given above, three are historical: I Esdras, which corresponds in content somewhat to Ezra and Nehemiah; I Maccabees, which is a simple and straightforward narrative of the revolt of Mattathias and his sons in 168 B.C. that terminated in the defeat of the Syrians and the establishment of the Hasmonean state; and II Maccabees, an inferior digest of the work of Jason of Cyrene, which supplements in some degree the content of I Maccabees. Tobit, Judith, The Rest of Esther, and The History of Susanna are romantic tales illustrating God's justice in vindicating his people. Bel and the Dragon, a spurious addition to the book of Daniel, belongs in the same category. The Wisdom of Solomon and Ecclesiasticus are philosophical treatises in the form of epigrams, somewhat like the book of Proverbs. The Song of the Three Holy Children and The Prayer of Manasses are expressions of devotion to God and of hope in his promises.

The language and style of all these books resembles that of the canonical Old Testament; but with the exception of the book of I Maccabees their historical allusions are not accurate and they have no solid connection with identifiable characters as authors. Their effect on the writers of the New Testament was slight, although occasionally there seem to be references to them in the text. Ecclesiasticus 44:16, "Enoch pleased the Lord, and was translated," may be echoed in Hebrews 11:5:

> By faith Enoch was translated that he should not see death; and he was not found, because God translated him: for he hath had witness borne to him that before his translation he had been well-pleasing unto God.

These two passages do not correspond so exactly that one can be called a quotation of the other. Both could originate from independent comments on the account given in Genesis.

A second list of works that have never been included in the Scriptures, whether Jewish or Christian, is given below. These consist of writings that were either never of canonical status, or were considered as representative of individual or group viewpoints.

The Book of Jubilees	200–150 B.C.
The Testimony of the Twelve Patriarchs	
The Psalms of Solomon	100–50 B.C.
III Maccabees	
IV Maccabees	
The Assumption of Moses	A.D. 1–50

Adam and Eve
The Martyrdom of Isaiah
The Book of Enoch
II Baruch
The Sibylline Oracles

In this list several of the books can be dated approximately, whereas others cannot. The Book of Enoch, for instance, is apparently composed of sections written at different times, all of which were finally combined not long before the Christian era. Some of its phraseology is paralleled in the New Testament, especially the well-known passage in Jude 14–15, which is an exact replica of Enoch 1:9:

> And to these also Enoch, the seventh from Adam, prophesied saying, Behold, the Lord came with ten thousands of his holy ones, to execute judgment upon all, and to convict all the ungodly of all their works of ungodliness which they have ungodly wrought, and of all the hard things which ungodly sinners have spoken against him.

The Book of Enoch, the Assumption of Moses, II Baruch, II Esdras, and parts of the Sibylline Oracles belong to the class of apocalyptic literature. Apocalyptic literature is predictive, generally using symbolism that seems grotesque and often inconsistent with itself. Uniformly it prophesies dire physical judgments on the wicked, from which the righteous shall be delivered by the supernatural intervention of God. Angels are frequently actors in the drama of apocalypse. Many apocalyptic works are pseudonymous, or are ascribed falsely to eminent men who never could have written them. For example, the Book of Enoch was not written by Enoch, but it was attributed to him because he had a reputation for piety and wisdom.

In style and imagery the Old Testament books of Ezekiel and Daniel have been classed as apocalyptic, although they could not rightly be called pseudonymous. Revelation, in the New Testament, is of the same literary type.

Apocalyptic literature was usually produced in a period of persecution, when people's hopes turned to future deliverance. It was intended to encourage believers to persist in their allegiance to God, and its imagery discouraged hostile readers from attempting to fathom its meaning. The fact that certain of the canonical books are apocalyptic does not disqualify them as inspired writings, since the inspiration of the Spirit appears in all kinds of literature within the covers of the Bible.

With the overthrow of Jerusalem in A.D. 70 Judaism ceased to be an independent political state and became solely a religious community. With the cessation of the temple sacrifices came the decline of the priesthood and the rise of the rabbinate. The study of the law took the place of offerings, and the teacher supplanted the priest. As the teachers sought to interpret the law, they codified the traditions that had grown up around it and ultimately reduced them to writing. The Pharisees looked on these traditions as contemporaneous with the written law and equally as binding, while the Sadducees repudiated them entirely.

Undoubtedly the Hebrew people observed ethical standards prior to the giving of the law at Sinai. Certain regulations and observances were connected with the lives of Noah and of Abraham as recorded in Genesis, and there could scarcely have been the perpetuation of unity during the bondage in Egypt had there not been some stable form of morals and worship to hold the people together. Whether these traditions were actually transmitted through the many vicissitudes of Israel's history to the first and second centuries A.D. is uncertain. One thing is certain—the mass of tradition contained in the Talmud includes much that is older than the writing of the book itself. The existence of the oral law is attested by the references Christ made to "the tradition of the elders" (Mark 7:3).

The collection of these traditions with the comments on them by early rabbis constitutes the Talmud. The name is derived from the verb *lammid*, which means "to teach." The Talmud comprises two elements, the Mishna and the Gemara. The Mishna is the oral law as it was known up to the end of the second century A.D. The Gemara is the interpretation of the oral law that the scholars of Babylon and Jerusalem produced between the beginning of the third century A.D. and the end of the fifth century. These interpretations or discussions were of two kinds: the Halakah, which dealt with the code of law, and the Haggadah, which was general preaching, or everything that was not Halakah.

The Halakah stated the rule or statute by which one is guided, the definite religious usage of the day. Strack says that "anything becomes Halakah (1) when it is held in acceptance for a long period; (2) when it is vouched for by recognized authority; (3) when it is supported by accepted proof from Scripture; (4) when it is established by majority vote. Any one or all of these reasons could establish a principle of the oral law."[8] Since no new principle of law could be established by invention, but rather by relation to an already existing principle, the rabbis became expert in manipulating the inferences from the existing law, oral and written, in order to cover all possible cases that might be brought before them. The records of these cases and the reasonings concerning them made the Halakoth.

The Haggadah included all scriptural interpretation that is nonhalakic

---

8. Hermann L. Strack, *Introduction to the Talmud and Midrash* (Authorized Translation from the Fifth German Edition. Philadelphia: The Jewish Publication Society of America, 1945), pp. 5–7.

in character. It was an attempt to develop the meaning of the implication of the law rather than to enlarge on its explicit statements. The argument of Jesus for the resurrection from Exodus 3:6 follows somewhat the pattern of Haggadic procedure (Matt. 22:31–33). Together, the Halakah and Haggadah are called the Midrash, a word derived from the Hebrew verb *darash,* meaning "to search," or "to conduct research." The research into the meaning of the law, oral and written, was thus made a part of the Talmud.

The Talmud contains sixty-three sections or tractates, each of which deals with some aspect of the law. Two Talmuds, representing the Palestinian and Babylonian schools of the Amoraim, or doctors, are in existence. The Palestinian Talmud, the shorter of the two, written in Western Aramaic, dates from the close of the fourth century. The Babylonian Talmud was written about the end of the fifth century in Eastern Aramaic dialect. Both are incomplete, lacking whole sections or parts of sections. In the thirteenth century the Talmud came under the ban of the church, and so many copies were destroyed or damaged that its survival was threatened. The marvel is that it exists at all.

To this day the Talmud is the standard of orthodox Judaism, regulative of faith and ritual practice. It sets the interpretation of the law and is often more directly influential on beliefs and life than is the Old Testament itself.

THE SECTS OF JUDAISM

Judaism was no exception to the human trend toward sectarianism in religion, even though its solidarity was greater than that of the other religions of the Roman world. Although all of the sects gave allegiance to the law, their emphases ranged from liberalism to rationalism and from mysticism to political opportunism.

The Pharisees

The largest and most influential sect in New Testament times was that of the Pharisees. Their name is derived from the verb *parash,* "to separate." They were the separatists, or Puritans of Judaism, who withdrew from all evil associations and sought to give complete obedience to every precept of the oral and written law. They originated as a separate group shortly after the times of the Maccabees, and by 135 B.C. they were well established in Judaism.

Their theology was founded on the entire canon of the Old Testament, which included the law of Moses (or Torah), the Prophets, and the Writings. In interpretation they used the allegorical method in order to allow for elasticity in applying the principles of the law to new questions that might be raised. They attached great value to the oral law or tradition, which they observed scrupulously. They believed in the existence of angels and spirits, in the immortality of the soul, and in the resurrection of the body. They practiced ritual prayer and fasting, and tithed their property meticulously (Matt. 23:23; Luke 11:42). They kept the Sabbath very strictly, allowing not even for healing the sick nor for the casual plucking of grain for eating by the wayside (Matt. 12:1–2).

Kohler lists seven types of Pharisees who were extremists:[9]

1. The "shoulder" Pharisee, who paraded his good deeds before men like a badge on the shoulder.
2. The "wait-a-little" Pharisee, who would ask someone to wait for him while he performed a good deed.
3. The "blind" Pharisee, who bruised himself by walking into a wall because he shut his eyes to avoid seeing a woman.
4. The "pestle" Pharisee, who walked with hanging head rather than observe alluring temptations.
5. The "ever-reckoning" Pharisee, who was always counting his good deeds to see if they offset his failures.
6. The "God-fearing" Pharisee, who, like Job, was truly righteous.
7. The "God-loving" Pharisee, like Abraham.

Although many of the Pharisees were so introspectively intent on obedience to the law that they often became fussily self-righteous, many among them were truly virtuous and good. Not all of them were hypocrites. Nicodemus, who earnestly sought out Christ during his earthly ministry, and who ultimately shared with Joseph of Arimathea the responsibility of burying Jesus' body, was a Pharisee. Saul of Tarsus, vehement persecutor of the church though he was, avowed that he was a Pharisee and the son of a Pharisee (Acts 23:6), and that "touching the righteousness which is in the law, [he was] found blameless" (Phil. 3:6). The moral and spiritual standards of Pharisaism may have tended toward self-righteousness and consequently toward hypocrisy, but they were high in comparison with the average of their day.

Of all the sects of Judaism, Pharisaism alone has survived. It became the foundation of modern orthodox Judaism, which follows the pattern of Pharisaic morality, ceremonialism, and legalism.

The Sadducees

The Sadducees, according to tradition, derived their name from the sons of Zadok, who was high priest in the days of David and Solomon. The sons of Zadok were the priestly hierarchy in the time of the captivity (II Chron. 31:10; Ezek. 40:46; 44:15; 48:11), and apparently the name per-

---

9. Kaufmann Kohler, "Pharises," in *Jewish Encyclopedia*, IX, 661–666.

sisted as the title of the priestly party in the days of Christ. Less numerous than the Pharisees, they possessed political power and were the governing group in the civil life of Judaism under the Herods.

As a party in Judaism, the Sadducees adhered to the strictly literal interpretation of the Torah, which alone they held to be canonical, having a higher authority than the Prophets and the Writings. There was consequently no room in their thinking for the oral tradition that the Pharisees studied with delight. As rationalists and antisupernaturalists, they denied the existence of angels and spirits (Acts 23:8) and did not believe in personal immortality. Their religion was coldly ethical and literal and was much more open to Hellenizing influences than was Pharisaism. Politically the Sadducees were opportunists and were quite ready to ally themselves with the dominant power if by so doing they could maintain their own prestige and influence.

Unlike the Pharisees, they did not survive the destruction of Jerusalem. The cessation of the priesthood, to which most of the Sadducees belonged, and the hostility with Rome, which had formerly protected the Sadducean clan, ended their existence as a group.

The Essenes

Little is known of this sect which Josephus described in detail in his *Wars of the Jews.* [10] The meanings of their name is uncertain, but it was connected by some with the Greek word *hosios,* meaning "holy."

The Essenes, unlike the Pharisees and the Sadducees, were a definite ascetic brotherhood that could be entered only by those who were willing to submit to the regulations of the group and to undergo ceremonies of initiation. They abstained from marriage and recruited their ranks by adoption or by receiving converts. Their communities held all property in common, so that none was rich and none was poor. Self-support was maintained by manual labor. They ate the plainest of food and dressed habitually in white garments when they were not working.

In behavior the Essenes were sober and restrained, not giving way to anger nor using oaths. They observed the Sabbath with utmost strictness and were exceptionally attentive to personal cleanliness. Any digression from the rules of their order was punished by expulsion from the community.

Theologically the Essenes were akin to the Pharisees in their close observance of the law and in their supernaturalism. They taught that the soul of man is intangible and immortal, imprisoned in a perishable body. At death, the good pass to a region of sunshine and cool breezes, while the wicked are relegated to a dark and stormy place of continual torment.

---

10. Josephus *Wars of the Jews* II.viii.2–13.

The Dead Sea and the Mountains of Moab, seen from the Wilderness of Judea.

The ascetic tendencies of the Essenes are comparable in many ways to the monasticism that grew up in early Christianity. Some of their doctrines seem to have sprung from contact with Gentile thought, for in their attitudes they resembled the Stoics. Curiously enough, they are never mentioned in the Gospels. Some writers have suggested that John the Baptist and Jesus were Essenes, so that Christianity was an outgrowth of Essenism. In spite of some superficial likenesses, the strict legalism of Essenism in contrast to the Christian emphasis on grace makes such a connection extremely improbable.

A new chapter in the history of the Essenes has been opened by the excavations at Qumran, a site about seven miles south of Jericho on the heights above the Dead Sea. The existence of buildings at this spot had been known for years, but they were thought to have been the ruins of a Roman garrison outpost. In the spring or early summmer of 1947 some Bedouin sheepherders discovered in a cave near Qumran eight large jars containing ancient scrolls. Three of these scrolls came into the possession of St. Mark's Syrian Orthodox Convent in Jerusalem, and were dated by their style of writing as belonging to the first century before or after Christ. Subsequent visits to the cave where these scrolls were found and to others near them brought to light more scroll material. A large hoard of manuscripts had evidently been secreted in the caves to preserve them from capture and consequent destruction. The dating indicated that they must

Part of the scroll of the Book of Isaiah from the collection of Dead Sea Scrolls.

have been consigned to their resting places in the caves about the time of the first Jewish revolt in A.D. 66–70.

In 1951 the ruins at Qumran were excavated. The exploration proved that they were not built originally as a Roman fort. They seemed to mark the living quarters of a large settlement, with a common dining hall, dormitories, cisterns, and scriptorium. All material evidence found in the ruins indicates that the community was flourishing in the era just preceding the destruction of Jerusalem in A.D. 70. The next question is: Who were the people that comprised the community?

The caves near the Dead Sea in which the famous scrolls were found. The second cave from the left is Cave No. 4, in which the main library of the Essenes was found.

Along with the manuscripts of the Old Testament found in the caves were other documents belonging to the former inhabitants. The *Manual of Discipline,* the *Damascus Document,* the *Thanksgiving Hymn,* and the *Order of Warfare* were cult documents, embodying the tenets and regulations of the Qumran community. From these works one may deduce that the people ate, lived, and worked together on a common basis. They had withdrawn from official Judaism, and had undertaken a monastic life in the wilderness. The organization was subordinate to the president of the congregation, who acted as arbiter in law, disciplinarian of the entire group, and the military leader in case of war. The congregation included men, women, and children. The governing council had both priests and laity in its ranks. Volunteers for this order underwent a period of probation lasting several months and finally were purified by baptism in order that they might enter the community. Within the group there was constant moral and spiritual discipline. The group was independent of all other movements, and was completely self-contained. Its energies were directed to the study of the law.

The theology of the Qumran sect is practically identical with that of Judaism. There is one God, the Creator, who has placed man in the world, and to whom man is responsible for his actions. He determines the course of history, and possesses all wisdom and all power. From his righteousness comes the pardon of sin, and in his mercy is all human life.

Subordinate to God are the good and evil principles that control life. Under their influence men are divided into the "sons of light" and the "sons of darkness." Because of the influence of these warring powers there are two ways of life, the way of righteousness that ends in personal happiness, and the way of evil that ends in disgrace and doom. This moral dualism is not reflected in a cosmological dualism, for evil is not eternal nor on a plane of equality with the good.

Recent scholarship tends to favor the identification of the Qumran community with the Essenes referred to in Josephus. There is similarity in geography and chronology, as well as in organization and customs. Some of the problems of identification may be solved by noting exceptions in the sources; for example, while Josephus said the Essenes abstained from marriage, he admits that there were also married members in the community (and female skeletons have been found in graves at Qumran).

It is likely that most of the discrepancies in testimony of writers such as Josephus, Pliny, and Philo may be accounted for by (1) the variety in reliability of the writers, and (2) the variety in the readers addressed. Except for Josephus, these writers wrote as outsiders; they did not always have firsthand information. The Qumran sectaries, however, have given us "primary documents," written from within the community. [11]

The Zealots

The Zealots were not a religious sect in the same class with the Pharisees or the Essenes. They were a group of fanatical nationalists who advocated violence as a means of liberation from Rome. Their creed was pointed: God is the only Lord; thus no tribute is to be paid to the Roman emperor. Apparently founded by Judas the Galilean in A.D. 6 (see Acts 5:37), they modeled themselves after "zealous" followers of Yahweh such as Phinehas and Elijah, of Old Testament fame, and the Maccabean fighters of the second century B.C. At the time of the siege of Jerusalem under Titus they formed one of the factions within the city, and the dissension they caused contributed heavily to its downfall. Perhaps they were connected with the "Assassins" mentioned in Acts 21:38. One of Jesus' disci-

---

11. See W. F. Albright and C. S. Mann, "Qumran and the Essenes: Geography, Chronology, and Identification of the Sect," in *The Scrolls and Christianity*, ed. M. Black (London: S.P.C.K., 1969), pp. 11–25; W. S. LaSor, *The Dead Sea Scrolls and the New Testament* (Grand Rapids: Wm. B. Eerdmans Publishing Company, 1972), pp. 131–141; G. Vermes, *The Dead Sea Scrolls: Qumran in Perspective* (Cleveland: Collins/World, 1978), pp. 116–136.

ples, Simon, had belonged to them, as his name indicates (Luke 6:15; Acts 1:13).

THE DIASPORA

Although Palestine was the traditional homeland of the Jewish race, by far the largest number of Jews in the Roman empire lived outside the borders of the Holy Land. Known as the Diaspora, or the Dispersion, they were found in almost all the large cities from Babylon to Rome and in many of the smaller settlements as well, wherever commerce or colonization had taken them. The scattering of the Jewish people began with the captivity of the northern kingdom in 721 B.C. when Sargon of Assyria deported inhabitants of Israel and settled them in new colonies in Assyria. The southern kingdom of Judah was conquered by Babylon in 597 B.C., and many of the upper class were carried away to Babylon. A second and third deportation followed, leaving only the poorest people of the land unmolested. Although several thousand returned from exile in the restoration under Ezra and Nehemiah, a large number chose to remain in the land of their captivity where they had established themselves and had begun to prosper.

The conquests of Alexander in the fourth century B.C. opened new opportunities for migration and settlement. The domination of the Near East by one great military power removed temporarily the petty hostilities between kingdoms that had made free travel almost impossible. As business opportunities increased and as the Seleucid and Ptolemaic successors of Alexander encouraged colonization by offering citizenship and exemption from taxation to those who would migrate to their own domains, many Jews took advantage of these offers and established new homes in the growing Hellenistic settlements. Some of them became temporary residents of the Greek cities, while others were granted citizenship and settled down in new homes and new occupations. In Alexandria one entire section of the city was Jewish, with its own governor and officials who were practically autonomous. Its population has been estimated at two million and it represented the largest single concentration of Jews in any one city of the world at that time.

In the Roman empire the Jewish settlements increased rapidly. The slaves that Pompey brought back from Palestine to Rome were ultimately freed and settled on the right bank of the Tiber near the docks. In 4 B.C. there were about eight thousand in the city. Under Julius Caesar and Augustus they were given legal standing, and in some cities such as Corinth they were freed from military service and the jurisdiction of the heathen courts.

Unquestionably the Greek influence affected the Jews of the Dispersion, and many of them lost the distinctive characteristics and faith that marked them off from other peoples. The majority of them, however, remained Jews. They clung tenaciously to their monotheistic faith based on the law of Moses. They kept contact with the temple at Jerusalem by pilgrimages to the annual feasts and paid the yearly tax of half a shekel. They observed the Sabbath and maintained synagogue services wherever there were enough of them to constitute a worshiping group.

Within the Diaspora were two distinct groups—the Hebraists and the Hellenists.[12]

The Hebraists

The Hebraists, or "Hebrews," were mentioned by Paul, who was one of them. He said that he was "circumcised the eighth day, of the stock of Israel, of the tribe of Benjamin, a Hebrew of Hebrews; as touching the law, a Pharisee . . ." (Phil. 3:5). The Hebrews were those Jews who retained not only the religious faith of Judaism but also the use of the Hebrew or Aramaic language and the Hebrew customs. Paul said that he was brought up "according to the strict manner of the law of our fathers" (Acts 22:3). His quotations from the Old Testament show that he was familiar with the Hebrew Bible as well as with its Greek version. Although he was born in Tarsus, a Greek city, and although he proudly claimed Roman citizenship (21:39; 22:25–29), he was still a thoroughgoing Jew, uncorrupted by the Gentile heathenism that surrounded him from youth. Doubtless there were many others like him. Probably the bulk of the Hebraists, however, lived in Palestine itself, where their worship centered in the temple. Acts pictures some of these Hebraists of the Diaspora in the Jews of Asia who accused Paul of desecrating the temple by bringing a Gentile into its sacred precincts (21:27–29).

The Hellenists

A far larger number of Jews, however, had absorbed the Graeco-Roman culture and had ceased to be Jewish except in matters of faith. They spoke Greek or whatever happened to be the language of the country where they dwelt, they adopted the customs of their neighbors, and in many cases were virtually indistinguishable as Jews. Syncretistic elements appeared in their worship, as in a synagogue at Dura-Europos on the Euphrates that had heathen mythology depicted in the mosaics and paintings on its walls.

---

12. On the problem of identifying these two names, see H. J. Cadbury, "The Hellenists," in *The Beginnings of Christianity, Part I, The Acts of the Apostles* (London: Macmillan, 1933), V, 59–74; F. F. Bruce, *The Acts of the Apostles* (Grand Rapids: Wm. B. Eerdmans Publishing Company, 1951), p. 151; E. F. Harrison, *Acts: The Expanding Church* (Chicago: Moody Press, 1975), p. 105. The term "Hellenists" (Acts 6:1) occurs here for the first time in Greek literature (see also Acts 9:29; 11:20). In the first instance it probably refers to Greek-speaking Jewish Christians; in the second to Greek-speaking Jews in the synagogues; and in the third to Gentiles.

Both classes of Jews are mentioned in Acts 6, where the division between them began to endanger the unity of the church. Apparently the Hellenists were somewhat broader in their sympathies than the Hebraists and were perhaps a bit more ready to see the wider implications of the Old Testament Scriptures. Stephen was probably one of them.

Counting both classes, the Jews in the Roman empire numbered about four and a half million. They were not generally popular because of their clannishness and because they would not join in the public worship of heathen gods. Frequently they were dubbed atheists by those who did not understand how anybody could worship an invisible God. On the other hand, their sobriety, industry, and upright morality commended them to their neighbors, who were compelled to acknowledge their ability and integrity.

On occasion the Jews could be turbulent, especially when their religious freedom was threatened. Under Claudius they were expelled from Rome because of an uprising, and there were serious riots in Alexandria later in the century. There is no evidence that the Jews of the Dispersion took any part in the Jewish war of A.D. 66 to 70, or that they offered any protest against the siege and capture of Jerusalem. Their apparent indifference to their national status even while they were exiles among the Gentiles is part of the paradox of the millenniums that is the Jew.

FOR FURTHER READING

Bacher, Wilhelm. "Synagogue," in *Jewish Encyclopaedia*, XI, 619–628. New York: Funk and Wagnalls, 1912.

Baron, Salo Untermeyer. *A Social and Religious History of the Jews*. Second Edition. Revised and Enlarged. Two volumes. New York: Columbia University Press, 1952. Good reference work. Written from standpoint of liberal Judaism.

Caldecott, W. S. and Orr, James. "Temple," in *International Standard Bible Encyclopaedia*, 2930–2940a. Grand Rapids, Mich.: Wm. B. Eerdmans Publishing Company, 1949. See especially pp. 2937–2940a for the Temple of Herod.

Charles, R. H. *The Testaments of the Twelve Patriarchs*. London: Society for Promoting Christian Knowledge, 1925. Pp. xxiii, 108.

Daube, David. *The New Testament and Rabbinic Judaism*. London: Athlone Press, 1956.

Davies, T. W. "Temple," in Hastings' *Dictionary of the Bible*, IV, 695–716. New York: Charles Scribner's Sons, 1902. Lucid and well documented.

Donald, James. "Diaspora," in Hastings' *Dictionary of the Apostolic Church*, I, 304–306. New York: Charles Scribner's Sons, 1922.

Edersheim, Alfred. *In the Days of Christ*. Chicago: Fleming H. Revell Company, n.d. Pp. vii, 342.

_____. *The Temple: Its Ministry and Services.* New Edition, Revised. Grand Rapids, Mich.: Wm. B. Eerdmans Publishing Company, 1950. Pp. xiv, 368.

Emmet, C. W. *Third and Fourth Books of Maccabees* in *Translations of Early Documents,* Series II, Hellenistic-Jewish Texts. London: Society for Promoting Christian Knowledge, 1918. Pp. xiv, 45; xxv, 75. Two books bound together.

Ferrar, William J. *The Uncanonical Jewish Books.* A short introduction to the Apocrypha and other Jewish writings, 200 B.C.–100 A.D. London: Society for Promoting Christian Knowledge, 1925. Pp. x, 112.

Finkelstein, Louis. *The Pharisees.* Two volumes. Philadelphia: The Jewish Publication Society of America, 1938. Pp. xxviii, 442, 793.

Hengel, Martin. *Judaism and Hellenism.* Two volumes. Philadelphia: Fortress Press, 1974.

Jeremias, Joachim. *Jerusalem in the Time of Jesus.* Translated by F. H. and C. H. Cave. Philadelphia: Fortress Press, 1969.

Levison, Nahum. *The Jewish Background of Christianity.* A manual of the political, social, and literary life of the Jews from 586 B.C. to A.D. 1. Edinburgh: T. & T. Clark, 1932. Pp. xi, 205.

Mackowski, R. M. *Jerusalem: City of Jesus.* Grand Rapids: Wm. B. Eerdmans Publishing Company, 1980. Pp. x, 221.

Metzger, Bruce M. *An Introduction to the Apocrypha.* New York: Oxford University Press, 1957. Pp. 274.

Moore, George Foot. *Judaism.* Two volumes. Cambridge: Harvard University Press, 1927.

Oesterley, W. O. E. *An Introduction to the Books of the Apocrypha.* New York: The Macmillan Company, 1935. Pp. x, 345.

_____. *A History of Israel.* Vol. II: *From the Fall of Jerusalem 586 B.C. to the Bar-Kokhba Revolt, A.D. 135.* Oxford: Clarendon Press, 1939. Pp. xvi, 500. Most thorough recent work. Contains full treatment of the Herods, the Diaspora, social and religious usages.

Pfeiffer, Robert H. *History of New Testament Times.* New York: Harper & Brothers, Publishers, 1949. Pp. xii, 561.

Robertson, A. T. *The Pharisees and Jesus.* New York: Charles Scribner's Sons, 1920. Pp. xii, 189.

Rosenau, William. *Jewish Ceremonial Institutions and Customs.* New York: Bloch Publishing Company, Inc., 1929. Pp. 190. Authoritative explanation of historical and modern Jewish usages.

Rost, L. *Judaism Outside the Hebrew Canon.* Nashville: Abingdon, 1971.

Safrai, S., et al. *The Jewish People in the First Century.* Two volumes. Assen: van Gorcum, 1974–1976.

Sandmel, S. *The First Christian Century in Judaism and Christianity.* New York: Oxford Press, 1969.

Smallwood, E. M. *The Jews Under Roman Rule.* Leiden: Brill, 1976.

Strack, Hermann L. *Introduction to the Talmud and Midrash.* Fifth Edition: Authorized Translation. Philadelphia: The Jewish Publication Society of America, 1945. An authoritative work on the Talmud.

Torrey, C. C. *The Apocryphal Literature.* New Haven: Yale University Press, 1945. Pp. x, 151.

CHAPTER 5

JEWISH BACKGROUND FOR THE NEW TESTAMENT, 200 B.C.–A.D. 200

THE NATURE OF JUDAISM

During these four hundred years, the rise and development of both religious parties and movements, as well as the literature, reveal "the vitality of Judaism and its manifold variety."[1] This culture was marked by a zeal for God and a determination to observe the Torah. During the days of the Maccabean wars against the Syrians the term "Judaism" first appears in the literature, reflecting the character of these patriots, namely, ". . . those who strove zealously on behalf of Judaism" (II Macc. 2:21; cf. 14:38).

Judaism was based on the conviction expressed in the opening words of the tractate Aboth: "Moses received the Law from Sinai and committed it to Joshua, and Joshua to the elders, and the elders to the Prophets; and the Prophets committed it to the men of the Great Synagogue."[2] The law, given by God to Moses, had been faithfully preserved through the ages, and was the foundation for the faith and life of Judaism. Due to a remarkable unity of belief and observance among the Jews—despite the well-known

---

1. R. H. Pfeiffer, *History of New Testament Times* (New York: Harper & Brothers, Publishers, 1949), p. 59.
2. *The Mishnah*, ed. H. Danby (London: Oxford University Press, 1933), p. 446.

diversities—this religion both flourished and survived the vicissitudes that overcame most of its contemporaries.[3]

The key theological emphases of Judaism at the time of the rise of Christianity (see Chap. 4 above) are reflected in the teachings of Jesus and the early disciples (e.g., in the speeches and prayers recorded in the book of Acts). Little is novel or new in the major affirmations of the New Testament (for nearly all the early believers were of Jewish extraction), save the confession that Jesus was the Messiah promised by the Prophets.

Yet of particular interest and importance is the question of the basic characteristics of the Jewish literature of the period 200 B.C. to A.D. 200, together with the developing oral tradition, and their relation to the New Testament. In particular, this complex literature included such works as the Apocrypha, the Pseudepigrapha, the Dead Sea Scrolls, and the writings of Philo of Alexandria and Flavius Josephus.[4] It must be recognized that this literature, none of which was held sacred by the Jewish people, was first based on the Scriptures, yet incorporating into those revealed truths many Jewish speculations, together with ideas also found in Persian and Greek religion. This may be seen in teachings regarding God and the world, angelology, the nature and relation of the soul and the body, the origin and nature of sin, the Messiah, and the Age to Come.

APOCRYPHA AND PSEUDEPIGRAPHA

While a brief description of the books included in these collections has been given in Chapter 4, some discussion of their content and significance is in order. On the one hand, some of these books could be regarded as conscious imitations of certain of the sacred books of the Jews. The Wisdom of Solomon and Sirach (Ecclesiasticus) are similar in form to the book of Proverbs; Jubilees is essentially a retelling of and commentary on the book of Genesis; II Esdras includes features reminiscent of works like Habakkuk and Daniel. Others are additions to Old Testament books, filling in details or glorifying famous people—among these are the Song of Azariah, Susanna, and Bel and the Dragon, relating to the book of Daniel;

---

3. G. F. Moore, *Judaism* (Cambridge: Harvard University Press, 1927), I, 111, ". . . this unity and universality . . . was not based upon orthodoxy in the theology but upon uniformity of observance." L. Jacobs sees Judaism as an amalgam of three ideas—belief in God, God's revelation of the Torah to Israel, and Israel as the people that lives by the Torah in obedience to God, and these ideas, despite varied interpretations of them, have remained constant from age to age (*Encyclopaedia Judaica*, ed. C. Roth, X, 378).

4. See M. Hengel, *Judaism and Hellenism* (Philadelphia: Fortress Press, 1974), I, 88ff., for other literature of the period.

the Prayer of Manasseh (cf. II Chron. 33:12–13); and The Additions to the book of Esther. Books such as the Testaments of the Twelve Patriarchs contain quasi-historical reminiscences of the lives of the twelve sons of Jacob together with sage exhortations concerning vice and virtue, modeled on the Testament of Jacob (Gen. 49), while the book of Enoch (along with II Esdras) is full of visions of heaven and earth, designed to reveal secrets of things present and things to come, especially about the Last Days. That it is a matter of first importance to be faithful to the law is extolled in the book of Tobit, a romantic tale set in the days of the Assyrian captivity. And the four books dealing with the Maccabees reflect the political, military, and religious strife that arose in defense of the law, when the Syrian king Antiochus IV threatened the very existence of that institution. A stirring story in itself, it forms the background for the insistence on being faithful to the law that appears so often in the words and deeds of its defenders in the pages of the New Testament.[5]

In a general sense, these writings encompass two main messages, one concerning the sacredness of the law and calling for fidelity to it, and the other concerning apocalyptic ideas designed to give hope in the present and a rationale for believing in a future salvation, that is, giving an eschatological perspective. That these two emphases existed together seems clear, for the apocalyptic works contain them both. Much of what is found in the New Testament is of the same order. The Torah as Jesus interpreted it was central for his followers—for example, "Whoever then relaxes one of the least of these commandments and teaches men so, shall be called least in the kingdom of heaven; but he who does them and teaches them shall be called great in the kingdom of heaven" (Matt. 5:19). Yet it was not the Torah as an end in itself. The Scriptures were given, not to bestow eternal life, but to bear witness to him who was the Life-Giver (John 5:39–40). "Christ," wrote Paul, "is the end (*telos*) of the law" to all who believe (Rom. 10:4), for in him the whole thrust of Torah is fulfilled. Thus God sent his Son "in order that the just requirements of the law might be fulfilled" in those who have been set free by the Spirit (Rom. 8:3–4).

Further, the store of apocalyptic in the New Testament is impressive. Interestingly, it is devoid of "a whole range of speculative interests," as well as a kind of sadness due to "hope deferred." Interest in calendars and chronology, far-ranging speculations about the future, especially the marvelous details of events of the End—these and similar items are treated lightly or not at all in the New Testament. Yet the great themes are found in both: God as Creator and Judge of mankind; the importance of Israel and

---

5. For a readable, concise summary of this literature, see D. S. Russell, *Between the Testaments* (Philadelphia: Fortress Press, 1960), pp. 75–91.

God's covenant with the seed of Abraham, and the destiny of his people; the expectation of the New Age with the glories of the reign of God (though this is seen in the light of the Incarnation and the drawing near of the Kingdom of God in Jesus Christ); and the ongoing conflict between light and darkness, flesh and spirit, and vice and virtue—all of which will be brought to a conclusion by God who "will make all things new."

THE DEAD SEA SCROLLS

Many writers have related the story of the amazing discoveries of ancient scrolls in the caves bordering the Dead Sea, particularly those in the areas of Qumran and Wadi Murabba'at (about twelve miles to the southeast of Qumran).[6] While much discussion has centered around questions of dating the scrolls, their authenticity and their origin, the assertion has been made that "for the study of New Testament background the discovery of the Dead Sea Scrolls is the most significant manuscript find ever made."[7]

Several types of documents have been found: (1) copies of canonical (Old Testament) books, including every one except Esther (the book of Isaiah was found in its entirety); (2) copies of the Apocrypha and the Pseudepigrapha, noncanonical writings; and (3) documents relating to the life of the community, including a variety of types.

Here we learn of a group conceiving itself to be "the true and ideal Congregation of Israel." By virtue of their faithfulness to God's covenant, their land of promise would be cleansed from guilt and liberated from oppression by the forces of evil. What had happened before, for example, in the days of Moses, would happen again. While "the end of days" was on them, their faithfulness to God and his covenant would assure them of deliverance. Had not the prophet Habakkuk written, ". . . the righteous shall live by his faith" (Hab. 2:4)?

Much as been said of both the similarities and the contrasts between the Qumran community and the early Christians. Some examples of these phenomena will now be given.

---

6. One of the most dependable and readable accounts is in F. M. Cross, Jr., *The Ancient Library of Qumran*, revised edition (Garden City, N.Y.: Anchor Books, 1961), pp. 3–30.

7. F. V. Filson, "The Dead Sea Scrolls and the New Testament," in *New Directions in Biblical Archaeology*, eds. D. N. Freedman and J. C. Greenfield (Garden City, N.Y.: Doubleday & Company, 1971), p. 142; M. Burrows, *The Dead Sea Scrolls* (New York: Viking Press, 1955), p. 327: "Everything that is important for Judaism in the last two or three centuries before Christ and in the first century A.D. is important also for Christianity."

BASIC CHARACTERISTICS OF THE QUMRAN COMMUNITY

1. Interpretation of the Scriptures was done by a method known as *pesher* ("interpretation"), in which the historical situation found in the prophetic passage was transferred, or applied, to their own time and situation. In the commentary on Nahum the "lion" of the prophet becomes Demetrius, the king of Greece (2:11–12); in the commentary on Habakkuk the "Chaldeans" become the Kittim (the Romans) (1:6).

2. The doctrine of salvation included faith in the Teacher of Righteousness (or, the Right-Teacher) and fulfillment of the law—both necessary to gain salvation. In the Habakkuk commentary (2:4) we read: "On account of their labor and of their faith in him who expounded the Law aright, God will deliver them from the house of judgment" (Gaster's translation).

3. Strict separatism was a distinctive mark of the Dead Sea community, and a continuing fight was waged against all wickedness and the forces of darkness. This involved a hatred of all enemies, and called down the wrath of God on all not part of the sect (see, e.g., The Manual of Discipline 3:13–4:26).

4. A highly disciplined life, reflected in a great number of rules and regulations, was intended to protect the purity of the community. Repeated ritual washings (rather than any known initiatory "baptism") were self-administered, permitted only to members in good standing. A common fellowship meal, consisting of bread and wine, was administered by a priest, and members were seated according to rank. This was a time to "worship together and take counsel together" (Manual of Discipline 6:1–6).

5. Within the community there was a strong eschatological orientation, pointing toward the dawning of God's kingly rule. This rule would be established by a forty-year war between the forces of light and the forces of darkness, a conflict including both human foes (the community vs. their enemies) and supernatural forces (the angels). In the document The War of the Sons of Light and the Sons of Darkness this final battle (cf. Ezek. 38–39) is given a full military dress, modeled on Roman patterns of military tactics and strategy. Near the end of the document are the words (ascribed to God), "Thine is the power, and in Thy hand lies [the issue of] war, and there is none [who can withstand thee]" (18:15).

6. Related to this eschatological hope was the expectation of "the coming of the Prophet" (cf. Deut. 18:18), and of both the priestly and the lay Messiah (of Aaron and Israel, respectively). As they waited, they were bound to do and teach the true interpretation of the law, and understanding was given (revealed) by God through a succession of inspired leaders,

each known by the title "The Right-Teacher," that is, "the *orthodox* expounder of the Word" (cf. Deut. 33:9–10).[8]

7. A highly structured society is described in the Damascus ("Zadok-ite") Document: first, the priests; second, the levites; third, the laymen; and fourth, the proselytes. This ranking determined the order of seating at public sessions, and the order in which opinions were invited in questions to be discussed. One priest held office over the masses (he must be between thirty and sixty years of age, and be knowledgeable in all regulations), while an "overseer" was over all the camps (a person from thirty to fifty years of age, adept in human relations and various languages). In another statement, in the Manual of Discipline, with respect to public sessions, priests occupied the first place, followed by the elders, then the rest of the people "according to their respective ranks." No one was allowed to speak before his rank had been reached.

8. Holiness was obligatory, and infractions of the spirit or regulations were punished by various levels of disciplinary action. For certain severe causes, such as pronouncing the Divine Name, or slandering the entire community, the offender was to be put out and never to return to formal membership in the community (Manual 6:26; 7:16, 23).

COMPARISONS WITH THE NEW TESTAMENT

1. In the New Testament the use of the *pesher* method of interpreting the Old Testament is not uncommon, and one frequently sees "this is that" occurring in the writings. Peter appealed to the prophecy of Joel (Acts 2:16); Paul to one of the Psalms (Eph. 4:8–10) or to the book of Deuteronomy (Rom. 10:6–8). Christ was regarded as the "stone" referred to by Isaiah and the Psalmist (I Pet. 2:6–8). Yet, whereas the Qumran writers understood the Scriptures to be predicting a series of leaders for the community, the early church saw Jesus as Prophet, Priest, and King, thus combining all three figures into one.

2. Habakkuk's word concerning the just one living by faith (Hab. 2:4) is taken by Paul as a foundation for teaching justification by faith alone (Rom. 1:17; Gal. 3:6). Christ is "the end of the law" for all who believe (Rom. 10:4); no one is justified before God by works of the law (Gal. 2:16). Christ is not simply Teacher, but Lord and Savior.

3. In Jesus' ministry there was an openness to and reception of people

---

8. The appearance of the Teacher is noted in the Zadokite Document: "For twenty years, however, they remained like blind men groping their way, until at last God . . . raised up for them one who would teach the Law correctly"; and see R. E. Brown, "The Teacher of Righteousness and the Messiah(s)," in *The Scrolls and Christianity*, ed. M. Black (London: S.P.C.K., 1969), p. 38.

Fragment of the Damascus (Zadokite) Document outlining the strict Sabbath regulations.

of all kinds, rather than asceticism or separatism. Criticism came from certain quarters, especially from the Pharisees and scribes, sensitive as they were to "holiness," because he mingled with tax-collectors and "sinners" (Luke 15:1–2; cf. Mark 2:16; Luke 7:39). Further, he counseled his disciples, "Love your enemies" (Matt. 5:44); Paul did likewise (Rom. 12:19–20), leaving vengeance to God.

4. While moral precepts are expounded in the New Testament (e.g., Matt. 5:21–7:12; I Cor. 6:1–20; I Pet. 2:11–17), one does not sense the detailed and obligatory kinds of regulations occurring in the Qumran literature. There is certainly an awareness of the need for righteous living, yet a

certain freedom of spirit pervades the teaching (Rom. 8:3–4; 14:1ff.; Gal. 5:18–24).

Baptism was clearly an initiatory rite in the early church, something related to repentance and involving the forgiveness of sins and the promise of the Holy Spirit (Acts 2:38–42). The practice was carried on by John the Baptizer, Jesus and his disciples, and the apostles. This rite was not repeated by the initiate, as in Qumran.

The meal instituted by Jesus for his followers was based on the familiar table fellowship meal, yet was centered on him ("my body" and "my blood") and was described as "the new covenant in my blood" (Luke 22:20), a note missing in the Qumran community. In the early church, the meal does not seem to have been administered by a priest (except in the sense that all believers are "priests" [I Pet. 2:5, 9]); nor was it observed according to rank. Rather, much is said against vying for places of prestige (Luke 22:24–27; John 13:12–17; both passages are included in the setting of Jesus' last meal with his disciples).

5. While the New Testament says much about "the kingdom of God,"[9] it is perceived as "at hand" (Mark 1:15), even "present" in the ministry of Jesus (Matt. 12:28; cf. Luke 17:20–21). There is, indeed, conflict between good and evil, even at present. Satan is the "evil one," and he has angels who accompany him (Matt. 25:41). Yet, even in the present age, Satan has been judged (John 16:11).

Still, the New Testament contains descriptions of a final conflict. In the early Pauline literature we read of "the day of the Lord" and "sudden destruction" (I Thess. 5:2–3), and of the vengeance to be inflicted "upon those who do not know God and . . . do not obey the gospel of our Lord Jesus Christ" (II Thess. 1:7–8). The Apocalypse tells of "the kingdom of our Lord and of his Christ" defeating the kingdom of the world, a triumph of Christ as King of kings and Lord of lords (Rev. 11:15; 19:11ff.). Satan and his hosts will be banished to the lake of fire and sulphur, along with all whose names are not found written in the book of life (Rev. 20:7–15).

6. The Community's expectation of "the coming of the Prophet and of both the priestly and the lay Messiah" (Manual 9:10) is centered in the New Testament on the single figure of Jesus the Messiah.[10] He is looked on

---

9. This phrase, "the kingdom of God," does not occur in the documents of Qumran, according to M. Burrows, *More Light on the Dead Sea Scrolls* (New York: Viking Press, 1958), p. 93; W. S. LaSor, *The Dead Sea Scrolls and the New Testament* (Grand Rapids: Wm. B. Eerdmans Publishing Company, 1972), pp. 156, 218.

10. K. G. Kuhn, "The Two Messiahs of Aaron and Israel," in *The Scrolls and the New Testament*, ed. K. Stendahl (New York: Harper & Brothers, 1957), pp. 63–64; E. Lohse, *The New Testament Environment*, tr. J. Steely (Nashville: Abingdon, 1976), p. 113.

as a Davidic type of Messiah (Matt. 1:1), a high priest appointed by God (Heb. 5:4–5), and the Prophet of whom Moses spoke (Acts 3:22–26; cf. John 6:14). Further, the figure of the Right-Teacher, while possibly paralleled in Jesus as Teacher of the Law, cannot be regarded as a "copy" in any serious way. His theology as well as his career stands in contrast to that of Jesus in most basic ways.[11] Jesus claimed to be Messiah, the Son of God; he saw his death as "a ransom for many"; and he predicted his rising from the dead after three days—all of which is in vivid contrast to the claims and the career of the Qumran Teacher (see, e.g., Mark 14:61–62; 10:45; 8:31).

7. The sort of rigid organization described in the Qumran writings is not reflected in those of the early church. There we discover a much greater flexibility, indeed a warning against seeking positions of superiority over others. While there may be some basic parallels in certain institutional features, for example, in the overseer figure found in both communities, the contrasts are present, too. Jesus warned his disciples against seeking positions over others (Mark 10:35–45); he himself dramatized the idea of being a servant (John 13:1–17). In the meetings of the early church, all were free to exercise their gifts (I Cor. 14:26ff.); no ranking among members of the group was predicated. For the sake of building up the members of the body, "God has so composed the body, giving the greater honor to the inferior part," in order that members may have the same care for one another (I Cor. 12:24–25).

8. As in Qumran, so in the New Testament much emphasis is laid on attaining holiness. Indeed, believers are called "saints" (lit. "holy ones"), meaning that God has "set them apart" as his people (I Cor. 1:2; I Pet. 1:2). Further, these saints are called to be holy in all their conduct (I Pet. 1:14–16), and to "strive . . . for the holiness without which no one will see the Lord" (Heb. 12:14). So, too, discipline was exercised against offenders, sometimes "delivering one to Satan" (I Cor. 5:3–5), or pronouncing divine judgment, resulting in death (Acts 5:1–11). Yet, even severe discipline (short of death) was meant to be remedial, looking forward to repentance and restoration to fellowship within the community (II Cor. 2:5–8). If an offender remained unrepentant, he was to be regarded as an outsider (Matt. 18:17), or to be cut off from fellowship (II Thess. 3:14–15).

---

11. See R. E. Brown, "The Teacher of Righteousness and the Messiah(s)," in *The Scrolls and Christianity*, p. 40.

FOR FURTHER READING

Burrows, M. *The Dead Sea Scrolls.* New York: Viking Press, 1955.

_____. *More Light on the Dead Sea Scrolls.* New York: Viking Press, 1958.

Charlesworth, J. H., ed. *The Old Testament Pseudepigrapha: Apocalyptic Literature & Testaments.* Garden City, N.Y.: Doubleday, 1984. Two volumes.

Cross, F. M., Jr. *The Ancient Library of Qumran and Modern Biblical Studies.* Revised Edition. Grand Rapids: Baker Book House, 1980.

DeVaux, R., *Archaeology and the Dead Sea Scrolls.* London: Oxford University Press, 1973.

Fairweather, W. *The Background of the Gospels.* Edinburgh: T. & T. Clark, 1908.

Gaster, T. H. *The Dead Sea Scriptures with Introduction and Notes.* Third Edition. Garden City, N.Y.: Doubleday, 1976.

Hengel, M. *Jews, Greeks and Barbarians.* Philadelphia: Fortress Press, 1980.

Metzger, B. M., ed. *The Oxford Annotated Apocrypha.* New York: Oxford University Press, 1977.

Mowry, L. *The Dead Sea Scrolls and the Early Church.* Chicago: University of Chicago Press, 1962.

Nickelsburg, G. W. E. *Jewish Literature Between the Bible and the Mishnah.* Philadelphia: Fortress Press, 1981.

Nickelsburg, G. W. E. and Stone, M. E. *Faith and Piety in Early Judaism: Texts and Documents.* Philadelphia: Fortress Press, 1983.

Pfeiffer, C. F. *The Dead Sea Scrolls and the Bible.* Grand Rapids: Baker Book House, 1969.

Stone, M. *Scriptures, Sects and Visions: A Profile from Ezra to the Jewish Revolts.* Philadelphia: Fortress Press, 1980.

Vermes, G. *The Dead Sea Scrolls.* New York: Penguin, 1975.

_____. *The Dead Sea Scrolls: Qumran in Perspective.* Cleveland: Collins & World, 1978.

PART II

THE GOSPELS: THE RECORDS OF THE LIFE OF CHRIST

The Period of Inception:
6 B.C. to A.D. 30

CHAPTER 6

THE NEW TESTAMENT: ITS
NAME AND CONTENT

THE NAME

THE name "New Testament," which is given to the second half of the English Bible, comes from the Latin *Novum Testamentum*, which is itself a translation of the Greek *Hē Kainē Diathēkē* (anglicized). The Greek term was generally used to mean "a last will or testament," as the Latin translation indicated, but this translation did not exhaust its meaning. The word really meant an arrangement made by one party that might be accepted or rejected by another party, but that he could not alter; and that, when accepted, bound both parties by its terms. Since a will is the best example of such an instrument, the Latin *Testamentum*, preserved in the English *Testament*, was used.

The term *covenant* used in the Revised Version is derived from the Old French *covenir*, "to agree," which in turn is derived from the Latin *convenire*, "to come together." It means an agreement, stipulation, or contract that involves both parties in the agreement. It implies more than a promise, for a promise obligates only the person making it, whereas a covenant obligates both parties concerned in it. In this respect it approximates the modern term "contract." Such is the meaning of the word *covenant* as used in Exodus 24:1–8, which describes the acceptance of the law by the people of Israel at Mt. Sinai. The fact that the Greek translator of the Old Testament uses *diathēkē* in this passage to render the Hebrew word for covenant indicates that *diathēkē* may on occasion have this meaning, and this usage is confirmed by the language of Luke 22:14–20, where the old covenant of Exodus 24:1–8 is contrasted with the new covenant that Jesus made with his disciples at the last supper. The general meaning of the Greek term must be the same in both instances, as the contrast of *old* and *new* implies. The New Testament, then, is the record of the character and establishment of a new dealing of God with men through Christ. God sets the terms; man can accept or reject them but cannot alter them, and when man accepts them, both he and God are obligated to fulfill their requirements. The Old Covenant involved a revelation of the holiness of God in a righteous standard of law that those who received it were solemnly enjoined to keep. The New Covenant embodies a revelation of the holiness of God in an utterly righteous Son, who empowers those who receive the revelation to become sons of God by making them righteous (John 1:12).

THE CONTENT

The contents of the New Testament consist of the revelation of this new covenant through the recorded words of Jesus Christ and of his followers. It comprises twenty-seven distinct pieces of writing by nine different authors, unless Paul is regarded as the author of Hebrews, in which case the number is reduced to eight. These documents were written over a span of a little more than half a century, probably from A.D. 45 at the earliest to about A.D. 100. The historical allusions in them cover the entire first century, and their background of cultural thought reaches back into the fourth or fifth century B.C.

The contents of the New Testament may be classified in three ways: by literary character, by authors, and by periods.

Literary Character

The first five books of the New Testament, Matthew, Mark, Luke, John, and Acts, are *historical* in character. All of them narrate a story. The first four sketch from different viewpoints the life and work of Jesus. Acts is a companion volume to Luke and carries on the story of Jesus' followers after the close of his earthly life, with special emphasis on the career of Paul, the missionary.

The following books are largely *doctrinal*: Romans, I and II Corinthians, Galatians, Ephesians, Philippians, Colossians, I and II Thessalonians, Hebrews, James, I and II Peter, I John, Jude. Most of these were written in the form of letters to churches for the purpose of instructing them in the elements of Christian belief and in the practice of Christian ethics. None of them, with the possible exception of Romans, was written as a formal argument. They were largely informal in approach and dealt with the current emergencies in the groups to which they were directed.

Still another group can be called *personal:* I and II Timothy, Titus, Philemon, II and III John. These were written as personal letters to individuals, not to groups, and were intended to be used for private instruction and counsel. Because their recipients were engaged in the leadership of the churches, however, the books took on a significance wider than that of private epistles and came to be regarded as public documents.

Revelation, the last book of the New Testament, is *prophetic.* It purports to deal with the future as well as with the present. Because of its highly symbolic style, involving visions and supernatural disclosures, it is also classed with *apocalyptic* literature.

This classification is not final or exclusive. There is much doctrine in the historical books and some prophecy in the doctrinal epistles. The classification holds only for general content.

Authors

These books may also be grouped by authors. All of the writers were Jews, except Luke. Three, presumably Matthew, Peter, and John, were members of the apostolic band. Mark, Jude, and James had been active in the early church, or had been in contact with the apostolic group even before the death of Jesus. Luke and Paul, while not eyewitnesses of the life of Christ, were well known to those who were, and were certainly able to compare notes with them if necessary. Of the author of Hebrews nothing is known from external evidence, hence his name does not appear in the summary.

Author	Book	Author	Book
Matthew	Matthew		Romans
Mark	Mark		I Corinthians
			II Corinthians
Luke	Luke		Galatians
	Acts		Ephesians
			Philippians
		Paul	Colossians
			I Thessalonians
	John		II Thessalonians
	I John		I Timothy
John	II John		II Timothy
	III John		Titus
	Revelation		Philemon
James	James	?	Hebrews
Jude	Jude	Peter	I Peter
			II Peter

Periods

The books of the New Testament were not written in the order in which they appear in the Bible. One must not assume that because the Gospels precede the Pauline epistles in literary order they are necessarily older. Furthermore, there may be a considerable difference between the date at which a writing was composed and the period with which it deals. Mark, for instance, describes the events in Jesus' life that took place within the last part of the third decade of the first century, but the Gospel may not have been circulated publicly until between A.D. 65 and 70.

In order to facilitate the study of the history of the first century, it may be divided into three periods of unequal length, each of which marks a definite stage in its development.

The first is the period of *inception,* which covers the lifetime of Christ from 6 B.C. to A.D. 30. This period is described by the four Gospels, which narrate with differing degrees of fullness the significant facts in the career of Jesus, and which give casual references to other historical events.

The second period, that of *expansion* (A.D. 30 to 60), witnessed the development of the missionary enterprise. Groups of preachers traveled the Roman roads in all directions, evangelizing and founding new churches in various important centers. The narrative of Acts affords chiefly a view of the Pauline mission to the Gentiles, with only occasional glimpses of the activities of other apostles and preachers. During this time the gospel progressed from Jerusalem to Rome, and doubtless into many other localities not noted by the author of Acts. Within this period fall also the majority of the Pauline epistles that were written during Paul's missionary career. Considerable knowledge of the growth of the Gentile church can be gleaned from them.

The third period from A.D. 60 to 100 may be called *consolidation.* In some respects it is the period of mystery, for little is told of the history of the church at this time. There is no consecutive account of it as the book of Acts affords for the preceding epoch, and what little history can be reconstructed must be pieced together from hints provided in various writings. To the early part of this period belong the Pastoral Epistles of Paul and the Petrine writings. Luke-Acts and Matthew were probably published between A.D. 60 and 70. Mark may have been composed at an earlier date, but if tradition be correct, it may not have been widely published until this era. Hebrews and Jude probably precede A.D. 70. The Johannine writings, the Fourth Gospel and the Epistles, may have appeared as late as A.D. 85 to 90. The Apocalypse should probably be assigned to the reign of Domitian in A.D. 96, or thereabouts.

A survey of this literature will show that in the last third of the first century the church was rapidly consolidating into a recognized institution. From being a scattered collection of isolated bands of believers, each with

CHART OF NEW TESTAMENT CHRONOLOGY

PERIOD	DATE	EVENT	HISTORY	PUBLICATION
Inception B.C. 6 to A.D. 30	B.C. 6 B.C. 4 A.D. 27 A.D. 30	Birth of Jesus Death of Herod Baptism Crucifixion	} Matthew Luke } Mark } John	

Expansion
 	
A.D. 30 to 60
	A.D. 31–33
	
	A.D. 45
	A.D. 49
	
	A.D. 52
	
	A.D. 54
	A.D. 55
	A.D. 56
	
	A.D. 60
		Paul's
		    Conversion
		
		Council of
		    Jerusalem
		
		Paul's First
		    Imprisonment
			}
			
			Acts
			
			Pauline
			Epistles
				
				James
				Galatians (Mark)
				
				I & II
				Thessalonians
				      Matthew (?)
				I Corinthians
				II Corinthians
				Romans
				Colossians,
				Ephesians
				Philemon
				Philippians
				      Luke-Acts

Consolidation
 	
A.D. 60 to
100
	
	A.D. 68
	A.D. 70
	
	A.D. 85
	
	A.D. 95
		Paul's Second
		    Imprisonment
		
		Destruction of
		    Jerusalem
			}
			
			General
			Epistles
			
			} Revelation
				I Timothy
				Titus
				I Peter
				II Timothy
				II Peter
				Hebrews Mark
				Jude
				
				I, II, III John John
				
				Revelation

its own problems and its own standards, it was beginning to acquire social and doctrinal solidarity and to be regarded as a potent factor in society.

The Gospels show that the narrative preaching about the life of the Lord Jesus had become an accepted type of evangelism and had crystallized into a pattern that was used for instruction of believers. Acts, the first history of the Christian church, is a conscious attempt to explain the fusion of Jew and Gentile into one body through Christian experience. The epistles of the period deal with heresies, which in themselves imply the existence of some orthodox framework of belief. The book of Hebrews and the Johannine writings show that the church had already been compelled to face the claims of the law and the inroads of a "progressive" faith that "advanced" by abandoning a sound Christology. The threat of persecution, too, is reflected in Hebrews, I Peter, and Revelation. The Pastorals indicate that even at the close of Paul's career many of these issues were current and that a decline of spiritual life had already affected some of the churches.

Exact chronological placement of the books of the New Testament is impossible. None of them is dated by figure, and only a few contain such unmistakable allusions to the time of their writing that they can be assigned to a given year of the Christian era. Opinions of scholars vary greatly on some of these books. John, for instance, has been dated from the fifth decade of the first century to the middle years of the second century. Most conservative scholars would locate it about A.D. 85, though it may be earlier. One can only approximate a correct order for these books; exactitude is impossible in consideration of present lack of knowledge.

The chart on p. 133 is intended to show approximately how the books are related to the time that they describe and in which they were written. Further discussion on the chronological problems will be offered in connection with each individual writing.[1]

In dealing with the Gospels, three chronological relations must be considered. The first is the time of which the Gospels speak and to which their narrative mainly relates. The second is the period in which their material was composed and in which it was shaped to the needs and usage of

---

1. The problems of producing an exact chronology of New Testament events and writings have been widely discussed. See G. B. Caird, "Chronology of the NT, The," *Interpreter's Dictionary of the Bible* (1962), I, 599–607; J. Finegan, *Handbook of Biblical Chronology* (Princeton: Princeton University Press, 1964); G. Ogg, *The Chronology of the Life of Paul* (London: Epworth Press, 1968); J. J. Gunther, *Paul: Messenger and Exile: A Study in the Chronology of His Life and Letters* (Valley Forge: Judson Press, 1972); W. R. Thompson, "Chronology of the New Testament," in *Zondervan Pictorial Encyclopedia* (1975), I, 816–829; R. Jewett, *A Chronology of Paul's Life* (Philadelphia: Fortress Press, 1979). For widely dissenting views, see J. Knox, *Chapters in a Life of Paul* (Nashville: Abingdon, 1968); J. A. T. Robinson, *Redating the New Testament* (London: S.C.M., 1967).

the church. The composition may have been wholly written or wholly oral, or it may have been partly both. The third is the actual date of publication, when the written copy of each Gospel first saw the light and began to be used as an authoritative document by some church or churches. The epistles were apparently written for some specific occasion and were "published" at some definite date without having been previously connected with the general body of preaching except where noted in the individual treatment of each book.

FOR FURTHER READING

See the lists of handbooks and commentaries and the articles in the Bible dictionaries on "The New Testament" (Bibliography, pp. 435–440).

A leaf from the Lindisfarne Gospels, dating from A.D. 700. Illustration shows the opening of the Gospel of Matthew: Christi autem generatio sic erat. Cum esset desponsata mater eius Maria Ioseph. . . . The small interlinear writing is an Anglo-Saxon gloss—the earliest form of the Gospels in English.

CHAPTER 7

THE GOSPELS AS LITERARY WORKS

CHRISTIANITY as a movement owes its origin to the person and work of Jesus Christ, its Founder and its Head. Except for a few fragmentary statements, the authentic records of his life are contained only in the four Gospels of Matthew, Mark, Luke, and John, which the Christian church has regarded as canonical from the earliest period of its history. Although numerous other Gospels purported to recount facts concerning his life that are not recorded in the famous four, the apocryphal Gospels, as they are called, are generally of later date and of doubtful reliability. They contain little information that is not a duplication of what the canonical Gospels impart and much of what they add is obviously fanciful and legendary. Furthermore, they often betray by their language that they were written to bolster the views of some particular sect that did not represent the mainstream of historic Christianity, but that was really a divergence from it or a rebellion against it.

Tatian, a Syrian Christian of the second century (A.D. 170), who devised the first harmony of the Gospels of which any trace has survived, used for his work only the four, although he must have known of others. Irenaeus, bishop of Lyons and Vienne, who lived about A.D. 180, put forward a rather quaint theory concerning the Gospels.

> It is not possible that the Gospels can be either more or fewer in number than they are. For, since there are four zones of the world in which we live, and four principal winds, while the Church is scattered throughout all the world, and the "pillar and ground" of the Church is

the Gospel and the spirit of life; it is fitting that she should have four pillars, breathing out immortality on every side, and vivifying men afresh.[1]

Irenaeus' reasons for believing that there should be only four Gospels may seem to be farfetched, but even if they are not regarded as scientifically valid, their context indicates that the content of the Gospel record was being debated in Irenaeus' day and that he defended vigorously the truthfulness of the canonical Gospels that appear in the Bible. He says, in fact:

> But that these Gospels alone are true and reliable, and neither an increase nor diminution of the aforesaid number, I have proved by so many and such [arguments].[2]

On the basis of both internal and external evidence these writings unmistakably stand in a class by themselves.

This book deals with the Gospels as four separate works, written at different times and in different places for distinct constituencies. Obviously they were read separately when first published rather than studied as parts of a harmonistic ensemble, and each was regarded by its writer and its audience as comprising a narrative complete for its purpose. From the beginning of the church at Pentecost until the middle of the second century no published harmony of the life of Christ existed, and the Gospels seem to have been circulated independently in different sections of the Roman empire. There is little specific testimony in the early Fathers concerning the use and distribution of these Gospels, but the nature and frequency of the quotations from them plus such casual observations as have survived from the works of these Fathers tend to confirm this impression.

According to Bishop B. F. Westcott, the main testimony of the Apostolic Fathers is to "the substance, and not to the authenticity of the Gospels." A. H. McNeile has added that (probably) the earliest known writing in which the plural term "Gospels" is used of the Memoirs of the Apostles is the *Apology* of Justin Martyr (see LXVI.1), and that by A.D. 160 or so the Gospels had come into prominence in both the East and the West.[3]

The Gospels themselves do not claim to be exhaustive accounts of all

---

1. Irenaeus *Against Heresies* IV.xi.8. Translation of Alexander Roberts and James Donaldson, *The Ante-Nicene Fathers* (American Reprint. Grand Rapids, Mich.: Wm. B. Eerdmans Publishing Company, 1951), I, 428.

2. Irenaeus *Against Heresies* III.xi.9.

3. B. F. Westcott, *A General Survey of the History of the Canon of the New Testament* (London: Macmillan, 1875), p. 52; A. H. McNeile, *An Introduction to the Study of the New Testament*, rev. by C. S. C. Williams (Oxford: Clarendon Press, 1972), pp. 319, 325.

that Jesus said or did. On the contrary, at least two of them deny explicitly any such possibility, and the other two negate it by implication. John states that "many other signs therefore did Jesus in the presence of the disciples which are not written in this book" (John 20:30), and Luke acknowledges that "many have taken in hand to draw up a narrative concerning those matters which have been fulfilled among us" (Luke 1:1). Matthew announced that he was writing "the book of the generation of Jesus Christ" (Matt. 1:1), and Mark entitled his work as "the beginning of the gospel of Jesus Christ, the Son of God" (Mark 1:1). Each Gospel was selective according to the purpose of the author, and is complete in the sense that it carries out his intent.

The individual differences of the Gospels are counterbalanced by strong resemblances of order, content, and phraseology. Numerous events in the life of Christ are narrated in all four. Since they are dealing with the same person, it is only natural that there should be substantial agreement on the selection and description of the main features of Jesus' career.

THE SYNOPTIC PROBLEM

The first three Gospels, however, display a closer interrelation in content and in manner of expression. They have consequently been called the Synoptic Gospels, from the Greek *syn*, "together," and *optanomai*, "to see," since they take a common view of the life of Christ. This interrelation has given rise to the Synoptic problem, so called, which is briefly this: If the three Synoptic Gospels are totally independent of each other in origin and development, why do they resemble each other so closely, even to exact verbal agreement in many places? If, on the other hand, they have a literary relationship to each other, how can they be three independent witnesses to the deeds and teachings of the Lord Jesus Christ? Neither part of this dilemma can rightly be suppressed or neglected. Facts must be explained by the best and most reasonable hypotheses available. Nevertheless, one should not assume that he has a final answer to the question when much evidence is still lacking, nor should he be satisfied with a purely naturalistic answer that will not do justice to the origin of the Gospels or to any other part of Scripture.

As a concrete example of the kind of passage that creates this problem one might take the healing of the leper described in Matthew 8:1–4, Mark 1:40–45, and Luke 5:12–16. All of them are narrating the same event, for the action is alike in all three, and the conversation is almost identical verbally. Each is introduced by a different sentence to fit the general context of the narrative, but the words of Jesus are nearly the same.

How shall the verbal agreement be explained? Why should three men writing independently show such exact accord in their language? Two school papers with as close an agreement between them as is exhibited in the Synoptics would instantly arouse suspicion on the part of the teacher that the writers either had copied from each other, or else that they had collaborated. Did the writers of the Gospels copy each other's works, or did they use a common source, or did they collaborate?

PROPOSED SOLUTION

Many theories have been proposed to account for these phenomena.[4] In general they may be classified in three ways: the theory of oral tradition, the theory of reciprocal borrowing, and the theory of documentary sources. Each of these theories has some merit, though not all three can be simultaneously correct.

The *oral tradition* theory is the oldest of the three, since it seems to have been the underlying assumption of the church fathers. Papias remarked that Matthew recorded the sayings of Jesus in Aramaic (Hebrew dialect) notes, and that every man interpreted them as he was able.[5] Mark, he said, was Peter's scribe and interpreter who wrote accurately all that he remembered, but did not necessarily put it in the original order of speaking or action. Irenaeus[6] (c.170) followed the same line of thought, calling Luke's Gospel a reproduction of Pauline preaching, and attributing the Fourth Gospel to the disciple of Jesus who leaned on his breast at the last supper.

The fathers were not infallible, and it is possible that they may have been mistaken. In the century between the fall of Jerusalem and the height of Irenaeus' career the church was too busily engaged in preaching and in defending itself to pay much attention to the technicalities of authorship. On the other hand, Papias and Irenaeus are the earliest direct witness to the authorship of the Gospels, and their testimony should not be rejected without a fair attempt to interpret it.

In each instance that they mention, they assume that the Gospel writer either possessed personal knowledge of Jesus' works and teachings, or else that he was reproducing the content of preaching that he had heard repeatedly from some apostolic authority. The theory assumes that the facts concerning Jesus had been collected and organized, then memorized, and finally delivered orally in a fairly fixed form.

Several factors lend plausibility to this view. First is the certainty that the message of the Gospels was preached before it was written. If Jesus were to be presented to the populace by his followers, they must tell a consistent

---

4. See H. C. Thiessen, *Introduction to the New Testament* (Grand Rapids, Mich.: Wm. B. Eerdmans Publishing Company, 1951; revised 1979), pp. 101–129.
5. Eusebius *Historia Ecclesiae* III.39.
6. *Ibid.* V.viii, 2–4; II.i.

story containing the significant elements of his career, and they must repeat these as they encountered new audiences or as they instructed the believers by repetition. Constant reiteration tends to crystallization of form; a repeated story will become stereotyped. Paul mentions the message that he "received" (I Cor. 15:3) and "preached" (Gal. 1:11) in terms that imply an underlying core of fact that he could not alter. He does not speak of using any written documents. Such documents may or may not have been known during his preaching career, although in II Timothy 4:13 he spoke of "books" and "parchments," which probably included some Scriptures. It is quite likely that written accounts of Jesus' life were circulated prior to the Neronian persecution of A.D. 64.

The second theory is *mutual interdependence*, namely, that two of the Gospels borrowed from the other. It would be profitless in this brief account to review every possible order that has been suggested. Such a theory, if accepted, would destroy the originality of the two Gospels that copied from the third. While the ancients were not bound by copyright laws, and regarded any written document as freely available for use as they pleased, it seems hardly credible that they should have copied each other indiscriminately.

Furthermore, if, for instance, Matthew copied from Luke, why should he have created so different an order of events, or have omitted so much material that the latter contains? No two scholars could agree on the same sequence of writing or on the same explanation of the phenomena. The conflicting theories are a good evidence of the insecurity of the hypothesis.

The most popular theory to date is the *documentary hypothesis* (first used in the form of the "two-document hypothesis"). It assumes that Matthew and Luke built their Gospels on the basis of Mark, plus a collection of the sayings of Jesus called "Q" from the German *Quelle*, meaning "source." The latter source is presumed to have been a document containing sayings of Jesus, although no such written source has yet come to light (but cf. Luke 1:1–2). Students of the Gospels have observed that while Matthew and Luke diverge greatly from each other in content and order, the content of Mark is reproduced almost wholly in the other two. Although Matthew and Mark may occasionally agree against Luke, and while Luke and Mark may agree against Matthew, Matthew and Luke do not agree against Mark. The phenomena are what one might expect if they had used Mark independently.

Some discourse material, like the Sermon on the Mount, common to Matthew and Luke does not appear in Mark. On the ground that collections of the sayings of Jesus are found in the papyri from an early date, and that the use of such a source would parallel the supposed use of Mark, the second source, "Q," has been reconstructed.

A further development of this view was proposed by Burnett Streeter.[7] He associated Mark with Rome (c. A.D. 60), "Q" with Antioch (c. A.D. 50), an "M" document (narrative and non-Lukan sayings peculiar to Matthew) with Jerusalem (c. A.D. 65), and an "L" document with Caesarea (c. A.D. 60), including non-Markan materials in Luke 3, 6, 9–18, 19, 22–24. From these four ancestors the first and third Gospels were descended, while Mark, one of the sources, survived independently.

The documentary theory, while plausible, has one or two weaknesses. It lays greater emphasis on contact with documents, or certain oral traditions in the form of sayings of Jesus, than on living contact between the authors during the period in which the Gospels were being written. These "living contacts" are a genuine possibility (whether or not the traditional authorships are affirmed). To begin, John Mark was an inhabitant of Jerusalem during the lifetime of Jesus and during the early years of the church up to the time of Herod Agrippa I in A.D. 44 (Acts 12:12). He subsequently visited the Gentile church in Syrian Antioch and participated in Gentile evangelism with Paul and Barnabas (13:4–5). He was constantly associated with the preachers of the church to the end of his life.

No certain facts are known about Matthew's career. He probably lived in Jerusalem for a part of the time that Mark was there, since the apostles did not leave Jerusalem until after the death of Stephen and the persecution following it (8:1).

It is noteworthy, however, that the allusions to Gospel writings in the earliest of the Fathers seem to accord best with the Gospel of Matthew, and to indicate that it was well known in Antioch at an early date.

Luke was acquainted with John Mark at a later time, for their names are mentioned together in Colossians (4:10, 14) and in II Timothy (4:11). Both were closely associated with Paul about the time of his imprisonment in Rome (c. A.D. 60–67). Luke may have lived at Antioch himself, for he shows considerable interest in the city, and one manuscript uses the first person plural pronoun in Acts 11:28, making the author a participant in the action.

While the foregoing facts do not prove conclusively that the authors of the Synoptics conferred with each other over the events they recorded, they do make plausible the possibility of a common tradition known to these men by personal contact and propagated as the general message of the church. The interchange and repetition of the narrative preaching about Jesus would explain much of the material common to the Synoptics, while the personal research and interests of the authors would explain the materials peculiar to each. The existence of such a core is corroborated by

---

7. B. N. Streeter, *The Four Gospels* (New York: The Macmillan Company, 1925/1936).

occasional references in the New Testament to preaching about Christ (I Cor. 15:1–11; Gal. 2:2, 7).

One may say with regard to "Q" that no trace of this hypothetical document has ever been recovered. Even those who advocate the documentary hypothesis admit that it was not a Gospel. Undeniably, collections of Jesus' sayings existed at an early date, for some have been recovered from the papyri, but there is no convincing proof of the independent existence of this shadowy scroll.

An attempt has been made in recent years to penetrate behind these documentary sources to the origin of the material from which they were constructed. The *Formgeschichte* ("form-history") school has contended that the sources were compiled from anecdotes about Jesus and from fragments of his teaching that were circulated independently by his followers. These stories have been classified in various categories, such as miracles, epigrams, edifying tales of good deeds, and historical recitals like the Passion narrative of Jesus' last days. According to this theory these biographical items were collected, put in a framework constructed by the author, and woven into a narrative that became either a Gospel source or a Gospel.

Further, this discipline cannot demonstrate the historical genuineness of the Gospel materials. The attempts of critics to locate the "life-setting" of sayings in the Gospels in some situation in the early church (rather than in the ministry of Jesus) is questionable at times. Reasonably, events and sayings for the life of Jesus might have been used in later times (e.g., I Cor. 7:10–11), but often the early church distinguished between Jesus' sayings and their own views (I Cor. 7:12, 25).

Yet, as has been observed, we may be made more aware of the influence of early Christian life and witness on the formation of the Gospel tradition by the insights of *Formgeschichte*. Documentary theories fail to account for some of the creative characteristics seen in the materials. Further, we are brought closer to the oral stage of the tradition, and to the words of Jesus himself.[8]

A further critical technique is known as *Redaktiongeschichte*, in which the Gospel writers "redacted" (i.e., shaped and presented), according to the distinctive approach of each, the existing traditional materials concerning the life of Christ that came to them. Thus the writers were more like creative writers than compilers (as in the *Formgeschichte* school); they were interpreters rather than collectors.[9]

---

8. F. F. Bruce, "Criticism," in *International Standard Bible Encyclopedia* (1979), I, 824. See the cautions noted by R. P. Martin, *New Testament Foundations* (Grand Rapids: Wm. B. Eerdmans Publishing Company, 1975), I, 134–136.

9. See, e.g., G. Bornkamm, G. Barth, and H. J. Held, *Tradition and Interpretation*

According to this methodology, the *theology* of each Evangelist is emphasized. Not only are the Gospels viewed as literary wholes, but they represent carefully crafted works, the editorial endeavors of each writer being evident in the shape and tone of the book. They do not simply "hand on the story," but edit the traditional materials so as to present a specific historical-theological view of Jesus' life and teachings.[10]

Less emphasis is placed on the origin of the Gospels, and more on the "life-setting" of the Evangelist. One asks, "What was the occasion or situation that caused the writer to assemble, shape, and produce his Gospel"?

None of the theories briefly sketched here has proved sufficient to account for the origin of the Gospels. Much more evidence is needed before a complete answer can be given to all of the questions involved. A few facts, however, seem reasonably certain:

1. The Gospel of Matthew represents the notes that Matthew took on Jesus' teaching, with a framework of narrative that closely—and at times verbally—resembles Mark. The resemblance could be explained on the basis of common tradition and living contact quite as well as by appropriation of written work.

2. The Gospel of Mark represents the main line of narrative preaching about Jesus. It was reproduced by a man who had contact with the apostles from the very inception of the church, and it was written while some of them, at least, were still alive. Its content was known at a very early date, whether the actual document had been published then or not.

3. The Gospel of Luke represents the independent account of Paul's traveling companion, who wrote in the seventh decade of the first century, and who incorporated both the narrative framework of apostolic preaching and the results of his own research. Many of the parables and miracles recorded in Luke are not identical with those of Matthew, and even the teachings of Jesus are organized differently. If Luke and Matthew both used a "Q," one of them certainly took liberties with it. Either Matthew arranged the bulk of its teaching topically, as in the Sermon on the Mount (Matt. 5–7), or else Luke scattered its teachings through his Gospel at will. It is more reasonable to assume that Luke may have met Matthew personally, or that his reproduction of the sayings of Jesus had its source in direct

---

in *Matthew* (Philadelphia: Westminster Press, 1963); R. P. Martin, *Mark: Evangelist and Theologian* (Grand Rapids: Zondervan Publishing House, 1972); I. H. Marshall, *Luke: Historian and Theologian* (Grand Rapids: Zondervan Publishing House, 1970).

10. A recent example will be found in R. H. Gundry, *Matthew: A Study in His Theological and Literary Art* (Grand Rapids: Wm. B. Eerdmans Publishing Company, 1982).

contact with the people who had first heard them and with the apostles who preached them.

Some other aspects of this question deserve consideration. One is that the dates of composition and publication may be widely separated. Matthew, for instance, could have collected his notes during Jesus' lifetime, but they may not have reached the public in organized form until a long time afterward. If so, they could have been used by others in the interim, and the final form need not have been identical with the former collection.

The final form in which these individual notes were written would be influenced by the predominant tradition and by the application of it to the individual need. Differences would arise from the varying application of Jesus' teachings to local needs and by adaptation for individual purposes. The same episodes can be used in different frameworks and can rightly be applied to very different circumstances. The disagreements in the accounts thus become negligible, since they do not predicate any deep inconsistency within the documents themselves.

The Gospels should be treated as honest attempts to arrange the life of Jesus for didactic purposes. Unquestionably it was the core of apostolic preaching, for it appears in Peter's address on the day of Pentecost (Acts 2:22–32), in his sermon in the house of Cornelius (10:36–43), and in Paul's address in Antioch of Pisidia (13:23–33). The Synoptists could not have been ignorant of this "oral tradition," as it is called; in fact, Luke's preface implies that the writer knew what had been handed down "by ministers of the word" (Luke 1:2). While the theory of oral tradition may not explain all of the Synoptic problem, it is worth more attention than has been accorded to it in recent years.

Finally, the purposes of the Evangelists should be taken into account. Granting that they possessed much material in common, they put it to different uses, and organized it into different frameworks under the direction of the mind of the Spirit. The very differences between the writers speak of independence; the similarities reflect a common background of information, a common subject of writing, and the common inspiration of God.[11]

---

11. Since a technical discussion of the Synoptic problem does not properly belong in a New Testament survey, the foregoing statement deals with the topic only in barest outline. For a fuller statement of the author's viewpoint, see M. C. Tenney, *The Genius of the Gospels* (Grand Rapids, Mich.: Wm. B. Eerdmans Publishing Company, 1951), pp. 1–119. An excellent small treatise of a more general nature is F. F. Bruce, *Are the New Testament Documents Reliable?* (Grand Rapids: Wm. B. Eerdmans Publishing Company, 1954), pp. 28–47. The bulk of critical literature on this subject is enormous, of which relatively little has been written from a conservative standpoint.

FOR FURTHER READING

For tools, see the Harmonies of the Gospels listed in the Bibliography. The introductions will supply the general approach to the Gospels. The bibliography on the Synoptic problem is immense in scope. Because the question belongs to biblical criticism rather than to survey, only selected readings are given. Conservative literature on this subject is scarce. The following works will be especially useful:

Barclay, Wm. *The First Three Gospels*. Philadelphia: Westminster Press, 1966.

Bartels, Robert A. *Kerygma or Gospel Tradition . . . Which Came First?* Minneapolis: Augsburg Publishing House, 1961.

Beare, Francis W. *The Earliest Records of Jesus*: a companion to the *Synopsis of the First Three Gospels* by Albert Huck. Nashville: Abingdon Press, 1962.

Bruce, F. F. *Are the New Testament Documents Reliable?* Grand Rapids, Mich.: Wm. B. Eerdmans Publishing Company, 1954. Pp. 28–47.

Burton, Ernest DeWitt. *A Short Introduction to the Gospels*. Chicago: University of Chicago Press, n.d. See particularly pp. 84–98.

Farmer, Wm. R. *The Synoptic Problem: A Critical Analysis*. New York: The Macmillan Company, 1964.

Hayes, Doremus A. *The Synoptic Gospels and the Book of Acts*. New York: The Methodist Book Concern, n.d. Pp. 1–354. Comprehensive coverage of the characteristic peculiarities of the Synoptic Gospels.

Holdsworth, W. W. *Gospel Origins*. New York: Charles Scribner's Sons, 1913. Pp. 1–211. Old, but useful for general information.

Jackson, Henry L. "The Present State of the Synoptic Problem," in *Cambridge Biblical Essays*, H. B. Swete, ed. London: Macmillan & Company, Ltd., 1909.

Jones, Maurice. *The Four Gospels*. London: The Society for Promoting Christian Knowledge, 1921. For argument for the Two-Document Theory, see pp. 10–19.

Kistemaker, S. *Gospels in Current Study*. Grand Rapids: Baker Book House, 1980.

McIntyre, D. M. *Some Notes on the Gospels*. Ed. by F. F. Bruce. London: Inter-Varsity Fellowship, 1943. Pp. 51.

Moorehead, William G. *Studies in the Four Gospels*. *Westminster Handbooks*. Philadelphia: The Westminster Press, 1900. Pp. 230.

Nickle, Keith F. *The Synoptic Gospels: An Introduction*. Atlanta: John Knox Press, 1980.

Pullan, Leighton. *The Gospels*. London: Longmans, Green, & Company, 1912. See particularly pp. 133–275.

Rollins, Wayne G. *The Gospels: Portraits of Christ*. Philadelphia: Westminster Press, 1963.

Scroggie, W. Graham. *A Guide to the Gospels*. London: Pickering & Inglis, 1948. Pp. 664.

Stonehouse, Ned B. *Origins of the Synoptic Gospels*. Grand Rapids: Wm. B. Eerdmans Publishing Company, 1963.

Streeter, Burnett H. *The Four Gospels*. New York: The Macmillan Company, 1925. Pp. 621.

Tenney, Merrill C. *The Genius of the Gospels*. Grand Rapids, Mich.: Wm. B. Eerdmans Publishing Company, 1951. Pp. 124.

Thiessen, Henry C. *Introduction to the New Testament*. Grand Rapids, Mich.: Wm. B. Eerdmans Publishing Company, 1951. Pp. xx, 347. Pp. 101–129 give a good, brief conservative treatment of this subject.

Westcott, B. F. *Introduction to the Study of the Gospels.* Seventh Edition. London: Macmillan & Company, 1888. Old, but still the best defense of the oral tradition theory. See pp. 164–212.

CHAPTER 8

THE GOSPEL OF MATTHEW

ORIGIN

THE first Gospel is traditionally ascribed to Matthew Levi, a tax collector or publican, whom Jesus called to be one of his twelve disciples (Matt. 9:9–13; 10:3). Practically nothing is known of him except his name and occupation. After the listing of the apostles in the book of Acts (Acts 1:13) he disappeared from the history of the church, except for allusions that are probably legendary. Nowhere in the First Gospel is he explicitly called its author, but the early writers of the church who discuss the authorship credit it to Matthew. Eusebius (c. A.D. 325) quotes Papias (c. A.D. 100) as saying that Matthew had composed in Aramaic the oracles of the Lord, which were translated into Greek by each man as he was able.[1] Irenaeus, about a century and a half earlier than Eusebius, stated that "Matthew also issued a written Gospel among the Hebrews in their own dialect, while Peter and Paul were preaching at Rome and laying the foundations of the church."[2]

Several inferences may be drawn from these early statements concerning the origin of the First Gospel. First, the Matthaean authorship was undisputed. Since Matthew was a comparatively obscure member of the apostolic band, there seems to be no good reason for making him the author of a spurious work. Any forger who sought fame for his production would

---

1. Eusebius *Historia Ecclesiae* III.xxxix.16.
2. Irenaeus *Against Heresies* III.i.1.

The Jordan River before it reaches the Dead Sea near the Jericho area.

have chosen to publish it under the name of a more renowned apostle. Second, the general agreement of early writers accords with the known character of Matthew. As a publican he must have been literate and accustomed to taking notes as a part of his business activity. Third, the tradition that this Gospel was originally written in Aramaic does not preclude the possibility that the author may have published later a Greek edition that quickly superseded the older writing.

DATE AND PLACE

Just when the Gospel was written is unknown. It can scarcely have been written before the first dispersion of the Jerusalem Christians (Acts 8:4), for the local church in Jerusalem would not have needed a written Gospel since the apostles were physically present to answer all questions and to impart authoritative teaching. It is doubtful whether it was written subsequent to A.D. 70, because the prophecy dealing with the overthrow of Jerusalem contains no allusion to the city's actually having fallen (Matt. 24:1–28). The testimony of Irenaeus, quoted above, would place its writing in the time of Nero "while Paul and Peter were in Rome." If this tradition is correct, it may have been composed by Matthew originally for non-Palestinian Aramaic-speaking converts, who did not have access to the apostles and who were consequently dependent on a written text for their knowledge of Jesus.

The testimony of Papias has been frequently rejected, since no trace of an Aramaic original has survived and the language of the Gospel bears no marks of being a Greek translation. Promiscuous translations such as Papias mentions would hardly yield the good Greek of the existing Gospel. On the other hand, it is possible that, seeing the demand for written information about the life of Jesus, the author made a Greek edition for the Gentile churches, perhaps for Antioch in particular. Since the Greek churches quickly outstripped the Aramaic churches in numbers and influence, the Aramaic original might have perished at an early date. Contradictory opinions have been expressed concerning the original language of this Gospel. In any case, the existing Greek text is early and should probably be regarded as an edition rather than as a translation from Aramaic.

Matthew's Gospel is admirably suited to a church that was still closely related to Judaism, though becoming increasingly independent of it. It breathes the atmosphere of Messianism, yet it has a message for "all the world." It preserves the essence of the Abrahamic covenant, which stressed God's benefits to Abraham and to his seed as a separate people, and yet added: "In thee shall all the families of the earth be blessed" (Gen. 12:3).

The place of writing could be Antioch. The quotations of the Gospels in the early patristic writings like those of Papias and Ignatius agree most closely with the text of Matthew, and show that this first Gospel was probably the favorite of the Syro-Jewish church. Furthermore, the church at Antioch was the first to have a markedly Gentile constituency that spoke both Aramaic and Greek. While absolute proof that the Gospel originated at Antioch is lacking, no other place is more suitable for it. It may, therefore, have been composed some time between A.D. 50 and 70 and have been circulated by those who worked in and from the church of Antioch.

CONTENT

The theme of the Gospel of Matthew is announced by its opening words: "The book of the generation of Jesus Christ, the son of David, the son of Abraham" (Matt. 1:1). The phraseology reminds one of the book of Genesis, which is divided into sections by the use of the same phrase, "the book of the generations of . . ." or "the generations of . . ." (Gen. 2:4; 5:1; 6:9, et al.). Each occurrence of this phrase marked a stage in the development of the Messianic promise. The links in the history of God's people are carried forward through Genesis, and one appears in Ruth 4:18, where the Messianic line ends with David. Matthew picks up the genealogy at this point and illustrates its fulfillment in the person of Jesus.

The structure of Matthew is built around a double outline that can be traced by recurring phrases in the book. The first is biographical and is quite similar to the framework of the biography of Jesus as given in Mark and Luke. The two points of division are Matthew 4:17, "*From that time* [italics ours] began Jesus to preach, and to say, Repent ye; for the kingdom of heaven is at hand*," and Matthew 16:21, "*From that time* [italics ours] began Jesus to show unto his disciples that he must go unto Jerusalem, and suffer many things of the elders and chief priests and scribes, and be killed, and the third day be raised up." The former of these two passages indicates the rise of Jesus' preaching career, which brought him into public prominence. The latter passage marks the beginning of the decline of his popularity and points toward the culmination of his career at the cross. The fact that these two foci of his life are so clearly marked in the Gospel indicates the avowed purpose of the author to present two aspects of Jesus' biography, and shows that he had a unitary concept of that life as a whole. The Gospel is no mere aggregation of fragmentary sayings and random stories, but it is definitely organized to show how the Messiah discharged the calling for which he came into the world.

The other structure of Matthew is peculiar to this Gospel. Whereas the previously mentioned outline is a biographical interpretation of the life of Jesus, this other outline is topical. The material is divided into five blocks of text, each of which is grouped around one dominant theme, and each of which ends with the phrase, "When Jesus had finished. . . ." With the introductory narrative and the concluding story of the Passion there are seven divisions in all, which are summarized in an epilogue that confronts the reader with the consequences of Jesus' Messianic claims. The sharp contrast of the action of the priests on the report of the guard at the tomb and the action of the disciples on the revelation of the risen Lord compel the reader to choose for himself which attitude he will take. Either he must align himself with the Jewish leaders who repudiated Jesus and would not acknowledge his claims under any circumstances, or else he must himself become a disciple.

OUTLINE

MATTHEW: THE GOSPEL OF THE MESSIAH

I. The Prophecies of the Messiah Realized	
The Advent	1:1–4:11
II. The Principles of the Messiah Announced	
The Inaugural Address	4:12–7:29
Challenge to Enter	(7:13–14)
III. The Power of the Messiah Revealed	
The Miracles	8:1–11:1
Challenge to Follow	(10:34–39)
IV. The Program of the Messiah Explained	
The Parables	11:2–13:53
Challenge to Acceptance	(11:28)
Challenge to Understanding	(13:51)
V. The Purpose of the Messiah Declared	
The Crisis of the Cross	13:54–19:2
Challenge to Testify	(16:13–15)
VI. The Problems of the Messiah Presented	
The Conflicts with Opponents	19:3–26:2
Challenge to Repentance	(23:37–39)
VII. The Passion of the Messiah Accomplished	
The Death and Resurrection	26:3–28:10
VIII. Epilogue	
Rumor and Reality	28:11–20
Challenge to Action	(28:16–20)

The first of these sections acquaints the reader of the Gospel with the background of the Messiah. His genealogy, stemming from Abraham, the initial recipient of God's promises, and from David, divinely chosen founder of Judah's royal house, is first stated in the opening verse and then demonstrated. The account of the virgin birth follows, together with the baptism and the temptation that prepared him for his public labors. In this section of three and a half chapters the phrase "that it might be fulfilled which was spoken by the Lord through the prophet," or some similar expression, occurs no less than five times. The advent of Jesus is thus depicted as the completion of the divine purpose that was revealed in the Old Testament and that was partially worked out in the historical process that preceded his coming.

The second section opens with the appearance of Jesus in Galilee after the imprisonment of John the Baptist. It is devoted largely to the declaration of the spiritual and ethical principles of the Messianic kingdom. Jesus summoned people to repentance and to faith in him, and as he declared to them the realm in which he was Lord, he sought to point out what the nature of that realm would be and how it could be entered.

Matthew alone uses the phrase "the kingdom of heaven," thirty-three times. Five times he speaks of "the kingdom of God" (6:33; 12:28; 19:24; 21:31; 21:43). The other Synoptics use the latter term in many passages where Matthew employs "kingdom of heaven." While Jesus asserted unmistakably that his kingdom would have an ultimate material manifestation (8:11; 13:40–43), he also made plain that it has a present spiritual existence (4:17; 12:28).

The spiritual principles of the kingdom were embodied in the Sermon on the Mount, of which Matthew gives the fullest record. It defined Jesus' position with regard to the law, for he said that he "came not to destroy, but to fulfil" (5:17). He demanded a righteousness that exceeded the standard of Jewish legalism, for it was inward, not outward; spontaneous, not legalistic; gauged by a person, not by a code. Its highest standard was God himself: "Ye therefore shall be perfect, as your heavenly Father is perfect" (5:48). In this respect he went beyond the law when he said: "Ye have heard that it was said to them of old time . . . but I say unto you" (5:21–22). The Sermon on the Mount is a direct assertion of his right to transcend the law. He did not revoke the law but he went beyond it by the sheer holiness of his person.

The criterion of righteousness in the Sermon on the Mount is not conformity with human ideals but knowledge of Christ, hearing his sayings, and doing them (7:23–24). The full import of Christ's person and work was yet to be realized, but the necessity of making him central to all of his teaching and to all of faith is stated here unmistakably.

In order that these principles might be validated in the thinking of potential believers, some proofs of Jesus' power were necessary. The third section of Matthew (8:1–11:1) is occupied first with a recital of miracles of various types that showed Jesus' power over disease (leprosy, 8:1–4; palsy, 8:5–13; fever, 8:14–17; paralysis, 9:2–8; issue of blood, 9:20–22; blindness, 9:27–31), demons (8:28–34; 9:32–34), the powers of nature (8:23–27), and death (9:18, 23–26). The commission to the Twelve that is described in Matthew 10 may be regarded as Jesus' delegation of power to these men and as his reassurance to them as they set out to exercise it. The preaching of the Messiah was not just the proclamation of a new ideal, but the demonstration of a new power—a concept that the book of Acts states became a reality in the later life of the church: "And with great power gave the apostles their witness of the resurrection of the Lord Jesus: and great grace was upon them" (Acts 4:33).

Such miraculous acts, whether of the Lord Jesus Christ himself or of his disciples, were not a sporadic and aimless show of power. Jesus was seeking to teach the multitude and inaugurate a program for his kingdom rather than to bewilder or amaze the crowds.

Beginning with the fourth section of Matthew (11:2–13:53) the parables are featured strongly. Not all of them belong to this part of the Gospel, but the greatest single aggregation of them is here in the thirteenth chapter. In figures taken from everyday life they portray the nature and program of the kingdom of heaven, particularly with reference to the future.

Jesus declared that the parables were intended both to reveal and to conceal truth, for when the disciples asked him why he used parables in speaking to the crowds, he said:

> Unto you it is given to know the mysteries of the kingdom of heaven, but to them it is not given.
>
> (Matt. 13:11)

Jesus intended that his instructions should be plain to those who were ready for it, and obscure to those who were rebellious.

In this list are eight parables:

1. The Soils	13:1–23
2. The Wheat and the Tares	13:24–30, 36–43
3. The Mustard Seed	13:31–32
4. The Leaven	13:33
5. The Treasure	13:44
6. The Pearl	13:45–46
7. The Net	13:47–50
8. The Householder	13:51–52

The list is divided at verse 36, where it is said that Jesus withdrew from the multitudes and went indoors, so that four parables were designed for the populace and four for his disciples.

The first four, then, present the kingdom of heaven to the crowd. Its inception by sowing the word of God, its reception by various types of hearers, the contrast of real and spurious response in the wheat and the tares, the amazing growth of the kingdom from a tiny beginning to a large tree, the dynamic forces of the kingdom as compared to leaven—all these were factors that he wanted the populace to know.

The last four parables deal with inner aspects of the kingdom: the cost of building it, the double destiny of those affected by it, and the intermingling of new and old elements in its teaching.

All the parables indicate that Jesus was not thinking of himself simply as a Jewish reformer, but as the sovereign of the earth and as a figure of world importance.

The eleventh and twelfth chapters, preceding the parables, contain additional discourses that bear on the nature and importance of his mission. The challenge of John the Baptist (11:2–19), Jesus' rejection by the Galilean cities (11:20–24), his authority over the Sabbath (12:1–14), and his authority over the demons (12:22–37)—all contribute to the understanding of his work as a supernatural person who had come to earth on an unusual errand.

The crisis of this mission is anticipated in the next section of Matthew (13:54–19:2). The rejection of Jesus by his fellow citizens (13:54–58), the threat of Herod in the death of John the Baptist (14:1–12), and the obtuseness of the disciples (15:1–16; 16:5–12) indicated tensions that brought from Jesus a declaration of the imminence of the cross, and also the revelation of himself in the transfiguration (16:21–17:8). From this point on in the narrative the cross loomed increasingly before Jesus and became the immediate objective of his earthly career.

Mount Tabor, believed by some to be the mountain on which Jesus was transfigured.

The declaration of the Messianic purpose led to conflict. In chapters 19:3 to 26:2 the problems of the Messiah are described and his conflicts with his opponents appear in definite events, such as the debates with the Herodians, the Sadducees, and the Pharisees (22:15–40). The denunciations of chapter 23 and the prediction of the desolation of Jerusalem in chapters 24 and 25 grew out of this conflict.

Conflict must come to a crisis, and in the life of the Messiah that crisis was the cross. Matthew 26:3 through 28:10 describes his Passion, death, and resurrection. Matthew stressed the Messianic character of his death by emphasizing its relation to prophecy. Four times Jesus alluded definitely to the Old Testament as applying to the events of his Passion (26:31, 54, 56; 27:9), and in replying to Caiaphas' questioning he used of himself the title Son of man (26:64), which in Daniel 7:13–14 was applied to a heavenly being.

The epilogue is a summary of the whole Gospel, clinching its teaching by illustrating the two attitudes toward Jesus: rejection in unbelief, or worship because of acceptance.

Each of the sections contains a challenge to the disciples, spoken by Jesus, which is obviously intended by the author to be a challenge to his reader also. At the close of the didactic section containing the Sermon on the Mount, Jesus called on the disciples to take the first step of entering the way that leads to life (Matt. 7:13–14). As soon as he had proved his power to them, he commissioned them as witnesses and challenged them to take up the cross and follow him (10:34–41). In the section dealing with the explanation of his program there is a double challenge: one to the multitude to come to him for rest (11:28) and one to the disciples asking if they had understood his words (13:51). He wanted to make sure that his claims brought both volitional and intellectual response. The prediction of the cross at the great turning point in his life evoked a call for committal: "Who say ye that I am?" (16:15). His rejection by Jerusalem constrained him to summon the rebellious city to repentance (23:37–39). With the denouement of the story, the Great Commission says, "Go ye therefore . . . ," the final appeal of the Gospel as a whole. Each section is thus applied practically to the action of the reader as he makes his way progressively through the book.

EMPHASIS

The Gospel of Matthew was written to show how Jesus of Nazareth enlarged and explained the revelation that had been begun in the Messianic prophecies of the Old Testament. Although it is strongly Jewish in its character, it was also written for the benefit of Gentiles, since the final commission enjoined the Twelve to make disciples "of all the nations"

(28:19). If it was originally composed for the benefit of the church at Antioch, where Gentile converts first came together in large numbers, the reason for its character would be plain. Matthew was seeking to show to these converts the meaning of Jesus' ministry in terms of the Old Testament that their Jewish colleagues believed, and from which they themselves had been taught.

Certain incidents are peculiar to Matthew. The vision of Joseph (1:20–24), the visit of the Magi (2:1–12), the flight into Egypt (2:13–15), the massacre of the infants (2:16), the dream of Pilate's wife (27:19), the death of Judas (27:3–10), the resurrection of the saints at the crucifixion (27:52), the bribery of the guard (28:12–15), and the baptismal commission (28:19–20) appear nowhere else in the Gospels. Among the parables, the tares (13:24–30, 36–43), the hidden treasure (13:44), the pearl (13:45–46), the dragnet (13:47), the unmerciful servant (18:23–35), the laborers in the vineyard (20:1–16), the two sons (21:28–32), the marriage of the king's son (22:1–13), the ten virgins (25:1–13), and the talents (25:14–30) are exclusively Matthaean.

Only three miracles are peculiar to Matthew: the two blind men (9:27–31), the dumb demoniac (9:32–33), and the coin in the fish's mouth (17:24–27). Matthew's use of miracles seems to be directed more to their use as proofs of Jesus' Messianic power than to the advancement of a narrative even though he duplicates many that appear in Mark and Luke.

Matthew's Gospel is didactic in emphasis. It contains the largest single block of discourse material found in the Gospels (chaps. 5, 6, and 7), as well as other long passages (chaps. 10, 13, 18, 23, 24, 25) that reproduce Jesus' teaching. These discourses comprise about three-fifths of the entire Gospel. Matthew evidently wanted to stress the content of Jesus' teaching as related to his person and to the law, in order that the full implications of the Messiah's coming might be clear.

In order to demonstrate the close tie-in of the career of Jesus with the Messianic promises, this Gospel makes much use of quotations from the Old Testament. There are at least sixty obvious examples, falling between 1:23 and 27:48. Most of them are drawn from Isaiah and the Psalms, yet the Old Testament as a whole is represented. Further, many of the passages include reference to "the fulfillment" of the words of the prophets. Jesus' career was more than a series of marvelous, historical events; it was "the fulfillment of the divine purpose in the promised Messiah."

CHARACTERS

Matthew lays less stress on the individual actors in his narrative than the other Synoptists do, nor does he introduce many whose names do not appear elsewhere. Joseph (1:18–25), Herod the Great (2:1–16), and the mother of James and John (20:20–21) are given more space than in Mark and Luke; but both Mark and Luke use character sketches more than does Matthew.

In general, the characters of Matthew's Gospel are identical with those of Mark, Luke, and John. John the Baptist, Mary (Jesus' mother), the twelve disciples, Caiaphas, the high priests, Pilate, Simon of Cyrene, Joseph of Arimathea, and many minor figures—all play their part in the narrative. They are, however, incidental to the teaching.

SPECIAL FEATURES

1. Matthew is the Gospel of Discourse.

In each of the sections is one long specimen of discourse, as the following table shows.

SECTION	DISCOURSE
I. The Prophecies Realized 1:1–4:11	Preaching of John 3:1–12
II. The Principles Announced 4:12–7:29	The Sermon on the Mount 5:1–7:29
III. The Power Revealed 8:1–11:1	The Commission 10:1–42
IV. The Program Explained 11:2–13:53	The Parables 13:1–52
V. The Purpose Declared 13:54–19:2	The Meaning of Forgiveness 18:1–35
VI. The Problems Presented 19:3–26:2	Denunciation and Prediction 23:1–25:46
VII. The Passion Accomplished 26:3–28:10	(No discourse: action)
VIII. Epilogue 28:11–20	The Great Commission 28:18–20

2. Matthew is the Gospel of the Church.

Matthew's Gospel is the only one in which the word "church" occurs (16:18; 18:17). Both of these passages were spoken by Christ, showing that he had a definite idea of the church as an institution to come. The very fact that these utterances of his are embodied in Matthew may indicate that it was written for a young and struggling church that needed encouragement and discipline.

Both passages in Matthew lay emphasis on the *authority* of the church—the former stressing its leadership, the latter the body as a whole. In particular, the context of 18:17 includes a pastoral tone—emphasizing the concern for a wayward member (i.e., "the lost sheep, 18:10–14) and an erring member (i.e., "If your brother sins against you," 18:15–20).

3. Matthew is the Gospel of the King.

Not only is the doctrine of the kingdom emphasized in Matthew, but through all of the Gospel the royalty of Christ is prominent. The genealogy in the first chapter follows the royal line of Judah. The alarm of Herod was caused because the birth of Jesus introduced a political rival. The entry into Jerusalem stresses his arrival as king, riding peacefully on an ass's colt (21:5, 7). In the eschatological discourse he predicts that he will sit "on the throne of his glory" (19:28; 25:31), an expression found in Matthew alone. The inscription over the cross, placed by Pilate, was "This is Jesus the King of the Jews" (27:37).

In keeping with the emphasis on a king stemming from David's line, Matthew contains nine references to Jesus as "the son of David" (a title found three times only in Mark and Luke respectively). As David had established Jerusalem as his capital, so in Matthew alone do we read of Jerusalem as "the holy city" and "the city of the great king" (5:35).

FOR FURTHER READING

Albright, W. F. and Mann, C. S. *Matthew: Introduction, Translation and Notes.* Garden City, N.Y.: Doubleday, 1971.

Broadus, John A. *Commentary on the Gospel of Matthew in The American Commentary.* Philadelphia: American Baptist Publication Society, 1886. Pp. li, 610. Good, popular commentary.

Gundry, Robert H. *Matthew: A Commentary on His Literary and Theological Art.* Grand Rapids, Mich.: Wm. B. Eerdmans Publishing Company, 1981. Pp. xviii, 652.

Kingsbury, Jack D. *Matthew.* Philadelphia: Fortress Press, 1977.

Lange, John Peter. *The Gospel According to Matthew.* Translated from the Third German Edition by Philip Schaff. Sixth Edition. Vol. I in *The Commentary on the Holy Scriptures.* New York: Charles Scribner & Company, 1867. Pp. xxii, 568. Very thorough.

Lenski, R. C. H. *The Interpretation of St. Matthew's Gospel.* Columbus, Ohio: The Wartburg Press, 1943. Pp. 1161.

McNeile, A. H. *Commentary on the Gospel According to Matthew.* New York: The Macmillan Company, 1915. Pp. 448.

Morgan, G. Campbell. *The Gospel According to Matthew.* New York: Fleming H. Revell Company, 1929. Pp. 321. Expository and doctrinal.

Plummer, Alfred. *An Exegetical Commentary on the Gospel According to St. Matthew.* Grand Rapids, Mich.: Wm. B. Eerdmans Publishing Company, 1953. Pp. xlvi, 451.

Robertson, A. T. *Commentary on the Gospel According to Matthew.* New York: The Macmillan Company, 1911. Pp. 294. Brief, and good for quick reference.

CHAPTER 9

THE GOSPEL OF MARK

ORIGIN

Of the author of this Gospel comparatively little is known. Nowhere does the book mention him by name; and relatively few passages give any hints concerning his interests and personality, to say nothing of his identity. Tradition identifies him as John Mark, the scion of a Christian family in Jerusalem, the assistant and understudy of Paul, Barnabas, and perhaps Peter. He was the son of Mary, a friend of the apostles, who is mentioned in Acts 12. The prayer meeting for the deliverance of Peter was held in her house, and it is possible that her home was the headquarters of the Christian leaders in Jerusalem. Evidently Peter sought it out as his first point of call after the deliverance from jail (Acts 12:12), which may indicate that he felt sure of finding his colleagues there at that time. It may have been in this house that the "upper room" was located where Jesus and the disciples ate the last supper, and where the pre-Pentecostal prayer meeting was held. If so, Mark was well acquainted with the leaders of the Christian movement almost from its inception.

The family from which Mark came was well-to-do, for his mother owned the house and kept slaves. Hayes suggests that he was "the spoiled son of a wealthy widow."[1] Barnabas, his cousin, was evidently a man of some property, for he sold a field, "and brought the money and laid it at the

---

1. Doremus A. Hayes, *The Synoptic Gospels and the Book of Acts* (New York: The Methodist Book Concern, n.d.), p. 105.

apostles' feet" (4:37). Their original home was probably Cyprus; at any rate, Barnabas came from there (4:36). Mark seems to have been brought up in an environment that combined piety and culture.

He was introduced to the ministry by his cousin Barnabas, who, after the visit to Jerusalem with Paul recorded in Acts 11:30, returned to Antioch, taking Mark with him (12:25). When Barnabas and Paul went on the first missionary journey, Mark went along as assistant or understudy (13:5). Mark stayed with them during their work in Cyprus, but when they left Cyprus for the mainland of Asia, he parted from them and returned to Jerusalem (13:13). The reason for this defection is not given, but the implication seems to be that either he did not feel called to this work or else that he suffered some emotional reaction. Perhaps he did not like Paul; perhaps he was not interested in the Gentile mission. The fact remains that he did not go on with the others.

After the return to Antioch and the subsequent Council of Jerusalem, Barnabas proposed that John Mark be taken on the next journey. Paul demurred because Mark "went not with them to the work" (15:37–39). The disagreement between them was so sharp that they severed connections. Barnabas took Mark and sailed to Cyprus, whereas Paul, with a new assistant, went on with the mission in Asia.

At this point, probably about the year A.D. 50, Mark disappears from the New Testament narrative and does not reappear for ten years. In the Epistle to the Colossians, however, Mark has again joined Paul's company at Rome, and the latter has recommended him to the Colossian church. At a somewhat later time, Paul characterized him as "useful to me for ministering" (II Tim. 4:11). The old disagreement must have been adjusted; Mark had evidently recovered himself in Paul's estimation. It is quite likely also that he was associated with Peter about the same time (I Pet. 5:13). Unquestionably he had been in the church from its very beginning and had been connected with its active witness from Jerusalem to Rome in the years between A.D. 30 and 65. Tradition, preserved by Eusebius, says that he founded the churches of Alexandria.[2]

DATE AND PLACE

The earliest witnesses to the Gospel of Mark generally connect it with the preaching of Peter in Rome in the seventh decade of the Christian era. Papias (c. A.D. 115), as quoted by Eusebius (A.D. 375),[3] said:

> And John the Presbyter also said this—Mark being the interpreter of Peter, whatsoever he recorded he wrote with great accuracy, but not,

---

2. Eusebius *Historia Ecclesiae* II.16.
3. *Ibid.* III.39.

however, in the order in which it was spoken or done by our Lord, for he neither heard nor followed our Lord, but as before said, he was in company with Peter, who gave him such instruction as was necessary, but not to give a history of our Lord's discourses: wherefore Mark has not erred in anything, by writing some things as he has recorded them; for he was carefully attentive to one thing, not to pass by anything he heard, or to state anything falsely in these accounts.

Eusebius[4] also quoted Clement of Alexandria (c. A.D. 180) to the effect that Peter's hearers urged Mark to leave a record of the doctrine which Peter had communicated orally, and that Peter authorized the Gospel to be read in churches. Origen, Clement's successor (c. A.D. 225), is alleged to have said that Mark wrote his Gospel as Peter explained it to him.[5] Irenaeus confirmed this tradition by saying that "after the death of Peter and Paul, Mark delivered to us in writing things preached by Peter."[6]

The reliability of these traditions may be open to question since they do not come directly from the first century, but it is noteworthy that they agree on the Markan authorship for the Second Gospel and that they all connect it with the preaching of Peter. The traditions disagree concerning the relation of the Gospel to the lifetime of Peter. The Anti-Marcionite Prologue to Mark and Irenaeus (both dated c. A.D. 180) agree that the Gospel was written after the death of Peter, presumably between A.D. 65 and 68, whereas Clement and Origen indicate that it was perfected during Peter's lifetime and authorized by him. There can be no doubt that this Gospel was produced by a man who knew some of the apostolic band and who had long and direct contact with their preaching.

From the foregoing facts certain deductions may be drawn:

1. Mark was brought up in the religious atmosphere of Judaism.

2. He may have been an eyewitness of some of the facts recorded in the Gospel that bears his name.

3. He was a close associate of the apostolic leaders of the early church, and would have been fully acquainted with their preaching about Jesus, and with the "good news" they propagated.

4. He himself had been a participant in the work of preaching, and had witnessed the beginning of the Gentile mission.

To these facts may be added one or two from a consideration of the Gospel:

1. The author stressed facts rather than themes or topics.

2. Possibly he was a witness of the arrest of Jesus in the garden. In Mark

---

4. *Ibid.* II. 15.
5. *Ibid.* VI. 25.
6. Irenaeus *Against Heresies* III. i. 1.

14:51–52 a young man is mentioned who had followed along with Jesus. No hint of his identity is given, nor is his place in the sequence clear. As far as the narrative is concerned, the omission of any reference to him would not break its continuity. It is difficult to resist the temptation to see here a personal reminiscence of an experience vivid to the author, but not significant to the main thread of the tale. Neither of the other Synoptics records this. If this does refer to Mark, then he was an eyewitness of the last hours of Jesus' life, and it is quite likely that posterity owes much of the records of those hours to him.

3. Again, in Mark 15:21 there is a reference to Simon the Cyrenian, "the father of Alexander and Rufus." These two men have no part in the story; they are mentioned only here. Why? Probably because they were known to the author and to his readers as personal acquaintances. If so, the date of the Gospel must be set within a generation of the cross, even if it is assumed that these men were children when the crucifixion occurred.

4. Another interesting fact emerges from a comparison of Peter's speech in Acts 10:34–43 with this Gospel. Eusebius asserts that Mark was Peter's assistant for a time, and there is some confirmation of it in I Peter 5:13. It is noteworthy that the sermon as recorded in Acts accords closely with the outline of the content of Mark. Did Mark, as tradition asserts he did, record in his Gospel the oral preaching of Peter?

From these considerations it may be concluded that this Gospel is the product of one of the junior preachers of the apostolic age, who was thoroughly acquainted with the message concerning Jesus and who recorded it as he heard it, without elaboration or embellishments of any kind. He made no attempt at a biographical interpretation; he merely allowed the facts themselves to speak for him. If it was written toward the end of his career, his own experience would have deepened and enriched his presentation of the message concerning Christ.

The foregoing discussion of the author has already covered much of the existing evidence concerning the date of the Gospel. It can scarcely have been later than A.D. 70 and may have been composed considerably earlier, if by "composed" is meant the collection and use of material in it, but not necessarily its publication. The close accord of Mark with Matthew and Luke, in which Gospels most of the material in Mark can be found, has led many to believe that Matthew and Luke used Mark as a source of information and that the written document must have antedated the other two Gospels. Such a conclusion would compel one to believe either that Mark was early, or that the others were late. If, however, these Gospels are three different written presentations of the apostolic message concerning the Lord Jesus Christ as inspired by the Holy Spirit, drawn from the common material that the apostles and their associates preached, there is a good possibility that they may have been produced simultaneously. For a further discussion of the subject, see the section on the Synoptic Problem in Chapter 7.

If a date in the sixties of the first century A.D. is granted, the life situation that occasioned this Gospel appears fairly clear. A crisis arose in the city of Rome that affected the Christian community there, namely, the persecution under Nero in A.D. 64. The vicious and irresponsible behavior of the Emperor, well attested by Tacitus (*Annals* XV.36–38), brought a threat on the Christians there. Well could the emphasis on the sufferings of Christ, beginning with "and he was with the wild beasts" (Mark 1:13), be appreciated by his followers. He who was to suffer and be killed (Mark 8:31; 9:31; 10:33–34) became a model for his disciples.

The Gospel of Mark is terse, clear, and pointed, a style that would appeal to the Roman mind, which was impatient of abstractions and literary inbreeding. There are many Latinisms in Mark, such as *modius* for "bushel" (4:21), *census* for "tribute" (12:14), *speculator* for "executioner" (6:27, A.V.), and *centurio* for "centurion" (15:39, 44, 45). For most of these there were Greek equivalents. Mark apparently used the Latin terms because they were more common or more familiar. The Gospel contains little emphasis on Jewish law and customs. When they are mentioned they are explained more fully than in the other Synoptics. The internal evidence of the Gospel fits fairly well the external tradition that the place of publication may have been Rome. At any rate, Mark was intended for the unevangelized layman of practical Roman mentality.

CONTENT

The Gospel of Mark is a historical narrative that sets forth a representative picture of the person and work of the Lord Jesus Christ. It is not primarily a biography, for it does not discuss the parentage, the early environment, the birth, the education, or the family of its principal character, nor does it attempt to furnish information about any particular phase of his life. It gives in close succession, probably in general chronological order, a series of episodes in Christ's career, with some detail concerning the last week that he spent on earth. It is almost entirely objective in its approach. Little comment is offered; the narrative tells its own story. If the last twelve verses of the Gospel, which are widely regarded as non-Markan because they do not appear in the text of the oldest manuscripts, are detached, the Gospel ends with singular abruptness. It is brief, pictorial, curt, clear-cut, and forceful. Like a snapshot album devoted to one person, it gives a series of characteristic poses of Jesus without attempting close continuity between them. Nevertheless Mark affords a satisfactory understanding of his person

Illuminated manuscript of the Gospel of Mark.

and work when the total impression of these individual episodes is put together.

The subject of the Gospel is adequately summed up in the opening verse, "The beginning of the gospel of Jesus Christ, the Son of God."[7] Whether the words are an ancient heading given to the Gospel, or whether they are the one chosen by the writer, they are an appropriate introduction to its content. The person of Christ dominates the narrative throughout its course. His works are the chief source of interest, and his death and resurrection in Jerusalem bring the story to a thrilling climax.

No attempt is made to hide or to exaggerate the supernatural element in his life. The miracles are almost always connected with some definite human need and are performed for the relief of some emergency, not for mere exhibitionism. There is a steady calm progress on the part of Jesus to the goal set for himself, and there is more than a hint of the surprising denouement in the resurrection (8:31; 9:31; 10:34). At the end the reader is left to make his own decision concerning the personality who is portrayed as man, and yet as more than man.

---

7. The words "the Son of God," which appear in the text of the A.R.V., are omitted from Nestle's Greek text and from that of Westcott and Hort, notwithstanding the united support of manuscripts B and D.

OUTLINE

An outline of Mark is difficult to construct because of the impressionistic character of the Gospel. For his effect on the reader the author apparently relied more on the total impact of the Gospel than he did on the climactic sequence of sections. The following, however, will afford a fair guide to the structure of the book.

MARK: THE GOSPEL OF THE SON OF GOD		Mark 1:1
(Topical Outline)	(Place)	
I. The Preparation		1:2–13
The Forerunner	Nazareth	1:2–8
The Baptism	to	1:9–11
The Temptation	Wilderness	1:12–13
II. The Opening		1:14–5:43
Ministry:		
Credentials		
Introduction:		
Works	Galilee	1:14–2:12
Continuation in		
Galilee:		
Teaching		2:13–4:34
Further Ministry:		
Authority	Decapolis	4:35–5:43
III. The Full Ministry:		
Conflict		6:1–8:26
Unbelief	Nazareth	6:1–6
Political Danger		6:7–29
Popular Acclaim		
(Retirement)	Desert	6:30–56
Traditionalism		7:1–23
Sensationalism		
(Retirement)	Tyre, Sidon,	
	Decapolis	7:24–8:26
IV. The Closing		
Ministry:		
Challenge		8:27–10:31
Revelation to		
Disciples		
(Retirement)	Caesarea Philippi	8:27–9:50
Challenge to Public	Judea and Perea	10:1–31

V. The Last Journey:		
Cross		10:32–13:37
(Topical Outline)	(Place)	
Teaching the	En Route to	
Disciples	Jerusalem	10:32–45
Healing the Sick	Jericho	10:46–52
Triumphal Entry	Jerusalem	11:1–11
Ministry in Jerusalem		11:12–12:44
Apocalyptic		
Prediction		13:1–37
VI. The Passion:		
Catastrophe		14:1–15:47
The Plot		14:1–2, 10–11
The Interlude at	Bethany	14:3–9
Bethany		
The Last Supper	Jerusalem	14:12–26
Gethsemane		14:27–52
The Trial Before		
Caiaphas		14:53–65
The Denial by Peter		14:66–72
The Hearing Before		
Pilate		15:1–20
The Crucifixion		15:21–41
The Burial		15:42–47
VII. The Resurrection:		
Commencement		16:1–8
Postscript		16:9–20

The foregoing outline is given in somewhat more detailed fashion than that of Matthew for the purpose of correlating several elements in the structure of Mark. Unlike Matthew, which follows chiefly the theme of the Messiah, Mark is concerned with the activity of Jesus as the Son of God, who is also the Servant of God. The basic outline is built on the changes in the geographical localities of his ministry. This Gospel says little about any ministry in Jerusalem prior to the Passion, although Jesus must have been there several times before his last visit. Not until he came to the crisis of his ministry did he remove from Galilee and the Decapolis. The trips to Tyre and Sidon, or to Caesarea Philippi, were attempts to withdraw from the tumult and conflict that attended his public ministry, in order that he might have opportunity to pray and to think alone, and to instruct his disciples in the truths that they perceived only too dimly.

The outline also shows a progression in the thought of Mark. The Greek word *euthys* or *eutheōs,* translated "straightway," "immediately," "forthwith," "anon," is used forty-two times, more times than in all the rest of the New Testament. It conveys the impression that however varied and detailed Jesus' ministry may have been, he was hurrying toward some unseen goal that he envisioned, but that was hidden to most of his contemporaries and only faintly perceived by the disciples at those rare intervals when his words illumined their understanding.

The outline attempts to classify the material in Mark. The first section (1:2–13) may be called an introduction, but is more properly an abbreviated account of the preparation of Jesus for his great work. Mark's treatment of this period of Jesus' life is much briefer than that of Matthew and Luke. There is no genealogy, the preaching of John is stated in its bare elements, and the temptation is not narrated in detail. The entire section deals with the credentials of Jesus, for he was endorsed by John, was anointed by the Holy Spirit, and was tested in the wilderness.

The second section (1:14–5:43) gives the initial impression of being simply a miscellany of representative events. Actually it contains a series of demonstrations of Jesus' authority. The miracle of the man sick with the palsy (2:1–12), which stands at the end of a list of healings, illustrated Jesus' power to forgive sins. The debate with the Pharisees over picking grain on the Sabbath (2:23–28), coupled with the healing of the man with a withered hand (3:1–6), established the principle of Jesus' lordship of the Sabbath. His authority over demons is mentioned in several passages (3:11, 20–30; 5:1–20). The storm on the Lake of Galilee revealed his power over the elements of nature (4:35–41). The raising of Jairus' daughter demonstrated his power over death (5:21–24, 35–43). Along with these proofs of Jesus' superiority Mark records much of his teaching, but the chief stress in the first part of his narrative is on the right of Jesus to speak and act as the Son of God and Son of man.

The third section (6:1–8:26) continues the teachings and miracles of the second, but gives a much larger place to the element of conflict. The unbelief of his fellow townsmen (6:6), the political pressure of Herod who had executed John the Baptist and might consequently look on Jesus with suspicion (6:27–29), the danger of popularity that could easily subvert his divine mission into demagoguery, and the traditionalism of the Pharisees (7:1–23) created pressures that Jesus had to resist. Finally, after one futile attempt to withdraw from the importunate crowds (6:31–34), he retired to Tyre and Sidon, Gentile territory where he would not be so well known (7:24). Even there he was asked for assistance. This section on the full ministry brings out the lights and shadows of Jesus' work. His compassion on the multitude, his readiness to minister to the needy, his wisdom in answering questions are contrasted with the unthinking greediness of the crowds.

The fourth section (8:27–10:31) commences with Jesus' retirement to

Caesarea Philippi. Mark, like the other Synoptics, treats this as the pivotal point of Jesus' career. Jesus challenged his disciples to make a personal confession of faith in him (8:27). He disclosed to them for the first time the necessity of his death, and then, in the transfiguration scene, revealed to them his real glory. Over and over again[8] he taught them that he must die and rise again, "but they understood not the saying, and were afraid to ask him" (9:32).

Section 5 enlarges on the consequences of this turn in Jesus' affairs by treating the final journey to the cross. In the teaching that Jesus gave to the disciples (10:32–40), in the healing of Bartimaeus, who was singled out by being named personally (10:46–52), and in the popular presentation of the dramatic entry into the city (11:1–10), he showed his attitude of service toward God and man. In the controversy with the various religious groups and in the apocalyptic discourse spoken to the disciples on the Mount of Olives, Jesus laid down the principles of thought and predictions for the future that explained more perfectly the outcome of his mission. He emphasized particularly the divine viewpoint of human life, culminating in his return at the close of the age. The tragedy of the cross is not minimized by Mark; but even before he recounts the events of the Passion, he indicates that Jesus would surmount triumphantly the apparent disaster that confronted him.

The section on the Passion (14:1–15:47) does not vary greatly in its essential facts from the story told in the other Gospels. The last few days of Jesus' life are given in closer chronological sequence than any other period of equal length in his life. Certainly it was the most vivid period and the most important. Mark's plain factual style enhances the value of the narrative and makes one ask why so marvelous a person, with such tremendous authority, should have come to so untimely an end.

Two answers to this question are given in the Gospel itself. One is the declaration of Jesus in Mark 10:45:

For the Son of man also came not to be ministered unto, but to minister, and to give his life a ransom for many.

The tragedy of the Gospel was an inevitable part of his service to men and of his redemption of them. The other answer is contained in the last section on the resurrection (16:1–8 [20]). The discovery of the empty tomb was proof that something had happened in Joseph's garden that could not be explained on any purely naturalistic basis. The positive testimony of the angel and the sudden terror of the women prove that the unexpected had happened and that Jesus had really risen.

The genuineness of the last twelve verses of Mark has been disputed on

---

8. Mark 9:31, *edidaskon,* imperfect tense.

textual grounds, for several of the oldest and most generally reliable manuscripts omit them entirely. Several endings are in existence, though the one that is familiar is the best of all of them. In any case, it represents an account that can be traced back to the end of the second century, and it bears strong affinities to the other accounts of the resurrection, so that there is good reason for believing that it contains authentic information. If Mark himself wrote it, he probably added it as an epilogue, since it begins with a resumé of what he has already stated in the first eight verses. It stresses the disbelief of the disciples (16:11, 13, 14, 16), as if to say that even after the crowning demonstration of Jesus' authority over death many were still incredulous and needed an added exhortation to faith.

EMPHASIS

As noted already, Mark is a Gospel of action. It has no prologue, except for the title. Direct citations from the Old Testament for purposes of prophetic interpretation are very few, although there are numerous quotations and allusions. Of seventy parables and parabolic utterances in the Gospels, Mark has only eighteen, though some of them comprise only a sentence apiece. For its size, however, Mark gives more space to the miracles than does any other Gospel; for it records eighteen out of a possible total of thirty-five. Luke, for instance, in ninety-one pages of Greek text narrates only twenty miracles, whereas the eighteen of Mark are included in fifty-three pages of the same text. Plainly, Mark was more interested in deeds than in speculation.

Mark is a Gospel of personal reactions. All through its pages are recorded the responses of Jesus' audience. They were "amazed" (1:27), critical (2:7), afraid (4:41), puzzled (6:14), "astonished" (7:37), bitterly hostile (14:1). There are at least twenty-three such references. The narrative presents its own appeal, and in the reflection of the popular mind one can see the evaluation of modern attitudes to Jesus. Besides these incidental notes of popular response are many recorded interviews of Jesus, and even observations of his personal gestures (3:5; 5:41; 7:33; 8:23; 9:27; 10:16).

All of these touches and others make Mark the Gospel of vividness. There are one hundred fifty-one uses of the historic present tense of the verb in Mark and many uses of the imperfect tense, both of which portray action as in process rather than simply as an event. Vivid phrases occur frequently: "The Spirit *driveth* him forth into the wilderness" (1:12); "when they had *broken it up* [the roof]" (2:4); "the unclean spirits . . . *fell down* before him" (3:11); "the waves beat into the boat, insomuch that the boat *was now filling*" (4:37); "he commanded them that all should sit down by companies *upon the green grass*" (6:39). The italicized phrases are a few samples taken at random from the text to illustrate the vigor and freshness of the Markan style—a style that shows unquestionably the oral testimony of an eyewitness who was telling exactly what he saw as it affected him and others.

The purpose of this Gospel seems to be primarily evangelistic. It is an attempt to bring the person and work of Christ before the public as a new message, "the gospel," without assuming much knowledge of theology or of Old Testament teaching on the part of the hearer. Its brief anecdotes, its epigrammatic sentences, its pointed applications of truth are just what a street preacher would use in telling of Christ to a promiscuous crowd. Although the Gospel is not primarily literary in style, it is integrated by the person of whom it speaks, and it gives a picture of Christ that is factual and inescapable.

CHARACTERS

Mark does not specialize in character sketches, although many of the personalities in his pages are etched more sharply than are those in Matthew. The young man in the garden who escaped from the soldiers (14:51–52), Alexander and Rufus (15:21), and Simon the leper (14:3) are mentioned as acquaintances of the author, and possibly of the readers. The allusion to Alexander and Rufus is particularly intriguing, for it implies that Mark's readers knew these men and were their contemporaries. If Rufus is identical with the man mentioned in Romans 16:13, the dating of Mark somewhere between A.D. 56 and 66 and its origin at Rome might be confirmed. Mark, however, does not mention as many persons as does Luke, nor does he use them as patterns to the same extent that Luke and John do. He seems to have been more interested in the progress of his story than in the analysis of individual characters. The naming of these persons suggests that later they may have become celebrities in the Christian community prior to the writing of this Gospel.

FOR FURTHER READING

Achtemeier, Paul J. Mark. Philadelphia: Fortress Press, 1975.

Anderson, Hugh. The Gospel of Mark. Grand Rapids: Wm. B. Eerdmans Publishing Company, 1981.

Earle, Ralph. The Gospel According to Mark in The Evangelical Commentary. Grand Rapids, Mich.: Zondervan Publishing House, 1957. Pp. 192.

Lane, William L. The Gospel According to Mark: The English Text with Introduction, Exposition, and Notes. Grand Rapids: Wm. B. Eerdmans Publishing Company, 1974.

Lenski, R. C. H. *The Interpretation of St. Mark.* Columbus, Ohio: The Wartburg Press, 1946. Pp. 775.

Lindsay, Thomas M. *The Gospel According to St. Mark* in *Handbooks for Bible Classes.* Edinburgh: T. & T. Clark, n.d. Pp. 1–272. Good, brief handbook, now somewhat out of date.

Martin, Ralph P. *Mark: Evangelist and Theologian.* Grand Rapids, Mich.: Zondervan Publishing House, 1973.

Morgan, G. Campbell. *The Gospel According to Mark.* New York: Fleming H. Revell Company, 1927. Pp. 350.

Robertson, A. T. *Making Good in the Ministry.* New York: Fleming H. Revell Company, n.d. Pp. 1–174. Deals with Mark's biography.

———. *Studies in Mark's Gospel.* New York: The Macmillan Company, 1919. Pp. 146. A series of lectures on special aspects of Mark.

Swete, H. B. *The Gospel According to St. Mark.* Third Edition. Grand Rapids, Mich.: Wm. B. Eerdmans Publishing Company, 1951. Pp. cxix, 434. Greek text.

Taylor, Vincent. *The Gospel According to St. Mark.* London: Macmillan & Company, Ltd., 1952. Pp. xx, 696.

CHAPTER 10

THE GOSPEL OF LUKE

ORIGIN

OF the three Synoptic Gospels Luke affords the greatest amount of information concerning its own beginning. Its author, who does not give his own name, supplied a literary introduction stating his aims in writing it, the methods that he employed, and his relationships to his contemporaries who had attempted the same thing. This introduction (Luke 1:1–4) is the key to the book, and to the book of Acts also, if Luke-Acts is regarded as a unit.

From the introduction a number of inferences may be drawn:

1. In the time of the writer a number of works were extant that contained only a partial, or possibly a garbled account of Jesus' life and work. The author would not have written a Gospel of his own had he been perfectly satisfied with any of those that he knew.

2. These accounts had attempted some systematic arrangement of available facts ("to draw up a narrative"—1:1).

3. These facts were well known to the Christian world and were accepted independently of the narratives. Luke says that they "have been fulfilled among us" (1:1).

4. The author felt himself at least as well informed as the others and as capable of writing an account on his own responsibility ("it seemed good to me also").

5. His information came from competent official sources ("who from the beginning were eyewitnesses and ministers of the word"—1:2).

6. He was conversant with the facts, either by observation or by

inquiry, and he was certainly a contemporary of the main course of action in the sense that he lived in the generation of those who had witnessed it. The term translated "having traced the course of all things"[1] is the same as the one used in II Timothy 3:10–11, where Paul said that Timothy had "followed" his "teaching, conduct . . . what things befell me at Antioch, at Iconium, at Lystra." The language does not imply that Timothy was present with Paul at every occasion in these cities, but it does indicate that he was a contemporary of Paul and that he had some firsthand knowledge of these affairs.

The word *anōthen*, translated "from the first" in the A.R.V., has been a source of some controversy. As used in the Johannine writings and in James (1:17) it means almost invariably "from above." It is used only twice by Luke, here and in Acts 26:5. In the latter passage, which is a speech of Paul, it cannot possibly mean "from above," but must mean "beforehand," "from some time back." Knowling says that Paul was referring to the beginning of his public education in Jerusalem.[2] Singularly enough, the only use of the word in the Pauline epistles (Gal. 4:9) means "back again," a reference to former time. While it could be rendered "from above" in Luke 1:3, such a translation is not necessitated by the context, and certainly would not be uniform with other Lukan and Pauline language.

The translation of an ambiguous term is always best determined by the current usage of the author; and since the rendering of the A.R.V. is in accord with that usage, it is retained here.

On this basis it may be understood that the author is claiming a contemporary knowledge of facts that was not acquired recently. His knowledge of Christ went back over a number of years of his life, during which he had associated with apostles, eyewitnesses, and possibly with personal friends or relatives of the Lord Jesus. The urge of the Holy Spirit that made him an author controlled the choice of incidents that he recorded and the language in which he wrote them.

7. Luke's knowledge covered all of the major facts. His Gospel contains many particulars that do not appear in the others and is the most generally representative life of Christ.

8. He professed to write accurately and in logical order. His use of the term "in order" does not necessarily presuppose chronological order, but it does mean that he had a definite plan of procedure and that he intended to adhere to it.

---

1. Greek *parēkolouthēkoti.*
2. R. J. Knowling in *Expositor's Greek Testament* (New York: George H. Doran Company, n.d.), II, 501. On the word *anōthen*, and the Prologue as a whole, see I. H. Marshall, *The Gospel of Luke: A Commentary on the Greek Text* (Grand Rapids: Wm. B. Eerdmans Publishing Company, 1978), pp. 39–44; J. A. Fitzmyer, *The Gospel According to Luke I–IX* (Garden City, N.Y.: Doubleday, 1981), pp. 287–302.

9. Luke's addressee was probably a man of the upper class who may be called here by his baptismal name, Theophilus, which meant literally "lover of God" or "loved by God." The epithet "most excellent"[3] was generally applied only to officials or to members of the aristocracy. Perhaps he was a convert of Luke, or a patron who assumed responsibility for circulating Luke's works.

10. This addressee had already been informed orally concerning Christ, perhaps through the preaching that he had heard, but he needed further instruction to stabilize him and convince him of the truth.

11. Luke's obvious purpose was to give to his friend complete knowledge of the truth.

From the foregoing deductions one may conclude that the author was a man who possessed literary gifts and knew how to make use of them in presenting the message of Christ. Who was he?

AUTHOR

The identity of the author depends on the relation of the Third Gospel to the book of Acts. If Luke and Acts were written by the same person, one can apply to Luke such evidence concerning the author as may be internal to Acts, and vice versa. In Acts the author was undoubtedly a participant in many of the events that he described, for he frequently used the pronoun "we." The "we" sections have become a useful guide for determining the interests, character, and possible identity of the writer.

The first of these is found in Codex Bezae (D), a manuscript of the sixth century, whose readings are often exceptional, as is this one. It is located in Acts 11:28, and reads:

> And there was great rejoicing, and when we gathered together, one of their number, named Agabus, spoke, indicating that a great famine was about to take place over the whole world. . . .

Since this reading occurs only in Codex Bezae it is generally rejected; but if it is genuine, it makes the writer a member of the early church at Antioch during the ministry of Barnabas and Saul.

The first generally accepted reference begins with Acts 16:10, at Paul's departure from Troas on his second missionary journey. The writer accompanied him from Troas to Philippi, where the references to the first person plural cease with the discussion of Paul's imprisonment (16:17, 19–34). Probably the writer was present at Philippi but was not arrested. The "we" sections reappear at Paul's return to Macedonia as recorded in Acts 20:6ff.

---

3. Greek *kratiste*. See Acts 23:26; 24:3; 26:25.

From this point the "we" sections remain throughout the book, although the writer does not seem to be in evidence during the imprisonment of Paul at Caesarea. Nevertheless, he accompanied Paul on the voyage to Rome (27:1ff.) and stayed with him until the end of the story.

The relation of Luke to Acts is close. Both documents are addressed to the same person, Theophilus. The introduction to Acts dovetails exactly with the content of Luke when it says that "the former treatise" concerned "all that Jesus began both to do and to teach" (Acts 1:1). The stress on the resurrection and the teaching ministry of the forty days accords well with the content of Luke 24. The emphasis in Acts on the place of the Holy Spirit is exactly like that of the Gospel. Harnack has shown that in vocabulary and in style there is a close agreement between the two narratives.[4] The argument is too long and complicated to be reproduced here, but the case for the unity of Luke-Acts seems to be fairly established. Such facts, then, as are true of the writer of Acts will be equally true of the writer of Luke, and may legitimately be used to fix his identity.

Accordingly, the author of Luke-Acts may have been an Antiochian Gentile, converted in Antioch not more than fifteen years after Pentecost. He became a friend and associate of Paul and traveled with him on the second journey after meeting him at Troas (Acts 16:10). He remained at Philippi as pastor of the church while Paul pursued his itinerant ministry in Achaia and, after a visit to Antioch (18:22), in Asia Minor (19:1–41). When Paul returned to Philippi on the third journey, the author again joined his company (20:6). He went with him to the mainland of Asia, and thence accompanied him to Jerusalem.

The four years of Paul's imprisonment give no reference to the writer's activities during that time, but at the close of the period he accompanied Paul to Rome, where Paul was about to stand trial before Caesar.

This man, whose diary forms the best source of knowledge about Paul's missionary travels, must have been a close associate of the great apostle. Of the known traveling companions of this period, none fits the requirements except Luke. Identification is established chiefly by process of elimination. The writer was not Timothy, nor any of those mentioned in Acts 20:4–6, for obviously the writer and Paul did not accompany these on their trip from Philippi to Troas, but went later. If the lists of associates in Colossians (4:7–17) and Philemon (23–24) are used, Aristarchus can be eliminated as one of the list in Acts 20; Mark is not the writer, since in Acts he is mentioned in the third person; Epaphras' field of labor was not Philippi, but the cities of Asia Minor; Demas ended his course in disgrace (II Tim.

---

4. Adolph Harnack, *Luke the Physician* (Translated by J. R. Wilkinson. *Crown Theological Library.* London: Williams and Norgate; New York: G. P. Putnam's Sons, 1907).

4:10); Jesus Justus evidently was Jewish by ancestry, whereas the writer of Acts was not. Only Luke remains as a possibility.

Internal evidence has some bearing on this conclusion. The author possessed high literary ability and was probably well educated. His language shows a definite Greek turn of mind. For instance, his use of the word "barbarians" in Acts 28:2 does not imply that the inhabitants of Malta were crude savages, but it means only that they were not a Greek-speaking people. He was a keen observer, for the twenty-seventh chapter of Acts gives the best account of ancient shipping that has come down from antiquity. A comparison of Mark 5:25–26 with Luke 8:43 shows that he had some interest in a physician's viewpoint, which would confirm the title given to Luke in Colossians 4:14: "Luke, the beloved physician."

External tradition supports the conclusion that Luke, the physician and the friend of Paul, was the writer of the Third Gospel. Justin Martyr of the second century used this Gospel.[5] Tatian employed it in the Diatessaron. Marcion included a revised form of it in his canon; and from the end of the second century onward it was widely quoted as Lukan. Tertullian alone quoted or alluded to the Lukan text more than five hundred times.

Since the identity of the author is reasonably well established, some notice should be taken of his character and achievements.

Briefly, he was a Greek-speaking Gentile by birth, who had received a good education and possessed considerable intellectual ability. He was probably one of the early converts of the first mission in Antioch. Nothing is known directly of his life until he met Paul at Troas, about A.D. 51. From Troas he went with Paul to Macedonia, where he became pastor of the Philippian church that was distinguished for its zeal and for its loyalty to its founder. Perhaps the "brother" mentioned in II Corinthians 8:22 is a reference to Luke. He may have been a blood-brother of Titus, who was himself connected with Antioch at an early date (Gal. 2:3). Corinthians suggests that this "brother" was of good repute in Achaia and that he was noted for his fame in the gospel. If the reference concerns Luke, he may have acted as Paul's representative all through Macedonia and Achaia while making headquarters at Philippi.

When Paul returned to Philippi on his third journey, Luke rejoined him and went with him to Palestine. During Paul's stay in Jerusalem and the imprisonment in Caesarea no mention is made of Luke; but he cannot have been far away, for he shared the journey to Rome and wrote the record of the shipwreck (Acts 27). He is mentioned in the Prison Epistles (Col. 4:14; Philem. 24), where he is classed among the "fellow workers." From this point the data are extremely fragmentary and uncertain. He seems to

---

5. Cf. Luke 22:44 with Justin Martyr *Dialogue with Trypho* CIII.

have been with Paul during the last imprisonment immediately preceding his death (II Tim. 4:11).

Luke was no mere spectator, viewing Christian truth from outside, but an active preacher and missionary himself. He was the first great church historian and literary apologist for Christianity. Since he was an associate of Paul his work might be expected to reflect the knowledge of Christ that was used in the preaching to the Gentiles.

DATE AND PLACE

Two termini fix within limits the time of the writing of Luke: it must have been written before Acts, and after the development of Christianity to the point where it would attract the attention of a Gentile inquirer like Theophilus. Acts was probably composed prior to the close of Paul's first imprisonment at Rome, since the abrupt ending of the book intimates that the author had no more to say. The Gospel was, of course, written after the close of the life of Jesus, and its prologue shows that already many others had attempted to write Gospels concerning the facts that were believed by a fairly extensive Christian community. Perhaps A.D. 60 would serve as a median date, for by that time Luke would have been a Christian at least ten years or more, and would have traveled in Palestine, where he could have met many of those who had known Jesus in the flesh. He may have occupied the time while Paul was in prison by investigating the background of the life of Jesus, concerning whom he had heard so much and for whom he himself had been a missionary.

Later datings have been assigned to Luke's Gospel on the ground of its alleged use of Mark, but the literary similarities between the Gospels can be explained on the basis of the common element of evangelistic preaching concerning Christ that was current in the apostolic church. Luke and Mark may have had personal contact at Antioch when John Mark first went there in the company of Barnabas and Saul. Although the date of A.D. 60 cannot be fixed dogmatically, it is as satisfactory as any later date would be.

No clue is given in this Gospel concerning its place of writing. Probably it was written outside of Palestine, though it may have been composed at Caesarea. Most suggestions, including Rome, Caesarea, Achaia, Asia Minor, and Alexandria, are mere guesses. There is not even any good early tradition relating to the place of its origin. All that can be said is that it was written somewhere in the Hellenistic world by a man who worked among Gentiles.

CONTENT

In general organization the Gospel of Luke follows the main sequence of events as given in Matthew and Mark, with many unique additions. The accounts of the birth of John the Baptist (1:5–25, 57–80) and of the birth and childhood of Jesus (1:26–56; 2:1–52), the genealogy (3:23–38), the preaching at Nazareth (4:16–30), the special summons to Peter (5:8–10), six miracles (5:1–11; 7:11–17; 13:10–17; 14:1–6; 17:11–19; 22:49–51), nineteen parables (7:41–43; 10:30–37; 11:5–8; 12:13–21; 12:35–40; 12:41–48; 13:6–9; 14:7–11; 14:16–24; 14:28–30; 14:31–32; 15:8–10; 15:11–32; 16:1–13; 16:19–31; 17:7–10; 18:1–8; 18:9–14; 19:11–27), the story of the encounter with Zacchaeus (19:1–10), the mocking of Jesus by Herod (23:8–12), and the postresurrection appearance of Jesus on the road to Emmaus (24:13–35) are all major additions in Luke's Gospel. The many other features peculiar to Luke are too detailed and numerous to catalog.

OUTLINE

The material of Luke is organized around the central concept of Jesus as a member of humanity who lived the perfect and representative life of the Son of man through the power of the Holy Spirit. The development of this concept is rooted in Luke 2:11, where the child was announced as "a Savior, who is Christ the Lord." The first of these titles speaks of his mission; the second and third identify him as the Messiah of Judaism.

The Mount of Olives.

Luke: The Gospel of the Savior of Men

The initial statement of Luke's preface declares that the Gospel was written to impart to its reader spiritual certainty concerning the things of which he had been orally instructed. The verb "instructed"[6] is generally used in the New Testament of information that is imparted formally rather than casually. Evidently Luke wanted to give Theophilus an authentic basis in this Gospel for correcting the teaching with which he was already familiar.

On this assumption one may conclude that Luke took special care to present all of his facts accurately, as indeed he says (1:3), and that he would organize them into some framework that would leave an integrated impression on the mind of the reader.

The section on the preparation of the Savior contains material that is not duplicated in the other Gospels. Matthew states that Jesus was born of a virgin, but he tells the story from the viewpoint of Joseph, whereas Luke tells it from the viewpoint of Mary. Nothing concerning the birth of John the Baptist can be found in Matthew or Mark.

The third section, the introduction of Jesus to his full ministry, opened with a direct connection with history, as if to show that he was not an idealized religious figure, but a very real participant in the history of mankind who could be localized in time and space. The genealogy is traced from Adam, and emphasizes human descent rather than the royal line. The account of the temptation is closely akin to that of Matthew except in order. Luke calls attention to the fact that the devil had "completed every temptation" (4:13), as if he wished to indicate that Jesus met all the representative temptations of humanity.

In opening the fourth section on the ministry of the Savior, Luke records the sermon in Nazareth in which Jesus announced his relation to prophetic Scripture. He set the proclamation of "the acceptable year of the Lord" as the goal of his ministry. The subsequent biographical material is quite similar to that which is found at this point in the other Synoptics, though Luke has added many individual touches.

The fifth section is peculiarly Lukan. With the exception of occasional paragraphs, very little of the text between Luke 9:51 and 18:30 occurs in the other Gospels. The parables of the good Samaritan (10:28–37), the rich fool (12:13–21), the fruitless fig tree (13:6–9), the seats at the marriage feast (14:7–14), the great supper (14:15–24), the lost coin (15:8–10), the prodigal son (15:11–32), the unjust steward (16:1–13), the rich man and Lazarus (16:19–31), and the Pharisee and the publican (18:9–14) are found only in Luke. Although they seem at first reading to be a random collection of Jesus' parables, they are illustrative of the meaning of his

---

6. Greek *katecheō*. Cf. Acts 18:25; Rom. 2:18.

mission. Each parable or narrative is a specimen of Luke's use of fresh material from the life of Christ to explain his significance for Gentile readers.

Luke's narrative of the Passion contains no large single paragraphs that deviate greatly from the general pattern of the Synoptic narrative as a whole. The order of the last supper (22:19–23), Jesus' comfort of Simon Peter (22:31–32), the episode of the bloodlike sweat (22:43–44), the arrangement of events in the house of Caiaphas (22:63–71), the appearance of Jesus before Herod (23:4–16), Jesus' address to the women of Jerusalem (23:27–31), and the penitent thief (23:39–43) add to the pictorial quality of the story, but do not alter its progress or meaning. Luke stressed the human sufferings and sympathies of Jesus as he showed how the Son of man endured the cross in obedience to the Father.

The account of the resurrection is strikingly new and different. The reality is the same as in the other Gospels, but the appearance of Jesus to the two men on the way to Emmaus clinches the argument of this Gospel. The actuality of Jesus' death, the despair of the disciples, the unexpected and convincing manifestation of his living presence, his interpretation of the Scriptures in terms of himself, and the spiritual conviction that seized them as he spoke to them were all compelling evidence that in the person of Christ something new had happened on the earth. The concluding words of the Gospel connect the historical reality with doctrinal truth and show that the revelation through Christ is the basis for the preaching of repentance and forgiveness of sins.

EMPHASIS

Tradition says that Luke was an artist, and that he painted pictures for the early church. Whether he ever painted on canvas may be uncertain, but unquestionably he was an artist in words. His is the most literary of the Gospels; his stories as he took them from the lips of Jesus or as he told them himself are gems of expression, and his vocabulary is rich and varied. Four beautiful songs or poems imbedded in his work have come down to the modern day as hymns of the church: the *Magnificat* (1:46–55), the song of Mary when she went to visit Elizabeth; the *Benedictus* (1:67–79) spoken by Zacharias at the birth of John; the *Gloria in Excelsis* (2:14) of the heavenly host at the birth of Jesus; and the *Nunc Dimittis*, Simeon's prayer at the dedication of the infant Jesus (2:28–32).

Luke's Gospel is predominantly historical. No other writer gives dating for his narrative as Luke does in 1:5, 2:1, and 3:1–2. No other attempts so complete a sketch of the career of Christ from birth to death, even though many periods of his life are not discussed in detail. There is no provincialism in his treatment of Christ; he looks at Jesus through the eyes of a cosmopolitan for whom there is neither Jew nor Gentile, Greek nor barbarian, bond nor free. Luke is impartial in the best sense of that term. His history is not a dull chronicle of happenings, but a live interpretation written into an integral whole by the inspiration of the Holy Spirit. Sir William Ramsay said:

> You may press the words of Luke in a degree beyond any other historian's, and they stand the keenest scrutiny and the hardest treatment, provided always that the critic knows his subject and does not go beyond the limits of science and justice.[7]

If Ramsay's praise seems exaggerated, one needs only to contrast Luke's writings with some of those of his contemporaries to realize that for sobriety, insight, and accuracy they are quite superior. Luke-Acts was written to give a spiritual analysis of the rise and growth of the Christian church, and as such it must be historical in method.

The Third Gospel emphasizes doctrine. Luke could scarcely have traveled with Paul and have ministered as a pastor and missionary without being aware of the importance of doctrinal teaching. Although he does not discuss theology topically, his vocabulary reveals his knowledge of it and his interest in it. Christ, the Son of God, who was acknowledged by the angels (1:35), by demons (4:41), and by the Father (9:35), is presented both as God and man. Salvation is a prominent teaching in Luke: ". . . the Son of man came to seek and to save that which was lost" (19:10) is a key sentence in the book; and several of the parables, particularly those of the fifteenth chapter, illustrate the meaning of salvation. The word "justify"[8] that is used so frequently by Paul appears several times in Luke-Acts, though not always in a theological sense. In one instance, however, that of the Pharisee and the publican (18:14), it is used unmistakably of a man's spiritual standing before God. Like the other Gospels, Luke lays a foundation for theology rather than developing it as a subject, but the doctrine of the person of Christ and the nature and meaning of repentance, salvation, sin, justification, redemption, and many others are patent to the reader.

The doctrine of the Holy Spirit is given special prominence; in fact, there are more references to the Holy Spirit in Luke than there are in Matthew and Mark combined. All of the chief actors of the Gospel—John the Baptist (1:15), Mary (1:35), Elizabeth (1:41), Zacharias (1:67), Simeon (2:25–26), and the Lord Jesus himself (4:1)—were empowered for their work by the Holy Spirit. The whole life of Jesus was lived by the Spirit. He was conceived by the Spirit (1:35), baptized by the Spirit (3:22),

---

7. William Ramsay, *The Bearing of Recent Discoveries on the Trustworthiness of the New Testament* (Fourth Edition; London: Hodder & Stoughton, Ltd., 1920), p. 89.
8. Greek *dikaioō*.

tested by the Spirit (4:1), empowered by the Spirit for his ministry (4:14,18), cheered by the Spirit (10:21), and he expected that his disciples would complete his work in the power of the Spirit (24:49). Acts, of course, develops this theme to a fuller degree by showing the nature and extent of the work of the Holy Spirit in the church.

Certain classes of people receive marked attention in this Gospel. Luke has much to say about women; the word "woman" occurs forty-three times, and only forty-nine times in Matthew and Mark combined. The character of Mary, Jesus' mother, is treated more fully in Luke than in Matthew. Elizabeth, the mother of John (1:5, 6, 39–45, 57), Anna the prophetess (2:36–38), the company of women that traveled among Jesus' disciples (8:2–3), the women who mourned his execution (23:27–28), and the women who were present at the cross and the tomb (23:55–56; 24:1–11) were all noted. Children receive more prominence in Luke than is usual in the annals of antiquity. Mark omits completely the birth and infancy of Jesus and of John; Luke gives three chapters to them. Three times Luke notes that Jesus performed a miracle on an only child (7:12; 8:42; 9:38). In his pages Jesus appears as the champion of the poor and oppressed. Seven or eight of his parables either are concerned with the contrast of poverty and wealth or stress economic need (7:41,43; 11:5–8; 12:13–21; 15:8–10; 16:1–13; 16:19–31; 18:1–8). All of these parables belong exclusively to Luke. The portrayal of the rich in the story of the rich man and Lazarus and in the parable of the rich fool is not complimentary, though it is not bitter. Although Luke himself belonged to the upper middle class, he associated voluntarily with the lower classes, and his Gospel was written to apply Christ to their needs.

Something should be said about Luke's skill in writing. Many of the parables of Jesus as Luke reproduced them would be noteworthy not only for their spiritual teaching, but also for their beauty of expression. The parable of the prodigal son in Luke 15 is one of the greatest short stories of all time, and its diction in the Greek is a marvel of combined simplicity and meaningfulness. No subject could be handled with more delicacy or sympathy than the account of Jesus' birth as given by Luke. The picture of the two on the road to Emmaus condenses the whole subject of the resurrection into a paragraph or two of exciting narrative, and includes also the essential teaching of the fact. Anyone who reads the Gospels as a literary critic would select Luke as outstanding.

CHARACTERS

Several new characters appear in this Gospel. Zacharias and Elizabeth his wife, Simeon, Anna, Zacchaeus, and Cleopas are not mentioned elsewhere, and each is a distinct type. Luke's literary characters are as interesting as his historical characters. Who could forget the patient and loving father of Luke 15 and his sons, one willful and irresponsible, the other haughty and unbending (15:11–32)? The Samaritan who risked life and purse to rescue the Jewish stranger beaten by robbers (10:30–37), the idle rich man who was gloating over his prosperity (12:13–21), the shrewd steward who rescued an income for himself from the wreck of his stewardship (16:1–13), and the snobbish Pharisee who prayed ostentatiously in the temple courts (18:9–14) are all types true to life. They may very well have been taken by Jesus from individual cases that he had observed and have been preserved for us in Luke's vivid narrative.

The cumulative effect of Luke's Gospel is precisely what is expressed in the purpose stated by the author. The narrative is so real and so well expressed that it makes one see Jesus as an actual figure of history, not just as the subject of an abstract essay. Luke 19:10, "For the Son of man came to seek and to save that which was lost," is amply illustrated by this Gospel. It portrays Jesus as the Son of man, showing how he lived among men, how he estimated them, and what he did for them.

FOR FURTHER READING

TECHNICAL AND HISTORICAL WORKS

Barrett, Charles K. *Luke the Historian in Recent Research.* London: Epworth, 1961.

Harnack, Adolph. *Luke the Physician.* Translated by J. R. Wilkinson. Crown Theological Library. New York: G. P. Putnam's Sons, 1907. Pp. xi, 231. Technical treatment of authorship for advanced students.

Hobart, William K. *The Medical Language of St. Luke.* London: Longmans, Green & Company, 1882. Pp. xxxvi, 305. Attempts to show that Luke's language is that of a physician.

Lenski, Richard Charles. *The Interpretation of St. Luke's Gospel.* Columbus, Ohio: The Wartburg Press, 1946. Pp. 1212.

MacLachlan, H. *St. Luke, the Man and His Work.* London: Longmans, Green, and Company, 1920. See pp. 1–223. Written from a liberal viewpoint. The book contains a mine of information on Luke's biographical and literary background.

Marshall, I. Howard. *Luke: Historian and Theologian.* Grand Rapids: Zondervan Publishing House, 1971.

Ramsay, William. *The Bearing of Recent Discoveries on the Trustworthiness of the New Testament.* Fourth Edition. London: Hodder and Stoughton, Ltd., 1920. Read pp. 222–300.

―――. *Was Christ Born at Bethlehem?* New York: G. P. Putnam's Sons, 1898. Pp. 1–280. A technical presentation of the historical material concerning the birth of Christ.

Robertson, A. T. *Luke the Historian in the Light of Research.* New York: Charles Scribner's Sons, 1923. Pp. 1–257.

Stonehouse, N. B. *The Witness of Luke to Christ.* Grand Rapids, Mich.: Wm. B. Eerdmans Publishing Company, 1951. Pp. 184. Conservative critical discussion of the content of Luke's account of the life of Christ.

COMMENTARIES

Creed, J. M. *The Gospel According to St. Luke.* London: Macmillan & Company, Ltd., 1942. Pp. xxix, 340.

Danker, Frederick W. *Luke.* Philadelphia: Fortress Press, 1976.

Ellis, E. Earle. *The Gospel of Luke.* Grand Rapids: Wm. B. Eerdmans Publishing Company, 1981.

Fitzmyer, Joseph A. *The Gospel According to Luke I-IX.* Garden City, N.Y.: Doubleday, 1981.

Geldenhuys, Norval. *Commentary on the Gospel of Luke* in *The New International Commentary on the New Testament.* Grand Rapids, Mich.: Wm. B. Eerdmans Publishing Company, 1951. Pp. 685.

Godet, F. *A Commentary on the Gospel of Luke.* Translated from the Second French Edition by E. W. Shalders and M. D. Cusin. Third Edition. New York: Funk and Wagnalls, Publishers, 1887. Pp. x, 574. Very thorough and quite satisfactory, though old.

Lindsay, Thomas M. *The Gospel According to St. Luke.* In *Handbooks for Bible Classes.* Two volumes. Edinburgh: T. & T. Clark, n.d. Pp. 268.

Marshall, I. Howard. *The Gospel of Luke: A Commentary on the Greek Text.* Grand Rapids: Wm. B. Eerdmans Publishing Company, 1978. Pp. 928.

Morgan, G. Campbell. *The Gospel According to St. Luke.* New York: Fleming H. Revell Company, 1931. Pp. 284.

Plumptre, E. H. *The Gospel According to Luke* in *The Handy Commentary.* New York: Cassell, Potter, Galpin, and Company, n.d. Pp. xx, 232.

Ragg, Lonsdale. *St. Luke* in *Westminster Commentary Series.* London: Methuen & Company, 1922.

CHAPTER 11

THE GOSPEL OF JOHN

ORIGIN

THE Gospel of John is the most unusual and perhaps the most valuable member of the quartet of canonical Gospels. Although it deals with the same broad sequence of events to be found in the pages of the others, it is quite different in structure and in style. It contains no parables and only seven miracles, five of which are not recorded elsewhere. The discourses of Jesus in it are concerned chiefly with his person rather than with the ethical teaching of the kingdom. Personal interviews are multiplied, and Jesus' relationship to individuals is stressed more than his general contact with the public. The Gospel is strongly theological, and it deals particularly with the nature of his person and with the meaning of faith in him.

Because of the marked differences between John and the Synoptics, its truthfulness has been questioned. The answer lies in its origin and purpose. Traditionally it was written by John the son of Zebedee, the last surviving member of the apostolic band, while he was spending the declining years of his life at Ephesus. Although this opinion has been persistently attacked, it still remains as good a probability as any other hypothesis that can be offered. So little is known concerning the Christian churches at large at the end of the first century that the framework for this Gospel is exceedingly difficult to reconstruct.

The earliest evidence for its existence is to be found in Papias, as quoted by Eusebius.[1] In this passage he alluded to John, who was one of the disciples of the Lord, and also to an elder John, a disciple of the Lord, who was his contemporary. Eusebius deduced that the two persons were different individuals, and cited the existence of two tombs in Ephesus, both of which were called John's in his day. Since Papias' works are not now extant, no independent judgment can be formed on the meaning of this statement. Possibly Eusebius misunderstood him. There is no reason why an apostle could not have also been called an *elder* (indeed, Papias refers to certain persons, including John, as "the presbyters" and "the Lord's disciples"), and Papias may simply have been saying that whereas the majority of the apostles did not survive their oral testimony, one or two of them remained until his day as the last witnesses in the flesh of what Jesus had said and done.

The theory that the Fourth Gospel was the product of some unknown presbyter by the name of John and not of John the apostle cannot be regarded as established. All the testimony of the fathers from the time of Irenaeus is overwhelmingly in favor of the Johannine authorship. Clement of Alexandria (A.D. 190), Origen (c. A.D. 220), Hippolytus (c. A.D. 225), Tertullian (c. A.D. 200), and the Muratorian Fragment (c. A.D. 170) agree in attributing the Fourth Gospel to John the son of Zebedee.

AUTHOR

From the Gospel itself certain facts about its author may be educed. First, he was a Jew who was accustomed to thinking in Aramaic, although the Gospel was written in Greek. Very few subordinate clauses appear in its text, and not infrequently Hebrew or Aramaic words are inserted and then explained. The author was familiar with Jewish tradition. In 1:19–28 he referred to the Jewish expectation of a coming Messiah. He knew the Jewish feeling toward the Samaritans (4:9) and their exclusive attitude in worship (4:20). He was acquainted with the Jewish feasts, which he explained carefully for the readers.

Second, he was a Palestinian Jew, who had personal acquaintance with the land and especially with Jerusalem and its environs (9:7; 11:18; 18:1). He was familiar with the cities of Galilee (1:44; 2:1) and with the territory of Samaria (4:5–6, 21). He seems to have been quite at home in the country he described.

---

1. Eusebius *Historia Ecclesiae* III. xxxix. 124, 127. A thorough examination of both external and internal testimony to the authentic authorship of this Gospel, with positive conclusions, may be found in D. E. Hiebert, *An Introduction to the New Testament* (Chicago: Moody Press, 1975), pp. 192–211.

Again, he was an eyewitness of the events he recorded. Both in 1:14, "we beheld his glory. . . ," and in 19:35, where he spoke in the third person, "he that hath seen hath borne witness," he claims to be stating what had been part of his personal experience. Small touches scattered throughout the Gospel confirm this impression. The hour at which Jesus sat on the well curb (4:6), the number and size of the pots at the wedding of Cana (2:6), the weight and value of the ointment that Mary used on Jesus (12:3, 5), and the details of Jesus' trial (chaps. 18–19) are points that have little to do with the main narrative but indicate the observer's eye.

Who was the author? Evidently he was with Jesus from the beginning of his career, for he mentions episodes that antedate the opening of the account of Jesus' ministry in the Synoptics. He must have belonged to the group of disciples mentioned in the narrative. According to the final chapter, he is to be identified with the "beloved disciple" who was a close associate of Peter, and who had been very near to Jesus at the last supper (13:23), at the trial (18:15–16), and at the cross (19:26–27). Only one of Jesus' most intimate associates would fit these circumstances. James was killed early in the history of the church (Acts 12:2). Peter, Thomas, and Philip are mentioned so frequently in the third person that none of them could have been the author. Although the author did not name himself, he took for granted that his readers knew who he was and that they would accept his authority in the matters of which he wrote. John the son of Zebedee is the best remaining possibility, and on the assumption of his authorship of the Gospel the following conclusions are founded.

The biography of John is fragmentary like all other biblical biographies. He was one of the sons of Zebedee (Mark 1:19–20), a fisherman of Galilee, and of Salome, who was probably the sister of Mary, Jesus' mother (cf. Matt. 27:56; Mark 15:40; John 19:25). He grew to manhood in Galilee and was a partner with his brother and with Andrew and Peter in the fishing business. He may have belonged first to the disciples of John the Baptist, and possibly was the companion of Andrew mentioned in John 1:40. If so, he accompanied Jesus on his first tour in Galilee (John 2:2), and later with his partners quit the fishing trade to follow him (Matt. 4:21–22).

The episodes of Jesus' life in which John shared are too numerous to list and treat separately. He was with Jesus in Jerusalem during the early Judean ministry. Perhaps the interview with Nicodemus was held at is home. He was a participant later in the mission of the Twelve, as described by Matthew (10:1–2). He needed Jesus' counsel as much as any other of the Twelve, for he and James seem to have possessed unusually ardent temperaments. Jesus called them "sons of thunder," or, by a more literal rendering, "sons of tumult" (Mark 3:17). Mark does not assign any reason for giving this name to them, but the usage of the Hebrew phrase "son of . . ." usually means that the term that completes it qualifies the man, as "sons of

Belial" means "worthless fellows." Their bigotry and truculence were revealed in their readiness to rebuke the man casting out demons because he
did not follow with them (Luke 9:49), and in their desire to call down fire
from heaven on the Samaritan villages that would not receive Jesus (9:52–
54). Both rashly asked their mother to petition Jesus that he would grant
them the seats of primacy in his kingdom (Matt. 20:20–28). Jesus sharply
rebuked these crudities of spirit, even though they may have been moti-
vated by loyalty to him and his work.

At the last supper John occupied a place of privilege and intimacy next
to Jesus (John 13:23). At the trial he obtained access to the court of the
high priest because he was known to the family (18:15–16). Perhaps he
had been the representative at Jerusalem of his father's fishing company,
and so had become acquainted with all of the prominent households of the
city. Apparently he witnessed the trial and death of Jesus and assumed the
responsibility for Jesus' mother when Jesus committed her to his care
(19:26–27). He stayed with Peter during the dark days of the interment,
and with him was one of the first visitors at the empty tomb. There, as he
looked at the empty grave clothes, he "saw and believed" (20:8).

The epilogue of this Gospel hints that he lived for a long time after the
beginning of the Christian era, for an explanation of his long life would
scarcely have been necessary otherwise. The epistles show that he rose to a
position of influence in the church and that he became a powerful expositor of the love of God as revealed in Christ. His death probably took
place at the close of the first century.

From these scattered items of John's biography, woven into the general
narrative of the life of Christ, one can see something of his personal
spiritual experiences. Intense in nature, he gave to Christ an undivided
loyalty that at times expressed itself crudely and rashly. As Christ tamed his
ardor and purified it of unrestrained violence, John became the apostle of
love whose devotion was not excelled by that of any other writer of the
New Testament. The fire of his nature appears in the vigor of his language.
John echoes the strictures of Jesus against unbelievers (8:44) when he calls
them "children of the devil" (I John 3:10). The same man, however, said:
"Beloved, let us love one another: for love is of God; and every one that
loveth is begotten of God, and knoweth God" (4:7). The two are not
inconsistent to an intense nature. John is an example of a man who could
have been a great sinner, but out of whom Christ made a great witness.

DATE AND PLACE

The date of the Fourth Gospel has been variously estimated from A.D. 40
to 140, or even later. It cannot be later than Tatian's Diatessaron, into
which it was incorporated about the middle of the second century. The

discovery of the Rylands fragment, which preserves a scrap from John 18:31–33, 37–38, shows that John was probably in use in the first half of the second century.[2] Goodenough argues that John may have been written as early as A.D. 40,[3] though few scholars accept so early a date. The best solution seems to be that John was produced in Asia Minor, possibly in Ephesus, toward the close of the first century, when the church had achieved a measure of maturity, and when there was need for an advance in the teaching concerning the nature of faith. It was apparently written in Gentile surroundings, for the feasts and usages of the Jews are explained for the benefit of those who were unfamiliar with them (John 2:13; 4:9; 19:31).

CONTENT

The key to the content of the Gospel of John is the author's own statement in John 20:30–31:

> Many other signs therefore did Jesus in the presence of the disciples, which are not written in this book: but these are written that ye may believe that Jesus is the Christ, the Son of God; and that believing ye may have life in his name.

Three words are prominent in this brief passage: *signs, believe, life.* The first of these words contains a clue to the organization of the Gospel around a select number of miracles, parallel in general character to those that are recorded in the Synoptic Gospels, but called *signs* here because of their special meaning in this Gospel. Seven were performed by Jesus publicly on other people or for the benefit of other people. They illustrate different areas of his power, and collectively bear witness to the central doctrine of the Gospel, his deity. They may be classified as follows:

TITLE	PASSAGE	AREA OF POWER
The Changing of Water into Wine	2:1–11	Quality
The Healing of the Nobleman's Son	4:46–54	Space
The Healing of the Impotent Man	5:1–9	Time
The Feeding of the Five Thousand	6:1–14	Quantity
The Walking on the Water	6:16–21	Natural Law
The Healing of the Blind Man	9:1–12	Misfortune
The Raising of Lazarus	11:1–46	Death

2. Frederick Kenyon, *Our Bible and the Ancient Manuscripts* (Revised Edition; New York: Harper and Brothers, Publishers, 1940), p. 128.

3. Erwin R. Goodenough, "John a Primitive Gospel," *Journal of Biblical Literature*, LXIV (1945), 145–182. Philadelphia: Society of Biblical Literature and Exegesis, 1945.

These seven miracles took place precisely in the areas where man is unable to effect any change of laws or conditions that affect his life. In these areas Jesus proved himself potent where man is impotent, and the works that he did testify to his supernatural ability.

The second word, *believe*, is the key word in the Gospel, occurring ninety-eight times. It is customarily translated *believe*, though sometimes it is rendered *trust* or *commit* (see 2:24). It usually means acknowledgment of a personal claim, or else it stands for the complete commitment of the individual to Christ. In it is the full meaning of the whole Christian life, for the tense of the verb used in this passage implies the continuing process of belief, involving also progress. John defines belief in Christ as receiving him (1:12), making him a part of one's life. Convinced by the *signs*, which were proofs of the power of Jesus' person, the believer would logically move on to a settled faith.

The third important word in the Gospel is *life*; in Johannine language, it is the sum total of all that is imparted to the believer in his salvation. It is the highest experience of which humanity is capable. "This," said Jesus, "is life eternal, that they should know thee the only true God, and him whom thou didst send, *even* Jesus Christ" (17:3). Life, according to John, is not just animal vitality or the course of human existence. It involves a kind of nature, a new consciousness, interaction with environment, and constant development. Christ is presented as the example of this life which is God's gift to the Christian and God's goal for the Christian.

These three words, *signs, belief, life*, provide logical organization for the Gospel. In the *signs* is the revelation of God; in *belief* is the reaction that they are designed to produce; in *life* is the result that belief brings.

OUTLINE

The development of the central theme of belief appears in the outline of the Gospel.

(*continued*)

III.	The Period of Controversy	5:1–6:71
	The Issues of Belief and of	
	Unbelief	
	Presented in Action	5:1–18
	Presented in Argument	5:19–47
	Presented in Demonstration	6:1–21
	Presented in Discourse	6:22–71
IV.	The Period of Conflict	7:1–11:53
	The Clash of Belief and of	
	Unbelief	
	The Conflict Described	7:1–8:59
	With Jesus' brethren	7:1–9
	With the populace	7:10–52
	The woman taken in adultery	7:53–8:11
	With the Pharisees and Jews	8:12–59
	The Conflict Illustrated	9:1–11:53
	By the blind man	9:1–41
	By the discourse on the	
	Shepherd	10:1–21
	By argument	10:22–42
	By the raising of Lazarus	11:1–53
V.	The Period of Crisis	11:54–12:36a
	The Declaration of Belief and of	
	Unbelief	
VI.	The Period of Conference	12:36b–17:26
	The Strengthening of Belief	
	Transition	12:36b–13:30
	Conference with the Disciples	13:31–16:33
	Conference with the Father	17:1–26
VII.	The Period of Consummation	18:1–20:31
	The Victory over Unbelief	
	The Betrayal	18:1–27
	The Trial Before Pilate	18:28–19:16
	The Crucifixion	19:17–37
	The Burial	19:38–42
	The Resurrection	20:1–29
VIII.	Epilogue	21:1–25
	The Responsibilities of Belief	

The structure of John's Gospel is so plain that its reader can hardly miss it. From beginning to end the theme of belief is followed consistently. Moreover, the Gospel is not an attempt to superimpose an artificial organization on existing facts. The inspired writer has selected certain episodes and teachings that represent the character and progress of the revelation of

God in Christ (1:19), and has arranged them in such a way as to sweep his reader along in the tide of spiritual movement toward an active confessional faith in Christ.

The Prologue (1:1–18) begins by using the term Word[4] to introduce the person of Christ. This term differs from those used in the other Gospels, for it does not connote any particular religious background. *Christ* is Jewish; *Lord* is Gentile; *Jesus* is human; but *Word* or *Logos* is philosophical. John thus makes the subject of his Gospel a universal figure, the incarnation of the Eternal Reason who is God, who came from God, and who reveals God as a son reveals a father. He is to be apprehended by those who receive him (1:12), and the conflict between those who receive him and those who do not is compared to the conflict between light and darkness.

The Period of Consideration (1:19–4:54) presents the person of the Word made flesh as he appeared to his contemporaries and as he was received by them. First he is proclaimed in the witness of his forerunner, John, and in his dealing with John's disciples. His essential mission, "the Lamb of God" (1:29), and his method of appealing to the needs and desires of his would-be followers connect him with preceding history and revelation. He utilized both the preaching of John and the prophetic Scriptures of the Old Testament to establish his position. In the works that he performed he demonstrated his inherent power over things, men, and institutions (2:1–22). The interviews that followed were fuller manifestations of his sufficiency for all men. The learned and gentlemanly Jewish teacher Nicodemus, the sharp-tongued and cynical Samaritan woman, and the importunate nobleman of Galilee, probably a Gentile, were all directed to faith in Jesus by different arguments and methods.

From Jesus' public presentation of himself arose controversy, for when he appealed to men to believe in him, many refused. He did not ask for a blind or unreasoning faith, but he took care always to appeal to facts and to define clearly the issues at stake in belief and in unbelief.

The healing of the man at the pool precipitated the Period of Controversy (5:1–6:71) because the miracle was performed on the Sabbath. Jesus indicated that his action was a sample of what his Father was continually doing, and thus tacitly claimed deity as his prerogative. In the discussion that followed (5:19–47) he argued for belief in himself on the basis of five witnesses: himself, the forerunner, the Father, the works he had performed, and the Scripture. The miracles of chapter 6, according to John, were directed chiefly to his disciples in order to evoke from them a committal to faith. These miracles and the discourses that followed are bound closely together, for the discourse is only the amplification of the truth

---

4. Greek *logos*.

Bodmer Papyrus II, the earliest substantial manuscript of John's Gospel (2nd–3rd cent. A.D.), showing John 6:59–70.

enacted in the miracles. The appeal for belief is very strong in this section, as if Jesus were desirous of having the disciples commit themselves to him before the heat of controversy might alienate them from him.

The Period of Conflict (7:1–11:53) carries the trends of the Period of Controversy to their logical crisis. The growing though hesitant faith of the disciples is contrasted with the stark cynicism of Jesus' brethren, with the wavering allegiance of the bewildered multitude, and with the venomous opposition of the Jewish hierarchy. Jesus' own evaluation of the conflict appears in the history of the blind man, where he expressed the necessity of doing the works of God while he still had opportunity, and also in the raising of Lazarus, which he regarded as a supreme test of faith and as the climactic proof of his power. The discourse material that is included between these two miracles in the tenth chapter is Jesus' last extended public statement of his mission. It declares the purpose of his death as clearly as did his utterance to the disciples at Caesarea Philippi that is recorded in the Synoptics. The outcome of the conflict is predicted in his words: "I lay down my life, that I may take it again" (10:17).

In the Period of Crisis (11:54–12:36a) appear the various tensions the conflict has created. Jesus retired from Jerusalem and its environs to Ephraim in order that he might be out of the storm center. The feeling of his friends was openly declared by the family of Bethany, who gave a dinner in his honor (12:1–2). The pilgrim multitude, who were present in Jerusalem for the Feast of the Passover, hailed him enthusiastically (12:20–21). Jesus himself realized that the die was cast, and removed himself from public contacts (12:36). Divine destiny, not popular vote, was the deciding factor in his life.

Up to this point Jesus' ministry was public; from here on it was private. The Period of Conference (12:36b–17:26) comprises the final instruction to the disciples after the last supper and also his prayer to the Father. The preparation of the disciples for the shock of the cross and the report to the Father that he had finished his work concluded the earthly ministry of Jesus.

The Period of Consummation (18:1–20:31) brings the fulfillment of the two clashing principles of belief and of unbelief. In the betrayal and crucifixion unbelief was unmasked. The weakness of Peter, the treachery of Judas, the jealous malice of the priests, and the cowardice of Pilate show how unbelief reaches its ultimate end. On the other hand, the constancy of the beloved disciple and the women and the generous action of Joseph and Nicodemus show how even an imperfect and uninstructed faith can maintain loyalty in spite of bewilderment and danger. The resurrection, of course, was the final justification of belief as well as the final vindication of the revelation through Jesus the Son of God.

EMPHASIS

The Gospel of John has many special features that strengthen the presentation of its main theme. The claims of Jesus are set forth in seven major I AM's:

1. The bread of life	6:35
2. The light of the world	8:12; 9:5
3. The door (of the sheepfold)	10:7
4. The good shepherd	10:11, 14
5. The resurrection and the life	11:25
6. The way, the truth, and the life	14:6
7. The true vine	15:1

John stresses the personal relation of Jesus to man. Twenty-seven interviews are noted, some of which are extensive and some of which are very brief. Included in the list are passages that can be classified under other headings, such as the miracle of the nobleman's son (4:46–54), or the trial before Pilate (18:28–19:16). On occasions like these the interest of Jesus in the individual is prominent rather than the action itself. In the Synoptics, for example, the trial before Pilate is an important feature of the denouement of Jesus' life, while in the Gospel of John Jesus' personal interest in Pilate and his effort to bring Pilate to a recognition of his claims are much more evident.

The Johannine vocabulary is so unusual that only a verse or two from this Gospel, quoted apart from its context, is easily recognizable. Certain key words are repeated constantly, not because the writer is limited in scope of thought, but because the central truths of the Gospel, like diamonds, need to be viewed from the angle of each facet. Some of these terms, like "life," "light," "darkness," "work," "world," "believe," "flesh," "hour," are either figurative or else have a special technical meaning in this Gospel. Others are abstract and somewhat philosophical in content: "truth," "true," "hate," "receive," "love" (two different verbs), "take away," "send," "beginning," "know" (two different verbs), "glory," "glorify," "witness" (verb and noun), "abide," "the Father." John's Gospel shows by its vocabulary that teaching on the Christian life had already crystallized into certain definite concepts that were expressed in fixed phraseology, and that then, as today, represented a whole new pattern of spiritual truth.

The Gospel of John emphasizes the deity of Jesus Christ, the Son of God. No other Gospel portrays more clearly his humanity, nor does any other assert so directly the prerogatives of deity: "The Word was God" (1:1); "I and the Father are one" (10:30); "Before Abraham was born, I am" (8:58); "He that hath seen me hath seen the Father" (14:9); and Thomas' ejaculation, "My Lord and my God" (20:28).

John also emphasizes the humanity of Jesus. He was weary (4:6), thirsty (4:7), impatient (6:26), wistful (6:67), severe (8:44), sorrowful (11:35), appreciative (12:7), troubled (12:27), loving (13:1), loyal (18:8), courageous (18:23). To his contemporaries who met him casually he was "the man that is called Jesus" (9:11); to those who lived with him he became "the Holy One of God" (6:69).

PURPOSE

As already stated, the purpose of this Gospel is apologetic. All of the Gospels were designed to inculcate belief in those who read them or heard them read. This Gospel was planned for those who already had some philosophical predilections, as the Prologue shows, and who were looking for an answer to Philip's demand: "Lord, show us the Father, and it sufficeth us" (14:8).

It is possible that John's Gospel was written as a conscious attempt to supplement the current accounts of the life and work of Jesus that had found written expression in the canonical Synoptic Gospels. One cannot state dogmatically that John knew and read Matthew, or Mark, or Luke. Nevertheless, the general omission of Jesus' Galilean ministry, the almost total absence of the parables, the definite reference to selectivity in the miracles (20:30), and the dovetailing of some of John's historical data with that in the Synoptics make one feel that the author was trying to give to the public fresh information that had not previously been used in writing. For instance, in the account of the last supper, John described the foot-washing scene and explained how Jesus wished to provide an object lesson in humility for the disciples. Apart from the assumption that such a lesson might be salutary for general application, he assigned no definite reason for it. Luke, however, told how the disciples were arguing among themselves "which of them was accounted to be greatest" (Luke 22:24). The two accounts thus interlock in meaning, and one may speculate whether John was not explaining how Jesus met the situation that Luke described as a personal addition to the Lukan account.

Based on a statement of Clement of Alexandria, cited by Eusebuis, one might argue for a kind of relationship between John and the Synoptics:

> But that John, last of all, conscious that the outward (Gr. *sōmatika*, "bodily") facts had been set forth in the Gospels, was urged on by his disciples, and, divinely moved by the Spirit, composed a spiritual (Gr. *pneumatikon*) Gospel.[5]

If we rightly understand "spiritual" to mean "the divine side of the subject," John's Gospel stands as a supplement to the message of the Synoptics. Some writers[6] have argued that John made use of the Synoptics, particularly Mark, possibly Luke, less probably Matthew. More likely it appears that material in John (e.g., Jesus' frequent presence in Judea) would help to illuminate such statements as appear in, for example, Luke 4:44; 14:34.

To say that John is independent of the Synoptics is one thing; to recall that all four are Gospels and describe the same person is another, of some importance. We need them all to grasp the total picture of Jesus.

CHARACTERS

One peculiarity of John's Gospel is its development of character in sketches separated by intervals of text. Nicodemus (John 3:1–15; 7:50–52; 19:39), Philip (1:43–46; 6:5–7; 14:8–11), Thomas (11:16; 14:5–6; 20:24–29), Mary and Martha (11:1–40; 12:2–8), Mary the mother of Jesus (2:1–5; 19:26–27), and others are mentioned naturally and easily as they are recalled in connection with the main narratives, and yet when the separate allusions to them are combined, they make a complete snapshot portrait of the person concerned. To some extent this procedure is true in the other Gospels, but it is largely confined to a few prominent characters such as

---

5. Eusebius *Historia Ecclesiastica* VI.xiv.7.
6. C. K. Barrett, *The Gospel According to St. John*, Second Edition (Philadelphia: Westminster Press, 1978), pp. 15–21.

Peter or Judas, whereas the Fourth Gospel uses both prominent and obscure characters as examples of belief and of unbelief.

FOR FURTHER READING

TECHNICAL, HISTORICAL, AND ANALYTICAL WORKS

Barrett, Charles K. *Essays on John.* Philadelphia: Westminster Press, 1982.

Barrett, Charles K. *The Gospel of John and Judaism.* Philadelphia: Fortress Press, 1975.

Ellis, E. Earle. *The World of St. John: The Gospel and the Epistles.* New York: Abingdon Press, 1965.

Gloag, Paton J. *Introduction to the Johannine Writings.* London: James Nisbet & Company, 1891. Pp. xiii, 440.

Hayes, Doremus A. *John and His Writings.* New York: Methodist Book Concern, 1917. Pp. 328.

Howard, W. F., Edited by A. W. Harrison. *Christianity According to St. John.* London: Duckworth, 1943. Pp. 221.

_____. *The Fourth Gospel in Recent Criticism and Interpretation.* London: The Epworth Press, 1931. Pp. 292.

Hunter, A. M. *According to John: The New Look at the Fourth Gospel.* Philadelphia: Westminster Press, 1968.

Iverach, James. "John, Gospel of," in *International Standard Bible Encyclopaedia*, III, 1720–1727. Grand Rapids, Mich.: Wm. B. Eerdmans Publishing Company, 1949.

Martyn, J. Louis. *The Gospel of John in Christian History: Essays for Interpreters.* New York: Paulist Press, 1978.

_____. *History and Theology in the Fourth Gospel.* New York: Harper & Row, 1968.

McIntyre, D. M. *Some Notes on the Gospels.* Edited for the Press by F. F. Bruce. London: The Inter-Varsity Fellowship, 1943. Pp. 51. Pp. 35–51 contain a succinct statement of the conservative side of Johannine criticism.

Morris, Leon. *Studies in the Fourth Gospel.* Grand Rapids: Wm. B. Eerdmans Publishing Company, 1969.

Nunn, H. P. V. *The Son of Zebedee and the Fourth Gospel.* London: Society for Promoting Christian Knowledge, 1927. Pp. x, 150. Good, conservative treatment.

Robertson, A. T. *Epochs in the Life of the Apostle John.* New York: Fleming H. Revell Company, 1935. Pp. 253.

Stanton, Vincent H. *The Gospels as Historical Documents.* Cambridge: University Press, 1920. Part III: The Fourth Gospel.

Tenney, Merrill C. *John: The Gospel of Belief.* Grand Rapids, Mich.: Wm. B. Eerdmans Publishing Company, 1951. Pp. 321. An aid to analytic study.

Thomas, W. H. Griffith. *The Apostle John: His Life and Writings.* Grand Rapids, Mich.: Wm. B. Eerdmans Publishing Company, 1948. Pp. 373.

White, W. W. *Studies in the Gospel by John.* New York: Fleming H. Revell Company, 1895. Pp. 130. Small handbook for study by inductive method.

COMMENTARIES

Bailey, R. F. *The Gospel of John: An Introductory Commentary*. London: Student Christian Movement, 1940. Pp. viii, 248.

Barrett, Charles K. *The Gospel According to St. John: An Introduction with Commentary and Notes on the Greek Text*. Second Edition. Philadelphia: Westminster Press, 1978.

Boice, James M. *The Gospel of John: An Expositional Commentary*. Four volumes. Grand Rapids: Zondervan Publishing House, 1975-1983.

Brown, Raymond E. *The Gospel According to John: Introduction, Translation and Notes*. Two volumes. Garden City, N.Y.: Doubleday, 1966-1970.

Godet, F. *Commentary on the Gospel of John*. Translated from the Second French Edition by Francis Crombie and M. D. Cusin. Four volumes. Edinburgh: T. & T. Clark, 1876.

Hendriksen, William. *Gospel of John* in *The New Testament Commentary*. Two volumes. Grand Rapids, Mich.: Baker Book House, 1953. Pp. 776.

Hunter, A. M. *The Gospel According to John*. Cambridge: University Press, 1965.

Lange, John Peter. *The Gospel According to John*. Translated from the German by Edward D. Yeomans and Evalina Moore. Edited by Philip Schaff. New York: Scribner, Armstrong & Company, 1872. Pp. xiv, 654.

Lenski, R. C. H. *The Interpretation of St. John's Gospel*. Columbus, Ohio: Wartburg Press, 1942. Pp. 1444.

Morgan, G. Campbell. *The Gospel According to John*. New York: Fleming H. Revell Company, n.d. Pp. 333.

Morris, Leon. *The Gospel According to John: The English Text with Introduction and Notes*. Grand Rapids: Wm. B. Eerdmans Publishing Company, 1971. Pp. xi, 936.

Moulton, Wm. F. and Milligan, Wm. *The Gospel According to John*. International Revision Commentary, Vol. IV. New York: Charles Scribner's Sons, 1883. Pp. xxxiii, 443.

Reith, George. *St. John's Gospel with Introduction and Notes*. Two volumes. Edinburgh: T. & T. Clark, 1926.

Sanders, Joseph N. *A Commentary on the Gospel According to St. John*. London: A. & C. Black, 1968.

Scroggie, W. Graham. *St. John: Introduction and Notes*. New York & London: Harper and Brothers, Publishers, 1931. Pp. 132. A devotional study with superb outlines.

Smith, D. Moody. *John*. Philadelphia: Fortress Press, 1976.

Westcott, B. F. *Commentary on John*. Grand Rapids, Mich.: Wm. B. Eerdmans Publishing Company, 1951.

———. *The Gospel According to John*. Two volumes in one. Grand Rapids, Mich.: Wm. B. Eerdmans Publishing Company, 1954. Pp. cxcv, 677.

CHAPTER 12

THE LIFE OF CHRIST

ONE would naturally expect that the Lord Jesus Christ would be sufficiently important to receive ample notice in the literature of his time, and that extensive biographical material would be available. He was observed by multitudes of people, and his own followers numbered into the hundreds (I Cor. 15:6), whose witness was still living in the middle of the first century. As a matter of fact, the amount of information concerning him is comparatively meager. Aside from the four Gospels, and a few scattered allusions in the epistles, contemporary history is almost silent concerning him.

THE SECULAR SOURCES OF INFORMATION

There are, however, a few references to Christ or to Christianity that can be cited.

Josephus, in his *Antiquities*,[1] made the following statement:

Now there was about this time Jesus, a wise man, if it be lawful to call him a man, for he was a doer of wonderful works, a teacher of such men as receive the truth with pleasure. He drew over to him both many of the Jews, and many of the Gentiles. He was [the] Christ. And when Pilate, at the suggestion of the principal men among us, had condemned him to the cross, those that loved him at the first did not

---

1. Josephus *Antiquities* XVIII.iii.3. See Philip Schaff, *History of the Christian Church* (Grand Rapids, Mich.: Wm. B. Eerdmans Publishing Company, 1950), I, 92ff., for an evaluation of this passage. It is considered by many to be a Christian interpolation into the text of Josephus.

One of the two main sites regarded as possible locations for the crucifixion and burial of Jesus.

forsake him; for he appeared to them alive again the third day; as the divine prophets had foretold these and ten thousand other wonderful things concerning him. And the tribe of Christians so named from him are not extinct at this day.

Tacitus, a Roman historian of the second century, in writing of the reign of Nero, alluded to the death of Christ and to the existence of Christians in Rome:[2]

But not all the relief that could come from man, not all the bounties that the prince could bestow, nor all the atonements which could be presented to the gods, availed to relieve Nero from the infamy of being believed to have ordered the conflagration. Hence, to suppress the rumor, he falsely charged with the guilt, and punished with the most exquisite tortures, the persons commonly called Christians, who were hated for their enormities. Christus, the founder of that name, was put to death as a criminal by Pontius Pilate, procurator of Judea, in the reign of Tiberius: but the pernicious superstition, repressed for a time, broke out again, not only through Judea, where the mischief originated, but through the city of Rome also. . . .

Suetonius' testimony is brief:[3]

Punishment [by Nero] was inflicted on the Christians, a class of men given to a new and mischievous superstition.

The younger Pliny, who was a correspondent of Trajan, spoke in one of his letters of the Christians as he had met them in Asia:[4]

They affirmed, however, the whole of their guilt, or their error, was, that they were in the habit of meeting on a certain fixed day before it was light, when they sang in alternate verses a hymn to Christ, as to a god, and bound themselves by a solemn oath, not to any wicked deeds, but never to commit any fraud, theft, or adultery, never to falsify their word, nor to deny a trust when they should be called on to deliver it up. . . .

Lucian, the satirist of the second century, spoke scornfully of Christ and of the Christians.[5] He connected them with the synagogues of Palestine, and alluded to Christ as

---

2. Tacitus *Annals* XV.44. The Oxford Translation, Revised (New York: Harper & Brothers, Publishers, 1858), p. 423.

3. Suetonius *The Lives of the Caesars, Nero* XVI. Loeb Classical Library. English translation by J. C. Rolfe (London: William Heinemann; New York: G. P. Putnam's Sons), II, 111.

4. Pliny *Letters* X.xcvi. Loeb Classical Library. English translation by William Melmoth, revised by W. M. L. Hutchinson (London: William Heinemann; Cambridge, Mass.: Harvard University Press, 1935), II, 403.

5. Lucian *The Passing of Peregrinus* 12–13. Loeb Classical Library. English translation by A. M. Harmon (London: William Heinemann, Ltd.; Cambridge, Mass.: Harvard University Press, 1936), pp. 13, 15.

. . . the man who was crucified in Palestine because he introduced this new cult into the world. . . . Furthermore, their first lawgiver persuaded them that they are all brothers one of another after they have transgressed once for all by denying the Greek gods and by worshipping that crucified sophist himself and living under his laws.

These brief notices of Christ and of Christianity were penned by men who were ignorant of the history of the movement and hostile to its tenets. They show that Christianity was already widespread by the second century and that the historic existence of Christ was generally acknowledged even by his foes. The nature of these references proves that he was regarded as an obscure fanatic whose cult had attained a prominence far greater than might rightfully have been expected. Up to the time of Nero, and in the circle of the court, Christianity was looked on by Romans in much the same way that Americans would appraise an importation of Japanese Shintoism.

THE PERIODS OF JESUS' LIFE

Since the data afforded by the four Gospels are not complete in the sense that they are exhaustive, a full biography of Jesus cannot be reconstructed from them. Of the four, Luke is perhaps the most representative, but he does not include the early Judean ministry, which is mentioned by John. None of these attempts a physical description of Jesus' person, although some facts about it must have been known to the writers. Only Luke gives a glimpse of his youth; for the most part, the thirty years of his life are passed over in silence. John alone follows any definite chronological scheme that is traceable to his allusions to the feasts Jesus attended; and one of those is ambiguous (John 5:1). The order of narration in any Gospel is not necessarily chronological, for each Gospel has its own objective and organizes its material for effect rather than for temporal sequence. It is an interpretation, not a chronicle. For this reason there are some differences of opinion on the preferred order of events in the life of Christ. The following outline agrees with the consensus of most scholars and treats the larger blocks of material in the Gospels rather than the smaller questions of detail that belong properly to a specialized study. The periods follow the conventional arrangement as given by Burton and Goodspeed,[6] Huck,[7] and others.

---

6. E. D. Burton and E. J. Goodspeed, A Harmony of the Synoptic Gospels (New York: Charles Scribner's Sons, n.d.), pp. xv, 279.

7. Albert Huck, A Synopsis of the First Three Gospels (Ninth edition, revised by Hans Lietzmann; English edition by Frank Leslie Cross. Tübingen: J. C. B. Mohr, 1936), pp. xx, 213.

HARMONY OF THE LIFE OF CHRIST

	MATTHEW	MARK	LUKE	JOHN
I. *Parentage and Infancy*				
Genealogy	1:1–17		3:23–38	
Birth of John the Baptist			1:5–25, 57–80	
Annunciation	1:18–25		1:26–38	
The Birth of Jesus	2:1		2:1–7	
The Angels			2:8–20	
The Circumcision and Presentation			2:21–39	
The Wise Men	2:1–12			
The Flight Into Egypt	2:13–23			
Childhood and Visit to Jerusalem			2:40–50	
The Silent Years			2:51–52	
II. *Preparatory Action*				
The Ministry of John	3:1–12	1:1–8	3:1–20	1:19–37
The Baptism of Jesus	3:13–17	1:9–11	3:21–22	
The Temptation	4:1–11	1:12–13	4:1–13	
III. *The Early Galilean Ministry*				
The Wedding at Cana				2:1–12
IV. *The Early Judean Ministry (Passover)*				
A Cleansing of the Temple				2:13–25
Interview with Nicodemus				3:1–21
Competition with John the Baptist				3:22–36
Withdrawal through Samaria				4:1–42
V. *The Return to Galilee*				
The Arrival	4:12	1:14	4:14	4:43–45
Healing of the Nobleman's Son				4:46–54
The Imprisonment of John and				
The Move to Capernaum	4:13–16			
The First Galilean Tour	4:17			
The Call of the First Disciples	4:18–22	1:16–20		
A Day of Work	8:14–17	1:21–34	4:31–41	
Traveling and Preaching		1:35–39	4:42–44	
Miracles and Discourses	8:1–4 9:1–17 12:1–21	1:40–3:12	5:1–6:19	

HARMONY OF THE LIFE OF CHRIST

	MATTHEW	MARK	LUKE	JOHN
The Appointment of the Twelve		3:13–19a	6:12–16	
The Sermon on the Mount	5:1–7:29		(6:20–49)	
The Centurion's Servant	8:5–13		7:1–10	
The Widow's Son			7:11–17	
The Inquiry of John the Baptist	11:2–30		7:18–35	
The Anointing of Jesus			7:36–50	
Another Preaching Tour			8:1–3	
The Protest of the Family	12:46–50	3:31–35	8:19–21	
Parables	13:1–53	4:1–34	8:4–18	
Miracles	8:18, 23–34; 9:18–26	4:35–5:43	8:22–56	

VI. *A Third Tour: The Peak of the Ministry*

	MATTHEW	MARK	LUKE	JOHN
Second Journey to Jerusalem				5:1–47
Rejection at Nazareth	13:54–58	6:1–6		
The Tour of the Twelve	9:36–11:1	6:7–13	9:1–6	
The Death of John	14:1–12	6:14–29	9:7–9	
The Return of the Twelve	14:13	6:30–32	9:10	
The Feeding of the 5,000	14:13–21	6:33–44	9:11–17	6:1–14
The Retirement and the Walking on the Sea	14:22–33	6:45–52		6:15–21
Discourse on the Bread of Life				6:22–71
The Discourse in the Synagogue	15:1–20	7:1–23		

VII. *The Retirement to the North*

	MATTHEW	MARK	LUKE	JOHN
In Tyre and Sidon	15:21–28	7:24–30		
In Decapolis	15:29–31	7:31–37		
Feeding of the 4,000— Discourse	15:32–16:12	8:1–21		
Healing of the Blind Man		8:22–26		
The Revelation of His Person	16:13–26	8:27–37	9:18–25	
The Transfiguration	16:27–17:13	8:38–9:13	9:26–36	
Healing of the Demoniac	17:14–21	9:14–29	9:37–43	
Prediction of Death and Resurrection	17:22–23	9:30, 32	9:43–45	

VIII. *The Last Ministry in Galilee*   17:24–18:35   9:33–50   9:46–50   7:1–9

(*continued*)

HARMONY OF THE LIFE OF CHRIST

	MATTHEW	MARK	LUKE	JOHN
IX. *The Later Judean Ministry*				
The Journey to Jerusalem via Samaria	19:1–2; 8:19–22	10:1	9:51–62	7:10
The Feast of Tabernacles				7:11–52
The Woman Taken in Adultery				7:53–8:11
Argument with Pharisees				8:12–59
The Man Born Blind				9:1–41
Discourse on Good Shepherd				10:1–21
The Mission of the Seventy			10:1–24	
The Parable of the Good Samaritan			10:25–37	
Mary and Martha			10:38–42	
The Lord's Prayer			11:1–13	
Controversy with Pharisees			11:14–54	
Public Teachings			12:1–59	
The Feast of Dedication				10:22–39
X. *The Perean Ministry*				[10:40–42]
Warnings			13:22–35	
Dinner with a Pharisee			14:1–24	
Challenge to the Multitude			14:25–35	
Teaching Publicans and Sinners			15:1–32	
Teaching the Disciples			16:1–17:10	
The Raising of Lazarus				11:1–44
The Withdrawal to Ephraim				11:45–54
XI. *The Last Journey to Jerusalem*				
Ministry in Samaria and Galilee			17:11–18:14	
Ministry in Perea				
Teaching on Divorce	19:1–12	10:1–12		
Teaching on Children	19:13–15	10:13–16	18:15–17	
The Rich Young Ruler	19:16–20:16	10:17–31	18:18–30	
Prediction of Death	20:17–19	10:32–34	18:31–34	
Ambition of James and John	20:20–28	10:35–45		
Approach to Jerusalem	20:29–34	10:46–52	18:35–19:28	
Arrival at Bethany				11:55–12:11
XII. *The Passion Week*				
Sunday				
The Triumphal Entry	21:1–9	11:1–10	19:29–40	12:12–19
Jesus' View of the City	21:10–11	11:11	19:41–44	
Monday				
Cursing of the Fig Tree	21:18–19	11:12–14		
Cleansing of the Temple	21:12–13	11:15–19	19:45–48	

HARMONY OF THE LIFE OF CHRIST

	MATTHEW	MARK	LUKE	JOHN
Healings in the Temple	21:14–17			
Tuesday				
The Withered Fig Tree	21:19–22	11:20–25		
Controversy	21:23–22:46	11:27–12:37	20:1–44	
Condemnation of Scribes and Pharisees	23:1–39	12:38–40	20:45–47	
Jesus' Observation of the Widow		12:41–44	21:1–4	
The Visit of the Greeks				12:20–36
Jewish Rejection of Jesus				12:37–50
The Apocalyptic Discourse	24–25	13:1–37	21:5–38	
Prediction of the Cross	26:1–5	14:1–2	22:1–2	
Anointing by Mary	26:6–13	14:3–9		12:2–8
The Betrayal	26:14–16	14:10–11	22:3–6	
Wednesday—no record				
Thursday				
The Passover Meal	26:17–29	14:12–25	22:7–30	13:1–38
Farewell Discourse				14:1–31
Discourse on Way to Gethsemane				15–16
The High-Priestly Prayer				17
In the Garden	26:30, 36–46	14:26, 32–42	22:39–46	18:1
Betrayal and Arrest	26:47–56	14:43–52	22:47–53	18:2–12
Trial Before Annas				18:12–14, 19–23
Trial Before Caiaphas	26:57, 59–68	14:53, 55–65	22:54, 63–65	18:24
The Denial of Peter	26:58, 69–75	14:54, 66–72	22:54–62	18:15–18, 25–27
Trial Before the Sanhedrin	27:1	15:1	22:66–71	
Death of Judas	27:3–10			
Friday				
Trial Before Pilate	27:2, 11–14	15:1–5	23:1–5	18:28–38
Before Herod			23:6–12	
Return to Pilate	27:15–26	15:6–15	23:13–25	18:39–19:16
Mockery by Soldiers	27:27–30	15:16–19		
The Way to Calvary	27:31–34	15:20–23	23:26–32	19:16–17
The Crucifixion	27:35–56	15:24–41	23:33–49	19:18–30
The Burial	27:57–60	15:42–46	23:50–54	19:31–42
Saturday				
The Women at the Tomb	27:61	15:47	23:55–56	
The Guard	27:62–66			
XIII. *The Resurrection*				
Sunday				
The Women's Visit	28:1–8	16:1–8	24:1–12	20:1–10
The Appearances of Jesus				

(*continued*)

HARMONY OF THE LIFE OF CHRIST

	MATTHEW	MARK	LUKE	JOHN
Mary Magdalene		16:9–11		20:11–18
Other Women	28:9–10			
Report of the Guard	28:11–15			
The Two Disciples		16:12–13	24:13–32	
Peter			24:33–35	
The Ten Apostles		16:14	24:36–43	20:19–25
The Eleven Apostles				20:26–31
By Sea of Galilee				21:1–14
Conversation with				
Peter				21:15–25
Disciples in Galilee	28:16–20	16:15–18		
Eleven at Olivet			24:44–49	
The Great Commis-				
sion and				
Ascension	28:18–20	16:19–20	24:50–53	

A review of the foregoing sketch of biographical material shows that there is a great deal of overlapping in the accounts. Much material is given at least three times by the Synoptics and is sometimes repeated by John. The sections in which all three agree are usually narrative portions concerning miracles or parables. Certain outstanding events, such as the baptism, the temptation, the feeding of the five thousand, the transfiguration, and the Passion week are recorded by all three of the Synoptics.

Luke and John have the largest amount of text that is not duplicated elsewhere. The section from Luke 9:51 to 18:14 is unique in its content, except as certain of the sayings are paralleled in Matthew for content, though not necessarily for context. Most of the Johannine material is different from that of the Synoptics, even when there is a general historical parallelism in sequence.

The Gospels are much more concerned with presenting a person than with writing a story. Not the completeness or the order of the account, but its significance is important. The differences between the varying reports indicate that they are supplementary, and probably undesignedly so as far as the human authors are concerned. The agreement of the accounts warrants amply the conclusion that a solid core of knowledge about Jesus was part of the fixed teaching of the early church, and that it was based on the valid testimony of eyewitnesses.

Much has already been said under the separate treatments of the Gospels that need not be repeated. Discernible in all of them, irrespective of their individual approach to the biography of the Lord, is a rise in his appeal to the public, a crisis at which he is rejected by the leaders, abandoned by the populace, and not well understood by his disciples. At the death of John the Baptist and the return of the Twelve from their preaching tour one can see that Jesus' ministry had passed its peak in popular appeal and that he slowly began the conscious descent to the cross. The retirement to the north and the later ministries in Judea and Perea were increasingly filled with controversy. Jesus' reactions to it indicated that he had little hope of convincing his enemies of his message, but he used it as a means for teaching the disciples who clung to him until the last.

The resurrection is the crowning event of Jesus' career. He predicted it on several occasions. Of the truthfulness of the Gospels and of their intent to proclaim that Jesus had physically risen from the dead there can be no legitimate doubt. All agree that the tomb was found empty on the first day of the week and that he appeared in tangible and recognizable form to his followers on numerous occasions.

None of these periods is chronicled exhaustively, not even the Passion week, in which Wednesday seems to have been omitted from the chronological account.

THE GEOGRAPHY OF JESUS' LIFE

The active life of the Lord Jesus was spent within the confines of Palestine, a territory comprising not more than ten thousand square miles. In infancy he was taken into Egypt by Joseph and Mary in order to escape the threat of Herod's anger (Matt. 2:13–14), and at the crisis of his ministry he visited Tyre and Sidon (15:21); but most of his travels were on the roads between Galilee and Jerusalem. If he crossed the Jordan to the east, he probably stayed in the cities and villages that bordered the river, so that he did not go far into the trans-Jordanian country.

The land of Palestine is located at the eastern end of the Mediterranean Sea, which washes its entire western shore. From Mt. Lebanon on the north to the southern end of the Dead Sea is a distance of approximately one hundred and seventy-five miles. From the coast to the Sea of Galilee on the north is only twenty-eight miles; from the coast to the Dead Sea on the south is about fifty-four miles. From north to south the land is divided by the Jordan River; it rises in the springs at the foot of Mt. Hermon and then flows southward through the Sea of Galilee to its terminus in the Dead Sea.

The land is divided into four general sections: the coastal plain, which extends northward from the desert along the Mediterranean up to Mt. Carmel; the hill country, which is rugged and largely barren; the valley of the Jordan, a deep gorge that, at the Dead Sea, is twelve hundred seventy-five feet below sea level; and a mountainous plateau east of the Jordan that is bordered on the east by the desert.

These four divisions provided Palestine with a variety of climate and material resources. The coastal plain had a few good harbors, but Joppa

One of the sources of the Jordan River, Nahr Baniyas.

(the modern Jaffa) and Ptolemais, north of Carmel, were embarkation points for the ships that plied the sea-borne trade of the eastern Mediterranean. Along the coastal plain ran the road that had from time immemorial been the communicating link between Egypt and the kingdoms to the

Aerial view of the Jordan River, looking north.

north and east. The climate along the shore was temperate and mild and the soil was fertile, so that agriculture flourished.

The hill country, where the Israelites had lived since the conquest of the land under Joshua, was rocky and barren. Jerusalem, near the end of the Dead Sea, and Samaria, near Mt. Ebal and Mt. Gerizim, were the two most important centers. The high elevation of the hill country gave it a moderate climate. Small farming, including the culture of grapes, small grains, and cattle, formed the principal occupation of the people.

Beginning at Mt. Carmel the plain of Esdraelon extended along the Kishon valley from the northwest in a southeasterly direction to the foot of Mt. Gilboa and thence connected with the valley that led to the Jordan. Because it was the sole good line of communication between the coastal plain and the center of the land, it was a military prey of great value and the plain was often the battleground for opposing armies of north and south when they fought for possession of Palestine. Megiddo, the key city of the region, gave its name to Har-Magedon, the Hill of Megiddo, or Armageddon, the site of the predicted last great conflict of this age (Rev. 16:16).

Within the hill country the majority of the population of Palestine lived. In the north was Galilee, the home country of Jesus. It was rugged terrain, but here and there the valleys gave opportunity for farming, while on the lake the fishing industry throve. The plain of Gennesaret that bordered the lake on the west was fertile and the lake was ringed with towns that had sprung up because of the business that grew there. Trade routes to the east passed through Galilee. Nazareth, Jesus' early home, was just to the northwest of one of these caravan routes. Many Romans and Greeks settled along the lake because of the healthy climate and because of business opportunities. Bethsaida, Chorazin, Capernaum, Magdala, the home of Mary, and Tiberias were some of these towns that Jesus frequented. Nazareth and Cana were farther inland.

The rocky hill country of Judah, terraced for agriculture.

South of Galilee was Samaria, the former center of the northern kingdom of Israel. The country is rough and hilly, less cultivable than Galilee. The twin mountains of Ebal and Gerizim, center of worship since the days of the conquest, dominated the landscape. The plain of Shechem, where Jacob settled and dug his well (John 4:5), supported a farming population.

South of Samaria was Judea, somewhat similar in terrain to Samaria. The lowlands bordering on the coastal plain were watered by occasional streams from the hills and by the winds that brought moisture from the Mediterranean. The center of the land was too rocky for much farming and the eastern part of Judea was almost wholly barren desert. The southern part, or the Negeb as it is still called, was fertile but dry, much like parts of the western United States. Irrigation has opened this territory to farming in recent years, though in the time of Christ it was practically uninhabitable.

The valley of the Jordan is one of the most unusual geological phenomena in the world. It is part of a rift that extends from the Taurus mountains in the north down through Arabia and the eastern tongue of the Red Sea into Africa. From its headwaters to the Dead Sea, which has no outlet, the Jordan has a fall of approximately three thousand feet. In Jesus' time it flowed first into Lake Huleh, a small body of water about three miles wide, located in the middle of a large swamp of reeds. In the modern resettlement of Palestine Jewish colonists have drained the lake to make farmland, so that it no longer exists; and the Jordan flows directly into the Sea of Galilee, called by the Romans the Lake of Tiberias. The lake is fourteen miles long, nine miles wide at its greatest expanse, and six hundred eighty-two feet below sea level. Because of the winds that often descend on it through the chimneylike defiles in the hills, the lake is subject to sudden violent storms. On the eastern side the banks are steep and the country is wild; on the western side are broad, cultivable slopes where, in Jesus' day, a number of towns and cities dotted the shore.

From the Sea of Galilee the Jordan winds a tortuous course to the Dead Sea. The gorge of the Jordan is narrow with steep sides, and is tropical in climate. The river is augmented by two other streams—the Jarmuk, which enters from the east four miles south of the lake, and the Jabbok, which joins it from the east about twenty miles north of the Dead Sea. The actual bed of the river is usually from one to two hundred feet wide, but in the rainy season the entire inner gorge is often flooded with its muddy waters. In ancient times there were no bridges, but the river could be crossed by fords in a few places.

The Dead Sea was called the Salt Sea, or the Sea of the Arabah (Josh. 3:16; II Kings 14:25), in the Old Testament. Because it has no outlet it is really a gigantic evaporating basin in which minerals and salts have been collecting for centuries. The water is extremely bitter to the taste and is so

General view of Tiberias on the Sea of Galilee.

impregnated with chemicals that one cannot sink in it. The cities of the plain that perished in the overthrow of Sodom and Gomorrah probably lie below the water of the southern tongue of the Dead Sea. The rocky desert to the south and southeast where Edom was located contained mineral deposits that were occasionally worked by the inhabitants.

Some farming was carried on in the Jordan valley wherever it was wide enough to allow for settlement. Its tropical climate permitted the raising of fruits and crops that would not thrive in the colder highlands.

Across the Jordan valley lies the eastern plateau; it stretches away to the Arabian desert. Toward the north is the Anti-Lebanon range of mountains, while toward the south bordering the Jordan are the hills of Gilead and Moab. On the slope of the Anti-Lebanons lies Damascus, the oldest continuously inhabited city in the world. South of it are the grasslands of Bashan, famous for their cattle. The northern section of this territory was known as Iturea in Christ's day, and the southern section was called Gaulanitis, from the city of Golan. Gilead, which extended from the Jarmuk River to the head of the Dead Sea and the upper part of Moab, between Gilead and the Arnon River, was the Perea of the New Testament.

In the time of Christ Palestine and Syria were closely linked by Roman rule and by settlements. The province of Syria included Phoenicia to Mt. Carmel and a strip of the coastal plain south of Joppa. The Roman governors of Syria kept a watchful eye on developments in Palestine and intervened occasionally if the local ruler or the Roman procurator did not seem to be acting wisely.

The Decapolis, a region south and east of the Sea of Galilee (originally a federation of ten cities settled by Greek-speaking people), contained a large foreign population. They did not constitute a single political unit, for they were under different rulers, some from Syria, some under Philip. They brought into Palestine a western type of civilization that was quite different from that of the Hebrew people and that must have familiarized even the rural population with Hellenistic customs and institutions. Although Jesus lived much of his life in Galilee, he could not have been unfamiliar with the language, customs, and beliefs of the Gentile peoples who dominated the world outside of Palestine.

The routes by which Jesus traveled and the places he visited are easily located on the map of Palestine (p. 174), which should be consulted in conjunction with the discussion of the Gospels. Jesus and his disciples toured Galilee and apparently visited most of the villages of the district. The majority of the cities that he entered are identifiable. Bethlehem and Nazareth are still flourishing villages. Cana, where he performed his first public miracle (John 2:1–11); Nazareth, where he spent his early years engaging in the carpenter's trade (Luke 4:34; Mark 6:3); Chorazin and Capernaum, where he preached frequently (Matt. 11:21, 23); Magdala, the home of Mary Magdalene (27:56); and Nain, where Jesus restored the widow's son to life—all were within twenty-five miles of each other. The site of Bethsaida is uncertain, but quite likely it was at the head of the Lake of Galilee east of the Jordan. The description of its location in John indicates that it was on the opposite side of the lake from Capernaum and Tiberias (John 6:1, 17, 25).

On the east side of Galilee was the region of Gerasa where Jesus cured the demoniac (Luke 8:26, 37). Probably it is to be identified with Kersa or Gergesa, which was located at a rather wild spot on a precipitous shoreline rather than with Gerasa, the modern Jerash, southeast of Galilee in the Decapolis.

Jesus' ministry in Judea was confined to the city of Jerusalem itself and to a few outlying villages. Bethany, where he ate with Mary and Martha, was a mile to the east on the slope of the Mount of Olives. Ephraim, to which he retired when the hostility became too great, was near the wilderness (John 11:54). Bethphage (Luke 19:29) was probably near Bethany. Emmaus, to which he walked with the two disciples after the resurrection, was about seven and a half miles west of Jerusalem on the road to Joppa.

Ruins of the synagogue at Capernaum.

The site is disputed, but a reference in Josephus[8] states that a place called Emmaus was only sixty stadia from Jerusalem, which accords exactly with Luke's description of the distance (24:13).

The references in the Gospels to Jerusalem itself are numerous. The temple, the pools of Siloam and of Bethesda with its porticoes (John 5:2), the valley of the Kidron between the city and the Mount of Olives (18:1),

---

8. Josephus *Wars of the Jews* VII.vi.6.

Ruins of Bethany. The towerlike structures in the upper right corner are said to be the remnants of the house of Simon the Leper, while the structure in the center is the so-called Tomb of Lazarus.

View of the Garden of Gethsemane, with the Mount of Olives in the background.

the garden of Gethsemane located on the side of the Mount of Olives (Luke 22:39), and Golgotha, "the skull" (23:33), were all landmarks familiar to Jesus and the writers of the Gospels.

THE TEACHING OF JESUS

In Mark's description of the activity of the Lord Jesus Christ there are fourteen references to the fact that he was engaged in teaching the multitude or his disciples. Luke and Matthew also speak frequently of his teaching work. Instruction was his delight; and its effectiveness is well attested by the way in which his disciples remembered his words and repeated them to others.

Methods

The method of teaching that Jesus used was not entirely novel. Some of the rabbis of his day, like Hillel, were famed for their wisdom and their ability to hold the attention of their people. All the pedagogical devices they employed were doubtless known to him, and he used them; but he used them far more effectively than they did. The people "were astonished at his teaching: for he taught them as having authority, and not as the scribes" (Mark 1:22). There was a directness, a freshness, and an authority in the teaching of the Lord Jesus Christ that made him more effective than his contemporaries. He was a master teacher whose skill in instructing the ignorant and the wayward was unsurpassed. What were his methods?

The method of teaching for which he is best known is the parable. A parable is an extended metaphor, the description of some common action or object as an illustration of spiritual truth. It is unlike an allegory because the latter may be purely fictitious, whereas the parable is always connected with ordinary, though perhaps unidentified, occurrences. Jesus' parables of the new and old wineskins (2:22), the seed that fell in different kinds of soil (4:2–8), the salt (Matt. 5:13), the good and bad fruit trees (7:16–20), the wise and foolish virgins (25:1–13), and the unfaithful steward (Luke 16:1–8) are excellent examples of this type of teaching. Each situation was taken from daily life, well known to Jesus' hearers. Each narrative was simply told with a minimum of detail. The point of the parable was clear and was sometimes stated in a concluding sentence, as in the parable of the ten virgins: "Watch therefore, for ye know not the day nor the hour" (Matt. 25:13).

The parable as a medium of teaching served several purposes. The average hearer would readily understand it because he would instantly recognize its relation to his daily life. Jesus may have taken some of his parables from current affairs so that his audience thought they could recognize the person of whom he spoke. The parables could easily be remem-

Aerial view of Jerusalem from the south.

bered, for they were neither lengthy nor abstract. Their spiritual application was always relevant to the hearer's need. Occasionally parables were given in sequence in order to present different aspects of the same subject, like those of Matthew 13 on the kingdom of heaven or like those of Luke 15 concerning God's reclamation of sinners.

A second method that Jesus used was the epigram—a terse, pungent statement that would stick in the mind of his hearer like a barbed arrow. In this category belong the Beatitudes (Matt. 5:3–12), or the statement "He that findeth his life shall lose it; and he that loseth his life for my sake shall find it" (10:39). Many of these epigrams contain paradoxes that make them all the more striking.

Occasionally Jesus employed argument in his teaching; but when he did so, he usually argued on the basis of Scripture rather than from abstract premises or assumptions. In this regard he differed from the Greek philosophers, who usually tried to establish some axiomatic truth by common agreement and then developed its implications into a system. Matthew 22:15–45 records debates that Jesus conducted with the Pharisees and the Sadducees. In each case his opponents introduced the argument; when he finally posed a question of his own, the argument was founded on a biblical statement. Jesus did not argue for argument's sake. When he did engage in debate, his logic was irresistible.

Another of the Master's favorite methods was that of question and answer. His questions were never trivial, but they were generally related to the deepest human problems. Sometimes they were startling: "For which is easier, to say, Thy sins are forgiven; or to say, Arise, and walk?" (9:5). "For what shall a man be profited, if he shall gain the whole world, and forfeit his life?" (16:26). Questions make men think, whether they are direct or rhetorical. The questions of Jesus always brought his hearers to an alternative, especially those that concerned himself, such as "Who do men say that I am? . . . But who say ye that I am?" (Mark 8:27, 29). Jesus also encouraged his disciples to ask questions. His teaching involved free discussion (John 13:31–14:24), in which they posed their problems and he answered them.

On some occasions Jesus used object lessons. He took a little child to illustrate humility (Matt. 18:1–6), and from the action of the widow who was contributing to the treasury he drew a lesson in giving (Luke 21:1–4). All the parables were implied object lessons, though the material of which Jesus spoke was not always present when he made the comparisons.

These samples of Jesus' method illustrate its variety and its success. He created the parable as a means of teaching, although approximations to it can be found in the Old Testament (Judg. 9:7–15; Isa. 5:1–7), and although the rabbis now and then employed the same general technique. He knew how to make the truth simple and cogent; his parables have lived when the others have been forgotten.

Purpose

All of the teaching of Jesus had a moral and spiritual purpose that was bound up with the mission on which he had been sent by the Father. "The words that I say unto you I speak not from myself: but the Father abiding in me doeth his works" (John 14:10). He regarded his teaching not simply as good advice or as hopeful speculation on universal theories. To him it was a declaration of moral and spiritual finalities. "Every one therefore that heareth these words of mine, and doeth them, shall be likened unto a wise man, who built his house upon the rock . . ." (Matt. 7:24). Jesus taught in order to give people the authoritative word of God on which their destiny depended.

Content

The body of teaching is scattered throughout the Gospels, and there is scarcely a page in any one of them that does not contain didactic utterances of Jesus. Some of it appears in blocks. The ethical teaching is concentrated in the Sermon on the Mount (Matt. 5–7). The parables of the kingdom have been gathered in Matthew 13; the eschatological teaching concerning the end of the age is found mostly in Matthew 24 and 25, and in the parallel passages in Mark 13 and Luke 21. John is filled with discourse: the teaching about his person (John 5:19–47), the bread of life (6:32–59), the nature of his person and mission (8:12–59), the shepherd and the sheep (10:1–30), and the farewell to the disciples, in which he sought to prepare them for his death (13:31–16:33). Some of these, such as the last one, were spoken on one occasion only; others, like the Sermon on the Mount, may have been repeated many times. Jesus made many preaching tours and undoubtedly he gave his parables and epigrams in various places as the need called for them.

The subjects Jesus treated were varied. Social adjustments (Matt. 5:21–26), sexual morality (5:27–32), oaths in speech (5:33–37), one's attitude toward evil (5:38–42), bestowal of charity (6:1–4), prayer (6:5–15; 7:7–12), fasting (6:16–18), economic life (6:19–34), marriage and divorce (19:3–12), relation to government (22:15–22), the nature of God (John 4:21–24), and others were discussed in turn. There is no hint that he ever sought to codify all of the teachings into one law to be obeyed, or into a philosophic system that would be logically impregnable. They were not organized around a system but around himself, and their value depends on who he is. Notable in the Sermon on the Mount is the phrase, "I say unto you," which marks the authority Jesus possessed and constantly asserted. To some his teaching may seem like an unsystematic collection of unrelated sayings, but in the light of his person these sayings take on new meaning. They are the flashing facets of a divine personality.

Doctrine

Certain teachings deserve special mention because of their doctrinal importance. Jesus presented God as a heavenly Father, whose fatherhood should be defined primarily in terms of his own relationship to God. "All things have been delivered unto me of my Father: and no one knoweth the Son, save the Father; neither doth any know the Father, save the Son, and he to whomsoever the Son willeth to reveal *him*" (Matt. 11:27). Nowhere in the Gospels did Jesus say "Our Father" and include himself with his disciples in the first person pronoun. On the contrary, he said to Mary Magdalene at the tomb: "I ascend unto my Father and your Father, and my God and your God" (John 20:17). In the model prayer that he gave to his disciples he taught them to pray "Our Father" (Matt. 6:9), expressing man's moral relationship to God. The divine fatherhood meant more to him than it did to them, since he was in a unique sense the Son of God. He was the Son of God by nature; the disciples could become sons of God only by receiving Christ (John 1:12).

The term "father," however, expressed God's attitude toward men. It connoted his love and justice (Matt. 5:44–45), his interest in and concern for his creation (10:29–30), his forethought and purpose (20:23), his forgiving attitude (Luke 15:11–32), and his final determination of their destiny (John 14:2). The Gospel of John has more references to Jesus' teaching concerning "Our Father" than any of the other Gospels, for the term appears more than one hundred times, and is Jesus' usual form of address to God.

Perhaps the greatest single topic that Jesus discussed was the kingdom. There has been an unusual amount of debate concerning its exact nature. Is it to be equated with a spiritual domination over the lives of men? Was Jesus speaking solely of restoring the independent Jewish monarchy? Is the kingdom identical with the church, or with the millennial reign, or with some revolutionary economic order that he sought to establish? All of these questions have been asked, and each has been answered in the affirmative by one group or another.

Apart from all speculation, certain facts are apparent in the Gospels. All of them mention the kingdom (Matt. 6:33; Mark 1:15; Luke 4:43; John 3:3), saying that Jesus preached it. John's Gospel speaks of it on only two occasions: in Jesus' interview with Nicodemus (3:3, 5) and in the trial before Pilate (18:36). To Jesus the kingdom was the entire sphere of the rule of God. Unquestionably it is spiritual in nature and not primarily political, but its full manifestation has not yet come, and shall not come until the King returns personally to reign (Matt. 25:1, 31).

In the teaching of Jesus no sharp difference is discernible between the meaning of the kingdom of heaven, a phrase used exclusively by Matthew, and the kingdom of God. Both were proclaimed by Jesus to be "at hand" (Matt. 3:2; Mark 1:15); the "mysteries" of both are mentioned in the parables (Matt. 13:11; Luke 8:10); both were preached from the days of John the Baptist (Matt. 11:12–13; Luke 16:16); the two phrases were used indifferently in the invitation to little children (Matt. 19:14; Mark 10:14). If any distinction can be drawn between them, one might say that the kingdom of heaven was used as a Jewish term, possibly in order to avoid offense by unnecessary repetition of the name of God, and that the teaching connected with it concerns the outward manifestation of the kingdom. Most of the passages dealing with the inward aspects of the kingdom use the expression "the kingdom of God" (Luke 17:20; John 3:3, 5; Luke 22:16, 18; 23:51).

The doctrine of the kingdom was linked with the Old Testament. In its ethic it called for repentance (Matt. 4:17), for obedience to the commandments of the law (5:19), for the wholehearted doing of the will of God (7:21). This was not synonymous with legalism, however; for Joseph of Arimathea, one of the earliest disciples, is described as "looking for the kingdom of God" (Luke 23:51). Jesus himself regarded the kingdom as yet to come in its fullness after his death and resurrection (22:16). The kingdom, then, is that rule which God shall establish over the earth when Christ returns. Its principles will conform to the highest spirit of holiness that is contained in the revealed law, and its perfection will come only through the work of Christ, who is both redeemer and king.

The teaching of Jesus concerning himself is of great significance. As a boy he informed Joseph and Mary of a peculiar obligation to his heavenly Father (2:49). He questioned his disciples concerning their belief in him (Matt. 16:15) and accepted with approval Simon's reply that he was "the Son of the living God" (16:16). Before his enemies he used language that predicated both preexistence and deity (John 8:42, 58; 10:30–33, 36;

View of Mount Zion in the Holy City.

Matt. 22:41–45). When believers worshiped him, he did not demur (John 9:38; 20:28–29), as Paul did on one occasion (Acts 14:11–18). The indirect implications of his teachings are equally conclusive, for he placed himself above the law (Matt. 5:21–22), and claimed authority to forgive sins (Mark 2:9–11). If the Gospel records are trustworthy at all, they declare unmistakably not only that Jesus was supernatural in his origin, but also that he claimed to be deity.

His estimate of his own mission is important. He came to preach the gospel of the kingdom (Luke 4:43), to call sinners to repentance (Matt. 9:13), to seek and to save the lost (Luke 19:10), to minister, and to give his life a ransom for many (Mark 10:45). He was sent by the Father (John 20:21), and just before his death he reported to the Father that he had accomplished his mission (17:4). Revelation and redemption had both been committed to him, and he completed both. On many occasions he predicted his death and resurrection (2:19; 3:14; 6:51; 12:24; Matt. 16:21; Mark 10:33–34), and also his return to judgment (Matt 25:31–46).

The many spiritual and ethical topics on which Jesus made pronouncements are too numerous to treat here. One common characteristic of his discourses is noteworthy: they were all based on the assumption that he had come to proclaim God's truth, that he had full authority to do so, and that man was obligated to follow his teaching. He represented himself as the Son of God, and as the Son of God his word is final.

FOR FURTHER READING

Andrews, Samuel J. *The Life of Our Lord upon Earth.* New and Revised Edition. New York: Charles Scribner's Sons, 1893. Pp. 651. Especially good on chronology.

Cullmann, Oscar. *Jesus and the Revolutionaries.* New York: Harper & Row, 1970.

Donehoo, James DeQ. *The Apocryphal and Legendary Life of Christ.* New York: The Macmillan Company, 1903. Pp. 531.

Edersheim, Alfred. *The Life and Times of Jesus the Messiah.* Eighth Edition, Revised. Two volumes. Grand Rapids, Mich.: Wm. B. Eerdmans Publishing Company, 1953. Pp. xlvii, 1523.

France, R. T. *I Came to Set the Earth on Fire.* Downers Grove, Ill.: InterVarsity Press, 1975.

Guthrie, D. *Jesus the Messiah.* Grand Rapids: Zondervan Publishing House, 1972.
_____. *A Shorter Life of Christ.* Grand Rapids: Zondervan Publishing House, 1970.

Harrison, E. F. *A Short Life of Christ.* Grand Rapids: Wm. B. Eerdmans Publishing Company, 1968. Pp. 288.

Henry, C. F. H., ed. *Jesus of Nazareth: Saviour and Lord.* Grand Rapids: Wm. B. Eerdmans Publishing Company, 1966. Pp. viii, 277.

Hoehner, Harold W. *Chronological Aspects of the Life of Christ.* Grand Rapids: Zondervan Publishing House, 1977.

Kingsbury, Jack D. *Jesus Christ in Matthew, Mark, and Luke.* Philadelphia: Fortress Press, 1981.

Marshall, I. H. *I Believe in the Historical Jesus.* Grand Rapids: Wm. B. Eerdmans Publishing Company, 1977. Pp. 253.

Ogg, George. *The Chronology of the Public Ministry of Jesus.* London: Longmans, Green, & Company, 1931. Pp. 407.

Robertson, A. T. *Epochs in the Life of Jesus.* New York: Charles Scribner's Sons, 1907. Pp. xi, 192. Good, brief study.

Smith, David. *In the Days of His Flesh: The Earthly Life of Our Lord and Saviour.* Twelfth Edition. London: Hodder & Stoughton, 1917. Pp. 549.

THE BIRTH OF CHRIST

Brown, R. E. *The Virginal Conception and Bodily Resurrection of Jesus.* Ramsey, N.J.: Paulist Press, 1973.

Machen, J. Gresham. *The Virgin Birth of Christ.* Second Edition. New York: Harper and Brothers, Publishers, 1932. Pp. 415.

Orr, James. *The Virgin Birth of Christ.* New York: Charles Scribner's Sons. 1907. Pp. 301.

THE RESURRECTION OF CHRIST

Craig, Wm. L. *The Son Rises: The Historical Evidence for the Resurrection of Jesus.* Chicago: Moody Press, 1981.

Fuller, Daniel B. *Easter Faith and History.* Grand Rapids: Wm. B. Eerdmans Publishing Company, 1965. Pp. 279.

Fuller, Reginald H. *The Formation of the Resurrection Narratives.* New York: Macmillan, 1971.

Gaffin, R. B. *The Centrality of the Resurrection.* Grand Rapids: Baker Book House, 1978.

Habermas, Gary. *Resurrection of Jesus: An Apologetic.* Grand Rapids: Baker Book House, 1980.

Hayes, Doremus A. *The Resurrection Fact.* Nashville: Cokesbury Press, 1932. Pp. 355.

Ladd, G. E. *I Believe in the Resurrection.* Grand Rapids: Wm. B. Eerdmans Publishing Company, 1975. Pp. 156.

Latham, Henry. *The Risen Master.* Cambridge: Deighton Bell and Company, 1901. Pp. xvi, 488.

Milligan, William. *The Resurrection of Our Lord.* London: Macmillan & Company, 1881. Pp. xiii, 304.

Morison, Frank. *Who Moved the Stone?* London: Faber & Faber, 1930. Pp. 304.

O'Collins, G. *What Are They Saying About the Resurrection?* Ramsey, N.J.: Paulist Press, 1978.

Orr, James. *The Resurrection of Jesus.* Cincinnati: Jennings & Graham, 1909. Pp. 292.

Sloan, Harold P. *He Is Risen.* New York and Nashville: Abingdon-Cokesbury Press, 1942. Pp. 186.

Sparrow-Simpson, W. J. *Our Lord's Resurrection.* London: Longmans, Green, and Company, 1905. Pp. 320.

———. *The Resurrection and Modern Thought.* London: Longmans, Green, & Company, 1911. Pp. ix, 464.

PART III

THE RECORDS OF THE EARLY CHURCH

The Period of Expansion:
A.D. 30 to 60

CHAPTER 13

THE ESTABLISHMENT OF THE CHURCH: ACTS 1:1 TO 8:3

Between the ministry of the Lord Jesus Christ and the church as it emerged into the full current of history there is a tremendous gap. How did it happen that the followers of Jesus, who were obscure provincial Galileans and Judeans, became world figures? What changed the timidity that drove these men to denial and flight at the crucifixion into a boldness that made them stalwart apologists for a new faith? How did preachers who were confessedly "unlearned and ignorant men" (Acts 4:13) make such an impact on the world that they created an entirely new culture that reshaped the face of all Western civilization? What was the origin of the theological truths contained in the New Testament and preached by the early missionaries? How is the teaching of the Epistles related to the teaching of the Gospels? How did it happen that a movement that began among Jews, that centered in a Jewish Messiah, and that was founded on the Jewish Scriptures became a religion espoused largely by Gentiles, as it is today?

These and similar questions are answered by the book of Acts, which is the only existing link between the ministry and teaching of Christ and the Christianity that appears full-blown in the epistles of Paul and of the other New Testament writers.

THE RECORD: ACTS

Acts in itself is not a unit, for it is obviously designed as a sequel to Luke. The author speaks of "the former treatise" (Acts 1:1), and his address to

Theophilus indicates a relationship to the Gospel that is addressed to the same person. The summary of that former treatise, as Acts gives it (1:1–2), accords exactly with the content of Luke and resumes the narrative at the point where Luke dropped it. There can be no reasonable doubt that Acts and Luke are two volumes of the same work. They were designed to fulfill the same general purpose of confirming personal faith and to provide an understandable historical record of God's revelation to men in the work of Christ, both through his personal career and through his church. Historically and spiritually Acts holds the answer to these problems.

Outline

Acts can be divided into five main sections:

I. Introduction	1:1–11
II. The Origin of the Church: Jerusalem	1:12–8:3
III. The Period of Transition: Samaria	8:4–11:18
IV. The Expansion to the Gentiles	11:19–21:16
The Pauline Mission: Antioch and the Empire	
V. The Imprisonment and Defense of Paul: Caesarea and Rome	21:17–28:31

Acts is constructed logically around the outline of geographical development given in 1:8: "ye shall be my witnesses both in Jerusalem, and in all Judea and Samaria, and unto the uttermost part of the earth." The first section after the introduction deals with the beginnings in Jerusalem. The second gives glimpses of work in Samaria, the coastal plain, and Caesarea. The last two sections take the message to the cities of the Mediterranean world, ending with Rome, the capital. The geographical expansion of the church was like waves of the tide, which rise higher after every recession, and move farther and farther up the beach.

The book of Acts may also be outlined according to its record of growth. In 2:47, 5:14, 6:7, 9:31, 12:24, 16:5, and 19:20 notations of increase in numbers or in quality of spiritual life show that Acts is concerned with the progressive development of the group. In the last part of the book from 19:20 to the end the emphasis is more personal than general. It stresses the events in the life of Paul as an individual rather than the church as an institution.

Acts may also be outlined in terms of the personalities that appear in it. Chapters 1 through 5 center in Peter; chapters 6 and 7, in Stephen; chapters 8 through 12 introduce several personalities, chief of whom are Barnabas, Philip, and Saul of Tarsus; and from chapter 13 to the end Paul is the dominant figure. A comparison between Peter and Paul is drawn in several instances: both were leaders, one to the Jews, one to the Gentiles. Peter labored largely in Jerusalem; Paul, in the Gentile world. Each had at least one discourse reproduced in full, which gives a summary of his preaching: Peter, on the day of Pentecost (2:14–40); Paul, at Antioch of Pisidia (13:16–42). Both performed miracles: Peter healed a lame man (3:1–10), and so did Paul (14:8–10). Peter brought swift judgment on Ananias and Sapphira (5:1–11), and Paul smote Elymas with blindness (13:6–11). Peter was freed from prison in Jerusalem (5:19–21; 12:1–11); Paul was released from jail at Philippi by divine intervention (16:19–30). Both stressed the work of the Holy Spirit (2:38; 19:2–6), and both made the resurrection a primary doctrine of their preaching (Peter: Acts 2:24–36; 3:15, 26; 4:2; 5:30; 10:40–41; Paul: 13:30–37; 17:3, 18, 31; 24:15, 21; 25:19; 26:8, 23). As one was the champion of the early church in Jerusalem, so the other was the founder of the first Gentile churches. There is, however, no intimation of antagonism between the two, nor was the work of either confined to one class of hearers. Peter brought the gospel to the house of the Gentile Cornelius, and Paul spoke to the Jews on every occasion that he could find. [1]

The reliability of Acts has often been challenged, but it has never been successfully impugned. There are difficulties to be encountered in equating its chronology with that of the epistles, and not all of the historical allusions in Acts can be confirmed because in many cases the requisite data are lacking. In those instances, however, where positive archaeological and literary data can be produced, Acts has been vindicated. John Knox, who thinks that "there is ample reason for being doubtful about some of the details" in Acts, admits that "there is every reason for trusting the essential historicity of the final chapters."[2]

Content

The very fact that Luke was desirous of writing an explanatory treatise on the development of Christian teaching and on the Christian mission implies that he possessed some insight into its overall significance. He was not merely a chronicler who drudgingly noted dry events on paper. He had the instincts of a historian, and he presented his facts with reference to the continuity of the theme that interested him. That theme was the growth of

---

1. Notice also the frequent references to "the word of God" (4:31; 6:2, 7; 8:14; 11:1; 13:5, 7, 44, 46, 48; 16:32; 17:13; 18:11; cf. 20:32) and to "the word of the Lord" (8:25; 12:24; 13:49; 15:35, 36; 19:10; cf. 14:3; 20:35). These are linked to geographical locations, and could suggest another type of outline for Acts.

2. John Knox, *Chapters in a Life of Paul* (New York: Abingdon-Cokesbury Press, n.d.), p. 43.

the church, particularly the transition from Judaism to Gentile Christianity. In this transition he took an active part, as his use of "we" indicates, and he was well qualified to deal with the theme of which he wrote.

Acts, then, does not pretend to be an exhaustive account of all the events that took place in the growth of the early church. No word is said of the expansion southward and eastward from Palestine, although there must have been Christians in Egypt and Syria from a very early date. There were believers in Damascus before Paul's conversion, but no account is given of the progress of the church there. The main narrative of Acts is concerned with the mission that took the gospel northward through Antioch to Asia Minor and from there to Macedonia, Achaia, and Rome.

The probable reason for this restriction is twofold. First, the writer himself was best acquainted with that aspect of the expansion of Christianity and consequently could use it with greater facility as illustrative of his main theme. Second, his main purpose was to instruct his reader in the certainty of the gospel. The continuity of that gospel from Jesus through the disciples to the hour at which he wrote must be demonstrated. Since Paul was the leader of the Gentile mission, he deserved primary attention, and the explanation of the transition from Jew to Gentile, from law to grace, and from Palestine to the empire did not call for a comprehensive survey of all that took place in the missionary growth of the Christian church. For Luke's purpose the presentation of this one phase was sufficient.

The chronological period covered by Acts extends from the crucifixion of Christ about A.D. 30 to the close of Paul's imprisonment in Rome in A.D. 60. The datings of events in Acts have been variously set by different scholars, but the figures given here will represent a fair average of their findings. Ancient writers did not date events by a calendar but by the accession or reign of officials. Absolute exactitude to the month and day is sometimes impossible to achieve. Certain fixed points of chronology stand out in Acts.

1. The death of Herod Agrippa I	Acts 12:20–23
2. The famine under Claudius	11:28
3. The proconsulship of Sergius Paulus	13:7
4. The expulsion of Jews from Rome under Claudius	18:2
5. The proconsulship of Gallio	18:12
6. The proconsulship of Felix	23:26; 24:27
7. The accession of Festus, Felix' successor	24:27

On this rather slender framework the arrangement of Acts depends. The allusions are made incidentally, as if the author took for granted that his reader would know the time well enough to fit events into their proper places without further detailed references. Their equation with the years of the first century is as follows:

Death of Herod	A.D. 44 (spring)
Famine under Claudius	44–48
Proconsulship of Sergius Paulus	Before 51
Expulsion of Jews from Rome	Probably 49
Proconsulship of Gallio	Probably 52–53
Proconsulship of Felix	52–56
Accession of Festus	57–60

The most doubtful of these points is the accession of Festus. Eusebius places it in the reign of Nero, and with this dating most of the available sources agree.[3] Felix was tried in Rome for malfeasance, but could not have come to trial before Nero's accession. In that case, Festus was not appointed until after Nero's reign began. The summer of A.D. 57 is the most probable date for Festus' arrival in Palestine, and the hearing of Paul followed shortly afterwards. If, allowing for time of travel, Paul reached Rome about the summer of A.D. 58, the narrative of Acts closed in A.D. 60.

The other events help to locate some of the important periods of the book of Acts. The death of Herod synchronized with the rise of the Gentile church, for after describing the beginning of the work in Antioch Acts 12:1 states that "about that time Herod the king put forth his hands to afflict certain of the church," and not long after the persecution his death took place. The famine under Claudius (11:28) occurred about the same time, between A.D. 44 and 48.

The proconsulship of Sergius Paulus in Cyprus, if before A.D. 51, means that Barnabas and Saul began their mission not later than A.D. 50, and probably earlier.

The accession of Gallio gives a fairly accurate point of reference for Paul's ministry in Corinth. The language of Acts 18:12 not only marks the dating of Paul's arrest and hearing before the proconsul, but it also seemingly implies that the Jews took advantage of Gallio's recent assumption of office in order to ask for a favor. If so, Paul's ministry may have preceded Gallio's arrival in the city, and although he did not leave Corinth immediately (18:18), it came toward the end of his stay of a year and a half (18:11). The ministry in Ephesus of two years and three months (19:8, 10) and the time of travel necessary to reach Jerusalem would bring Paul to the latter

---

3. Eusebius *Historia Ecclesiae* II.xxii.1.

ACE

BYZANTIUM

BITHYNIA

PONTUS

GALATIA

CAPPADOCIA

ROAS

ADRAMYTTIUM

ASSOS

PERGAMUM

A S I A

LYCAONIA

ANTIOCH

ICONIUM

TARSUS

PISIDIA

LYSTRA

DERBE

CILICIA

ANTIOCH

EPHESUS

LAODICEA

PAMPHYLIA

ATTALIA

SELEUCIA

MILETUS

COLOSSAE

PATMOS

LYCIA

PATARA

MYRA

SYRIA

RHODES

SALAMIS

CYPRUS

PAPHOS

DAMASCUS

SSUS

SEA

SIDON

TYRE

PTOLEMAIS

CAESAREA

AIR HAVENS

AN

SEA

JERUSALEM

ALEXANDRIA

AUL'S MISSIONARY JOURNEY'S

st Journey ———————

nd Journey ———————

rd Journey ....

ourney to Rome ---------

MEMPHIS

EGYPT

THE NEW
TESTAMENT
WORLD

destination about the summer of A.D. 55 or 56, and would end the two years' imprisonment at Caesarea at the time of Festus' administration.

Luke's interest was not primarily chronological, although he paid more attention to such details than did most of the writers of the New Testament. Acts stressed the gradual decline of the Jewish church and the rise of Gentile Christianity.

The first question that the disciples asked the risen Lord concerning his program was, "Dost thou at this time restore the kingdom to Israel?" (1:6). The audience at Pentecost was Jewish (2:5), and the preaching was addressed to "men of Israel" (2:22). The church at Jerusalem was predominantly Jewish, although there were two groups among them, the Hebraists of Palestine and the Hellenists of the Dispersion (6:1). The preaching was in Jewish terms and consisted of the presentation of Jesus as the Messiah who had risen from the dead.

Throughout this first period of the apostolic mission the church was established in Jerusalem. At the outset it was characterized as "the Way" (9:2), or "the sect of the Nazarenes" (24:5), a subordinate group in Judaism, perhaps in a category similar to that of the Essenes. The preaching of Stephen, which brought a violent reaction on the part of the Jewish leaders and the consequent dispersion of the disciples, compelled the leaders to seek other fields. The evangelization of Samaria, Antioch, and the Gentile world at large followed.

The period of transition (8:4–11:18) is not covered in detail. The work of only a few of the refugees from persecution is given, but enough is told to show how spontaneously the Gentile trend began and how effective it was. The conversions of the Ethiopian eunuch and of Cornelius, both probably Gentile proselytes, and the enthusiastic response of the Samaritans to the preaching of Philip marked the new trend away from the establishment of the Messianic kingdom to the growth of the visible church.

The Gentile mission (11:19–28:31) began with the establishment of the church at Antioch. There the disciples were called Christians and took a new place in the world. They were known not just as a sect of Judaism, but as an independent body maintaining a different kind of faith (11:26). The Antioch church became a center of teaching, and from it the first mission to the Gentiles went forth. At Antioch was fought out the battle for Gentile freedom, which culminated in the decision of the council at Jerusalem that exempted the Gentile converts from observance of the ceremonial law.

The Pauline program described in Acts 15:35 to 21:14 was illustrative of the development of the church. Although Paul generally appealed "to the Jew first" (Rom. 1:16), the greatest response came from Gentile proselytes and heathen, and the churches that sprang up in the wake of his mission included both Jew and Gentile. On several occasions Paul made unmistakably clear that he was turning to the Gentiles (Acts 13:46; 18:6; 19:9–10; 21:19; 26:20, 23; 28:28). The general rejection of the message by the Jews confirmed his appointment as an apostle to the Gentiles (26:16–18), accelerated the growth of the church independently of the synagogue, and brought the final severance between Judaism and Christianity.

His review of the growth of Christianity reveals the pattern of church life: its power, its objective, its methods, its essential organization and discipline, and its missionary expansion. Acts is not only a history of a given period in the life of the church, it is a handbook for Christians. It illustrates the procedure and the effectiveness of a church built on the principles that the Holy Spirit administers.

Another aspect of Acts is its apologetic character. The relation of Christianity to the Roman government is traced from its origin to the time of Paul's hearing in Rome. Since the writer was a friend of Paul and a companion of the final journey to Rome, one cannot help wondering whether he was not trying to prove to his reader that Christianity was not a source of political danger, but that it was wholly a spiritual movement. J. Ironside Still, in his work St. Paul on Trial,[4] argues that Acts was written as a brief for the defense when Paul appeared before Caesar. Although his theory is not generally accepted, his recognition of the apologetic character of Luke-Acts deserves consideration. Theophilus, to whom Luke-Acts was directed, would not have needed certainty if there had been nothing to make him uncertain. Perhaps the disfavor exhibited toward the gospel by the Jews and Gentiles alike had made him look on it with suspicion. In any case, Luke-Acts demonstrated that a new supernatural revelation had invaded the field of history. It was not confined to any one nationality or group, nor to any existing faith. Nurtured within Judaism, it perpetuated its truth but transcended it by proclaiming that the Messiah had come. Since it was nonpolitical in character it deserved to be treated as a permitted religion, at least on a plane of tolerance equal with the other religions of the empire. For Theophilus, of course, the apologetic was more direct than this, and could be stated in the words of Acts 4:12:

> And in none other is there salvation: for neither is there any other name under heaven, that is given among men, wherein we must be saved.

THE FOUNDATION: ACTS 1:1 TO 8:3

The first period in the history of the early church can be characterized as that of establishment. At the outset there is no evidence that the believers broke sharply with Judaism. Pentecost was a Jewish feast before it became a

---

4. J. Ironside Still, St. Paul on Trial (New York: G. H. Doran Company, n.d.).

Christian anniversary. The preaching of the apostles interpreted the Old Testament Scriptures and stressed Jesus' Messianic office, even avowing that if the nation repented, the Messiah Jesus would return (3:19–20). The addresses of Peter were gauged for a Jewish audience, and so was the great appeal of Stephen. When the apostles went to worship they went to the temple (3:1), and Stephen debated in the synagogues (6:9–10) of the foreign residents in Jerusalem.

Nevertheless the church was not simply a natural outgrowth of Judaism, a new prophetic movement centered about the person of the Galilean Jesus. Luke's Gospel makes unmistakably plain that the career of Jesus from birth to death was miraculous and that he came among men as the Son of God (Luke 1:35). The opening of Acts says that ". . . he . . . showed himself alive after his passion by many proofs, appearing unto them by the space of forty days" (1:3). The resurrection is paramount all through Acts and is the foundation of doctrinal preaching. The church, according to Luke, is a new thing among men.

Within the four years more or less that elapsed between the death of Christ and the persecution that rose about Stephen the church had become a distinct body with its own peculiar organization, beliefs, and purpose.

Pentecost

The birthday of the church was Pentecost. The eleven disciples, Mary the mother of Jesus, his brethren, a number of the women who had followed him, and a large group of unnamed believers, totaling about one hundred and twenty, were gathered for prayer in accordance with the command of Christ. Judas, who had already died, had been replaced by Matthias. On the day of Pentecost, as they were assembled in one place, the Holy Spirit came on them with visible and audible signs. They spoke with new languages, so that their hearers were able to understand in their own dialects "the mighty works of God" (2:5–13).

The coming of the Spirit was the fulfillment of the prediction of John (Luke 3:15–16) and of the promise by Jesus (24:49). Peter declared it to be a fulfillment of the prophecy of Joel (Acts 2:16–21) and a proof of the resurrection of Christ (2:32–36). It fused the believers into one group, giving them a unity that they had not previously possessed, and it emboldened them to brave the perils of persecution (2:4; 4:8, 31; 6:8–15).

Early Preaching

Preaching during this early period of the church's life was centered in the life and person of Christ. Unlike modern preaching, which is usually either the logical development of some topic or the elaboration of a single text, the apostolic preaching was a narration of the life and work of Jesus, with a defense of his resurrection, and was followed by a call to repentance and faith in his name. The sermons of Peter and Stephen that are recorded in this part of Acts were apologetic in character, because they are answers to challenges that were flung at the preachers by a curious or hostile audience.

The apostolic preaching was strongly biblical in content. The New Testament had not been written at this time, but the addresses were saturated with Old Testament quotations and prophecies. Peter introduced his sermon at Pentecost with a long quotation from Joel, and he made another long quotation from the Psalms to show the Messianic promise of the resurrection. Stephen's address was a historical review of the unbelief of the nation that culminated in the rejection of Jesus. Both the precepts and the precedents of Scripture constituted the foundation of the apostolic message.

The burden of this preaching was the necessity of belief in the risen Messiah, repentance both personal and national, and the receiving of the Holy Spirit (2:38). It was accompanied by instruction, so that as the number of the believers increased, they were bound together in common knowledge and common action (2:42).

Organization and Leaders

The first church in Jerusalem was not a highly organized body, owning property and maintaining a strong ecclesiastical system. The apostles, because of their preaching and teaching functions, were naturally the leaders, but the government of the church was essentially democratic. When complaints were voiced that the widows of the Hellenistic Jews were being neglected in the distribution of daily food, the apostles suggested the appointment of qualified men to oversee this part of the church's activity. The choice was made by the "multitude" (6:5), and the new officials were duly appointed.

Much has been said about the so-called communism of the early church, by which a redistribution of goods was made for the benefit of the poor (2:45; 4:34–35). It is true that the multitude "had all things common," but the giving was voluntary, not compulsory, and was apparently calculated for the emergency in Jerusalem where there were many "poor among the saints" (Rom. 15:26). There is no record of a similar system in other churches, although relief of the poor was a general practice.

The meetings of the early Christians, which were held both in the temple and in private homes (Acts 2:46), were characterized by teaching, breaking of bread, and prayer (2:42).

The leaders of the early period were Peter, John, and Stephen. Of the three, John was least prominent, being mentioned only in company with Peter. Peter was the preacher who dominated the scene. He made the opening address on the day of Pentecost, and he defended the position of the Christian believers before the Sanhedrin when he and John were accused (4:5–8). Peter's boldness and spiritual power were an amazing contrast to his vacillation at the time of his denial of Jesus.

Stephen, who was one of the seven appointed for relief work, and who became the outstanding apologist of the early church, was not one of the original twelve disciples. If his name has any bearing on his background, he was a Hellenistic Jew who probably came to Jerusalem as a pilgrim, and after his conversion stayed with the church. As a debater in the foreign synagogues he was without a peer (6:9–10). He did not confine his activities to social work, but became an apologist and evangelist as well as the church's first martyr.

THE FIRST DISPERSION

At the violent death of Stephen and because of the sternly repressive measures taken by the Jewish leaders to crush the new movement, the majority of the Christians in Jerusalem were scattered abroad throughout Judea and Samaria. From this point to the last chapters of Acts little is said of the Jerusalem church. It was strongly Judaistic in character and maintained some observance of the law, as the later controversies showed (15:1; 21:17–26). The scattering of its adherents, however, resulted in numerous missionary projects, of which a few are narrated in the next section on the transition (8:4–11:18).

FOR FURTHER READING

Note: Much of the material for further reading listed here also applies to chapters 14 through 17 since it is arranged by topics.

TOOLS

Burton, Ernest D. *The Records and Letters of the Apostolic Age.* New York: Charles Scribner's Sons, 1923. Pp. viii, 238.

Clark, George W. *Harmony of the Acts of the Apostles.* A New and Revised Edition. Philadelphia: American Baptist Publication Society, 1897. Pp. 408.

Goodwin, Frank J. *A Harmony of the Life of St. Paul.* Grand Rapids, Mich.: Baker Book House, 1950. Pp. 240.

THE APOSTOLIC AGE

Bartlet, James Vernon. *The Apostolic Age* in *Ten Epochs of Church History.* Vol. I. New York: Charles Scribner's Sons, 1900. Pp. xvi, 542.

Bruce, F. F. *The Spreading Flame: The Rise and Progress of Christianity.* Grand Rapids, Mich.: Wm. B. Eerdmans Publishing Company, 1953. Pp. 432.

Caird, G. B. *The Apostolic Age.* London: G. Duckworth & Company, 1955.

Foakes-Jackson, F. J. and Lake, Kirsopp, Editors. *The Beginnings of Christianity.* Five volumes. London: Macmillan & Company, Ltd., 1920–1933. Thorough treatment of background and text.

Purves, George T. *The Apostolic Age.* New York: Charles Scribner's Sons, 1900. Pp. xx, 343.

Ropes, James Hardy. *The Apostolic Age.* New York: Charles Scribner's Sons, 1921. Pp. xi, 327. Liberal viewpoint.

LIVES OF PAUL

Barrett, Charles K. *Essays on Paul.* Philadelphia: Westminster Press, 1982.

Bruce, F. F. *Paul, Apostle of the Heart Set Free.* Grand Rapids, Mich.: Wm. B. Eerdmans Publishing Company, 1977. Pp. 491.

Conybeare, W. J. and Howson, J. S. *The Life and Epistles of St. Paul.* New Edition. Grand Rapids, Mich.: Wm. B. Eerdmans Publishing Company, 1949. Pp. xxii, 850.

Davies, William D. *Paul and Rabbinic Judaism.* Revised Edition. London: S.P.C.K., 1955.

Hayes, Doremus A. *Paul and His Epistles.* New York and Cincinnati: The Methodist Book Concern, c. 1915. Pp. 508. Contains bibliography.

Moe, Olaf. *The Apostle Paul.* Translated by L. A. Vigness. Minneapolis, Minn.: Augsburg Publishing House, c. 1950. Pp. 578.

Ramsay, William. *St. Paul, the Traveller and the Roman Citizen.* New York: G. P. Putnam's Sons, 1909. Pp. xvi, 394.

Robertson, A. T. *Epochs in the Life of Paul.* New York: Charles Scribner's Sons, 1909. Pp. xi, 337.

————. *Paul, the Interpreter of Christ.* New York: G. H. Doran Company, c. 1921. Pp. 155.

Sanders, E. P. *Paul and Palestinian Judaism.* Philadelphia: Fortress Press, 1977.

Smith, David. *The Life and Letters of St. Paul.* New York: G. H. Doran Company, 1920. Pp. xv, 704.

Stalker, James. *The Life of St. Paul.* New Edition. Edinburgh: T. & T. Clark, 1885. Pp. xi, 240. Elementary handbook.

Wood, C. T. *The Life, Letters, and Religion of St. Paul.* Edinburgh: T. & T. Clark, 1946. Pp. xv, 418.

CHRONOLOGY

Gunther, J. J. *Paul: Messenger and Exile.* Valley Forge: Judson Press, 1972.

Jewett, Robert. *A Chronology of Paul's Life.* Philadelphia: Fortress Press, 1979.

Knox, John. *Chapters in a Life of Paul.* New York: Abingdon-Cokesbury Press, 1950. Pp. 168. See chaps. III, IV, V for the chronology of Paul's life. Knox regards the book of Acts as of secondary authority, and not wholly reliable in its chronology of Paul's life.

Lightfoot, J. B. *Biblical Essays.* New York: Macmillan & Company, 1893. "The Chronology of St. Paul's Life and Epistles," pp. 215–233.

Ogg, George. *The Chronology of the Life of Paul.* London: Epworth Press, 1968.

Ramsay, William. *Pauline and Other Studies.* New York: A. C. Armstrong and Sons, 1906. See "The Pauline Chronology," pp. 345–365.

GENERAL INTRODUCTION

Fairweather, Wm. *The Background of the Epistles.* Edinburgh: T. & T. Clark, 1935. Pp. xxiii, 399.

Gloag, Paton J. *Introduction to the Pauline Epistles.* Edinburgh: T. & T. Clark, 1874. Pp. xvi, 480.

Guthrie, Donald. *Introduction to the Pauline Epistles.* Chicago: Inter-Varsity Press, 1961. Pp. 319.

COMMENTARIES ON ACTS

Bruce, F. F. *The Acts of the Apostles.* Grand Rapids, Mich.: Wm. B. Eerdmans Publishing Company, 1952. Pp. viii, 491. Greek text.

————. *Commentary on the Book of the Acts* in *The New International Commentary on the New Testament.* Grand Rapids, Mich.: Wm. B. Eerdmans Publishing Company, 1956. Pp. 555.

Carter, Charles W. and Earle, Ralph. *The Acts of the Apostles* in *The Evangelical Commentary.* Grand Rapids, Mich.: Zondervan Publishing House, 1959. Pp. 434.

Dunnett, W. M. *The Book of Acts.* Grand Rapids, Mich.: Baker Book House, 1981.

Foakes-Jackson, F. J. *The Acts of the Apostles* in *The Moffatt New Testament Commentary.* New York: Harper & Brothers, Publishers, 1931. Pp. xx, 236.

Haenchen, Ernst. *The Acts of the Apostles: A Commentary.* Translated by B. Noble and G. Shinn; ed. by R. McL. Wilson. Philadelphia: Westminster Press, 1971.

Hengel, Martin. *Acts and the History of Earliest Christianity.* Translated by John Bowden. Philadelphia: Fortress Press, 1980.

Lenski, R. C. H. *The Interpretation of the Acts of the Apostles.* Columbus, Ohio: The Wartburg Press, 1944. Pp. 1126.

Marshall, I. Howard. *The Acts of the Apostles* in *The Tyndale New Testament Commentaries.* Grand Rapids, Mich.: Wm. B. Eerdmans Publishing Company, 1980. Pp. 427.

Morgan, G. Campbell. *The Acts of the Apostles.* New York: Fleming H. Revell Company, 1924. Pp. 547. Excellent analytical and devotional commentary.

Munck, Johannes. *The Acts of the Apostles.* Introduction, translation, and notes. Revised by Wm. F. Albright and C. S. Mann. Garden City, N.Y.: Doubleday, 1967.

Rackham, Richard B. *The Acts of the Apostles.* Twelfth Edition. London: Methuen & Company, Ltd., 1939. Pp. cxv, 524.

Stifler, J. M. *An Introduction to the Study of the Acts of the Apostles.* New York: Fleming H. Revell Company, n.d. Pp. 287.

Scroggie, W. Graham. *The Acts of the Apostles.* New York and London: Harper & Brothers, Publishers, n.d. Pp. 186. Devotional studies. Unusually good outline.

Thomas, W. H. Griffith. *The Acts of the Apostles.* London: Marshall Brothers, Ltd., n.d. Pp. 110. A series of studies.

CHAPTER 14

THE TRANSITION: ACTS 8:4 TO 11:18

THE sudden persecution that burst like a storm at the death of Stephen marked a sharp change in the affairs of the church. Up to this time the believers had been tolerated, or else the arrests, interrogations, and imprisonments had been spasmodic. The genuineness of the miracles that had been performed (4:15–16) and the popular favor that they enjoyed (2:47) prevented the ruling priesthood from treating the church too drastically. Stephen's arraignment of the nation for the rejection of Christ, however, so enraged them that they did not wait for legal action but stoned him on the spot (7:54–60). The fall of this leader and the bitter hostility of the Jewish officials might have brought the church to an end had not God's intervention saved the day.

THE PREACHING IN SAMARIA

Evidently the seven who had been appointed to care for the widows of the Jerusalem church had not been content to remain servers of tables. Stephen became an apologist; Philip became an evangelist. Driven from Jerusalem, Philip made his way to Samaria, where he opened a preaching campaign.

Samaria was inhabited by a population of mixed ancestry. When the northern kingdom of Israel fell before the Assyrians in 721 B.C. they deported a large number of people to Assyria, replacing them with settlers

245

from other lands. In the resulting mixture of population both the Jewish blood and the Jewish worship were affected. The Samaritans were half Gentile by descent, and they retained some of the features of heathen worship, although they also adhered to Jehovah (II Kings 17:24–33). In the time of the restoration under Ezra and Nehemiah they constituted a separate commonwealth (Neh. 4:1–2, 7–8) that was a serious rival of the group in Judea. They maintained a temple in Mt. Gerizim that the Jews regarded as schismatic (John 4:20, 22). The tension between the two peoples was so strong that the Jews who traveled between Judea and Galilee usually avoided Samaria by crossing the Jordan and using the roads on its eastern bank.

Philip's preaching among the Samaritans was, therefore, a surprising action for a Jew. It showed that he had a vision of the possibilities of his message for other peoples than his own. The response was amazing. The Samaritans forsook their superstitions and believed on Christ.

The mission of Philip was reinforced by the aid of Peter and John, who visited Samaria to see what had been accomplished and to make sure that the Samaritans received the Holy Spirit. The book of Acts recounts four occasions on which the Holy Spirit came to people in a spectacular manner: to the disciples at Pentecost (2:1–4), to the Samaritans (8:17), to the Gentiles in the house of Cornelius (10:44–46), and to the disciples of John the Baptist at Ephesus (19:6). Each of these instances represents the introduction of the Holy Spirit to a different class of people. Collectively they mark the beginning of the Spirit's work in the lives of individual believers at the opening of the church era. The gift of the Holy Spirit was the proof of conversion (Rom. 8:9) and the stamp of divine approval on the apostles' work.

THE ETHIOPIAN EUNUCH

The eunuch was an official of the Ethiopian court who was probably a proselyte returning from a pilgrimage to Jerusalem. The interview of Philip with this man was illustrative of several principles in the growth of the church. As in the case of the Samaritans, racial backgrounds and prejudices were overcome, the ministry to an individual was proved to be as important in the eyes of God as a mass revival, and the method of preaching Jesus from the Old Testament was demonstrated. Acts does not relate the consequences of this interview and makes no allusion to the effect of the gospel in Ethiopia. It does indicate that the period of transition from

Hellenistic round tower at Samaria.

Jerusalem as the center of Christianity to the Gentile world involved a large number of contacts and that the message went in many directions.

THE CONVERSION OF PAUL

The ministry of Philip illustrated the outreach of the church to new localities and groups; the conversion of Saul of Tarsus was the provision of a new leader. Next to the work of Christ himself, the conversion of Saul was probably the most important event in the history of Christianity, for it not only removed an active enemy of the gospel, but it also transformed him into one of its chief propagators.

Saul of Tarsus appears first in the pages of Acts as a young man holding the garments of those who stoned Stephen and "consenting unto his death" (8:1). Three separate accounts of his conversion are given in Acts: one by Luke in chapter 9 as an integral part of the general historical account, and two that are included in quoted speeches of Paul (22:1–21; 26:2–23). Each had a different emphasis. The first account is historical, as part of the movement of the church; the last two are personal, and were given as defenses of Paul's life and doctrine before hostile or questioning audiences. Taken together with certain passages from his epistles,[1] they afford the sum total of available data concerning the great crisis of his life.

Saul, or Paul as he is generally known, was born into a strict Hebrew family near the beginning of the first century. His native city was Tarsus, a busy metropolis in Cilicia, situated on the northeast corner of the Mediterranean Sea. From Tarsus a land road went north and west through the pass in the mountains known as the Cilician Gates, and the docks of the city were a center of shipping. The university of Tarsus was noted for its courses in philosophy and medicine, and the temple of Aesculapius, the god of healing, served as a hospital and clinic for the use of the medical students. Whether Paul ever attended the university is doubtful, but he can scarcely have escaped its influence on the thinking and life of the city.

He was educated strictly in good Jewish fashion, learning the Hebrew language and the Scriptures, and also the trade of tent-making (18:3). He was acquainted with Aramaic, which he probably spoke at home, and with Greek, which was the prevalent language of Tarsus. Possibly he knew a little Latin too, though proof of his knowledge is lacking.

At the age of twelve he was sent to Jerusalem to study with Gamaliel (22:3), and according to his own testimony he made good progress in his studies (Gal. 1:14). By conviction he was a Pharisee, and his zeal was

---

1. For full data see Frank J. Goodwin, *A Harmony of the Life of Paul* (Grand Rapids, Mich.: Baker Book House, n.d.), pp. 19–25.

measured by the intensity with which he persecuted the church (Acts 26:9–11). By the time that he came to manhood he was already a leader in Judaism. The language of Acts 26:10, ". . . I gave my vote against them," if taken literally, implies that he was a member of the Sanhedrin. If that is so, he must have been thirty or more years of age at the martyrdom of Stephen, since a man was not eligible for membership in that body until he had attained maturity.

The moral antecedents of his conversion are suggested by his account of his inner life as given in Romans 7. Plagued by the consciousness of sin aroused by the law, he found that the good that he wanted to do he could not produce, and the evil that he sought to avoid was always present with him (Rom. 7:19). Whether Romans 7 applies to the converted or to the unconverted man has long been debated by theologians, but there can be little doubt that it refers to man under the law as Paul was. Certainly the law itself could produce the consciousness of sin even apart from the gospel. Paul's zeal for persecution, then, may have been the effort of a misguided conscience to do something for God that would compensate for the evil in his soul.

The death of Stephen was also a rankling thorn in his mind. According to Paul's way of thinking, Stephen was a blasphemer and stood condemned by the law. Nevertheless, Stephen's argument was essentially sound and could not be refuted. Furthermore, the vision of the risen Christ that Stephen professed to have and the joy that illumined his face in spite of impending death gave his life a reality that the legalistic arguments of Saul could not shake. He alluded to this event in his speech from the castle of Antonia (Acts 22:19–20) as an experience he could not forget. His conversion may not have been caused by it, but it formed part of the foundation for the transformation that took place on the road to Damascus.

The conversion itself was distinctly a supernatural revelation of the risen Christ to this implacable persecutor. Paul classes it as the last of Jesus' postresurrection appearances (I Cor. 15:8). No theory of disease or hallucination can account for it adequately. Luke notes that it took place at a definite locality near Damascus (Acts 9:3); that it was accompanied by a great light (9:3) that Paul says was brighter than the noonday sun (26:13); that an audible voice spoke to Paul that was heard by the men with him (9:7), although they did not understand what was said (22:9). Paul himself suffered physical effects (9:8) that could be observed by those who accompanied him. The objective character of the conversion is above doubt.

The subjective factor also deserves some attention. When the unknown voice spoke to him from the blazing light of the heavenly glory, Paul's natural question was, "Who art thou?" (9:5). The answer, "I am Jesus" (9:5), would have been unbelievable to him had not his experience

"The street which is called Straight" in Damascus.

with Stephen prepared him for it. In one flash of revelation he saw that Stephen was right, that all of the arguments of Judaism against Stephen and the disciples had been wrong, and that a new world of revelation had been opened to him. Parallel with the reversal of his theological thinking came a call to service in the Gentile world. He acceded and was filled with the Spirit for his new task (9:10–19).

The ministry of Paul began immediately in Damascus. Galatians says that he visited Arabia at this time (Gal. 1:17). Probably he did so between his initial testimony in the synagogues (Acts 9:22) and his final departure from Damascus (9:23–25). Quite possibly the shock to his thinking was so great that he had to retire for a while to readjust his beliefs to the new light that had come in Christ. His sudden reversal of position was as disconcerting to him as it was to his associates.

Paul's new faith in Jesus as the Messiah brought him into a clash with his former Jewish colleagues in Damascus (9:23), and for his own safety he was obliged to flee the city. In Jerusalem he was regarded with cold suspicion by the disciples, who, logically enough, looked on him as a wolf adopting the sheep's garb in order to raid the flock. Under the sponsorship of Barnabas, however, he was accepted into the apostolic circle (9:27). He maintained a bold program of preaching, especially among the Hellenistic Jews, quite similar to the work that Stephen had done. So great was his success and so violent was the reaction against him that the church sent him away to Tarsus (9:30) where the opposition that he aroused would endanger them less.

Paul, according to all testimony (9:15; 22:21; 26:17; Rom. 15:16; Gal. 1:16; 2:7–8; Eph. 3:1–7), was God's choice as the apostle to the Gentiles. His conversion was part of the transition from the Jewish-centered church of Jerusalem to the Gentile church of the Roman world.

THE PREACHING OF PETER

The conversion of Paul brought into the church a new personality who was destined to become the outstanding apostle to the Gentiles, but the Spirit of God was also working with the personalities within the church, chief among whom was Peter. Beginning with the period of transition, he began to enlarge his ministry by preaching in the coastal plain of Sharon, where his activities were concentrated in the cities of Lydda and Joppa (Acts 9:32–43).

The important case in this period was the conversion of Cornelius, a Roman centurion, who was in command of a military detachment at Caesarea. Evidently he had already been interested in Judaism, for he is called "a devout man, and one that feared God with all his house" (10:2). Probably he was an adherent of the Jewish faith who had not formally become a proselyte but who had put his trust in Jehovah, the only God, and who had attached himself to the synagogue. He was typical of many Gentiles of that time who, disgusted with the irrationalities and excesses of paganism, had sought something better elsewhere. In Judaism he found a loftiness of theology and a purity of ethic that were missing in his previous experience, and so he embraced it enthusiastically.

The divine direction of Peter to the house of Cornelius is important in the history of Acts for a number of reasons. First, it indicated that God's provision of salvation was not to be confined to one race or people. Cornelius, the Roman Gentile, had as much right to hear the message of Christ as any Jew in the synagogues of Palestine.

Second, the conversion of Cornelius was the opening wedge for bringing Gentiles into the church. Peter's initial reaction to the divine command was a refusal to participate in anything that was unclean (10:14; 11:7–12). At God's behest he went to a Gentile home, preached, and subsequently remained for a few days (10:48). The conversion of these Gentiles was so convincing that Peter proposed their baptism and accepted them into fellowship (10:44–48).

The reception of these Gentiles precipitated a question within the church that remained a point of controversy for some time thereafter. Should a Jewish Christian eat with the uncircumcised Gentiles who did not observe the law? If the Gentiles became believers, how much of the law should they observe? Was legal observance the final criterion of righteousness or of a right relation with God? Not all of these questions were raised immediately by the conversion of Cornelius, but the whole principle of law versus grace was brought forward in the thinking of the church by the accession of the Gentiles, and the subsequent missionary movement made it even more acute.

The immediate answer of Peter illustrates the point that the history of Acts seeks to teach. The transition from law to grace was not an evolutionary drift, nor was it the policy of expediency, nor a whim of a few leaders. It was prompted by the Holy Spirit (10:19), explained by Spirit-led preaching (10:43), and confirmed when the Spirit came on the Gentile believers (10:44; 11:15–18). "To the Gentiles also God [had] granted repentance unto life."

The sermon of Peter in the house of Cornelius is an excellent example of evangelistic preaching in the apostolic age. It is really a brief historical summary of the life of Christ, emphasizing his death, his resurrection, and his coming to judgment. In general substance it is virtually an outline of the gospel narrative. The novel element in it is its universality: "To him bear all the prophets witness, that through his name *every one that believeth* [italics ours] on him shall receive remission of sins" (10:43). Up to this time Peter had been preaching to the "men of Israel" (2:22), the descendants of Abraham, Isaac, and Jacob (3:13, 25), the "rulers and elders" (4:8). Here he adapted the message to an audience that did not possess the heritage of the covenant and of the law, and he said that it was directed "to every one that believeth." Paul later developed the implications of this message more fully, but the rule of grace and the doctrine of justification by faith were certainly latent in Peter's preaching.

The period of transition was thus marked by a change in the geographical scene of operations from Jerusalem to the wider sphere of Palestine as a whole, including Samaria and extending to Syria and Damascus. There was a change in constituency, for the Samaritans, the Ethiopians, and even Roman Gentiles were included. The preaching message began to expand as the purpose of God in reaching the Gentiles became increasingly evident, and the center of its thought shifted from the restoration of the kingdom to forgiveness of sins. The church began to face the problem of the interpretation of the law as it should—or should not—be applied to the Gentiles. A new leadership was provided for the missionary expansion that came as a result of the persecution and that was accelerated by the response to the preaching of this period. A new stage of growth was opening before the church, for which the period of transition had been a preparation.

FOR FURTHER READING

See the resources listed at the end of Chapter 13.

CHAPTER 15

THE GENTILE CHURCH AND THE PAULINE MISSION: ACTS 11:19 TO 15:35

THE missionary movement to the Gentiles as portrayed in Acts began with the establishment of the church of Antioch in Syria. The founding of this church was part of the sudden expansion that came in the period of transition. There is a definite link between Acts 8:4 and 11:19, for the latter says:

> They therefore that were scattered abroad upon the tribulation that arose about Stephen travelled as far as Phoenicia, and Cyprus, and Antioch, speaking the word to none save only to Jews. But there were some of them, men of Cyprus and Cyrene, who, when they were come to Antioch, spake unto the Greeks also, preaching the Lord Jesus.   (Acts 11:19–20)

The Cypriote and Cyrenian believers who preached at Antioch departed from the general exclusive procedure of their fellows by preaching to Greek Gentiles. Luke's comment here indicates that his presentation of the period of transition emphasized the exceptions rather than the usual procedure of preaching. Antioch, which was evangelized in that period, was so exceptional that it became the fountainhead of an entirely new missionary enterprise.

The city of Antioch where believers were first called Christians.

THE CHURCH AT ANTIOCH

The city of Antioch was founded by Seleucus Nicator in 300 B.C. Under the early Seleucid kings it enlarged rapidly. The earliest city was purely Greek, but in later days Syrians settled outside the walls and were taken into the city as it grew. The third element of the population was Jewish, many of whom were descendants of colonists imported from Babylon. They possessed equal rights with the Greeks and maintained their own synagogue worship. Under Roman rule Antioch prospered, for it was the military and commercial gateway to the Orient, ranking next to Rome and Alexandria in size.

The year of founding the church in Antioch is not stated. Apparently it took place not long after the death of Stephen, probably between A.D. 33 and 40. Some time would be required for the church to attain sufficient importance in size and character to bring it to the attention of the church in Jerusalem (11:22). They delegated Barnabas to visit Antioch, where he labored for an indeterminate period, and then went to Tarsus to ask Paul to become his assistant (11:22–26). They labored together for at least a year after that (11:26) before Agabus prophesied the famine that came to pass "in the days of Claudius" (11:28). The implication of the text is that the prophecy was given before the accession of Claudius in A.D. 41, and that the famine came later. Another chronological note is afforded by the reference to Herod Agrippa I (12:1), who died in A.D. 44. Probably the work in Antioch began around A.D. 33 to 35. If the "famine relief" took place about A.D. 44, Barnabas may have begun his connections with Antioch about A.D. 41, which would mean that Paul first came on the scene in A.D. 42.

While this chronology cannot be considered as final, it fits fairly well with Paul's known movements. If he was converted in A.D. 31 or even 32, and spent three years in the region of Damascus (Gal. 1:18), he could have returned to Jerusalem before A.D. 35. If he spent a year or two in Jerusalem before returning to Tarsus (Acts 9:28–30), he could have been preaching in Tarsus and Cilicia for five years before Barnabas persuaded him to join him in his new undertaking. This seems a rather long silence, but Luke's silence on other matters of equal interest shows that it is not exceptional.

The church at Antioch was important because it possessed certain distinctive features. First, it was the mother of all the Gentile churches. The household of Cornelius could scarcely be called a church in the sense that the group at Antioch was, for it was a household rather than a general congregation. From the Antioch church went the first recognized mission to the unevangelized world. At Antioch began the first controversy over the status of Gentile Christians. It was a center where the leaders of the church met. At one time or another, Peter, Barnabas, Titus, John Mark,

Judas Barsabbas, Silas, and, if the Western text is correct,[1] the author of Acts himself, were all connected with this church. It is noteworthy that practically all of these men were engaged in the Gentile mission and were mentioned in Paul's epistles as well as in Acts.

The written Gospels may have originated at Antioch. The possibility of contact between Mark and Luke as well as the fact of their later association at Rome may have some bearing on the much discussed Synoptic problem. Ignatius, bishop of Antioch at the close of the first century, seems to have quoted almost exclusively from Matthew when he alluded to the Gospels, as if Matthew were the only Synoptic Gospel that he knew. Streeter[2] argues at length for the Antiochene origin of Matthew on the basis of its use by Ignatius and in the Didache, both of which he identifies as Syrian documents. If these three Gospels struck their roots into the living oral teaching of the church at Antioch, their ministry to the world is in a measure the legacy of this church to the Gentile believers of yesterday and today.

The church at Antioch was also distinguished for its teachers. Of those mentioned in Acts 13:1, only Barnabas and Paul were known from later references, but their ministry must have made the church famous as a center of teaching. Antioch virtually superseded Jerusalem as the home of Christian preaching and as the headquarters of evangelistic missions.

Perhaps the ascendancy of Antioch was hastened by the persecution of Herod in A.D. 44. The church at Jerusalem had always been financially weak, since many of the poorer members had to be subsidized by gifts. The famine must have weakened it still further, in spite of relief from Antioch (11:28–30). The persecution under Herod brought the death of James, the son of Zebedee (12:2), and Peter barely escaped with his life (12:17). The interlude of 12:1–24 gives only a brief glimpse of the situation in Jerusalem, but it shows a devout church under tremendous pressure, struggling to maintain its very existence.

The most outstanding fact about the church at Antioch was its testimony. "The disciples were called Christians first in Antioch" (11:26). Previously the believers in Christ had been looked on as a sect of the Jews, but with a Gentile constituency and with a growing system of doctrine that was quite different from that of the Mosaic law, the world began to see the difference and to label them accordingly. "Christian" meant "belonging to Christ" as "Herodian" meant "belonging to Herod." The name was proba-

---

1. Acts 11:28, Codex D: *synestrammenon de hēmon ephe heis ex auton*, translated, ". . . and when we were gathered together, one of them said. . . ." According to this text, the writer of Acts included himself among the Antiochenes.

2. Burnett H. Streeter, *The Four Gospels* (New York: The Macmillan Company, 1925), pp. 12, 500–523.

bly given in derision, but the character of the disciples and the testimony that they bore gave it a complimentary meaning.

THE MISSION TO THE GENTILES

By A.D. 46 or thereabouts the church at Antioch had grown into a stable and active group. They were instructed in the faith, their reputation was so well established in the city that they were given a classification of their own as Christians, and they had sponsored a relief expedition to Jerusalem to carry a contribution for those who were suffering because of famine. In the course of regular worship there came a call to "separate Barnabas and Saul" (13:2) for a special work. In obedience to this direction of the Holy Spirit the two men were consecrated by the church to the new task and were sent on their mission.

Cyprus

The first sphere of activity was Cyprus, which was Barnabas' native soil (4:36). The church may have had some interests there, since the first evangelists in Antioch included in their number "men of Cyprus" (11:20). Barnabas and Saul, with John Mark as their assistant, visited the synagogues and there preached the new message. In the conflict with Elymas for the attention of the proconsul, Paul came to the fore. Recognizing the diabolical character of Elymas' sorcery, he rebuked him publicly and pronounced judgment on him. The proconsul, amazed at the swift retribution that fell on Elymas, "believed" (13:12).

No statistical results of the campaign in Cyprus are given, but one important change took place. In Acts 13:2 the team is described as "Barnabas and Saul," giving Barnabas the place of prominence as the senior missionary, and calling Paul by his Jewish name. In Acts 13:13 the phraseology changes to "Paul and his company," using Paul's Gentile name. From this turn in the narrative Paul is in the place of prominence. The ministry in Cyprus brought out his qualifications for leadership and placed him in undisputed command of the mission.

At this same period two other things happened. Paul left Cyprus and moved to Asia Minor, and John Mark withdrew from the party and returned to Jerusalem. For Paul it was the beginning of a worldwide project of carrying the gospel to untrodden regions. For Mark it may have seemed to be an unwarranted deviation from an established program. Whether he was jealous for his relative, Barnabas, who had been relegated to second place, or whether he was afraid of entering the wild territory of central Asia Minor, or whether he had some doctrinal difference with Paul is not told. In any case he refused to go farther and turned back.

Antioch of Pisidia

The address of Paul in the synagogue at Antioch of Pisidia is quoted at length by Luke (Acts 13:16–43). In its general style it is quite similar to that of Stephen, for its approach is the historical review of God's dealing with the nation of Israel. The central theme is introduced in verse 23: "Of this man's seed hath God according to promise brought unto Israel a Saviour, Jesus. . . ." The development of the theme does not vary greatly from the apostolic preaching recorded in the early chapters of Acts, but when Paul came to the climax of this address he introduced one element that was new:

> Be it known unto you therefore, brethren, that through this man is proclaimed unto you remission of sins: and by him every one that believeth is justified from all things, from which ye could not be justified by the law of Moses.
>
> (Acts 13:38–39, emphasis ours)

Although Peter had proclaimed the resurrection and the forgiveness of sins through Christ (2:32, 36, 38; 3:15, 19; 5:30–31; 10:40, 43), not until this time had anyone preached so explicitly that men could be justified individually before God solely on the ground of faith. To be justified means to be declared righteous, or to be regarded as legally righteous. To obtain by faith a standing with God that would enable one to possess assurance of salvation would mean that the works of the law were unavailing and unnecessary. It was a new and bold advance in the truth concerning Christ.

The immediate result was twofold. There was a tremendous response to Paul's preaching, for "the next sabbath almost the whole city was gathered together to hear the word of God" (13:44). On the other hand, Jewish opposition became bitter and stooped to jealousy and slander (13:45). The ultimate result was that Paul announced that he would turn to the Gentiles, of whom a number believed (13:48). The Gentiles, rather than the Jews, became the core of the new church in Antioch of Pisidia.

Iconium, Lystra, and Derbe

The same situation was duplicated in the town of Iconium, situated a little to the southeast of Antioch. A flourishing church was built in the synagogue, but the division of opinion became so strong that the preachers were expelled from the city and took refuge in the outlying cities of Lystra and Derbe.

In Lystra Paul encountered paganism. The priest of Jupiter-before-the-city (14:13), seeing the healing of the cripple that Paul performed and thinking that Paul and Barnabas were gods come down to earth, attempted to offer sacrifice to them. Paul's horrified protest against the error affords an insight into his method of approaching the pagan mind, which was ignorant of the Old Testament. He and Barnabas appealed to the one God who had given "rains and fruitful seasons" (14:17), a point of contact that the simple agriculturalists of that region would appreciate whether they had any formal theology or not.

The stay at Lystra was terminated by the incursion of Jewish agitators from Pisidian Antioch and Iconium, who persuaded the ignorant and fickle people that Paul was a dangerous propagandist. Stoned and dragged out of the city as dead, he recovered consciousness and went on to Derbe to preach there. Having gathered a group of believers in that city, Paul and Barnabas retraced their steps, strengthening and organizing the churches that they had founded. They returned to Syrian Antioch to report on the things that God had done with them, and to show how ". . . he had opened a door of faith unto the Gentiles" (14:27).

The importance of this itinerary can scarcely be exaggerated. It brought Paul into the foreground as a leader of the church and placed him on a par with the apostles (cf. Gal. 2:7–9). It contributed to the education of John Mark, even though he seems to have made a conspicuous failure. Initial contact with Timothy probably dated from this journey, for Paul alluded to his experience in this region when he wrote to Timothy many years later (II Tim. 3:11). Above all, it marked a new departure in the theological thinking of the church, for out of the events of this journey came the Pauline doctrine of justification by faith.

THE COUNCIL AT JERUSALEM

The rapid growth of the Gentile church under the mission of Paul and Barnabas brought into focus a new problem. If the Gentiles became be-lievers in Jesus as the Messiah, and if they accepted him as Savior and Lord, to what extent should they be required to observe the precepts of the law? The Lord Jesus Christ had placed himself and his teachings above the law and had indicated that he was superior to Moses and to the prophets as a son is superior to the servants in the household. The full import of his words had not gained immediate recognition, but the slow trend within the Christian movement under the leadership of the Holy Spirit had been away from legalism and toward faith. With the mission to Gentiles who knew nothing of the law and who had entered into the Christian fellowship solely by belief, the division of opinion within the church became acute. Peter's debate with the Jewish Christians in Jerusalem after his visit to the house of Cornelius was an early sign of the tension. Only when he reported that the Holy Spirit came on the Gentiles as he had come on the Jewish believers at Pentecost did the Jewish Christians admit that Gentiles might be saved at all (Acts 11:18).

The legalistic element in the Jerusalem church remained active, how-

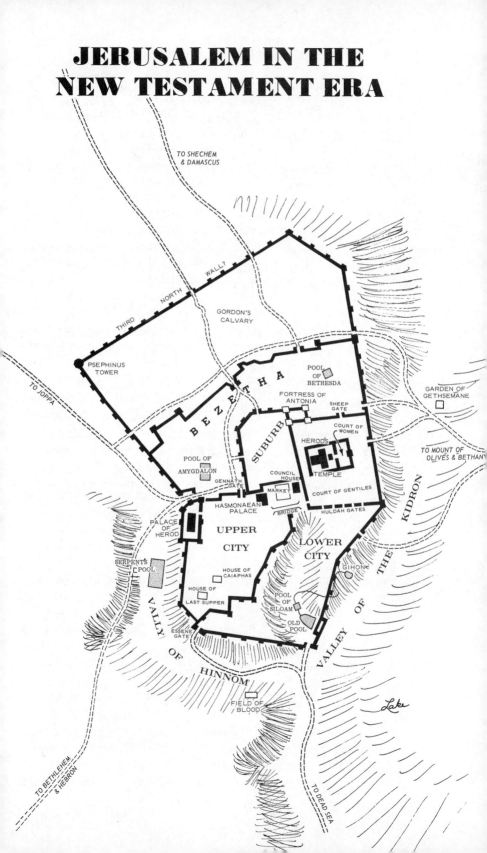

JERUSALEM IN THE NEW TESTAMENT ERA

TO SHECHEM & DAMASCUS

TO JOPPA

NORTH WALL?

THIRD

GORDON'S CALVARY

PSEPHINUS TOWER

B E Z E T H A

POOL OF BETHESDA

FORTRESS OF ANTONIA

SHEEP GATE

GARDEN OF GETHSEMANE

S U B U R B

COURT OF WOMEN

HEROD'S TEMPLE

TO MOUNT OF OLIVES & BETHANY

POOL OF AMYGDALON

GENNATH GATE

COUNCIL HOUSE

MARKET

COURT OF GENTILES

HASMONAEAN PALACE

BRIDGE

HULDAH GATES

PALACE OF HEROD

UPPER CITY

LOWER CITY

K I D R O N

SERPENT'S POOL

HOUSE OF CAIAPHAS

GIHON

V A L L E Y   O F   T H E

HOUSE OF LAST SUPPER

POOL OF SILOAM

ESSENE GATE

OLD POOL

V A L L E Y   O F

V A L L E Y   O F   H I N N O M

FIELD OF BLOOD

Lake

TO BETHLEHEM & HEBRON

TO DEAD SEA

ever. After Paul and Barnabas returned to Antioch and told of the success of their preaching, ". . . certain men came down from Judea and taught the brethren, *saying,* Except ye be circumcised after the custom of Moses, ye cannot be saved" (15:1). To the Gentiles this teaching must have been a shock. They had not been brought up on the law, and their spiritual experience since their conversion had proved quite satisfactory without the observance of all the ceremonies. Furthermore, they had found in Christ a deliverance from the legalism and the ceremonialism of their own religions. Why should they now put themselves back under another bondage?

The Judaizers, on the other hand, argued that circumcision had been established by the law of Moses as a sign of God's covenant (Exod. 12:48), and that the divine will had insisted on it rigidly. As a matter of fact, it antedated the Mosaic law, for God had required it of Abraham as a mark of the covenant that was established through him (Gen. 17:9–14). The outward significance of the rite was applied to the inward life even under the law, which speaks of being circumcised in heart (Deut. 10:12–16), but in actual practice it had probably become a routine ceremony.

The argument became so sharp that the church at Antioch decided to send delegates to discuss the matter with the apostles and elders at Jerusalem. Paul, Barnabas, and some others went to Jerusalem and were welcomed by the church. They gave a full report of their successful work among the Gentiles. Opposition came from a group of Pharisees who contended naturally enough for the strict observance of the law.

A free discussion followed in which both sides participated. Luke notes three decisive contributions.

The speech of Peter carried weight because he spoke as the initial leader of the church in Jerusalem and as one who had already experienced the practical aspects of the question. He pointed out that (1) it was God's choice that the Gentiles should hear the message of Christ (Acts 15:7); (2) that they had been given the Holy Spirit without any discrimination against them (15:8); (3) that the ceremonial law was an unbearable yoke on the Jews themselves (15:10); and (4) that salvation was by grace for the Jew as well as for the Gentile (15:11). Peter's argument from church experience brought the matter up to date.

Paul and Barnabas reported on the work among the Gentiles, stressing the "signs and wonders" that had been effected (15:12). The implication of their argument was that God would not have prospered their mission if he had not approved their methods. Their appeal was pragmatic.

The final speech was given by James, who was generally considered to be a champion of the strict observance of the law (Gal. 2:12). He pointed out the scriptural argument that God had intended to save the Gentiles, who would seek after him. James recommended that they not be required to keep all the law, but that they be requested to abstain from certain practices that would be particularly offensive to their Jewish brethren, namely, (1) idolatry, (2) fornication, (3) eating of meat from strangled animals, and (4) eating of blood. These regulations were suggested more as a basis of fellowship than as a platform of ethics, although the first two dealt with moral issues that had to be faced irrespective of Jewish law.

In some of the manuscript texts of Acts the third phrase, ". . . and from what is strangled," is omitted.[3] Should this reading be correct, the last term, ". . . and from blood," might be interpreted to mean bloodshed or murder. In that case all three requirements would be ethical or moral, and the regulation would mean that these standards would be expected of the Gentiles as essential to moral character.

James called attention to the additional fact that if any Gentiles really desired to adopt Judaism, there had been synagogues in every major city of the empire for generations. It would be easy to ascertain the meaning of the law from them. His suggestion encouraged the assumption that the Christian message, though akin to that of the synagogue in many ways, nevertheless had new and distinctive features of its own. Such an admission on James' part took him out of the category of the Judaizers who claimed his authority for insisting on the necessity of circumcision.

The decision that followed the discussion favored the recommendation of James. Not only the "official board," but also the whole church agreed to send back delegates to Antioch with Paul and Barnabas, bearing written record of the proceedings of the group (15:22–23). The communication contained several important provisions: (1) a repudiation of the initial group of Judaizers who had begun the controversy (15:24); (2) approbation of Barnabas and Paul (15:25); (3) the authorization of Judas and Silas as delegates (15:27); and (4) the decision of "the Holy Ghost and us" to insist on the "necessary" abstinence from idolatry, from blood, from things strangled, and from fornication.

The decision was well received by the church at Antioch. Judas and Silas remained for a short time to participate in the work (15:32–33) and finally returned to Jerusalem. Paul and Barnabas resumed their work of teaching, and peace descended on the church.

THE LITERATURE OF PROTEST

The controversy over circumcision for Gentiles was no mere tempest in a teapot that affected only the superficial peace of the churches at Jerusalem and Antioch and that was settled by a few concessions to Jewish

---

3. Omitted by D, gig, Irenaeus lat., Ephraem Syrus.

prejudice. Several deeper questions were involved. What was the place of the law in the plan of God? Was obedience to the law in addition to faith in Christ necessary for salvation? If the Gentiles did not need to keep the law, just what relation existed between salvation by faith and ethical behavior? What connection is there between faith and works? These and similar problems were reflected in many of the books of the New Testament that were written in the decade between A.D. 50 and 60, but two of these writings dealt so clearly with this subject that they may be called the literature of protest.

The date of these books is a disputed subject. The clues that are used by one group of commentators as proof for an early date may be used by the opposing school to argue for a late date. While a complete discussion of this topic does not lie within the scope of this book, reasons for the earlier date of writing will be given in treating each epistle. They represent in any case a trend of thought closely connected with the period centering around the council of Jerusalem.

THE EPISTLE OF JAMES

The Epistle of James is ascribed traditionally to James, the brother of the Lord, who was moderator of the council. The author's name appears in the salutation, and his Jewish interest is immediately apparent in his greeting to the twelve tribes of the Dispersion. The epistle seldom refers to systematic Christian doctrine. The name of Jesus Christ appears only twice (1:1; 2:1), and there is a possible reference to him in 5:8. The synagogue is mentioned as the place of meeting rather than the church (2:2). The illustrations are taken from the Old Testament, or else are drawn from rural life. In style and content the Epistle of James bears a striking similarity to the teachings of Jesus, particularly to the Sermon on the Mount. The same proverbial epigrammatic statement of truth, the same homely figures of speech drawn from everyday country life, the same directness of address, and the same topics of discussion appear in James. The scantiness of James' christological discussion, the heavy emphasis on ethics, and the obvious parallels with the teaching of Jesus seemingly indicate that the epistle was written at a time when the church was still within the general circle of Judaism and before it had become an independent religious movement.

If it is objected that the epistle is addressed to the Jews of the Dispersion who would not have been converted at so early a date, one need only recall that there were synagogues in Jerusalem that represented the Dispersion as early as the time of Stephen (Acts 6:9), and that James had a wide acquaintance with the pilgrims who came annually from all parts of the world to celebrate the various feasts (21:20–21). While one may not be able to prove conclusively that the book of James was written as early as A.D. 45 to 50, its content fits that era fairly well.

The Author

If James was the brother of Jesus mentioned in the Gospels (Mark 6:3), their exact relationship remains to be defined. Was James a child of Joseph by a former marriage, which would make him really a stepbrother, or was he a half brother, a son of Joseph and Mary, or was the word "brother" loosely used to mean "cousin"? All three theories have been advanced at various times, and usually the first and third have been defended by those who have argued for the perpetual virginity of Mary. The third seems to be the least likely to be acceptable, for the references to Jesus' sisters and brothers (Mark 6:3; Matt. 13:55; John 2:12; 7:3, 10) imply a contact between them and Jesus that was within rather than outside the immediate family. If they were older than Jesus, and not sons of Mary, the patronizing and unbelieving attitude that they took is all the more explicable (John 7:3–5). The fact that Jesus committed his mother to John rather than to some of his brethren would easily be accounted for by the fact that none of them would have a sufficient interest in their stepmother to assume responsibility for her. On the other hand, the fact that they came with her to remonstrate with Jesus concerning his public preaching (Matt. 12:46–50) may show that they were her sons.[4]

In any case, James was brought up in the same environment as Jesus and was in close touch with him throughout the years that led up to his ministry. His background would be practically the same as that of Jesus. As an interpreter of truth he would have the advantage of knowing its historical and geographical context thoroughly. James, while not a believer during the life of Jesus (John 7:2–8), was a witness of the resurrection (I Cor. 15:7) and was among those waiting for the Spirit on the day of Pentecost (Acts 1:14). On the withdrawal of Peter from Palestine (12:17) he took over the leadership of the Jerusalem church. He was noted for strict adherence to the law (Gal. 2:12) and was later the champion of the Jews who had felt uneasy about Paul's reputation (Acts 21:17–26). It would be extreme to say that he was opposed to Paul, but he stood for a stricter application of the law to the life of the Christian than Paul did in his ministry to the Gentiles.

There is no indication that James opposed Paul's teaching as a matter of principle. According to Galatians he gave Paul the right hand of fel-

---

4. A very satisfactory brief treatment of this subject may be found in A. T. Robertson, *Practical and Social Aspects of Christianity* (Second Edition; New York: George H. Doran Company, n.d.), pp. 16–18.

lowship (Gal. 2:9–10), and in Acts his demeanor was certainly not that of an antagonist. He was solicitous to remove all misapprehensions the Jews might have concerning Paul's real attitude. On the other hand, he may have feared that with release from the system of the law might come lax and careless behavior that would dishonor the name of the Christian believers. He wrote his epistle to foster a practical ethical life for the same reason that Paul wrote the practical applications of his epistles.

Outline

The Epistle of James is difficult to outline because of the variety of topics discussed in it and because these topics do not seem to follow any fixed pattern. There is, however, a basic structure in James that accords generally with the following scheme.

JAMES: THE TRUE STANDARDS OF LIVING

I. Salutation	1:1
II. The Nature of True Religion	1:2–27
Stability	1:2–11
Endurance	1:12–18
Action	1:19–27
III. The Nature of True Faith	2:1–3:12
Avoidance of Discrimination	2:1–13
Avoidance of Inactive Profession	2:14–26
Avoidance of Boastful Officiousness	3:1–12
IV. The Nature of True Wisdom	3:13–5:18
Wisdom Defined	3:13–18
Wisdom in Spiritual Life	4:1–10
Wisdom in Legal Relationships	4:11–12
Wisdom in Commercial Plans	4:13–17
Wisdom in Labor Problems	5:1–6
Wisdom in Waiting for the Lord	5:7–11
Wisdom in Language	5:12
Wisdom in Affliction	5:13–18
V. Conclusion: The Purpose of Wisdom—An Effective Testimony	5:19–20

James, like the book of Proverbs in the Old Testament, deals with practical application of truth to everyday situations. In vivid, homely language it sets forth the ethical requirements of the Christian life.

Problems

The second chapter of James, which says "Ye see that by works a man is justified, and not only by faith" (2:24), has been a puzzle to many people.

Martin Luther called James "an epistle of straw" because it seemed to contradict the teaching of Romans and Galatians on justification by faith alone. James is not really an attack on faith, but a protest against the hypocrisy of pretending to have faith without demonstrating it in works. "Show me thy faith apart from *thy* works, and I by my works will show thee *my* faith" (2:18). Every truth has its perversion, and the doctrine of salvation by faith may easily have degenerated into the acceptance of a creed without a corresponding holiness of life. James does not deny the necessity of faith. He insists that faith must produce results. Like Paul, he took his illustration from the life of Abraham, the founder of the Jewish race and the first beneficiary of God's covenant relations with his people. Paul cited this instance of Abraham's response to God's promise as proof that salvation is by faith, not by works (Rom. 4). James used Abraham's sacrifice of Isaac to prove that faith must be manifested through works in order to be real (Jas. 2:21–24). The two instances are not contradictory, for Abraham had to exercise faith to come into relationship with God at the outset, and that faith was manifested by his obedience in doing what God had commanded him to do. The two principles are supplementary, not contradictory.

THE EPISTLE TO THE GALATIANS

The second piece of writing that emerged from the general controversy over keeping the law was Paul's epistle to the Galatians. As James was written from the standpoint of a strict Jew who worked to avoid all semblance of looseness and license in the use of ethical freedom, "the perfect law of liberty" (Jas. 1:25), so Galatians was written by a champion of freedom who saw that neither Gentiles nor Jews could be delivered from their sins by self-effort in keeping a set of ethical principles. Galatians accordingly has been called "the Magna Charta of spiritual emancipation"[5] because it declared that " 'Christ redeemed us from the curse of the law, having become a curse for us . . . that we might receive the promise of the Spirit through faith" (Gal. 3:13–14).[6]

Destination

Galatia is the name given originally to the territory in north-central Asia Minor where the invading Gauls settled in the third century before

---

5. See F. W. Farrar, *Messages of the Books of the Bible* (London: Macmillan & Company, Ltd., 1909), I, 258.

6. For a full discussion of Galatians and its antecedents, see the author's book *Galatians: The Charter of Christian Liberty* (Grand Rapids, Mich.: Wm. B. Eerdmans Publishing Company, 1957), p. 216.

Christ and maintained an independent kingdom for many years. Gradually the Gallic population was absorbed into the other peoples living there, and after a number of political changes the territory became the property of Rome in 25 B.C. The Romans incorporated this northern section into a larger division of land that they made a province and called by the name of Galatia. Galatia, then, under Roman rule, could mean Galatia proper, which the Gauls had founded, or it could be applied to the whole province, which included the southern cities of Antioch, Iconium, Derbe, and Lystra.

To which of these did Paul refer when he wrote his epistle to the churches of Galatia (Gal. 1:2)? The usage of the New Testament appears in seven passages. In Galatians 1:2 and 3:1 the people of the churches are addressed, but no hint is given of their location beyond the mere use of the name. In I Corinthians 16:1 Paul spoke of "the churches of Galatia" whom he had asked for a contribution for the poor in Jerusalem. In the same context he referred to Macedonia (16:5), Achaia (16:15), and Asia (16:19). Since these last three names refer to Roman provinces, it seems probable that Galatia in the context should also mean the province as a whole.

The two other passages that allude to Galatia are found in Acts. The former of the two, Acts 16:6, says, "And they went through the region of Phrygia and Galatia. . . ." The expression is peculiar and could be translated better "the Phrygian and Galatian region," or "the Phrygio-Galatic country." Since Paul and his company were on their way westward, the territory must have been adjacent to Asia and Mysia, which they were prevented from entering. The second allusion occurs in Acts 18:23, "the region of Galatia, and Phrygia, in order." Here the same terms are used, but in reverse order. Perhaps both refer to the mountainous country that lay on the borders of Galatia and that had been ethnically Phrygian. Whether the Lukan and Pauline usages of these terms coincided exactly or not, both referred to the same general region included within the bounds of the Roman province of Galatia. The problem is this: Was Galatians written to the churches in the southern part of the province, which Paul and Barnabas evangelized on the first journey, or was it written to a group of churches in Galatia proper, which were founded on the second and third journeys?

The latter of these views, which is the older, has been defended by J. B. Lightfoot[7] and a number of other scholars. It assumes that Paul's visit to Galatia proper began on the second journey when he left the southern territory of Derbe, Lystra, and Iconium, and traveled through "the region

---

7. J. B. Lightfoot, *St. Paul's Epistle to the Galatians* (Tenth Edition; London: Macmillan & Company, 1890), pp. 18–35.

of Phrygia and Galatia" mentioned in Acts 16:6. According to this view, Paul traversed the territory of old Galatia, including the cities of Pessinus, Ancyra, and Tavium, and finally reached Troas after a long journey. A similar trip on the third journey is stated in Acts 18:23.

The South Galatian theory, as the other view is called, was championed by Sir William Ramsay,[8] who contended that "the churches of Galatia" were those of Antioch of Pisidia, Iconium, Derbe, and Lystra, which Paul established on his first missionary journey. They were subsequently revisited on the later journeys (Acts 16:1-6; 18:23). The second tour of these southern churches did not preclude completely a northern swing in his last itinerary, for the language of Acts 16:2, 4, and 6 shows that Paul covered the territory around Derbe and Lystra, and that he then went along the Phrygio-Galatic border to Mysia and Bithynia, at which point he turned westward to Troas.

The importance of the difference of interpretation is that the South Galatian theory allows for an earlier dating of Galatians and for a better explanation of its historical setting. If Galatians was not written until after Paul toured the Galatic territory on his second or third journey, and consequently long after the council of Jerusalem, it is difficult to explain why he made no appeal to the decision of that council in settling the controversy of law versus grace. Irrespective of whether the decision was regarded as a concession by the Jewish church to the Gentiles in order that the latter might make their own decisions, or whether it was an expression of an authoritative dogma, it could have been quite useful in convincing the Galatians that the teaching of the Judaizing faction was insupportable. The fact that no action of the council is so much as mentioned probably indicates that it had not yet taken place.

This conclusion is strengthened by the internal evidence of Galatians. Paul reviewed his biography up to the time of writing. He spoke of his conversion and call (1:15-16), his stay in Damascus (1:17), his first visit to Jerusalem (1:18), his ministry in Syria and Cilicia (1:21), and the visit to Jerusalem with Barnabas (2:1-10), which has been equated with the "famine visit" of Acts 11:30, or with the council of Acts 15. If it was the latter, there is a strange silence in Galatians concerning many of its important features that would have been quite pertinent to the argument of the letter. If the visit of Galatians 2 was the "famine visit," it explains why Barnabas and Paul felt that they had such a free hand in Antioch, and why Paul included relief for the poor in his subsequent missions. The episode of Peter's defection (Gal. 2:11ff.) can be much more easily explained if it preceded the council, for the confusion and discussion that it precipitated

---

8. William M. Ramsay, A *Historical Commentary on St. Paul's Epistle to the Galatians* (New York: G. P. Putnam's Sons, 1900), pp. xi, 478.

could hardly have taken place in Antioch after the decision had been rendered and after the letters had been sent to the Gentile churches.

Date

If the South Galatian theory is adopted, it means that Paul and Barnabas on their first tour preached in the cities of southern Galatia, and on their return trip organized the converts into church groups (Acts 14:21–23), closing their mission about A.D. 48. After their return to Antioch, Peter paid a visit to the city, and openly fellowshiped with the Gentile converts. He had not been there long before some men came down from Jerusalem who professed to follow the strict observance of the law that James practiced, and who argued that unless the converts were circumcised, they could not be saved (15:1). Peter, overawed by their attitude, withdrew from eating with the Gentiles. In the meantime the same controversy had broken out in Galatia, agitated perhaps by local Jewish influences, which were quite strong (14:2). Paul therefore, on the eve of the council, wrote this letter to the Galatian churches, in order to settle for them by correspondence the question that he expected to debate in the coming assembly in Jerusalem. This conclusion is confirmed somewhat by a comparison of Peter's speech in Acts 15:7–11 with the structure of Galatians as a whole. His emphasis on his personal calling and experience, on theological argumentation, and on the practical development of grace parallels the general outline of Galatians and also reflects Paul's conversation with him as reported in Galatians 2. If Galatians can be fitted into this situation, it was written from Antioch, just prior to the council in A.D. 48 or 49.

Not all scholars agree with this solution, and admittedly it involves some difficulties. The chronological problems are great. If the "famine visit" with which Galatians 2:1–10 has been equated took place fourteen years after Paul's first trip to Jerusalem, and if his conversion was three years before that, he must have been converted about A.D. 31. The relief journey to Jerusalem cannot have been much later than A.D. 46, and even allowing for counting fractions of years as whole years, the interval between it and his conversion must have been at least fifteen years. In that case, his conversion occurred about three years after the crucifixion of Christ. If the passage in Galatians 2:1–10 is interpreted as a private aspect of the council, the chronological and psychological difficulties are sharpened. The following diagram will give a fairly satisfactory perspective of the chronology involved.[9]

---

9. For current discussions of problems in Pauline chronology, see references noted in Chap. 6 above, n. 1.

CHART OF EARLY PAULINE CHRONOLOGY

Event	Reference	Time
Resurrection: Pentecost	Acts 1:3, 5; 2:1	A.D. 30
Conversion of Paul at Damascus	Acts 9:1–18	31/33
Visit to Arabia	Gal. 1:17	
Return to Damascus		
Paul's First Visit to Jerusalem	1:18	33/35
Interview with Cephas		
Spent fifteen days in city		
Departure to Syria and Cilicia	1:21	
Early ministry in Antioch		
Second visit to Jerusalem	2:1–10	46
Accompanied by Barnabas and Titus		
Motivated by revelation		
Private interview		
Complaint about "false brethren"		
Agreement with James, Cephas, and John		No interval stated in text
First Missionary Journey		
Return to Antioch	2:11ff.	
Visit of Cephas		
Controversy		
Writing of Galatians		
Council of Jerusalem	Acts 15:1–35	48/49

Content

Galatians was not written as an essay in contemporary history. It was a protest against corruption of the gospel of Christ. The essential truth of justification by faith rather than by the works of the law had been obscured by the Judaizers' insistence that believers in Christ must keep the law if they expected to be perfect before God. When Paul learned that this teaching had begun to penetrate the Galatian churches and that it had alienated them from their heritage of liberty, he wrote the impassioned remonstrance contained in this epistle.

The tone of the book is warlike. It fairly crackles with indignation, though it is not the anger of personal pique but of spiritual principle. "Though we, or an angel from heaven, should preach unto you any gospel other than that which we preached unto you, let him be anathema" (1:8), cried Paul as he reproved the Galatians for their acceptance of the legalistic error.

Outline

The structure of Galatians is symmetrical and logical. Its outline is as follows:

GALATIANS: THE DEFENSE OF CHRISTIAN LIBERTY

Introduction:	1:1–9
Salutation: The Ground of Liberty	1:1–5
Occasion: The Challenge to Liberty	1:6–9
I. The Biographical Argument: An Independent Revelation	1:10–2:21
Independent of Human Teaching	1:10–17
Independent of Judean Churches	1:18–24
Independent of Judaizing Brethren	2:1–10
Independent of Apostolic Pressure	2:11–18
Independent of Selfish Interest	2:19–21
II. The Theological Argument: The Failure of Legalism	3:1–4:31
From Personal Experience	3:1–5
From Old Testament Teaching	3:6–14
From Priority of Promise	3:15–22
From Superiority of Mature Faith	3:23–4:7
From Danger of Reaction	4:8–11
From Contrast of Motives	4:12–20
From Contrast of Bondage and Liberty	4:21–31
III. The Practical Argument: The Effect of Liberty	5:1–6:10
Introductory Statement	5:1
The Consequences of Legalism	5:2–12
The Definition of Freedom	5:13–15
Individual Practice	5:16–24
Social Practice	5:25–6:10
Conclusion	6:11–18
The Motive of Liberty: The Cross	6:11–16
The Price of Liberty: Suffering	6:17
The Benediction of Liberty	6:18

Evaluation

If the early date for Galatians is correct, the book is the earliest of Paul's extant writings. It summarizes the heart of "the gospel which [he preached] among the Gentiles" (Gal. 2:2). In it he showed that man's chief problem is obtaining a right standing with God. Since he is incapable of establishing this himself because "a man is not justified by the works of the law" (2:16), it must be provided for him by another. Christ has given this standing, for he "gave himself for our sins, that he might deliver us out of this present evil world" (1:4). His provision is available to those who put their full trust in him, for "the promise by faith in Jesus Christ [is] given to them that believe" (3:22). This standing is not simply a legal fiction, applied only externally or ceremonially, but it becomes part of the inner life through union with Christ. "I have been crucified with Christ; and it is no longer I that live, but Christ liveth in me: and that *life* which I now live in the flesh I live in faith, *the faith* which is in the Son of God, who loved me, and gave himself up for me" (2:20). Salvation is thus not only the application of a new life, but also its impartation.

The books of James and Galatians thus illustrate two aspects of Christianity that from the very beginning have seemed to be in conflict, though in reality they are supplementary. James insists on the ethic of Christ, a demand that faith prove its existence by its fruits. Nevertheless James, no less than Paul, emphasizes the need of the transformation of the individual by the grace of God, for he says, "Of his own will he brought us forth by the word of truth, that we should be a kind of firstfruits of his creatures" (Jas. 1:18). Galatians stresses the dynamic of the gospel that produces the ethic. "Christ redeemed us from the curse of the law, having become a curse for us . . . that upon the Gentiles might come the blessing of Abraham in Christ Jesus; that we might receive the promise of the Spirit through faith" (Gal. 3:13–14). Nor was Paul less concerned than James about the ethical life, for he says: "*Use* not your freedom for an occasion to the flesh, but through love be servants one to another" (5:13). Like the two sides of a coin, these two aspects of Christian truth must always accompany each other.

Thus the Gentile mission, with its enlarged declaration of Christian truth, was launched. The doctrine of justification by faith apart from the law was recognized by the church and was accepted. Christianity was ready for a new era of development.

FOR FURTHER READING

JAMES

Adamson, James B. *The Epistle of James* in *The New International Commentary on the New Testament.* Grand Rapids, Mich.: Wm. B. Eerdmans Publishing Company, 1976. Pp. 227.

Davids, Peter H. *The Epistle of James: A Commentary on the Greek Text.* Grand Rapids, Mich.: Wm. B. Eerdmans Publishing Company, 1982. Pp. xxviii, 226.

Dibelius, Martin. *James: A Commentary on the Epistle of James.* Philadelphia: Fortress Press, 1976.

Knowling, R. J. *The Epistle of St. James.* Second Edition. *Westminster Commentaries.* London: Methuen & Company, Ltd., 1910. Pp. lxx, 160.

Laws, Sophie. *The Epistle of James.* New York/San Francisco: Harper & Row, 1980.

Mayor, J. B. "James, The General Epistle of," in Hastings' *Dictionary of the Bible,* II, 543a–548. New York: Charles Scribner's Sons, 1901.

———. *The Epistle of St. James.* Second Edition. London: Macmillan & Company, Ltd., 1897. Pp. cclx, 255. An advanced commentary with Greek text.

Patrick, W. *James, the Lord's Brother.* Edinburgh: T. & T. Clark, 1906. Pp. xii, 369.

Robertson, A. T. *Practical and Social Aspects of Christianity.* Second Edition. New York: George H. Doran Company, n.d. Pp. ix, 271.

Tasker, R. V. G. *The General Epistle of James* in *The Tyndale New Testament Commentaries.* Grand Rapids, Mich.: Wm. B. Eerdmans Publishing Company, 1957. Pp. 144.

THE PAULINE EPISTLES

Lightfoot, J. B. *Notes on Epistles of St. Paul from Unpublished Commentaries.* London: Macmillan and Company, 1895.

Moorehead, Wm. G. *Outline Studies in Acts-Ephesians.* Grand Rapids, Mich.: Baker Book House, repr. 1953. Pp. 247.

———. *Outline Studies in the New Testament: Philippians to Hebrews.* New York and Chicago: Fleming H. Revell (1905). Pp. 249.

GALATIANS

Beet, J. A. *A Commentary on St. Paul's Epistle to the Galatians.* Fifth Edition. London: Hodder & Stoughton, 1885. Pp. xxiv, 232.

Betz, Hans Dieter. *Galatians: A Commentary on Paul's Letter to the Churches in Galatia.* Philadelphia: Fortress Press, 1979.

Brown, John. *An Exposition of the Epistle to the Galatians.* Evansville, Ind.: The Sovereign Grace Book Club, 1957. Pp. 427.

Bruce, F. F. *The Epistle to the Galatians: A Commentary on the Greek Text.* Grand Rapids, Mich.: Wm. B. Eerdmans Publishing Company, 1982. Pp. xx, 305.

Findlay, George G. *The Epistle to the Galatians. The Expositor's Bible.* New York: Armstrong and Company, n.d. Pp. 461.

Lenski, R. C. H. *The Interpretation of St. Paul's Epistles to the Galatians, to the Ephesians, and to the Philippians.* Columbus, Ohio: The Wartburg Press, 1937. Pp. 911.

Lightfoot, J. B. *St. Paul's Epistle to the Galatians.* London: Macmillan & Company, Ltd., 1921. Pp. 384. Greek text; very reliable.

Luther, Martin. *Commentary on Galatians.* A New Edition, corrected and revised by Erasmus Middleton. Grand Rapids, Mich.: Wm. B. Eerdmans Publishing Company, 1930. Pp. 536.

Machen, J. Gresham. *The Origin of Paul's Religion.* Grand Rapids, Mich.: Wm. B. Eerdmans Publishing Company, 1947. Pp. 329. The relation between Galatians and Acts is discussed in Chapter III, pp. 71–113.

Ramsay, William. *A Historical Commentary on St. Paul's Epistle to the Galatians.* New York: G. P. Putnam's Sons, 1900. Pp. xi, 477.

Ridderbos, Herman N. *The Epistle of Paul to the Churches of Galatia* in *The New International Commentary on the New Testament.* Grand Rapids, Mich.: Wm. B. Eerdmans Publishing Company, 1953. Pp. 238.

Tenney, Merrill C. *Galatians: The Charter of Christian Liberty.* Grand Rapids, Mich.: Wm. B. Eerdmans Publishing Company, 1951. Pp. 200. A manual covering ten different methods of book study, using Galatians as an example.

See also the materials for further reading found at the end of Chapter 13.

CHAPTER 16

THE PAULINE PROGRAM: ACTS 15:36 TO 21:16

AFTER the close of the council of Jerusalem, Paul and Barnabas returned to Antioch and spent some time teaching and preaching (15:35). Probably the dispute over the question of circumcision had resulted in intellectual confusion within the church that could be disentangled only by careful instruction. The missionary incentive, however, had not been forgotten and before long a new enterprise was begun.

A comparison of Acts 15:36 with 13:1–2 will show that the new mission was Paul's suggestion, whereas the original mission to Cyprus was proposed by the church as a whole. The leadership that Paul had assumed halfway through the former journey (13:13) had now become an established fact. Furthermore, the proposal of Paul disclosed an important aspect of his missionary policy:

> Let us return now and visit the brethren in every city wherein we proclaimed the word of the Lord and see how they fare.

Evangelization should be followed by consolidation through instruction and organization of the converts.

Unfortunately a dispute arose between Barnabas and Paul that, for the time being at least, severed their partnership. Barnabas desired to take with

Panel from the arch of Titus showing Roman soldiers carrying the spoils taken from the Jerusalem temple. Titus and his father Vespasian built the Arch to commemorate their victory over the Jews and the fall of Jerusalem in A.D. 70.

them his cousin John Mark, whose service had been unsatisfactory on the previous trip. Doubtless he wanted to give the young recruit a second chance. Paul, realizing the seriousness of the task they were about to undertake, thought that Mark would be a bad risk, and refused to accept him as a colleague. Both men were right to a degree. Mark was too valuable a man to be thrown aside for one mistake; at the same time the life of the young churches should not be jeopardized by a careless or unreliable worker. The solution that they reached was the best possible one for the circumstances. Barnabas took Mark with him to Cyprus, his home territory, where any possible defection on Mark's part would do less harm and where Mark would not be subjected to so great a strain as in the pioneer country of Asia. Paul chose Silas, a delegate to Antioch from the Jerusalem council, and struck north through Syria and Cilicia toward the frontiers of Asia Minor.

At this point Barnabas disappears from the narrative of Acts. Apparently Paul did not break fellowship with him completely, for later he mentioned him (I Cor. 9:6) as still engaged in the work of the Lord and as still within the circle of his acquaintance at the time when he wrote I Corinthians. The episode is illustrative of how two men of excellent character can differ on an important issue, and yet both be partially right. Barnabas' sponsorship of Mark was vindicated by the favorable spiritual growth of the latter, and Paul's jealousy for the pioneer fields brought many new laborers into the work and probably averted a second disappointment similar to Mark's withdrawal from Perga.

THE SECOND MISSION TO ASIA MINOR

The expedition set out on its journey in A.D. 49, after the interval of teaching in Antioch. They traveled by land "through Syria and Cilicia, confirming the churches" (15:41). In this way each of the two groups began by revisiting the churches that had previously been founded, for Paul had labored a long time in these regions before he was summoned to Antioch. Still traveling overland, they made their way northward from Tarsus through the Cilician Gates, and then westward along the caravan route that lay through southern Galatia. Probably it was late spring or early summer before they left the parched plains and ventured to cross the mountains into the hinterland.

Eventually they reached Derbe and Lystra, which had been the last outposts of their previous tour. Here an unusual event occurred. Paul found Timothy, a young convert, whose mother was a Jewess and whose father was a Greek. His mother was probably a convert of Paul's previous visit.

Timothy had been thoroughly trained in the Old Testament Scriptures by his Jewish mother and grandmother (II Tim. 1:5; 3:14–15) and was highly regarded by the Christians of the region. Recognizing Timothy as a potential leader and a valuable assistant for work in that territory, Paul decided to add him to his company.

The status of Timothy, however, posed a new problem for Paul. As the son of a Gentile father, and uncircumcised, he might be rejected by the Jewish population who had already proved hostile to Paul and his message. On the other hand, if Paul had him circumcised, would he not seemingly be making a concession to the Judaizers who had already plagued Galatia and whose position Paul had already attacked in his epistle? On this very journey Paul was publicizing the results of the council of Jerusalem (Acts 16:4), and the circumcision of Timothy would seem inconsistent with all for which he had contended. Nevertheless he did have him circumcised. Timothy was half a Jew by birth and wholly a Jew by training. The act was not a repudiation of the principle that Gentiles need not submit to the law, for Timothy was not rated as a Gentile. It was a personal concession that violated no principle but removed an obstacle to further work among the Jews of this region. The Gentile converts would probably not be greatly disturbed, since they would class Timothy as a Jew anyway and since they were not compelled to submit to the rite themselves.

Apparently the epistle and the personal visit of Paul brought peace to the Galatian churches. No details are given of this trip except that "the churches were strengthened in the faith, and increased in number daily" (16:5).

Having completed the visitation of Galatia, Paul looked for new fields to enter. He preached along the western border of Galatia, which was Phrygian in nationality ("the Phrygio-Galatic region"), as he proceeded along the road toward Asia (16:6). Being directed not to enter Asia, he looked northward to Mysia and Bithynia, but these provinces also were closed to him. In perplexity he made his way to Troas, the westernmost port of Asia, wondering what his next move should be.

THE MISSION TO MACEDONIA

Two important events occurred at Troas. First of all, there appeared a night vision of a Macedonian man beseeching Paul: "Come over into Macedonia, and help us" (16:9). Instantly Paul accepted the vision as the answer to his perplexity, believing it to be the call of God. This decision was momentous. Had Paul turned eastward, it is conceivable that today the Western world might have been receiving missionaries of the gospel from the Orient instead of sending them there. The evangelization of Europe and all of the effect of the gospel on Western civilization began with Paul's response to the Macedonian call.

Second, at Troas he was joined by Luke, the missionary diarist and writer of Luke-Acts. The tenth verse of the sixteenth chapter contains an abrupt change in person that shows that the author at this point became a participant in the action. "And when he had seen the vision, straightway *we* sought to go forth into Macedonia . . ." (16:10, italics ours). Although the author never named himself in the account that he wrote, the use of the first person plural pronoun betrayed his presence and enables the reader to reconstruct to some extent the relation between the author and the episodes that he described.

Philippi

Leaving Troas, probably in the month of August, Paul and his company crossed the Aegean Sea to Neapolis in Macedonia, the seaport of Philippi. Philippi lay ten or twelve miles inland up the Gangites River. The city was named for Philip, the father of Alexander the Great, who had founded it as a center for mining the gold and silver that were available nearby. Through it passed the trade that flowed from Neapolis along the great Egnatian highway to its western terminal at Dyrrhachium, the port on the Adriatic Sea.

Philippi was the leading city of its district and was a Roman colony (16:12). Colonial status made its inhabitants citizens of Rome, privileged to vote in Roman elections and to have a Roman type of government. Such cities guarded their political privileges jealously and sought to avoid any action that would bring them into disfavor with Rome. Knowing this sentiment, Paul wrote to them later, saying, "For our citizenship is in heaven," or, as Moffatt translated it, "For ye are a colony of heaven" (Phil. 3:20), as if to say that spiritually they were as much a part of the eternal city as politically they were attached to Rome.

Since there was no large colony of Jews in Philippi, there was no synagogue where Paul could begin his preaching. A small prayer meeting outside the city by the river was the only nucleus that he could find, and he resorted thither. Lydia, a Thyatiran dealer in dyestuffs and textiles, and a proselyte, opened her home to him as his headquarters.

During his ministry in the city he expelled a demon from a slave girl, a clairvoyant who had been a source of wealth to her masters. Angered by the loss of their business, they accused Paul and Silas of teaching "customs which it is not lawful for us to receive, or to observe, being Romans" (Acts 16:21). This appeal to political prejudices resulted in the imprisonment and beating of Paul and Silas, who were released from jail by an earthquake. Their claim of Roman citizenship exempted them from further punishment but their ministry in Philippi was ended, and they left for other fields. Here in the story the "we" section ends, and a fair inference may be drawn that the writer remained in Philippi. His obvious interest and pride in the city, his knowledge of detail concerning it, and the fact that with the return of Paul to Philippi at a later date the "we" sections are resumed constitute fair proof that he remained to act as pastor for the new church and perhaps to serve as an evangelist for Macedonia.

Thessalonica

Traveling along the Egnatian highway from Philippi, Paul and his companions passed through Amphipolis and Apollonia en route to Thessalonica, the modern Salonika. It was founded about 315 B.C. by Cassander, who named it in honor of his wife, the half sister of Alexander the Great. It was a free city, with officers called *politarchs* (17:6), a seaport, a center of trade, and the capital of the province.

The Jewish colony in Thessalonica had a synagogue where Paul preached for three weeks. Luke defined briefly but carefully the type of message that Paul gave to men of Jewish background. Its major premise was that the Messiah of the Scriptures must die and rise again from the dead—a new idea to the Jews, who thought of the Messiah only as a king. The minor premise was that Jesus of Nazareth fitted the prophetic description and should be identified with the Messiah (17:3). The conclusion is not stated, but its content is obvious. If Jesus of Nazareth is the predicted Messiah he should be accepted instantly by all true Jews.

A sharp difference of opinion followed. Some of the Jews believed, and there was a great response among the proselyte Greeks. Paul, alluding to this instance in the first letter that he wrote to the church, said that they accepted his message "not *as* the word of men, but, as it is in truth, the word of God" (I Thess. 2:13), and that they "turned unto God from idols, to serve a living and true God" (1:9). Several times in the Thessalonian epistles he referred to the tension between the converts and the Jews who had refused his message, and he could not hide his exasperation over the petty jealousy that hindered his giving the gospel of Christ to the Gentiles (2:15–16). The opposition became so intense that the evangelists could not remain in the city. They fled by night to Beroea where they again began preaching in the synagogue.

Beroea

The visit to Beroea was more peaceful than that in Thessalonica. The Jews received Paul's message and diligently examined the Scriptures to see whether or not he was telling the truth. Although they may not have been any more ready to accept his preaching than their fellow religionists of Thessalonica (Acts 17:11), they were at least more candid in their attitude. Believers were multiplying when a delegation from Thessalonica descended on them and commenced to attack Paul. Realizing that nothing could be done, the believers sent him on his way as if he were to take ship at the sea; but instead of proceeding to a port, he turned south and went to Athens where he was beyond the reach of the Jews.

In spite of persecution the Thessalonian church flourished, as the Pauline correspondence shows. When Paul left Beroea, Silas and Timothy remained behind to complete the work that he could not finish. Evidently Timothy joined him at Athens and brought news of the turmoil in Macedonia, which had involved the churches in affliction and temptation. Paul promptly sent him back to encourage the church and to prepare a report as to how they were standing the test (I Thess. 3:1–5). Silas also probably returned to Macedonia, perhaps to Philippi. At any rate, Paul was left alone in Athens and did not see his helpers again until they joined him later at Corinth (Acts 18:5).

THE THESSALONIAN LETTERS

I THESSALONIANS

Content

Although these letters belong chronologically to Paul's stay in Corinth about the end of A.D. 51, they are considered here because of their relation to the church. They were written within a few months of each other while Paul was engaged in the ministry in Achaia. The first letter was written on the receipt of the report that Timothy brought back to Corinth, and it included his name and that of Silas in its greeting. Its content is generally twofold: praise for the steadfastness of the Thessalonians under persecution by the Jews and the correction of certain errors and misunderstandings that had grown up among them. The main doctrinal theme concerned the return of Christ, a topic that is scarcely mentioned in Galatians unless it appears in Paul's allusion to waiting for the hope of righteousness (Gal. 5:5). It was no novelty in apostolic preaching, for Peter intimated that Jesus Christ had been received into the heavens until the time of restoration of all things spoken by the prophets (Acts 3:21), and Paul himself in his speech in Athens said that Christ would be the judge of the world (17:31). James, too, had spoken of the coming of the Lord (Jas. 5:7–8). The Thessalonian epistles, however, contain the earliest full discussion of this truth in Christian literature.

Outline

Evaluation

The problems in this epistle are quite different from those mentioned in Galatians. In general they reflect the problems of Gentile converts, not those of Jewish believers. The questions of fornication and of idleness were much less likely to appear in a Jewish community because the law, which was instilled into Jewish children from their earliest years, settled these questions in advance. The Gentiles had no such background. Sexual relations were governed chiefly by pleasure and convenience; and although the pagan moralists set certain limits on license, they did not speak with an authoritative "Thus saith the Lord." The social solidarity that the Jew possessed because of his family and his loyalty to the commonwealth of Israel did not characterize the Gentile converts, who by their very conversion had been cut loose from such social bonds as paganism had to offer. To create a sense of brotherhood and mutual responsibility the Thessalonians were commanded to labor industriously and to behave discreetly "toward them that are without" (I Thess. 4:12).

The teaching on the Lord's coming was not entirely new, for Paul spoke later of having taught these things while he was with them (II Thess. 2:5). He may have known some of the teachings of Christ on this subject, for he says, "This we say unto you by the word of the Lord" (I Thess. 4:15), and he used the figure of the thief in the night (5:4), which Jesus used for the same teaching (Matt. 24:43; Luke 12:39–40). The first part of the discussion concerning the translation of the living and the resurrection of the dead (I Thess. 4:13–18) was evidently prompted by the concern of the Thessalonians for those who had died. They believed that the Lord would come, but what would happen to those who died before he came? The second part of the discussion (5:1–11) was evoked by the desire to know when Christ would return. Paul replied that the answer lay in spiritual consciousness rather than in speculative calculation. If they were alert and active, waiting eagerly for the return of Christ, they would be preserved from wrath and would not need to fear.

II THESSALONIANS

Content

The second epistle to the Thessalonians was written to remove the misapprehension that "the day of the Lord is just at hand" (II Thess. 2:2). Perhaps the vehemence with which Paul preached the doctrine had led to a misunderstanding of his preaching or of the allusions contained in his first letter. It may be that they had received some teaching from a spurious source, for he urged them not to be "quickly shaken from your mind . . . either by spirit, or by word, or by epistle *as from us*" (2:2, italics ours), which may mean that he was repudiating some teaching falsely attributed to him by others. In any case, he undertook to provide them definite criteria by which they might recognize the approach of "the day of the Lord."

Unfortunately the criteria, which were clear to Paul and to the Thessalonians, are not so easily understandable today. The veiled reference to the "hinderer" (2:6–7) is difficult to interpret. Apparently three major events will presage the Lord's coming: (1) a sudden acceleration of apostasy from godliness (2:3), (2) the removal of some restraining influence (2:6–7), and (3) the complete unveiling of the incarnation of evil who will be animated by Satan and who will oppose and exalt himself above all that is called God (2:4, 9). Nowhere else in the Pauline epistles does this particular aspect of eschatological teaching occur. It was, however, an integral part of Paul's current instruction, and he preached it in the churches. The passage indicates that the mystery of lawlessness and the mystery of Christ develop concurrently in the world, and that ultimately there will be an inevitable clash in which Christ must and will triumph. The triumph itself will be his personal return to earth to destroy the antichrist and to reward his saints.

The exhortation of the third chapter is an expansion of the charge given in I Thessalonians to "study to be quiet, and to do your own business, and to work with your hands" (I Thess. 4:11). Some of the Thessalonians had become so enamored of the idea that the Lord's coming could release them from the evils and tensions of the world that they had given up working and were waiting for the appearance of the Deliverer. They were out of step with the rest of the church and were dependent on others for their support (II Thess. 3:6–11). Paul urged them to earn their own living and to mind their own business.

Outline

II THESSALONIANS: THE EXPECTATION OF THE CHURCH

I. Salutation	1:1–2
II. Expectation in Persecution	1:3–12
Thanksgiving for Growth	1:3–4
Explanation of Purpose	1:5
Expectation of Outcome	1:6–10
Prayer	1:11–12
III. Explanation of Events	2:1–17
Alarms Quieted	2:1–2
Apostasy Predicted	2:3–7
Antichrist Revealed	2:8–12
Attitude of Faith Encouraged	2:13–17
IV. Exhortations to Readiness	3:1–15
To Prayer	3:1–5
To Industry	3:6–15
V. Benediction and Salutation	3:16–18

Evaluation

First and Second Thessalonians are among the first of Paul's writings. They testify to the fact that the message Paul preached was no novelty, but that it had already been a settled body of faith for some time. Paul's reference to his preaching among them (II Thess. 2:15) the same things that he wrote in his letter shows that he had a well-defined system of belief, and his use of the word "tradition" (2:15; 3:6) corroborates this impression. For Paul "tradition" did not mean a loosely transmitted rumor of doubtful authenticity. It meant rather a body of instruction that may have been oral, but was carefully preserved and exactly formulated. He used the cognate verb in describing his transmission of the facts of the life of Christ, which for him constituted the gospel (I Cor. 15:3: *delivered*), and Luke used the same verb to describe the narration of the facts of the life of Christ by eyewitnesses (Luke 1:2). The "tradition" must have included ethical precepts, for he implied that it was a rule of conduct that the brethren could follow (II Thess. 3:6).

This tradition, furthermore, was not only authentic but authoritative. In Galatians Paul said that his gospel was exclusive in its truth and that no other could be substituted for it. In II Thessalonians 3:14 he said:

And if any man obeyeth not our word by this epistle, note that man, that ye have no company with him, to the end that he may be ashamed.

If he was insisting on his authority as purely personal, he could scarcely escape being called a religious egotist and tyrant. If, on the other hand, he had received his message from God, so that his utterance was the word of God mediated through him by the Holy Spirit (I Thess. 2:13), he had a right to his authority.

Practically every major doctrine in the catalogue of faith is represented in these two small epistles. Although they were not written as doctrinal treatises, nor primarily to present the author's general theological views, they contain a well-rounded body of theological teaching.

Paul and those who received his epistles believed in one living God (I, 1:9), the Father (II, 1:2), who has loved men and has chosen them to enjoy his salvation (II, 2:16; I, 1:4). He has sent deliverance from wrath through Jesus Christ, his Son (I, 1:10), and has revealed this deliverance through the message of the gospel (I, 1:5; 2:9; II, 2:14). This message has been confirmed and made real by the power of the Holy Spirit (I, 1:5; 4:8). The gospel concerns the Lord Jesus Christ, who was killed by the Jews (I, 2:15). He rose from the dead (I, 1:10; 4:14; 5:10). He is now in heaven (I, 1:10), but he will come again (I, 2:19; 4:15; 5:23; II, 2:1). To him is ascribed deity, for he is called Lord (I, 1:6), God's Son (I, 1:10), and the Lord Jesus Christ (I, 1:1, 3; 5:28; II, 1:1). Believers, (1) receiving the word of God (I, 1:6), (2) turn from idols, serve God, and wait for the return of Christ (I, 1:9–10). Their normal growth is in sanctification (I, 4:3, 7; II, 2:13). In personal life they are to be clean (I, 4:4–6), industrious (I, 4:11–12), prayerful (I, 5:17), and cheerful (I, 5:16). Theoretically and practically the Thessalonian letters embody all the essentials of Christian truth.

THE MISSION TO ACHAIA

Athens

The city of Athens was one of the wonders of the ancient world. In its golden age, the fifth century B.C., it had probably held within its walls more literary genius, more philosophical brilliance, and more architectural beauty than any other city of antiquity. In the time of Paul its political and commercial importance had declined greatly, but a faint aura of intellectuality and of culture still hung over it. The people of Athens were deeply conscious of their heritage and they prided themselves on their past. Many of the finest buildings of Athens' heyday, such as the Erechtheum and the

Parthenon, were still intact. The intellectual atmosphere of the city preserved the philosophical tradition, and if the teachers who frequented the
porticoes and street corners lacked the creative genius of Plato and Aristotle, they had at least an appreciation of the thinkers of the past that could
not be duplicated readily elsewhere.

While Paul was awaiting at Athens the arrival of Silas and Timothy
from Macedonia, he gave himself as usual to the ministry. Two spheres of
activity were open to him: the synagogue, where he met the usual congregation of Jews and proselytes, and the marketplace, where he encountered the pagan thinkers. Here he met a new type of opponent, the
educated and cynical pagan, who was ready to hear anything but not ready
to believe it. Luke devoted considerable space to the singular clash of the
Jewish Christian Paul, whose passionate hatred of idolatry collided with
the skeptical tolerance of pagans who might not take their own gods
seriously, but who would not take his message seriously either.

Paul's preaching intrigued their curiosity and they took him to the
Areopagus for a hearing. Literally, the Areopagus was Mars' Hill, a small
rocky elevation in Athens where there was an area large enough for a public
conference. Ramsay contends with some show of reason that *Areopagus*
here means not so much the place as the group that took its name from the
place, the governing council of the city that controlled educational pol-

The famous Parthenon on the Acropolis, Athens.

icies and passed on the licensing of foreign teachers.[1] There is no indication that he was on trial because a charge had been made against him. He was simply making an official statement of the chief tenets of his teaching.

The speech itself (17:22–31) was a masterpiece of condensation. Beginning with the point of contact furnished by the lavish display of architecture and statuary that adorned the city, most of which was dedicated to the worship of the gods, he made a plea for the one God who made the heavens and the earth and who governs the destinies of men. In contrast to the vague absentee deity of Epicureanism he spoke of God as immanent; in contrast to the pantheistic *Logos* of Stoicism he emphasized God's personality and the necessity for repentance, which was the opposite of Stoic fatalism.[2] For most Greeks, Paul's reference to resurrection was untenable. They considered the body inferior to the soul, and in the words of the poet Aeschylus, "Once a man dies and the earth drinks up his blood, there is no resurrection." Following his speech, interrupted as it was by his hearers (v. 32), there were some, though few, converts. Among them was a member of

---

1. William Ramsay, *St. Paul, the Traveler and the Roman Citizen* (New York: G. P. Putnam's Sons, 1909), pp. 243–248.
2. For a description of Epicureanism and Stoicism, see above, pp. 75–77.

The Theseum, to the west of the Agora (marketplace), is the best preserved Greek temple in the world.

General view of the Acropolis, Athens.

the court of the Areopagus, one Dionysius, along with a woman named Damaris, "and others with them" (v. 34).

Apparently the ministry in Athens was a disappointment to Paul. He created no great stir in the synagogue, and the pagan population dismissed him with ridicule. He was accustomed to being thrown out of town, but he was not used to being subjected to contemptuous indifference. Evidently it cut deeply into him, for he wrote to the Corinthians concerning his arrival among them after leaving Athens: "I was with you in weakness, and in fear, and in much trembling" (I Cor. 2:3). Possibly this timorous attitude had physical causes, but it seems more likely that the unusual dismissal Athens gave him unnerved him and caused him to rethink his whole procedure in apologetics.

Corinth

From Athens Paul went to Corinth, a city of totally different character. The city had been sacked and burned by the Romans in 146 B.C. In 46 B.C. it was rebuilt by Julius Caesar and became the acknowledged political capital of Achaia, which was a senatorial province. Corinth was the residence of the governing proconsul, as Acts 18:12 states.

Located in the isthmus that connected the Peloponnesus to the mainland, between the Gulf of Lechaeum on the west and the Aegean Sea on the east, Corinth became a center of trade. Rather than sailing around

The Erechtheum with its famous Porch of the Maidens on the Acropolis.

Cape Malea on the southern tip of the Peloponnesus, where navigation was dangerous, many shipmasters preferred to transship their cargoes at Corinth and to send them westward from Lechaeum to the Adriatic ports of Italy. Corinth, with its two seaports, Lechaeum on the west and Cenchrea on the east, enjoyed a monopoly of trade and rapidly grew wealthy.

In government it was a Roman colony like Philippi. Its population was cosmopolitan. The inhabitants had been killed or displaced when the city was first destroyed, and when it was rebuilt new elements settled there. Jews came for the trade, Romans were there on official business or were descendants of the original colonists, Greeks gravitated toward the city from the countryside, and the commerce brought the usual miscellany of sailors, salesmen, bankers, and people from every corner of the Mediterranean world.

Rapid growth in wealth promoted a false culture. Corinth was a "boom town," offering luxury, display, sensuality, and sport. Morally, Corinthians were regarded as inferior even according to the loose standards of paganism. They were usually represented on the Roman stage as drunk. "To live as do the Corinthians" was a euphemism for the vilest kind of life. The temple of Aphrodite in Corinth at one time lodged one thousand priestesses who were professional prostitutes, and the ebb and flow of travel and commerce brought to the city a floating population that included the scum of the Mediterranean. Wealth and dire poverty, beauty and wretchedness, culture and squalor rubbed elbows at Corinth.

Since Paul had spent no great length of time at Athens, his arrival at Corinth may be dated in the fall of the same year that he left Macedonia. The administration of Gallio before whom he was tried probably began with the opening of the proconsular year in July of A.D. 52. Paul's total stay in Corinth was a year and a half (18:11), but how much of that preceded his trial and how much of it followed is uncertain. Luke says that after Gallio dismissed his case he remained in the city for "many days" (18:18). Perhaps the most acceptable dating would bring him to Corinth in the fall of A.D. 51, and would place his departure from the city in the early spring of A.D. 53.

As already noted, the scorn with which his message was greeted at Athens brought him to Corinth in a depressed frame of mind. His colleagues had not returned from Macedonia, and his funds were probably running short. When he reached Corinth, he found employment at his old trade of tent-making with Aquila and Priscilla, who had been expelled from Rome by the edict of Claudius. Whether they were converts to Christianity before they came to Corinth, or whether they became believers through contact with Paul is not known. In any case, he found shelter, employment, and fellowship with them.

In a short time Silas and Timothy returned from Macedonia, bringing the news of the growth of the churches. At this time the contribution to Paul's support of which he spoke in the Philippian letter may have come:

> . . . when I departed from Macedonia, no church had fellowship with me in the matter of giving and receiving but ye only; for even in Thessalonica ye sent once and again unto my need.
>
> (Phil. 4:15–16)

This passage implies that the Macedonian churches gave more generously after he left. Encouraged by the good tidings and by the support from Macedonia, he preached more vigorously and more definitely that Jesus was the Messiah (Acts 18:5).

The reaction in the synagogue was such that Paul withdrew, vowing that he would leave them to their unbelief and go to the Gentiles. He quit the synagogue, transferring his headquarters to the home of a proselyte, Titus Justus, who lived nearby. The ruler of the synagogue became a believer, and many of the Corinthians believed and were baptized.

Paul's ministry in Corinth at this time seems to have been under considerable strain. He was reorganizing his missionary procedure, for he said in I Corinthians that he "came not with excellency of speech or of wisdom, proclaiming . . . the testimony of God" (I Cor. 2:1). He could

The remains of the ancient Agora and of the old city of Corinth, Greece, with the Acrocorinthus in the background.

not recall exactly how many he baptized (1:16). The eighteen months of pioneering in this corrupt and idolatrous city must have taken a heavy toll of his physical and nervous strength. It may be that his return from Achaia to Palestine was occasioned by illness, though Luke says nothing of it.

In company with Aquila and Priscilla, Paul left Corinth and set out for the east. They stopped at Ephesus en route, where Aquila and Priscilla took up new headquarters and began their ministry. Paul preached in the synagogue, but only for a short time since he was desirous of reaching Palestine quickly.

No details are given of his journey, and there is only the barest mention of his arrival at his destination. He landed in Caesarea, greeted "the church" (Acts 18:22), whether at Caesarea or at Jerusalem is not clear, and then proceeded to Antioch—his last visit to the church that had originally commissioned him. Probably the eastern part of the journey consumed most of the summer, so that by the fall of A.D. 53 he was once again on the road westward (18:22–23).

Late summer and early fall may have been spent in the tour of Galatia and Phrygia. The disturbance in the Galatian churches that began at the time of the Council (A.D. 48 or 49) may not have died down completely, so that Paul had to "establish" the disciples. Before winter set in, Paul was back at Ephesus where he began his mission in Asia; it was the longest and perhaps the stormiest ministry of his experience.

THE MISSION TO ASIA

Ephesus

The city of Ephesus was one of the oldest of the settlements on the west coast of Asia Minor and the leading city of the Roman province of Asia. Its origin is shrouded in antiquity, but it was a prominent settlement in the eighth century B.C. and was taken over by the Greeks at an early date. It was located about three miles from the sea on the Cayster River, which at that time was navigable, so that Ephesus was a seaport. The valley of the Cayster penetrated far inland, making a caravan route to the East. Roads from Ephesus communicated with all the other large cities of the province and with the lines of commerce that connected with the north and east. It was a strategic point for evangelism, since workers from Ephesus could maintain contact with the whole Asian hinterland.

The outstanding feature of Ephesus was its great temple of Artemis, a local deity who was later identified with Artemis of the Greeks and with Diana of the Romans. Her image was a many-breasted figure with a female face, having a solid block of stone instead of legs. The first temple was probably begun in the sixth century B.C., but was not finished until 400 B.C. It was burned to the ground in 356 B.C. and replaced by a newer and larger structure, four hundred twenty-five feet by two hundred twenty feet, which was subsidized by contributions from all of Asia. It was considered one of the wonders of the world and was an outstanding center for pilgrims who came to worship at its shrine.

Not only was the temple a center for religious worship, but because its halls and grounds were regarded as sacred and inviolable, it also became an asylum for the oppressed and a depository for funds.

A crude picture of the temple appeared on Ephesian coins, accompanied by the very title that is used in Acts for the city, NEOKOROS, or "temple-sweeper" of Artemis (19:35). Unlike most of the people, who were caught up in the routine state worship, the inhabitants of Asia and of Ephesus in particular exhibited an almost fanatical devotion to Artemis. Its intensity appeared in the action of the mob in the amphitheater, which for two hours shouted, "Great is Diana of the Ephesians" (19:34).

The Agora at Ephesus. The building to the left is the library.

Ephesus was rated a free city and maintained its own government. The ultimate authority lay in the popular assembly when legally convoked (19:39), while the leaders or senate of the city acted as the central legislative body. The secretary or "town clerk" was the responsible official: he was entrusted with keeping records and with presenting business to the assembly (19:35). The influence of labor was also strong, for it was the guild of silversmiths who protested that Paul's evangelizing activities had imperiled their trade in religious souvenirs, the silver shrines that were miniature copies of the temple.

Paul encountered several important problems in Ephesus. The first was the question of the survival of the teaching of John the Baptist, whose disciples were still active after John's life had closed. Apollos, an educated Alexandrian Jew, had already been preaching in Ephesus concerning Jesus, "knowing only the baptism of John" (18:24–25). Undoubtedly he knew that the Messiah was coming, that he had already been anointed to serve God, and that preparation for his ministry must include repentance and faith. His knowledge was not so much false as partial; he had not gone far enough. He was preaching in the synagogues and apparently evoked some response.

Under the tutelage of Priscilla and Aquila his understanding was broadened. A contrast of phrases here is enlightening: Luke says that he "had been instructed in the way of the Lord" (18:25), but that "Priscilla and Aquila . . . expounded unto him the way of God *more accurately*" (18:26, italics ours). Leaving Ephesus with the recommendation of the believers there, he went over to Achaia and became a strong apologist for the Christian faith, especially among the Jews (18:28). Later he became one of Paul's trusted friends and colleagues (I Cor. 16:12; Titus 3:13).

Apollos departed from Ephesus before Paul arrived, but others like him were there. These men, disciples of John the Baptist, were deficient in personal spiritual experience. So obvious was this fact that when Paul came into contact with them, he asked them if they had received the Holy Spirit when they believed. Their answer was that they had not so much as heard whether the Holy Spirit had come. In view of John's prediction that Jesus would baptize with the Holy Spirit, it seems inconceivable that they had never heard his name; but they might never have heard of the fulfillment of the promise at Pentecost. The reply of Paul proved that the baptism of John was insufficient to produce a full Christian experience, for the believer must not only repent of sin, but also be filled with the Spirit. The first problem at Ephesus, then, was to bring sincere but immature believers up to date.

A second important problem of the Asian mission was the occult. The Jewish exorcists represented by the seven sons of Sceva, and the hundreds of nameless persons who burned their books of magic are proof of the wide extent to which superstition and demonology prevailed. The answer to this problem was twofold. On the positive side, the power of Christ was demonstrated to be greater than that of the exorcists and demon cults. The sick were healed, the obsessed were delivered, and those who practiced the occult arts were so convicted of the evil of their ways that they voluntarily destroyed the books of magic on which they had relied (Acts 19:19). On the negative side, the exclusive character of the gospel was demonstrated. A Christian did not *add* his Christianity to his other religions; he discarded them. Christianity was essentially intolerant of all rivals, and nowhere is this principle better demonstrated than at Ephesus.

The ministry of Paul in Ephesus was singularly effective. For more than two years (19:8, 10) he was able to preach unhindered, first in the synagogue and later in the school of Tyrannus (19:9). He performed special miracles (19:11) and reached the populace of Ephesus and the province as a whole more thoroughly than he did the people of any other place. Luke notes that "all they that dwelt in Asia heard the word of the Lord, both Jews and Greeks" (19:10), that "mightily grew the word of the Lord and prevailed" (19:20), and that so many had believed that idolatry suffered economic loss (19:26–27). The church at Ephesus became a missionary center and was for centuries one of the strongholds of Christianity in Asia Minor.

THE CORINTHIAN CORRESPONDENCE

BACKGROUND

During Paul's stay in Ephesus he maintained relations with the churches of Achaia that he had founded on the preceding journey. The church at Corinth was a vexing problem to him because of its instability. Since it was largely composed of Gentiles who had no training in the Old Testament Scriptures, and whose religious and moral antecedents were the exact opposite of Christian principle, much teaching was required to bring them to spiritual maturity (I Cor. 3:1–3).

The ministry of Apollos among them was helpful in many ways. He attracted many of the Corinthians by his learning and his polished presentation of truth. He was especially effective in dealing with Jews, since he knew the Old Testament well and could argue publicly in convincing fashion (Acts 18:27–28). Paul appreciated his ministry and commended him (I Cor. 16:12).

It is possible that Peter visited Corinth, although no detail is given concerning his work. Paul mentioned his name as known to the Corinthians (1:12) and implied that he also was engaged in itinerant preaching (9:5). It is scarcely probable that a certain faction in the Corinthian church would claim him as their champion had there not been some contact with him personally at that time.

THE "LOST LETTER"

While Apollos and possibly Cephas were visiting Corinth and preaching there, Paul was on the tour that took him back to Palestine and thence to Ephesus. During this period, or shortly after his return to Ephesus, he wrote a letter to which he alluded in I Corinthians 5:9: "I wrote unto you in my epistle to have no company with fornicators. . . ." The moral atmosphere of Corinth was such that absolute separation from evil was necessary if the church was to survive. Evidently there had been some misunderstanding of his injunction, for in I Corinthians he explained that he was not advocating withdrawal from the world, but that there should be separation from professing Christians who persisted in this sin.

The full content of the previous letter will never be known, since it has been lost. An ingenious hypothesis has been offered that fragments of this "lost letter" were preserved in the manuscript collection at Corinth, and that I Corinthians 6:12–20 and II Corinthians 6:14–7:1 are parts of it that were incorporated into the body of the later epistles.[3] The hypothesis rests solely on subjective impression, and however plausible it may seem, there is no good external evidence to support it. It is certain that the problem of moral purity was of supreme importance at Corinth, as it was elsewhere throughout the Gentile world, and that it was one of the earliest issues with which Paul had to deal.

I CORINTHIANS

Date

The response to the first letter was quite unsatisfactory. Apollos and Cephas had moved to other fields, and the church, bereft of adequate leadership, had fallen into confusion. Disquieting rumors concerning it began to drift back to Ephesus through slaves of a Corinthian family who were in Ephesus on business. Finally three members of the church, Stephanas, Fortunatus, and Achaicus, brought a contribution to Paul and also a letter containing certain questions that the Corinthians wanted clarified. In response Paul wrote I Corinthians. It was composed near the end of his sojourn at Ephesus, for he had already formulated his plans for leaving Asia and for making an extended visit to Macedonia and Achaia (I Cor. 16:5–7). It must have been composed during the winter or in the fall, for he spoke of staying at Ephesus until Pentecost because of the success that was attending his work (16:8). He was engaged in raising the contribution for the poor in Jerusalem, which he took with him on his last journey to that city (Acts 24:17), so that he contemplated returning to Palestine again in the near future. Probably it was written in the winter of A.D. 55, during the peak of his work at Ephesus.

Content

First Corinthians is the most varied in content and style of all the epistles of Paul. The topics discussed range from schism to finance and from church decorum to the resurrection. Every literary device known to writing is employed in its pages: logic, sarcasm, entreaty, scolding, poetry, narration, exposition—in short, it is written in the same style as Paul would have carried on in a conversation with the elders of Corinth had he been present with them. It is thoroughly informal in its approach rather than

---

3. See David Smith, *Life and Letters of St. Paul* (New York: George H. Doran Company, n.d.), Appendix I, p. 654.

being a set essay on theological subjects. There is, however, a central theme. Findlay has called it "the doctrine of the cross in its social application."[4] It reflects the conflict that took place when Christian experience and Christian ideals of conduct came into conflict with the concepts and practices of the pagan world. The problems discussed in it are by no means outdated, for they are still to be found wherever Christians come into contact with a pagan civilization.

Outline

I CORINTHIANS: THE PROBLEMS AT CORINTH

I. Salutation	1:1–9
II. Reply to Report from "house of Chloe"	1:10–6:20
Party Strife	1:10–3:23
Defense of Paul's Ministry	4:1–21
Criticism of Immorality	5:1–13
Criticism of Lawsuits	6:1–11
Reply to Libertinism	6:12–20
III. Reply to Questions in Letter	7:1–16:9
Marriage	7:1–24
Virgins	7:25–40
Things Sacrificed to Idols	8:1–11:1
Evaluated by the idol	8:1–13
Evaluated by freedom	9:1–27
Evaluated by relation to God	10:1–22
Evaluated by relation to others	10:23–11:1
Problems of Worship	11:2–34
The covering of the head	11:2–16
The Lord's table	11:17–34
Spiritual Gifts	12:1–14:40
The Resurrection of the Body	15:1–58
The Collection	16:1–9
IV. Concluding Salutations	16:10–24

The structure of I Corinthians depends on the order of topics that had been brought to Paul's attention by the visitors from Corinth and by the letter the Corinthians had written. How much news had been imparted by Apollos and by the trio who brought the contribution is not told. He made direct reference to "them *that are of the household* of Chloe" (1:11) who had

---

4. G. G. Findlay, *The First Epistle of Paul to the Corinthians* in *The Expositor's Bible* (Grand Rapids, Mich.: Wm. B. Eerdmans Publishing Company, repr. 1947), II, 739.

informed him of the parties that had grown up within the church and of the immorality and litigation that disturbed their peace. These topics he discussed at length in the first six chapters. Beginning with the seventh chapter a new phrase appears: "Now concerning the things whereof ye wrote . . ." (7:1), and its subsequent repetitions (7:25; 8:1; [11:2]; 12:1; [15:1]; 16:1) mark off the subdivisions of his reply to their written questions.

Evaluation

First Corinthians affords a better insight into the problems of a pioneer church than almost any other writing in the New Testament. Each problem was met by applying a spiritual principle rather than by recommending a psychological expedient. For schism, the remedy is spiritual maturity (3:1–9); for fornication, church discipline until the offender repents and is restored (5:1–5); for litigation, arbitration within the Christian community (6:1–6). In the case of marriage between a believer and an unbeliever, the concern of the believer is to save the unbeliever, not to alienate him or her (7:16); for the problem of the unmarried virgins, self-control or lawful marriage (7:36–37). In the casuistic questions of food offered to idols and of details of worship, the relation of the believer to God is the deciding factor (10:31; 11:13, 32). Similarly the gifts are administered by God (12:28) within the church.

First Corinthians contains some allusions to church life and practice that are puzzling to modern Christians. The status of "virgins" in chapter 7, where the word "daughter" (7:36–38) does not occur in the original text, the "delivering unto Satan" (5:5) in church discipline, and baptism for the dead (15:29) are usages for which no explanation is given, although they were evidently well known to Paul and his readers. Their mention does not mean that they were widely practiced. Baptism for the dead, too, may have been a local custom in the Corinthian church that was not necessarily approved, but that was used by Paul as a practical point of appeal in his argument for the resurrection.

First Corinthians was dispatched to its destination by Timothy (16:10). Paul had tried to persuade Apollos to undertake the task of straightening out the church's problems, but he declined. Perhaps he thought that his presence could only increase the schismatic tendency among the followers. Paul had some misgivings concerning Timothy's effectiveness, for he urged the Corinthians not to frighten him or despise him (16:10–11).

Nothing is said concerning the outcome of Timothy's mission, but it seems to have been a failure. In II Corinthians Paul spoke twice of his plans and said, "This is the third time I am ready to come to you" (II Cor. 12:14;

13:1). Since his first visit to Corinth was the founding of the church, and since his letter was written from Macedonia after leaving Ephesus where he was waiting to come to Corinth, there must have been an unrecorded visit somewhere between Timothy's visit and Paul's departure from Asia. Such a call need not have occupied any great length of time, for transit from Ephesus to Corinth could be made easily. Luke does not record any such trip in Acts, but neither does he record many other episodes that might have been equally interesting or important. A survey of II Corinthians will show that Paul doubtless did go to Corinth to attempt to accomplish what Timothy had not been able to do, and that while there he had been grossly insulted and his counsel had been rejected. Rival self-styled "apostles," who drew their support from the churches and who boasted of their Jewish ancestry and of their activity as ministers of Christ, had invaded Corinth and belittled Paul to the church (see II Cor. 10–11). Furthermore, the offending members of the church had been decidedly unrepentant (12:21). The situation was tense.

Paul decided that he would not return to Corinth until the church adopted a different attitude (1:23). He had hoped that he might raise some money in Achaia for the Jerusalem collection. In anticipation of carrying through the original plan of a final visit to Macedonia and Achaia, he sent Titus ahead to deal with the church, while he closed the work at Ephesus and went to Troas en route westward.

Perhaps Paul wrote once again to Corinth at this time. There has been some speculation as to whether II Corinthians represents one epistle or two. In II Corinthians 2:4 Paul spoke of a previous letter that he wrote "with many tears," and that was intended to convince the Corinthians of his love for them. I Corinthians does not seem to fit the description, and II Corinthians as it stands was written subsequently. A number of scholars have suggested that II Corinthians 10 through 13 may be a third epistle, written between I Corinthians and II Corinthians 1 through 9, which Paul wrote to defend himself and which he sent to the church by the hand of Titus (II Cor. 7:8–13).[5] Others have contended that the intermediary severe letter was lost.[6] As in the case of the first letter, there is no satisfactory external evidence for partitioning II Corinthians. Every manuscript of the Pauline epistles contains it as it is, so that its integrity cannot be challenged on grounds of manuscript variation. If chapters 10 through 13

---

5. For a full exposition of this view, see David Smith, *Life and Letters of St. Paul*, pp. 325–371. Compare also James Moffatt, *Introduction to the Literature of the New Testament* (New York: Charles Scribner's Sons, 1911), pp. 119–123.

6. See H. C. Thiessen, *Introduction to the New Testament* (Grand Rapids, Mich.: Wm. B. Eerdmans Publishing, Company, 1951), pp. 209–210.

do represent a third epistle, while chapters 1 through 9 represent a fourth, there is no trace of original separation in the manuscript tradition.[7]

When Paul reached Troas after leaving Ephesus, he looked eagerly for Titus, but Titus did not appear (2:12–13). Paul, oppressed with worry over what might have happened at Corinth, went across to Macedonia, where his troubles multiplied (7:5). While he was laboring there and arranging with the Macedonian churches for their gifts to Jerusalem, Titus suddenly arrived with the good news that a revival had broken out in the Corinthian church and that its attitude had changed from one of carelessness and obstinacy to one of repentance. With joy Paul sat down and penned II Corinthians as a preparation for a third visit that he hoped would have only happy consequences. If the whole epistle were written at this time, he included a lengthy defense of his ministry (2:14 to 7:4) and the financial request for the Corinthians and their colleagues of Achaia to match the Macedonian contributions to Jerusalem (chaps. 8–9).

II CORINTHIANS

Content

The content has already been discussed to some extent. The epistle differs from I Corinthians in dealing with personal matters rather than with doctrinal teaching or ecclesiastical order. The human Paul is much in evidence: his feelings, desires, dislikes, ambitions, and obligations are all spread before his readers. This epistle contains less systematic teaching and more expression of personal feeling than even I Corinthians, and its structure is not as clear-cut as is that of the former epistle.

Outline

II CORINTHIANS: THE EPISTLE OF PAUL'S MINISTRY

I. Salutation	1:1–2
II. Explanation of Personal Conduct	1:3–2:13
III. The Defense of the Ministry	2:14–7:4
The Nature of the Ministry	2:14–3:18
The Sincerity of the Ministry	4:1–6
The Perseverance of the Ministry	4:7–15

---

7. W. G. Kümmel, *Introduction to the New Testament* (Revised Edition; Nashville: Abingdon Press, 1975), p. 292 concludes: "Looking at the whole question, the best assumption is that II Cor as handed down in the tradition forms an originally unified letter."

Evaluation

Second Corinthians affords an insight into the career of Paul that none of the other epistles gives. It was written not only to defend him against the occasional criticisms of the Corinthian church, but also against the slanders and accusations that his enemies raised against him wherever he was preaching. The controversy that began in Galatia had created a powerful group of Judaizing opponents, who did not scruple to use any methods, fair or foul, in order to discredit him. Not only did he have to contend with the spiritual inertia and the evils of traditional paganism, but he also had to face the active malice of jealous and prejudiced leaders who professed to be Christians.

The accusations brought by his opponents were numerous. They charged him with walking "according to the flesh" (10:2). They said that he was a coward, for he wrote letters that resounded like thunder but in actual presence he was about as authoritative as a mouse (10:10). He did not maintain himself in dignity by taking support from the churches, but demeaned himself by working (11:7). They claimed that he was not one of the original apostles, and so was not qualified to teach (11:5; 12:11–12), and that he had no credentials that he could show (3:1). They attacked his personal character by saying that he was fleshly (10:2), boastful (10:8, 15), and deceitful (12:16), and they insinuated that he embezzled the funds that were being entrusted to him (8:20–23).

The accusers themselves were apparently Jews (11:22) who were "ministers of Christ" (11:23) and who, by means of the clever use of recommendations from other churches (3:1), had obtained entrance into the Pauline churches. Doubtless they were responsible for some of the schism in Corinth. They were haughty and domineering (11:19–20), but were not ready to do pioneering work or to suffer for Christ (11:23ff.). They were, in short, "false brethren."

This picture, drawn by inference from the language of Paul, shows that the church of the apostolic age had its struggles and its sins. The marvel is not that it was imperfect; the marvel is that it survived. Only a divine dynamic could have given enduring vitality to so weak and sensual a group as the Corinthian church.

The positive teaching of the epistle makes it one of the most valuable in the New Testament. Its picture of the ministry, its statement of the prospects beyond death (chap. 5), and its teaching on giving (chaps. 8–9) are all outstanding passages.

THE LAST VISIT TO CORINTH

The arrival of Titus in Macedonia with the reassuring word of a change in the attitude of the Corinthian church (II Cor. 7:6–16) enabled Paul to pursue his journey without fear. Luke simply says that he spent three months in Achaia, but gives no details. In the spring of A.D. 56 he made plans to return to Jerusalem with the offering, when he learned that a plot against his life had been hatched by his Jewish enemies (Acts 20:3). Realizing that they would easily do away with him on shipboard, he dispatched his companions to Troas, while he, in company with Luke, went north to Philippi by the land route, and then sailed for Troas just after the close of the Feast of Unleavened Bread, which came immediately after the Passover.[8]

The way in which the "we" section reappears at this point in Acts (20:5–6) indicates that Luke had been traveling with Paul in Achaia. Robertson suggests,[9] following an ancient tradition, that perhaps Luke is identical with "the brother whose praise in the gospel *is spread* through all the churches; and . . . who was also appointed by the churches to travel with us in *the matter of* this grace" (II Cor. 8:18–19). No name is mentioned, and the anonymous person could be any one of the companions of Paul listed in Acts 20:4. On the other hand, the definite article when used with terms denoting members of a family may be translated as a possessive pronoun. If Titus and Luke were brothers, the early connection of both of them with Antioch and the silence concerning both in the book of Acts could be explained more easily. At any rate, Luke at this time was Paul's active helper in the campaign throughout Macedonia and Achaia, and he became Paul's closest associate in the years of imprisonment that followed.

THE PROJECTED MISSION

Paul had planned the return to Jerusalem to be only an interlude in a larger mission. Already he had his eyes on a grander goal than any of the cities

---

8. Above, p. 94.
9. A. T. Robertson, *Luke, the Historian in the Light of Research* (New York: Charles Scribner's Sons, 1923), p. 21.

that he had evangelized previously. Rome beckoned him, for he was a citizen of the empire. If he could reach Rome with the gospel, it could easily be disseminated to all parts of the empire, for all roads led to Rome.

With true missionary statesmanship he laid out his course of action. Luke says that "after these things were ended [the ministry at Ephesus], Paul purposed in the spirit, when he had passed through Macedonia and Achaia, to go to Jerusalem, saying, After I have been there, I must also see Rome" (Acts 19:21).

THE EPISTLE TO THE ROMANS

Background

In preparation for this next step in his missionary enterprise, he wrote the Epistle to the Romans. It was sent from Corinth, which is the traditional view, or from Philippi, just prior to sailing for Troas,[10] for Paul states in its closing chapters that he had concluded his preaching as far as Illyricum (Rom. 15:19), that he had in hand the offering that the churches of Macedonia and Achaia had taken for the poor at Jerusalem (15:26), and that he was on the eve of sailing to Jerusalem to deliver it (15:25). He expected that his presence in Judea might not be well received by some, but he intended to return shortly in order to visit Rome, and even to go to Spain (15:24, 28, 32). Granting that Romans 16 is an integral part of the epistle, it was sent to Rome by Phoebe, a deaconess of the church of Cenchrea, who was traveling in that direction (16:1).

.Paul had numerous friends at Rome. He had tried frequently to visit them, but had been hindered (15:22; 1:13) on each occasion. The church could not have been a large one and probably it consisted chiefly of Gentiles, since in addressing them he classed them as Gentiles (1:13), and since the later account of his visit to Rome as given by Acts indicates ignorance concerning Christian truth on the part of the Jews. They had heard of the movement, but had not investigated it for themselves, nor had any others reported to them about it (Acts 28:21). The Gentile church of Rome had in it a small minority of Jews at the most; and the Jews who lived in Rome, having come to the city since the expulsion under Claudius, had not made the acquaintance of those who were in the church.

The origin of the church in Rome is unknown. There were present at Jerusalem on the day of Pentecost "sojourners from Rome" (2:10) who may have returned with the message of Christ. Aquila and Priscilla had come from Rome, and, according to Romans 16:3, had returned there. No hint is

---

10. See Theophilus M. Taylor, "The Place of Origin of Romans," in *Journal of Biblical Literature*, LXVII (1948), 281–295.

given in the New Testament that Peter had anything to do with the founding of this church. It seems to have begun spontaneously among believers, the majority of whom had probably migrated to Rome from other parts of the world.

Paul had several reasons for being interested in this church. His desire to see the imperial city, the need of the Christians for instruction, his wish to forestall any Judaizing activity in a group of great potential importance, and his hope of support from them as he undertook a tour to Spain (Rom. 15:24)—all contributed to his resolve to spend some time with them.

Romans was written as a substitute for immediate personal contact and as a preparation for making the Roman church a missionary center comparable to Antioch, Ephesus, Philippi, and the other cities where Paul had labored. Romans, therefore, unlike Corinthians, is not devoted so much to the correction of errors as to the teaching of truth. Although it does not comprise all the fields of Christian thought—eschatology is notably lacking in its content—it does give a fuller and more systematic view of the heart of Christianity than any other of Paul's epistles, with the possible exception of Ephesians. Most of the Pauline epistles are controversial or corrective in nature; Romans is chiefly didactic.

Content

The central theme of Romans is the revelation of the righteousness of God to man, and its application to his spiritual need. Its theme is thus basic to all Christian experience, for man cannot do business with God until a proper approach has been established. The epistle is directed particularly to Gentiles. Paul stated that he was an apostle to the Gentiles (1:5); he sketched the religious history of the Gentile world as the prelude to revelation (1:18–32); he asserted that God's salvation is for "Gentiles also" (3:29) and that there is "no distinction" between Jew and Greek in the way of faith. Romans avers that salvation is universal in its scope.

The development of this theme of the righteousness of God can best be seen in the outline.

Outline

ROMANS: THE GOSPEL OF GOD'S RIGHTEOUSNESS

I. Introduction	1:1–17
Salutation	1:1–7
Author	1:1–5
Destination	1:6–7a
Greeting	1:7b
Occasion	1:8–15
Theme	1:16–17

Evaluation

Romans has long been the mainstay of Christian theology. Most of its technical terms, such as justification, imputation, adoption, and sanctification, are drawn from the vocabulary of this epistle, and the structure of its argument provides the backbone of Christian thought. Its logical method is obvious. First, the theme is announced: ". . . the gospel . . . is the power of God unto salvation to every one that believeth" (1:16). The need for that power is shown by the fall of the world, Jew and Gentile alike, so that "there is none righteous, no, not one" (3:10). If, then, all are helpless and condemned, relief must come from without by providing for them both a legal and a personal righteousness. This is found in Christ, "whom God

THE PAULINE PROGRAM: ACTS 15:36 TO 21:16   307

set forth *to be* a propitiation, through faith, in his blood, to show his righteousness because of the passing over of the sins done aforetime" (3:25). Since the sinner cannot earn his salvation, this righteousness must be accepted by faith. Individually and racially man is restored to his right position before God through the grace manifested in Christ.

Chapters 6 through 8 deal with the personal problems that rise out of the new spiritual relationships. "Shall we continue in sin, that grace may abound?" (6:1). "Shall we sin, because we are not under law, but under grace?" (6:15). "Is the law sin?" (7:7). "Who shall deliver me out of the body of this death?" (7:24). All these questions are answered by the description of the personal life in the Spirit given in chapter 8.

The section comprising chapters 9 through 11 deals with a broader question. Has God, by instituting salvation for all by faith, invalidated the covenant with Israel that was established through the law? Paul points out that the choice of the Gentiles is quite in keeping with God's original procedure of choosing Jacob rather than Esau. It is no less right for God to choose the Gentiles for salvation than it was right for him to choose Israel to be the vehicle of his revelation. His will is ultimate; beyond it there is no court of appeal. Furthermore, Israel's unbelief had forfeited her standing, so that the Gentile is now being given his day before God. The time may come when the Gentiles' opportunity will close (11:25), and then the believers of Israel shall enter into their heritage. The present dealing of God with Gentiles is neither arbitrary nor accidental, but is in full accordance with the divine plan.

The practical section of Romans makes close ethical application of the salvation described in the first eleven chapters. The redeemed individual is obligated to live a righteous life: "whether we live . . . or die, we are the Lord's. For to this end Christ died and lived *again*, that he might be Lord of both the dead and the living" (14:8–9). The conclusion (15:14–33) expresses Paul's own sense of debt to Christ for making known the gospel "not where Christ was *already* named" (15:20). He translated the obligation of the gospel of righteousness into missionary terms.

Romans is a superb example of the integration of doctrine with missionary purpose. Had Paul not believed that men were lost and that God had provided a righteousness for them, he would not have been a missionary. Had he not been an active missionary, he never would have formulated so systematic a presentation of truth as Romans. It illustrates what he did when he "established" the converts in his churches.[11]

---

11. Compare the language of Rom. 1:11 and Acts 18:23. Apparently the word "establish" (Greek *sterizō*) had the connotation of "instruction."

THE MISSION CONCLUDED

Two brief stops on the way to Palestine are described at some length by Luke in Acts 20. The first was the meeting in Troas at which Paul preached. It is one of the earliest existing descriptions of Christian worship. The meeting was on the first day of the week, in the evening. The disciples gathered to break bread together, presumably the love-feast, or *Agape,* which culminated in the Lord's Supper, described in I Corinthians 11:17–26. Preaching or discourse was part of the service. In this case Paul preached and taught through the night because he was leaving on the next day and might not return.

The second stop was at Miletus, a sizable port on the west coast of Asia. Paul had taken a fast ship that bypassed Ephesus, in order that he might reach Jerusalem by Pentecost. When the ship touched at Miletus, he summoned the elders of the church at Ephesus in order to give them a farewell message. Luke used the speech to epitomize Paul's missionary policies and achievements to date. It is the utterance of a great soul who had given his life unreservedly into the hands of Christ and who had been fully directed by the Holy Spirit in his ministry. It discloses his own consciousness that trouble awaited him at Jerusalem (Acts 20:22–23) and that his work in Asia was ended (20:25), for he contemplated going farther west on his next trip. Perhaps he realized that old age was beginning to overtake him, and that there would not be time to retrace his first steps as he had done in former journeys for the purpose of confirming the believers. With an affectionate farewell he parted from them (20:36–38).

The remainder of the voyage was uneventful, except for repeated warnings to Paul to stay away from Jerusalem (21:4, 10–11). In spite of the pleas of his friends, Paul persisted in his original plan, and the others assented reluctantly, saying, "The will of the Lord be done" (21:14).

With this visit to Jerusalem closed the most active part of Paul's missionary career. In a little less than a decade he had won the freedom of the Gentile believers from the yoke of legalism. He had built a strong chain of churches from Antioch of Syria and Tarsus of Cilicia straight across southern Asia Minor to Ephesus and Troas, and from there through Macedonia and Achaia to Illyricum. He had chosen and trained companions like Luke, Timothy, Silas, Aristarchus, Titus, and others who were well qualified to maintain the work with him or without him. He had commenced an epistolary literature that already was regarded as a standard for faith and practice. In his preaching he had laid the groundwork for future Christian theology and apologetics, and by his plans he pursued a statesmanlike campaign of missionary evangelism. His plans for a trip to Rome and Spain showed that he wanted to match the imperial commonwealth with an imperial faith. Notwithstanding his bitter and active enemies, he had established the Gentile church on a firm foundation and had already formulated the essence of Christian theology as the Spirit of God revealed it to him.

FOR FURTHER READING

THESSALONIANS

Bruce, F. F. *1 and 2 Thessalonians*. Word Biblical Commentary 45. Waco, Tex.: Word Books, 1982.

Ellicott, Charles J. *Commentary on the Epistles of St. Paul to the Thessalonians* in *Classic Commentary Library*. Grand Rapids, Mich.: Zondervan Publishing House, 1957. Pp. 167.

Hendriksen, William. *I and II Thessalonians* in *The New Testament Commentary*. Grand Rapids, Mich.: Baker Book House, 1955. Pp. 214.

Lenski, R. C. H. *The Interpretation of St. Paul's Epistles to the Colossians, to the Thessalonians, to Timothy, to Titus and to Philemon*. Columbus, Ohio: The Wartburg Press, 1937. Pp. 986.

Milligan, George. *St. Paul's Epistles to the Thessalonians*. Grand Rapids, Mich.: Wm. B. Eerdmans Publishing Company, 1952. Pp. cix, 195. Based on Greek text; very thorough.

Morris, Leon. *The First and Second Epistles to the Thessalonians* in *The New International Commentary on the New Testament*. Grand Rapids, Mich.: Wm. B. Eerdmans Publishing Company, 1959. Pp. 274.

Plummer, Alfred. *A Commentary on St. Paul's Epistle to the Thessalonians*. London: R. Scott, 1918. Pp. xxviii, 116.

———. *A Commentary on St. Paul's Second Epistle to the Thessalonians*. London: R. Scott, 1918. Pp. xxiii, 118.

Ward, Ronald A. *Commentary on 1 and 2 Thessalonians*. Waco, Tex.: Word Books, 1973.

CORINTHIANS

Barrett, Charles Kingsley. *A Commentary on the First Epistle to the Corinthians*. First Edition. New York: Harper & Row, 1968.

Barrett, Charles Kingsley. *A Commentary on the Second Epistle to the Corinthians*. New York: Harper & Row, 1973.

Conzelmann, Hans. *I Corinthians: A Commentary on the First Epistle to the Corinthians*. Translated by James W. Leitch; bibliography and references by James W. Dunkly; edited by George W. MacRae. Philadelphia: Fortress Press, 1975.

Edwards, T. C. *A Commentary on the First Epistle to the Corinthians*. Fourth Edition. London: Hodder & Stoughton, 1903. Pp. 491.

Godet, F. *Commentary on St. Paul's First Epistle to the Corinthians*. Translated from the French by A. Cusin. Two volumes. Edinburgh: T. & T. Clark, 1889. Pp. vii, 428, vii, 493. Very thorough.

Grosheide, F. W. *Commentary on the First Epistle to the Corinthians* in *The New International Commentary on the New Testament*. Grand Rapids, Mich.: Wm. B. Eerdmans Publishing Company, 1953. Pp. 415.

Hodge, Charles. *Commentary on First Corinthians.* Grand Rapids, Mich.: Wm. B. Eerdmans Publishing Company, 1959. Pp. 373.

———. *Commentary on Second Corinthians.* Grand Rapids, Mich.: Wm. B. Eerdmans Publishing Company, n.d. Pp. 314.

Hughes, Philip Edgcumbe. *Paul's Second Epistle to the Corinthians.* The English text with introduction, exposition, and notes. *New International Commentary on the New Testament.* Grand Rapids, Mich.: Wm. B. Eerdmans Publishing Company, 1962. Pp. xxxvi, 508.

Lenski, R. C. H. *The Interpretation of St. Paul's First and Second Epistle to the Corinthians.* Columbus, Ohio: The Wartburg Press, 1935. Pp. 1383.

McFadyen, John E. *The Epistles to the Corinthians.* London, etc.: Hodder & Stoughton, 1911. Pp. 428.

Menzies, Allan. *The Second Epistle of the Apostle Paul to the Corinthians.* London: Macmillan & Company, Ltd., 1912. Pp. lvii, 111.

Morgan, G. Campbell. *The Corinthian Letters of Paul.* New York: Fleming H. Revell Company, c. 1946. Pp. 275. A popular commentary in lecture style.

Morris, Leon. *The First Epistle of Paul to the Corinthians* in *The Tyndale New Testament Commentaries.* Grand Rapids, Mich.: Wm. B. Eerdmans Publishing Company, 1958. Pp. 249.

Tasker, R. V. G. *The Second Epistle of Paul to the Corinthians* in *The Tyndale New Testament Commentaries.* Grand Rapids, Mich.: Wm. B. Eerdmans Publishing Company, 1958. Pp. 192.

ROMANS

Barrett, Charles K. *A Commentary on the Epistle to the Romans.* New York: Harper & Row, 1957.

Cranfield, C. E. B. *A Critical and Exegetical Commentary on the Epistle to the Romans* in *International Critical Commentary.* Two volumes. Edinburgh: T. & T. Clark, 1975, 1979. (Reissued as *Romans: A Shorter Commentary.* Grand Rapids, Mich.: Wm. B. Eerdmans Publishing Company, 1985. Pp. xvii, 388.)

Gifford, Edwin Hamilton. *The Epistle of St. Paul to the Romans.* London: John Murray, 1886. Pp. 238.

Godet, F. *Commentary on St. Paul's Epistle to the Romans.* Translated from the French by Rev. A. Cusin. Translated, revised and edited by T. W. Chambers. Second Edition. New York: Funk & Wagnalls, 1885.

Harrisville, Roy A. *Romans.* Minneapolis: Augsburg Publishing House, 1980.

Hodge, Charles. *Commentary on the Epistle to the Romans.* New Edition; revised and in great measure rewritten. Grand Rapids, Mich.: Wm. B. Eerdmans Publishing Company, 1951. Pp. 716. A theological commentary.

Käsemann, Ernst. *Commentary on Romans.* Translated and edited by G. W. Bromiley. Grand Rapids, Mich.: Wm. B. Eerdmans Publishing Company, 1980. Pp. xxix, 428.

Lenski, R. C. H. *The Interpretation of St. Paul's Epistle to the Romans.* Columbus, Ohio: The Wartburg Press, 1945. Pp. 933.

Liddon, Henry P. *Explanatory Analysis of St. Paul's Epistle to the Romans.* London: Longmans, Green & Company, 1893. Pp. vi, 309.

McQuilkin, Robert C. *The Message of Romans.* Grand Rapids, Mich.: Zondervan Publishing House, 1947. Pp. 178.

Moule, Handley C. G. *The Epistle of St. Paul to the Romans. The Expositor's Bible.* New York: A. C. Armstrong & Son, 1894. Pp. xvi, 437.

Murray, John. *The Epistle to the Romans* in *The New International Commentary on the*

New Testament. Two volumes in one. Grand Rapids, Mich.: Wm. B. Eerdmans Publishing Company, 1968. Pp. xxv, 408, xvi, 286.

Newell, William R. *Romans Verse by Verse.* Chicago: Moody Press, n.d. Pp. 577.

Stifler, James M. *The Epistle to the Romans.* New York: Fleming H. Revell Company, 1897. Pp. 275.

Thomas, W. H. Griffith. *Romans I-XVI: A Devotional Commentary.* Grand Rapids,
Mich.: Wm. B. Eerdmans Publishing Company, 1953. Unusually good teaching outlines.

CHAPTER 17

THE PAULINE
IMPRISONMENT: ACTS 21:17
TO 28:31

THE last section of Acts, containing the account of Paul's imprisonment, trials, and voyage to Rome, seems almost like an anticlimax. About one quarter of the book is given to a discussion of events that seemingly had no bearing on the doctrinal or missionary advance of the church. Instead of showing how the church expanded into Rome and Spain, the account leaves Paul under custody in his own hired house and tells nothing of the hearing before the emperor nor of Paul's subsequent ministry if the hearing ended in release. The story ends abruptly and, to the usual way of thinking, unsatisfactorily.

The abruptness of Acts' ending may be accounted for by assuming that the author wrote all that he knew. If he were attempting to bring Theophilus up to date, he would want to inform him as quickly as possible and, having given him the latest developments in Paul's career, there would be nothing left to say. The disproportionate emphasis on the imprisonment may mean that Luke could write more freely and fully of what he himself had witnessed, but there is probably an even better reason for the detail concerning the period. Christianity had become increasingly separate from Judaism, and its independence was more and more apparent to the observant public. The view that Rome took of it would have a very important effect on its future, for if it were to be regarded as a dangerous revolutionary movement, immediate suppression would follow. In this account, written for Theophilus, who was possibly a Roman official, Luke desired to show that Christianity had no political pretensions and that its relations with the Roman power had always been friendly. Persecution had come from the Jews on religious grounds, but all charges that it was subversive of Roman authority, as at Philippi (Acts 16:20–21), were false. Furthermore, these chapters of Acts have great biographical and theological value because they reveal more of the inner thought and teaching of Paul than do most of the other passages in Acts.

JERUSALEM

Paul's arrival in Jerusalem brought an immediate clash within the Jewish church in spite of his attempts at pacification. At the suggestion of James, Paul undertook the financial responsibility of helping some Jewish Christians to discharge the Nazirite vow (21:23–24).[1] Paul himself had undertaken the vow on a previous occasion (18:18), and James thought that it would afford him a good means of demonstrating that he had no aversion to keeping the law voluntarily. By so doing he could stop the various rumors that were being circulated about him that he was teaching all the Jews of the Dispersion not to circumcise their children nor to keep the customs of the law (21:21).

The project was well under way when the inevitable clash occurred. The Jews from Asia (20:19), who had been his bitter opponents at Ephesus and elsewhere, assuming that he had brought his Gentile companions into the forbidden sanctuary of the temple, accused him publicly of so doing and mobbed him. The ensuing riot took on such proportions that the Roman military tribune had to intervene with his armed cohorts. They rescued Paul from the fury of the mob and conducted him to the Castle of Antonia for further examination.

Paul gained permission from the tribune to speak from the castle steps (21:40) and, addressing the crowd in Aramaic, made his defense. The crowd listened respectfully as he told of his conversion. No objection was voiced to the reality of the blinding light, which to a Jewish mind would connote the Shekinah glory of God,[2] nor to the glorification of Jesus, nor to the concepts of baptism and repentance. Only when Paul mentioned a call to the Gentiles did the hatred of the mob burst into flame and he had to be removed to the castle for safety.

In the examinations and hearings that followed, two facts were brought into prominence: Paul's innocence of any political or criminal

---

1. For the nature of the vow, see Num. 6:1–20.
2. The Shekinah was the brilliant glory that accompanied the manifest presence of God. See Exod. 3:1–5; II Chron. 7:1–3; Isa. 6.

offense, and his Roman citizenship. He was in protective custody for four years. Two years were spent in Caesarea, because Felix hoped to extort a bribe from Paul for releasing him (24:26). He failed to discharge him when his procuratorship ended, for he thought that thus he could curry favor with the Jews (24:27). At the accession of Festus, Paul, realizing that the Jews would never relent in their hatred nor withdraw their accusations, feared that Festus would listen to them and leave him to languish indefinitely in prison. To take the case out of Festus' hands, he appealed to Caesar (25:10–12). Festus, knowing that Paul was a Roman citizen, was obligated to comply with his demand, and dispatched him to Rome to stand trial. Waiting for the hearing consumed another two years (28:30). Whether Paul was released because the case had not come to trial within the prescribed time, or whether he was tried and discharged as innocent is not told.

This period of enforced inactivity was by no means fruitless. Even in Jerusalem Paul was not forbidden to maintain contact with the outside world (23:16), and in Rome he dwelt in his own hired house where he carried on a ministry to all who called on him there (28:30–31). He could not travel, but he had liberty to teach and write within the limits of his own cell or house.

Seafront of ancient Caesarea from where Paul set sail for Rome.

The epistles that were written during this period testify that the growth of the church was not brought to a halt by Paul's imprisonment, and that the literature that Paul produced was of more solid and didactic nature than anything he had written up to that time, with the possible exception of Romans. The Prison Epistles as a group deal more with general teaching and less with individual questions than do the earlier Travel Epistles. They reveal a church that was not simply the initial aggregation of converts, eager, uncertain, perplexed by current problems, and somewhat disorganized, but a church that was maturing rapidly. There are indications that a second generation of Christians was beginning to emerge whose problems were those of complacency rather than of confusion. They had already been instructed in the elements of the faith, and they needed to receive the deeper teaching that would enlighten and stabilize them.

In spite of the change in Paul's plans that the imprisonment effected, his sense of destiny and his faith that the purpose of God was sending him to Rome did not alter. The voice he heard in the vision in Jerusalem that came just after his appearance before the Sanhedrin said: "As thou hast testified concerning me at Jerusalem, so must thou bear witness also at Rome" (23:11). The promise was renewed in the midst of the peril of the shipwreck by the angel of God, who said, "Fear not, Paul; thou must stand before Caesar" (27:24), and Paul's response was characteristic: "I believe God" (27:25). The entire period is an exemplification of the slow but sure operation of divine providence in Paul's ministration of the gospel.

The development of his message is also indicated by the repeated allusions in his defense to the resurrection of Christ. Allowing for the fact that the addresses in this section are apologetic rather than didactic, they show that in Paul's thinking the resurrection had taken a central place. In his defense before the Sanhedrin he said, "Brethren, I am a Pharisee, a son of Pharisees: touching the hope and resurrection of the dead I am called in question" (23:6). In the hearing before Felix he defined the belief of the "sect" to which he belonged by saying that he hoped "that there shall be a resurrection both of the just and unjust" (24:15). Even Festus, the Roman governor, who could hardly be called theologically minded, introduced Paul to Agrippa declaring that the Jews "had certain questions against him of their own religion, and of one Jesus, who was dead, whom Paul affirmed to be alive" (25:19). In the reply to Agrippa's invitation to speak for himself, Paul asked, "Why is it judged incredible with you, if God doth raise the dead?" (26:8). Following the account of his conversion, which presupposed the activity of a risen Christ, Paul avowed that his message was founded on prophecy, "how that the Christ must suffer, and how that he first by the resurrection of the dead should proclaim light both to the people and to the Gentiles" (26:23).

This stress on the resurrection is, of course, evident in all of Paul's epistles from the first (Gal. 1:1; I Thess. 1:10; 4:14; I Cor. 15:1–8; II Cor. 5:15; Rom. 1:4). The amplification of its meaning for the believer is developed in the sixth and eighth chapters of Romans, but its claims on his ethical and devotional life appear most clearly in Colossians and Ephesians. It may be that during the enforced retirement of his imprisonment Paul was able to contemplate more fully the meaning of the truth that was familiar to him and to formulate in greater detail its consequences for the Christian life.

THE EPISTLES

The four Prison Epistles, Philippians, Colossians, Ephesians, and Philemon, were the products of this period from A.D. 56 or 57 to A.D. 60 or 61. Some critical questions have been raised concerning them. Were they written at Caesarea, or at Rome? Are they all genuinely Pauline? What was their destination?

Undoubtedly they were written during the period of imprisonment, for all of them make reference to Paul's bonds (Phil. 1:12–13; Eph. 3:1; 4:1; 6:20; Col. 1:24; Philem. 1). Probably the traditional view that they were written from Rome is correct, for the allusions to Caesar's household (Phil. 4:22) and to the praetorian guard (1:13) would apply better to Rome than to Caesarea. He seemed to be in a center of travel, where his friends came and went with ease, which would be much more characteristic of Rome than of Caesarea.

Some questions have been raised in recent years concerning the genuineness of Ephesians. Goodspeed and others contend that it was written by a man who first collected and edited the Pauline epistles in order to provide an introduction for the collection. The letter, however, bears the name of Paul; the personal references are all in keeping with the known facts of his life; and its close resemblance to Colossians may be accounted for by the fact that both were written at approximately the same time so that the prevailing ideas of the two were similar. There is no convincing external evidence that Ephesians was written by another than Paul, and the internal evidence that is cited is susceptible of more than one interpretation.[3] It is possible that Ephesians was an encyclical letter, written not only to Ephesus, but generally for the churches of Asia that had been the field of Paul's last extended ministry before the imprisonment. The phrase "at

---

3. The strongest case for the non-Pauline authorship of Ephesians has been proposed by Edgar J. Goodspeed in his An Introduction to the New Testament (Chicago: The University of Chicago Press, n.d.), pp. 222–239. His argument, however, is based almost wholly on internal evidence. The case for Pauline authorship will be found in detail in D. Guthrie, New Testament Introduction (Third Edition; Downers Grove, Ill.: Inter-Varsity Press, 1970), pp. 490–508.

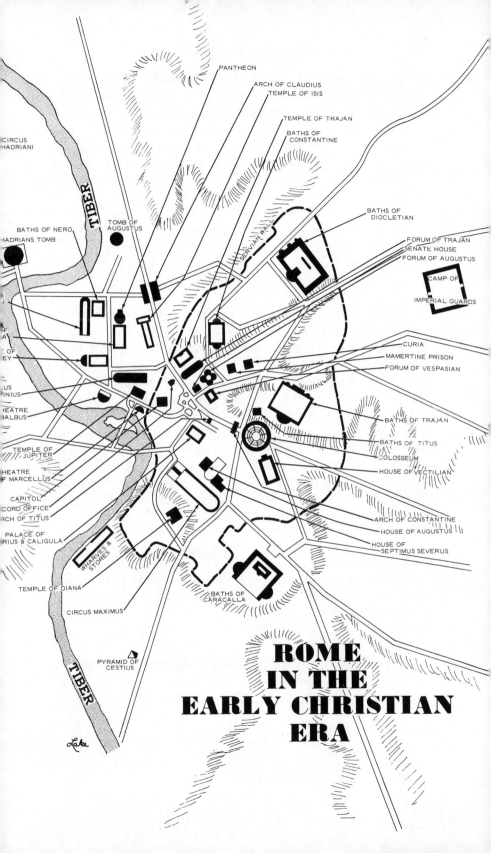

PANTHEON

ARCH OF CLAUDIUS
TEMPLE OF ISIS

TEMPLE OF TRAJAN

BATHS OF
CONSTANTINE

CIRCUS
HADRIANI

BATHS OF
DIOCLETIAN

SERVIAN WALL

BATHS OF NERO
HADRIANS TOMB

TOMB OF
AUGUSTUS

FORUM OF TRAJAN
SENATE HOUSE
FORUM OF AUGUSTUS

CAMP OF
IMPERIAL GUARDS

A

OF
EY

CURIA

MAMERTINE PRISON

FORUM OF VESPASIAN

US
PINIUS

HEATRE
BALBUS

BATHS OF TRAJAN

BATHS OF TITUS
COLOSSEUM

HOUSE OF VECTILIAN

TEMPLE OF
JUPITER

HEATRE
F MARCELLUS

CAPITOL
CORD OFFICE
RCH OF TITUS

ARCH OF CONSTANTINE

HOUSE OF AUGUSTUS

PALACE OF
RIUS & CALIGULA

HOUSE OF
SEPTIMUS SEVERUS

WHARVES &
STORES

TEMPLE OF DIANA

BATHS OF
CARACALLA

CIRCUS MAXIMUS

PYRAMID OF
CESTIUS

TIBER

TIBER

Lake

ROME
IN THE
EARLY CHRISTIAN
ERA

Ephesus" of 1:1 is lacking in some of the oldest manuscripts.[4] One wonders why no personal greetings are appended to this letter which was traditionally sent to a church where Paul labored for three years, unless he intended it for general reading by many churches. Its broad teaching, which does not deal with specific situations in a local church, confirms this impression. If it was a circular letter to the churches of Asia, undoubtedly one copy was sent to Ephesus. Since Ephesus was the largest church of the province, the copy in its possession would be the most accessible and the one most frequently reproduced. The destination of each of the other Prison Epistles is clearly indicated by the superscription that it bears, and has never been a subject of argument.

PHILEMON

Background

Philemon was written at the same time and under the same circumstances as Ephesians and Colossians. Onesimus, a slave of Philemon who was a businessman of Colosse, had absconded with some of his master's property and had gone to Rome to lose himself in the crowds of that great city. In some way he came in contact with Paul and was converted (Philem. 10).

Realizing the necessity of making right the wrong that Onesimus had done, Paul sent him back to his former master with this note, requesting that he be received and forgiven. Paul agreed to pay for the financial loss that Onesimus had caused (18–19). He added that he hoped for release in a short time, after which he planned to visit the churches again.

Content and Outline

Although this epistle is intensely personal rather than theological, it contains the finest picture of the meaning of forgiveness that can be found in the New Testament. Further, it is an example of Paul's adeptness in dealing with a touchy social problem. The outline will be a sufficient summary.

PHILEMON: A PICTURE OF CHRISTIAN FORGIVENESS

I. Salutation: The Family	1–3
II. The Fellowship	4–7
III. The Favor	8–20
IV. The Farewells	21–25

---

4. *En Epheso* does not appear in P[46], B*, or Aleph.

Evaluation

In this letter are found all the elements of forgiveness: the offense (11, 18), compassion (10), intercession (10, 18–19), substitution (18–19), restoration to favor (15), and elevation to a new relationship (16). Every aspect of the divine forgiveness of sin is duplicated in the forgiveness that Paul sought for Onesimus. It is a practical lesson in the petition of the prayer, "Forgive us our debts as we also have forgiven our debtors."

EPHESIANS

Background

The necessity for writing Philemon and sending a letter back to Asia afforded an opportunity to send others also. Ephesians, as a general encyclical to be distributed through the Ephesian church, and Colossians, a direct communication to the church at Colosse, were composed at this time, probably in A.D. 60 or 61. The messenger was Tychicus, whom Onesimus accompanied (Eph. 6:21; Col. 4:7–9). With Paul at the time of writing were Aristarchus, who had been one of the delegates to Jerusalem (Acts 20:4), Epaphras, an Asian, Luke "the beloved physician," and Demas. Mark had rejoined Paul at this time and was evidently contemplating a journey to Asia (Col. 4:10), for Paul commended him to Colosse. Jesus Justus, a Jewish colleague, is otherwise unknown. The fact that these men are mentioned both in Colossians and in Philemon indicates that the epistles were written about the same time.

Ephesians was written after many churches had been founded and after Paul had opportunity to contemplate the meaning of the new organism that had come into being. It is the one writing in the New Testament in which the word "church" means the church universal rather than the local group. It was intended to inform the Gentiles of their new calling, and it disclosed the mystery of the body of Christ in which there is neither Jew nor Gentile, bond nor free.

Content

Throughout the Epistle to the Ephesians runs the one theme of the church. The epistle was not directed to novices in the Christian faith, but to those who, having achieved some maturity in spiritual experience, wished to go on to fuller knowledge and life. Certain themes recur constantly in the book. The sovereign purpose of God in establishing the church permeates the first half of the epistle (1:4, 5, 9, 11, 13, 20; 2:4, 6, 10; 3:11) in which the divine plan of redemption is elaborated. In the second half the conduct of the believer is emphasized in the word "walk," which describes his model for conduct (4:1, 17; 5:1, 8, 15) as contrasted with his former behavior in the world (2:1). The sphere of the Christian's activities is "in the heavenlies" (1:3, 10, 20; 2:6; 3:10; 6:12), a phrase that refers to spiritual rather than to geographical locality. The dynamic of the church's life is the Holy Spirit, who is the seal of acceptance (1:13), the means of access to God (2:18), the source of revealed truth (3:5), the secret of universal power (3:16), the bond of unity (4:3–4), the mentor of thinking and speech (4:30), the stimulus of joy (5:18), and the armorer for conflict (6:17).

The textual divisions of Ephesians given below follow each other logically, leading the Christian from an understanding of the origin of his salvation in the thought and action of the triune God to the practical application of that salvation in everyday life.

Outline

Evaluation

If Romans is a sample of the kind of teaching that Paul would give to churches on his first visit to them, Ephesians is a specimen of his "Bible conference" technique. Much of its material can be duplicated in his other epistles, and there is little theology or ethics in Ephesians that cannot be found in essence elsewhere. The total complex, however, is integrated into a new picture of the church as a single functioning body, created out of Jew and Gentile, equipped with standards of its own, and engaged in a spiritual conflict. Its goal is "the unity of the faith . . . the knowledge of the Son of God . . . the measure of the stature of the fulness of Christ" (4:13).

COLOSSIANS

Background

Colossians and Ephesians are twin epistles; in fact, their resemblance is so great that some who doubted the Pauline authorship of Ephesians have averred that it is only a copy of Colossians with additions. The town of Colosse was located in the hinterland of Asia on a rocky ridge overlooking the valley of the Lycus River, not far from the cities of Hierapolis and Laodicea. During the period of the Persian Wars in the fifth century B.C., Colosse had been a town of considerable importance, but as Hierapolis and Laodicea grew, its commerce declined. It had been especially noted for the glossy black wool that was grown by the shepherds in the adjoining hill country. In Paul's day it was decadent, although still a good-sized city.

Paul himself had probably not visited Colosse or its neighboring cities, since he says that they had "not seen [his] face in the flesh" (Col. 2:1). It must have been evangelized during his stay in Asia, perhaps by Timothy and Epaphras (1:7) who went from place to place while Paul preached in Ephesus.

The heresy of Colosse that evoked this epistle was a local development that arose because of the peculiar situation of the city. Colosse was on the trade route from the East, along which oriental religions as well as oriental merchandise were transported to Rome. The Colossians were Phrygian Gentiles (1:27) whose religious antecedents were highly emotional and mystical. They were seeking to attain the fullness of God, and when teachers came among them with a philosophy that promised a mystic knowledge of God, they were entranced by it. Among its tenets were voluntary humiliation, probably by ascetic practices (2:18, 20–21), the worship of angels, who may have been reputed intermediaries between God and man (2:18), abstinence from certain foods and drinks, and the observance of feasts and ceremonial days (2:16). It is quite likely that these teachings also included a strain of Jewish legalism, brought in from contacts with the Jewish population of Asia Minor. Paul's references to ceremonialism (2:11) and to the fact that the ceremonies and feasts were a shadow of things to come (2:17) sound more like Judaism than heathenism. The Colossian heresy, then, was of the same order as the Galatian heresy, except that it centered about the person of Christ rather than about salvation by grace versus salvation by works.

Many interpreters of Colossians regard this heresy as a syncretism (i.e., a mixing or blending) of Jewish and oriental elements. There appears to be ascetic veneration of the "elemental spirits of the universe" (2:8 RSV) along with a Jewish ritualism concerned with various matters of food and ceremony (2:16). This is likely not a formal Gnostic system, such as

Ruins of the temple of Telesterion at Eleusis, Greece. Eleusis was the seat of the cult of the mysteries in ancient Greece.

became known in the late first and early second centuries, but may have contained elements found in that later complex of thought.[5]

The answer to this heresy lay not in extended argument, but in a positive presentation of the person of Christ. Paul pointed out that all philosophies, spiritual powers, ceremonial observances, and restrictions were secondary to the preeminence of Christ.

Content

Outstanding in Colossians is the passage from 1:14 to 22, which sets forth Paul's Christology. Curiously enough, it was not a separate treatise, but part of a prayer with which Paul opened the paragraph in 1:9. Beginning with a relative clause explanatory of the phrase "the Son of his love" (1:13), it continued with a description of Christ in terms that could be applied only to deity, summarized finally in the astounding statement that "in him dwelleth all the fulness of the Godhead bodily" (2:9). In creation, in redemption, in the church, and in personal life Christ must be preeminent.

Redemption is prominent in the teaching of Colossians. In Christ we have forgiveness of sins (1:14). Through the blood of his cross we are reconciled to God (1:20, 22). The bond written in ordinances that was against us has been abolished in the cross (2:14). The subjective application of death and resurrection is also taught in Colossians: "If ye died with Christ . . . why . . . do ye subject yourselves to ordinances? . . . If then ye were raised together with Christ, seek the things that are above, where Christ is, seated on the right hand of God" (2:20; 3:1).

Outline

COLOSSIANS: CHRIST PREEMINENT	
I. Salutation	1:1–2
II. Christ Preeminent in Personal Relationships	1:3–2:7
In Personal Contacts	1:3–8
In Personal Presentation	1:9–23
In Personal Purpose	1:24–2:7
III. Christ Preeminent in Doctrine	2:8–3:4
False Philosophy versus Christ	2:8–15
False Worship versus Christ	2:16–19
False Asceticism versus Christ	2:20–3:4

5. See F. F. Bruce, *Commentary on the Epistles to Ephesians and Colossians* (Grand Rapids, Mich.: Wm. B. Eerdmans Publishing Company, 1957; reissued 1984), pp. 230–232; R. P. Martin, *Colossians and Philemon* (Grand Rapids, Mich.: Wm. B. Eerdmans Company, 1981), pp. 10–19.

IV. Christ Preeminent in Ethics   3:5–4:6
    Negatively: "Put off . . ."   3:5–11
    Positively: "Put on . . ."   3:12–17
    In Family Relationships   3:18–4:1
    General   4:2–6
V. Concluding Personal Greetings   4:7–18

Evaluation

Colossians was written as an antidote to a blasé intellectualism that prated of mysteries, secret knowledge, and wisdom, while discounting Christ by a false philosophy. Paul shows that in Christ God is perfectly pictured (1:15), that in him all the fullness of deity resides (1:19), and that in him are hidden all the treasures of wisdom and knowledge (2:3). Moreover, the ethical demands of the Christian life are closely linked with its intellectual standards. "Set your mind on the things that are above, not on the things that are upon the earth" (3:2). The practical section of the book that follows this injunction (3:5–4:6) is connected to it by a "therefore," which establishes the relation of conscious effort between knowledge and behavior. Paul was no purveyor of idle theories. For him the gospel had clear ethical consequences.

PHILIPPIANS

Background

Philippians is the most personal of all the epistles of Paul that were not written to individuals. In the four pages that it occupies in an ordinary-size Bible there are no less than one hundred uses of the first person pronoun. Paul was not talking about himself in any boastful spirit, nor was he engaged in defense of his personal ministry, as in II Corinthians. The Philippian church had been intensely loyal to him, and he felt that he could speak to them freely of his tribulations and spiritual ambitions.

Practically a decade had passed since Paul, Silas, and Luke had first entered Philippi. From the beginning people had responded to his message. This church included many women, possibly friends of Lydia, who had labored with him in the gospel (Phil. 4:3). Some of them, like Syntyche and Euodia, did not always agree among themselves (4:2). At the outset of his ministry in Macedonia the church had supported him, but as his travels had taken him farther afield, they had not done very much for him. The news of the disaster in Jerusalem and his consequent imprisonment in Rome had revived their sympathetic interest (4:10–14), and they had again made a contribution to his need. Epaphroditus, their messenger, had brought to Paul their gifts, and had been taken seriously ill. Paul counted his recovery an answer to prayer (2:25–27), and was sending him back to Philippi with the letter that he wrote (2:28–29). He stated that Epaphroditus had risked his life to bring the gifts, though the nature of the danger was not revealed. Perhaps he incurred disease through his travels and contacts; perhaps he laid himself open to suspicion by communicating with a man who was a political prisoner.

The date of Philippians is uncertain, but it seems most reasonable to believe that it was written toward the close of Paul's two years in Rome. Lightfoot thinks that it may have been earlier than the Asian epistles, because its language has greater affinity with that of the Travel Epistles than with that of the others.[6] Language affinity is a very tenuous argument, since an author may change his style and vocabulary not only with the advance of his years but also with the needs of the situation for which he was writing. While it is true, as Lightfoot points out, that Philippians does resemble Romans more in its vocabulary and general style than it does Ephesians or Colossians, it was intended for a church that was more European than Asian and that was not affected by the mysticism and legalism that plagued Colosse.

Several other factors enter into the background. Some time must be allowed for the news of Paul's arrival in Rome to reach Philippi, and for the church there to send Epaphroditus to him with the gift. Paul's reputation among the praetorian guard (1:13) and the penetration of the gospel among the members of Caesar's household (4:22) required an interval of time. The two factions among the preachers, those that envied and disliked Paul and those that stood with him (1:15–16), did not develop overnight. Furthermore, his view of his trial shows that he was uncertain of the outcome and that while he was resigned to whatever might happen, he appeared confident that he would be released for further service (1:23–26; 2:17, 24).[7]

No particular schism or heresy within the Philippian church itself seems to have called for disciplinary action. The references to the Judaizers in 3:2 picture them as a potential rather than as a present danger; and while Paul's language is vehement, his main purpose is not so much to refute their error as to arouse the Philippians to walk worthily of their heavenly citizenship (3:17–21).

---

6. J. B. Lightfoot, *St. Paul's Epistle to the Philippians* (Eighth Edition; London: Macmillan and Company, 1888), pp. 30–46.

7. On place of origin, see D. E. Hiebert, "Philippians, Letter to," *Zondervan Pictorial Encyclopedia of the Bible*, IV, 764–765; G. B. Caird, *Paul's Letters from Prison* (Oxford: University Press, 1976), pp. 2–6.

Content

Two topics predominate in the text of Philippians. One is *the gospel*, which Paul mentions nine times. He speaks of "the fellowship in the gospel" (1:5, Greek text), the "confirmation of the gospel" (1:7), "the progress of the gospel" (1:12), "the defence of the gospel" (1:16), "worthy of the gospel" (1:27), "striving for the faith of the gospel" (1:27), "service in the gospel" (2:22, Greek text), "labor in the gospel" (4:3), "the beginning of the gospel" (4:15). Paul used the term as denoting a body of faith, a message, and the sphere of activity bounded by preaching. No definition of the gospel is given in Philippians, but the heart of the gospel is contained in two phrases that give respectively the historical and the personal aspects: he became "obedient *even* unto death, yea, the death of the cross" (2:8), and "having a righteousness . . . which is through faith in Christ" (3:9). The former is the good news that Christ died for men; the latter assures men that they can possess his righteousness before God. These are the two aspects of the gospel.

The second topic in Philippians that Paul stressed is *joy*. His outlook in Rome certainly was unpleasant, since his enemies were seeking to under-

Representation of an ancient Roman ship.

mine his work, and sudden execution was a possible outcome of the trial. Philippians is anything but pessimistic. Paul rejoiced in every remembrance of the Philippians (1:3) because Christ was preached, whether sincerely or hypocritically (1:18), in the growth of humility in his followers (2:2), in his personal sacrifice for Christ (2:17), and in the gifts and goodwill of his friends (4:10). All through the epistle the brilliant joy of faith is contrasted with the somber background of untoward circumstance and impending disaster.

Outline

PHILIPPIANS: THE PERSONAL EPISTLE

I. Salutations	1:1–2
II. Thanksgiving for Personal Fellowship	1:3–11
Gratitude	
Confidence	
Prayer	
III. Encouragement in Personal Circumstances	1:12–2:18
Paul's Personal Courage	1:12–26
Paul's Encouragement to the Philippians	1:27–30
Christ, the Model for Service	2:1–11
The Objective of Service	2:12–18
IV. Personal Relations with Messengers	2:19–30
V. Personal Warning against Legalism	3:1–4:1
Personal Example	3:1–16
Exhortation to the Philippians	3:17–4:1
VI. Concluding Counsel and Greetings	4:2–23
Unity	4:2–3
Joy	4:4–7
Thought	4:8–9
Thanksgiving	4:10–20
Salutations	4:21–23

Evaluation

Philippians is a note of thanks for favors received and an expression of Paul's personal Christian life. The two outstanding passages in this epistle, 2:5–11 and 3:2–15, express respectively the supreme obedience of Christ to the will of God and the supreme passion of his servant, Paul, to achieve the goal for which Christ had called him. The former passage was not written primarily as an essay in Christology, but was given incidentally to illustrate the nature of humility to which Paul was exhorting the Philippians. The very fact that Paul took its truth for granted in using it as an illustration confirms the theological truth that it contains. People take for granted what they believe in common; they argue when differences arise.

Much ink has been spilled over the meaning of the phrase "emptied himself" (2:7). To what extent did Christ relinquish the prerogatives of deity when he came among men? The Lord Jesus Christ voluntarily divested himself of visible glory in order to take on himself the garment of humanity and in order to meet the penalty of human sin on human ground, but he did not cease to be God. Along with Colossians 1, Hebrews 1 and 2, and John 1, this is one of the outstanding passages relating to the doctrine of the incarnation.

The other passage, Philippians 3, provides an insight into the driving motive in the life of Paul. His amazing devotion and unflagging zeal place him among the great leaders of history who have devoted their lives to a cause in which they believed utterly. To him, however, all of life was summed up in Christ. To "gain" him, to "know" him, to "be found" in him, to attain the goal set in him engaged all of Paul's attention. Philippians depicts a totalitarian life in Christ.

Ruins of buildings that graced the ancient Roman Forum.

RESULTS OF THE PAULINE IMPRISONMENT

The outcome of the period of imprisonment is not difficult to assess, even though there may be some questions as to whether Paul was released or not. In spite of his confinement at Caesarea and at Rome, Paul's ministry was not ended. Through his assistants and friends, who are mentioned in the salutations of his epistles, he maintained constant communication with the churches. The enforced retirement provided more time for prayer and contemplation, out of which came the priceless revelation of the Prison Epistles. His appeal to Caesar brought Christianity directly to the attention of the Roman government and compelled the civil authorities to pass judgment on its legality. If it was to be allowed as a *religio licita,* a permitted cult, the persecution of it would be illegal, and its security would be assured. If, on the other hand, it was adjudged to be a *religio illicita,* a forbidden cult, then the ensuing persecution would only advertise it and offer an opportunity for a demonstration of its power. In the decade of the Gentile mission from A.D. 46 to 56, and in the four years of Paul's imprisonment, the church came out from under the banner of Judaism and formed its own ranks as an independent movement. It was now ready for even greater advances in missionary expansion.

FOR FURTHER READING

EPHESIANS

Barth, Markus. *Ephesians* in *Anchor Bible.* Two volumes. Introduction, Translation, and Commentary. Garden City, N.Y.: Doubleday, 1974.

Bruce, F. F. *The Epistles to the Colossians, to Philemon, and to the Ephesians* in *New International Commentary on the New Testament.* Grand Rapids, Mich.: Wm. B. Eerdmans Publishing Company, 1984.

Cable, John H. *The Fulness of God.* Chicago: The Moody Press, 1945. Pp. 160. Helpful in Bible class work.

Findlay, G. C. *The Epistle to the Ephesians. The Expositor's Bible.* Grand Rapids, Mich.: Wm. B. Eerdmans Publishing Company, 1947. Pp. xii, 440.

Hodge, Charles. *Commentary on the Epistle to the Ephesians.* Grand Rapids, Mich.: Wm. B. Eerdmans Publishing Company, 1950. Pp. 398.

Miller, H. S. *The Book of Ephesians.* Houghton, N.Y.: The Word-Bearer Press, 1931. Pp. 250. A mine of information on Ephesians.

Moule, H. C. G. *Ephesian Studies.* London: Hodder & Stoughton Company, 1900.

Paxson, Ruth. *The Wealth, Walk, and Warfare of the Christian.* New York: Fleming H. Revell and Company, 1939. Pp. 223.

Robinson, J. Armitage. *St. Paul's Epistle to the Ephesians.* Second Edition. London: Macmillan & Company, Ltd., 1909. Pp. ix, 314. Greek text.

Westcott, B. F. *St. Paul's Epistle to the Ephesians.* Grand Rapids, Mich.: Wm. B. Eerdmans Publishing Company, 1952. Pp. lxviii, 212. Greek text.

COLOSSIANS AND PHILEMON

Garrod, G. W. *The Epistle to the Colossians*. London: Macmillan & Company, Ltd., 1898. Pp. 176.

Jones, Maurice. *The Epistle of St. Paul to the Colossians*. London: Society for Promoting Christian Knowledge, 1923. Pp. 119.

Lightfoot, J. B. *The Epistles of St. Paul: Colossians and Philemon*. London: Macmillan & Company, 1892. Pp. viii, 428. Greek text.

Martin, Ralph P. *Colossians and Philemon* in *New Century Bible Commentary*. Grand Rapids, Mich.: Wm. B. Eerdmans Publishing Company, 1981.

———. *Colossians: the Church's Lord and the Christian's Liberty*. An expository commentary with a present-day application. Grand Rapids, Mich.: Zondervan Publishing House, 1973.

McDonald, H. Dermot. *Commentary on Colossians and Philemon*. Waco, Tex.: Word Books, 1980.

Moule, C. F. D. *The Epistles of Paul the Apostle to the Colossians and to Philemon*. Cambridge: University Press, 1957.

Moule, H. C. G. *Colossian Studies*. New York: George H. Doran Company, n.d. Devotional commentary.

Robertson, A. T. *Paul and the Intellectuals*. New York: Doubleday, Doran, & Company, 1928. Pp. 217.

Westcott, B. F. *A Letter to Asia*. London: Macmillan & Company, Ltd., 1914. Pp. vi, 263.

PHILIPPIANS

Lightfoot, J. B. *St. Paul's Epistle to the Philippians*. Eighth Edition. London: Macmillan & Company, 1888. Pp. xii, 350. Greek text.

Moule, H. C. G. *Philippian Studies*. Fifth Edition. London: Hodder & Stoughton, 1904. Pp. xii, 265.

Müller, Jac. J. *The Epistles of Paul to the Philippians and to Philemon* in *The New International Commentary on the New Testament*. Grand Rapids, Mich.: Wm. B. Eerdmans Publishing Company, 1955. Pp. 200.

Plummer, Alfred. *Commentary on St. Paul's Epistle to the Philippians*. London: R. Scott, 1919. Pp. xxiii, 115.

Robertson, A. T. *Paul's Joy in Christ*. New York: Fleming H. Revell Company, 1917. Pp. 267.

Tenney, Merrill C. *Philippians: The Gospel at Work*. Grand Rapids, Mich.: Wm. B. Eerdmans Publishing Company, 1956. Pp. 102.

See also the material for further reading at the end of Chapter 13, especially the section "Lives of Paul."

PART IV

THE PROBLEMS OF THE EARLY CHURCH

The Period of Consolidation:
A.D. 60 to 100

CHAPTER 18

THE INSTITUTIONAL CHURCH: THE PASTORAL EPISTLES

BACKGROUND

No single consecutive history is available that gives in written form the fortunes of the church from the close of the book of Acts to the end of the first century. Only the individual books of the canon, with such additional hints as may be gleaned from the writings of the early church fathers, can supply any knowledge of events in this period. The uncertainty of placing exactly the dates and places of origin of these writings adds to the problem, so that a consistent picture of this era is almost impossible to reconstruct.

A definite change took place after the imprisonment of Paul. The man himself was different, for although he was unready to quit the ardent pursuit of his calling as Philippians showed (Phil. 3:12), time was against him. In Philemon he described himself as "Paul the aged" (Philem. 9), and in Philippians he indicated that death might not be far distant (Phil. 1:20–21). He was relying increasingly on the aid of his younger associates, who were still free and better able than he to carry on the work of preaching.

The Pastoral Epistles, I Timothy, Titus, and II Timothy, belong at this stage in his career. Their genuineness has been disputed because of the differences between them and the general body of Pauline literature in vocabulary, in style, and in content. They still bear Paul's name, and their connection with his known biography is sufficiently strong to warrant their acceptance, since his vocabulary and style may vary with age and circumstances. There is a marked difference in both between the Prison Epistles and the Travel Epistles, so that a further difference between the others and the Pastoral Epistles is not surprising.

The biographical data that they supply seemingly indicate that Paul must have been acquitted on his first hearing before the emperor and that he enjoyed thereafter a short period of free ministry. His original plan had been to deposit the offering of the Gentile churches at Jerusalem, and then to hasten westward in order to strengthen the church in Rome, from which he would proceed to Spain. Four years at least had elapsed since he had been the master of his own plans, but finally he was released. The allusions to his movements in the Pastorals bear no relation to the account given in Acts, and in many particulars do not correspond with it at all. The inevitable deduction is that the three epistles must have been written later, when Paul was traveling again.

The chronological relations of the Pastorals to the Prison Epistles seem clear from their reference to Paul's companions. Many of these are identical with those of the Prison Epistles, but are located in places that show that they had left Paul's immediate vicinity. Timothy had been left at Ephesus while Paul was en route to Macedonia (I Tim. 1:3), whereas on the last trip that Timothy took with Paul the order of procedure was from Macedonia to Asia (Acts 20:4–6), and Timothy did not remain in Ephesus. Demas had deserted Paul (II Tim. 4:10), whereas the Prison Epistles included him among the group at Rome (Philem. 24). Titus was left in Crete (Titus 1:5), and then went to Dalmatia (II Tim. 4:10), but on none of the journeys in Acts did Paul go to Crete, nor did he have Titus with him when he finally did go there during the voyage to Rome. Mark was in Asia (4:11) where Paul had recommended him according to one of the Asian letters (Col. 4:10). Luke was still with him (II Tim. 4:11). Tychicus had gone on his errand to Ephesus (4:12). Paul himself had visited Ephesus (I Tim. 1:3), Crete (Titus 1:5), Nicopolis (3:12), Corinth (II Tim. 4:20), Miletus (4:20), and Troas (4:13), and was presently located in Rome (1:17). He was in prison (1:16) and was quite sure that the end of his life was not far away (4:6–7). Altogether the situation was very different from that described by the Prison Epistles.

Within the range of the Pastoral Epistles there was probably some lapse of time. I Timothy pictures Paul as traveling and active, counseling his young lieutenant concerning his pastoral duties. Titus is quite similar in its outlook. II Timothy, however, is definitely a terminus, for Paul evidently was confident that he would not survive the winter (II Tim. 4:21). His first hearing, at which nobody defended him, had ended favorably (4:17), but his accusers had become more vicious (4:14), and his condemnation and execution would be only a matter of time. The temper of Nero was very uncertain, and the chances of further clemency from him would be small.

The Pastorals belong together. If vocabulary and style can be used as a criterion for determining their relationship to each other, they certainly must have been written by the same man and under the same general circumstances. They are, therefore, a fair basis for judging the state of the church in the seventh decade of the Christian era.

I TIMOTHY

Assuming that Paul was acquitted in A.D. 60 or 61 after his appeal to the emperor, he resumed his missionary activities. Contrary to his original expectations (Acts 20:38), the way was open for him to revisit the Asian churches. There had been some defection among them, for Paul counseled Timothy to "charge certain men not to teach a different doctrine, neither to give heed to fables and endless genealogies . . ." (I Tim. 1:3–4). They had desired to be teachers of the law, though they were inexperienced and untaught in its mysteries (1:7). In addition to those who were intellectually confused stood those who were morally abandoned, such as Hymenaeus and Alexander (1:20), who had been put under stringent discipline. Profitless argument (1:6) and spiritual shipwreck had followed these trends.

The organization of the church had increased in complexity. Offices had become fixed and were sought by some as affording desirable eminence, so that the prestige of the office rather than its usefulness became the chief objective. Bishops, deacons, and elders are all mentioned, though probably the first and third of these classes are identical.[1] Widows who were supported by the church were "enrolled," and they assumed some responsibility for the social service of the church (5:9). The services had certain regular features: prayer with uplifted hands (2:8), modesty and unobtrusiveness on the part of the women (2:11), reading, preaching, and teaching (4:13), the laying on of hands to confer a spiritual gift (4:14). As the second and third generations of believers arose, the theology of the church was increasingly taken for granted and became decreasingly vital. Wrangling and argument developed over points of difference; heresy became a growingly imminent danger.

Timothy's Biography

Timothy himself is an interesting study. Born in Lystra of a Greek father and a Jewish mother, he was brought up in the Jewish faith and was taught the Scriptures from childhood. Paul made him an understudy in his second journey (Acts 16:1–3), and Timothy remained with him ever after. He shared in the evangelization of Macedonia and Achaia and aided Paul during the three years of preaching at Ephesus, where he became thor-

---

1. Cf. Acts 20:17 and 28. The persons mentioned belonged to Ephesus.

oughly acquainted with the city and with the needs of the local church. He was one of the delegates appointed to Jerusalem (20:4) and probably went with Paul all the way back to that city. He was with Paul in Rome during the first imprisonment, for his name appears in the headings of Colossians (1:1) and Philemon (1). After the release he traveled with Paul and evidently was left at Ephesus to straighten out the tangle that had developed there, while Paul went on to visit the churches in Macedonia. At the end of Paul's life he joined him at Rome (II Tim. 4:11, 21), and he himself suffered imprisonment (Heb. 13:23), from which he was later released.

Timothy was a trustworthy but not a forceful character. He gave the impression of immaturity, although he must have been at least thirty years of age when Paul assigned him to the pastorate at Ephesus (I Tim. 4:12). He was timid (II Tim. 1:6–7) and was subject to stomach trouble (I Tim. 5:23). The epistles that bear his name were intended to encourage and strengthen him for the tremendous task that Paul had bequeathed to him.

Outline

Content

An integrated outline of this epistle is difficult to achieve because of its conversational style and intensely personal tone. Some sentences seem irrelevant to their context, such as the injunction to "be no longer a drinker of water" in 5:23. These are just the sort of sayings that one might expect in casual conversation where the speaker interjects them as he thinks of them without planning a formal essay. The preamble (1:3–17) sketches the emergency for which Paul had left Timothy at Ephesus. He recalls for Timothy his own experience, which serves as a pattern of the call to the ministry. He reminds Timothy frequently of the responsibility of this calling (1:18; 4:6, 12, 16; 5:21; 6:11, 20), as if to keep him from quitting a difficult task. The official commission, introduced by the phrase "This charge I commit unto thee . . ." (1:18), deals with matters of organizational importance in the church. The corporate devotional, official, and doctrinal problems are aired, and pastoral administrative policies are outlined. Under the section on personal admonitions (4:6–6:19) Paul outlines the relation of the preacher to his own ministry and to the groups in the congregation, showing how to deal with each of them. The final appeal to Timothy as a man of God is a classic, and in the four imperatives, *flee, follow, fight, keep* (6:11–12, 14), Paul sketched the elements of personal ministerial life.

TITUS

Background

In order of time Titus followed I Timothy. Paul, having left Ephesus, went to Macedonia and perhaps sailed from there to Crete, where he had been a visitor on his voyage to Rome. On this occasion he spent some time there, but left Titus to complete the establishment of the church and to rectify its errors. One wonders whether Paul felt that his time was short and that he wanted to return to Ephesus, for he spoke of sending Tychicus to Crete (Titus 3:12) at a later date. His ultimate goal was Nicopolis (probably in Epirus), where he planned to winter.

The situation in Crete was discouraging. The church was unorganized, and its members were quite careless in behavior. If the injunctions of chapter 2 are any indication of what the churches needed, the men were lax and careless, the older women were gossips and winebibbers, and the young women were idle and flirtatious. Perhaps the preaching of the gospel of grace had given the Cretans the impression that salvation by faith was unrelated to an industrious and ethical life. Six times (1:16; 2:7, 14; 3:1, 8, 14) in this short epistle Christians are urged to do good works. Although Paul says that salvation cannot be earned by good works (3:5), he affirms with equal vigor that believers must be careful to maintain good works.

The disturbance in Crete had been caused by a combination of the ethical laxity that sprang from the natural tendencies of the Cretans (1:12–13) and the disputation over Jewish fables and commandments that were promoted by a Judaizing group (1:10) who were godless (1:16), unruly (1:10), divisive (1:11), and mercenary (1:11). These teachers differed from those that troubled the Galatians in that their error was moral perversity, whereas that of the Galatians was stringent legalism. Both are condemned by this epistle.

Both I Timothy and Titus were written to counsel an understudy who was working out the problems of a difficult pastorate. Titus, the recipient of this epistle, had been an acquaintance and associate of Paul for fifteen years or more. He was a Gentile convert of the early days in Antioch, whose conversion was so convincing that he served as Exhibit A of the uncircumcised Gentile believers when Paul and Barnabas went up for the conference at Jerusalem (Gal. 2:1, 3). He must have been with Paul during his third journey, for he acted as Paul's emissary during the trying days of the church's rebellion in Corinth, and he was successful in bringing them back to penitence and loyalty (II Cor. 7:6–16). He had traveled widely in Macedonia to collect the funds that Paul was raising and had his hearty approval (8:16, 19, 23). He may have been included in the "us" of Acts 20:5, though he is not mentioned by name anywhere in Acts. The last allusion to him in the New Testament states that he had gone to Dalmatia (II Tim. 4:17). He seems to have been a stronger character than Timothy and better able to cope with opposition.

Outline

TITUS: SOUND DOCTRINE

I. Salutation: The Source of Sound Doctrine	1:1–4
II. The Administration of Sound Doctrine	1:5–16
The Appointment of Elders	1:5–9
The Exposure of False Teachers	1:10–16
III. The Preaching of Sound Doctrine	2:1–15
Application	2:1–10
To aged men	
To aged women	
To young women	
To young men	
To himself	
To slaves	
Definition	2:11–15
IV. Counseling by Sound Doctrine	3:1–11
V. Concluding Salutations	3:12–15

Content

The general content of Titus is like that of I Timothy, except for a stronger emphasis on creedal formulation. In two passages Paul states the closest approach to a formulated creed in the whole New Testament (2:11–14; 3:4–7). Note the elements contained in these passages:

1. The personality of God (2:11; 3:6).
2. The qualities of his love and grace (2:11; 3:4).
3. His title of Savior (2:10; 3:4).
4. The saviorhood of Christ (2:13; 3:6).
5. The Holy Spirit (3:5).
6. The implication of the triune being of God (3:5–6).
7. The essential deity of Christ (2:13).
8. The vicarious atonement of Christ (2:14).
9. The universality of salvation (2:11).
10. Salvation by grace, not by works (3:5).
11. The incoming of the Holy Spirit (3:5).
12. Justification by faith (3:7).
13. Sanctification (purification) of his own people (2:14).
14. Separation from evil (2:12).
15. Inheritance of eternal life (3:7).
16. The return of Christ (2:13).

The foregoing points constitute a fair digest of New Testament theology.

Titus is a good summary of the doctrinal teaching of the church as it emerged into the institutional stage. Although it was written to a pioneer missionary, he represented a church that had passed the pioneer era and that had settled policies and faith. The word "sound" implies that a recognized standard of doctrine had been acknowledged, to which correct life and teaching must conform.

II TIMOTHY

Background

Whether Paul ever fulfilled his desire to visit Spain is not known. Clement of Rome (A.D. 95) said in his letter that Paul ". . . taught righteousness to all the world, and when he had reached the limits of the West he gave his testimony before the rulers. . . ."[2] If Clement was writing from Rome, it would be as strange for him to refer to Rome as "the bound of the west" as for a man living in Chicago to call that city the western boundary of the United States. Clement did not mention Spain, and it is possible that he was simply surmising what Paul had done on the assump-

2. I Clement V.7. See Kirsopp Lake, *The Apostolic Fathers* (London: William Heinemann, 1919), I, 17.

tion that he had fulfilled his avowed intention. It would be interesting to know whether Paul actually did preach there, and whether the early churches in North Africa and Britain might have been founded by his converts.

Any trip to Spain at this time, then, must be purely speculative, and its appearance on the map is at best a probability. If Paul's travels follow rigidly the lines marked out in the Pastorals, he stopped at Corinth (4:20), where Erastus chose to remain, at Miletus, where he left Trophimus sick, and at Troas (4:13). The exact order of these steps is not prescribed by the narrative. He did not stop at Ephesus, but sent Tychicus there. He must have been arrested suddenly and taken to Rome, for he left his plans unfinished. The books that he dropped at Troas he may have intended to retrieve later, but he had no opportunity to do so. The place of his arrest is uncertain; it might have been Troas or Nicopolis.

The cause of his arrest is also uncertain. If Alexander the coppersmith mentioned in II Timothy 4:14 is identical with the Alexander of Acts 19:33, one might venture a guess that he was a Jewish metallurgist who was disgruntled with Paul on two counts: Paul's preaching of free grace for Gentiles, and the decline of the trade in shrines at Ephesus because of Paul's vigorous inroads into heathenism. The situation at Ephesus had been tense. Paul spoke in II Corinthians 1:8 of "our affliction which befell *us* in Asia, that we were weighed down exceedingly, beyond our power, insomuch that we despaired even of life." In Acts 20:19 he referred to "plots of the Jews" the had been formed there. Perhaps Alexander, still rankling over Paul's escape from Ephesus and over the loss of trade that his fellow workmen had suffered, denounced him to the Roman authorities and finally brought about his condemantion. Alexander was known to Timothy also, and Paul's counsel to beware of him implies that he was operating where Timothy was, perhaps in Ephesus.

The general tone of the Pastoral Epistles reveals a church that was fighting for its life against the malicious jealousy of a frustrated Judaism and against the corrupt indifference of a decadent paganism. Paul, the representative of the passing generation of missionary pioneers, was delegating his responsibilities to younger and more vigorous assistants, some of whom, like Titus and Timothy, were worthy successors, and others of whom, like Demas, were recreant (II Tim. 4:10). II Timothy was his last message to his helpers and friends before he passed from the scene.

Outline

II TIMOTHY: THE FAREWELL MESSAGE

Content

The content of this last epistle is an intermingling of personal sentiment and administrative policy, of reminiscence and instruction, of sadness and confidence. Its main purpose was to strengthen Timothy for the arduous task that Paul himself was about to relinquish. He laid down the pastoral pattern by first reminding Timothy of his own personal experi-

Temple of Apollo in what once was a large settlement known as Bassae near Phigalia, Greece.

ence, and by including him in it: "who saved *us*, and called *us* with a holy calling . . . according to his own purpose and grace" (II Tim. 1:9, italics ours). With this calling in mind, he urged Timothy to undertake his problems as a soldier goes to war (2:3), trusting his general to plan the campaign, and serving wholeheartedly and uncomplainingly in the ranks wherever he is needed. In personal life and in public relations with the church he should always be the Lord's servant, not contentious, but ready to help all people to understand the truth of God.

The picture of the last days, like the similar passage in I Timothy 4:1–3, was a piece of prophecy characterizing the conditions to which the church might look forward. The antidote that Paul prescribed for the influx of evil was the knowledge of the Scriptures, "which are able to make thee wise unto salvation through faith which is in Christ Jesus" (II Tim. 3:15).

The final charge (4:1–6) is a classic, and should be studied carefully by every candidate for the ministry.

EVALUATION

The Pastoral Epistles as a group are the most valuable source extant for understanding the life of the church in the transition period between the close of the pioneer days and the emergence of the institutional organization that is portrayed in the Epistles of Ignatius. Two or three tendencies are worthy of notice.

For one, the growth of heresy is more apparent. Opposition to truth and doctrinal divergences appear in all the Pauline Epistles. Galatians attacks legalism, I Corinthians states that some did not believe in the resurrection of the body, Colossians reflects the inroads of some philosophic cult. These, however, were sporadic and local, with the possible exception of the Judaizing tendency, but even that varied in its character and intensity in different places. In the Pastorals these same errors appear, but they are intensified and constitute a future menace that the younger preachers must meet.

Because of this menace, there is a greater stress on formulated creed in the Pastorals than in the earlier writings. The specific doctrinal formulas in Titus, the injunction to "hold the pattern of sound words which thou hast heard from me" (II Tim. 1:13), and the frequent sentences in creedal form (I Tim. 1:15; 2:3–5; 3:16; 4:10; II Tim. 1:10; 2:8; 3:16) impress the reader that the Pastorals were written to a church that was beginning to put its faith into articulate terms. Such creedal expressions were current, for the formula "Faithful is the saying" is used to introduce a number of them as if they were commonly employed in the oral teaching of the church (I Tim. 1:15; 3:1; 4:9; II Tim. 2:11; Titus 3:8). The phrase "sound doctrine" also occurs frequently (I Tim. 1:10; 6:3; II Tim. 1:13; 4:3; Titus 1:9; 2:1, 8).

The word "sound" means literally "healthful" and is usually connected with good works as well as with correct principles. Creed and life are never divorced in the Bible.

Although the self-consciousness of the church as an institution had begun to emerge (I Tim. 3:15), it had not become a fixed hierarchy or a machine organization. Spiritual vitality and conduct were more important than ritual and politics, and the missionary motive was still keen. In spite of incipient persecution and heresies, the church was still growing apace.

FOR FURTHER READING

The historical background for this period may be found in the later chapters of the biographies of Paul and in the general reference works listed at the ends of chapters 13 and following.

Dibelius, Martin and Conzelmann, Hans. *A Commentary on the Pastoral Epistles.* Translated by P. Buttolph and A. Yarbro; edited by H. Koester. Philadelphia: Fortress Press, 1972.

Falconer, Sir Robert. *The Pastoral Epistles.* Introduction, Translation, and Notes. Oxford: The Clarendon Press, 1937. Pp. viii, 164.

Guthrie, Donald. *The Pastoral Epistles* in *The Tyndale New Testament Commentaries.* Grand Rapids, Mich.: Wm. B. Eerdmans Publishing Company, 1957. Pp. 228.

Hendriksen, William. *Timothy and Titus* in *The New Testament Commentary.* Grand Rapids, Mich.: Baker Book House, 1957. Pp. 412.

Hillard, A. E. *The Pastoral Epistles of St. Paul.* The Greek Text with Commentary. London: Rivingtons, 1910. Pp. 147.

James, J. D. *The Genuineness and Authorship of the Pastoral Epistles.* London: Longmans, Green, & Company, 1906. Pp. 165.

Kelly, J. N. D. *A Commentary on the Pastoral Epistles.* Grand Rapids, Mich.: Baker Book House, 1981.

Liddon, H. P. *Explanatory Analysis of St. Paul's First Epistle to Timothy.* London: Longmans, Green, & Company, Ltd., 1897. Pp. 93.

Parry, R. St. John. *The Pastoral Epistles, with Introduction, Text and Commentary.* Cambridge: The University Press, 1920. Pp. clxviii, 104.

Shaw, R. D. *The Pauline Epistles.* Edinburgh: T. & T. Clark, 1903. Pp. xi, 508. See pp. 422–495.

Simpson, E. K. *The Pastoral Epistles.* Grand Rapids, Mich.: Wm. B. Eerdmans Publishing Company, 1954. Pp. 174.

CHAPTER 19

THE SUFFERING CHURCH:
I PETER

BACKGROUND

THUS far the New Testament has said little about the relation between Christianity and the Roman government. The few political references in the Gospels deal with the local rule of the Herods rather than with the imperial system, with the exception of Jesus' famous utterance: ". . . Render therefore unto Caesar the things that are Caesar's; and unto God the things that are God's" (Matt. 22:21). Acts invariably represents the contacts between Christianity and the Roman officials in a favorable light, but it gives the impression that those contacts were few. The epistles of Paul do not discuss political theory and merely enjoin the Christians to be subject to the powers that be, because they are ordained of God (Rom. 13:1–6).

This comparative silence concerning political relations that could hardly have been unimportant under a totalitarian government may be explained in several ways. First, Christianity was primarily spiritual, not political. "My kingdom is not of this world," said Jesus to Pilate: "if my kingdom were of this world, then would my servants fight . . ." (John 18:36). The application of the principles that Jesus taught had political consequences, but neither he nor the apostles were revolutionists or agitators.

Again, as has been observed, Christianity grew up within Judaism, which was a *religio licita*, a cult permitted and protected by the state. Rome's policy was tolerance wherever religious observances did not conflict with

344

the state's claims. As long as the Christians created no disturbance, they were simply ignored.

The Christians who did come into contact with Rome in the earlier part of the first century left a favorable impression on the Roman authorities. Paul stood on his rights as a citizen on at least two occasions and demanded recognition for them (Acts 16:36–39; 22:24–29), but he could also say that he had never been guilty of subversive activities or of raising insurrection (24:12). The church had followed a policy of peaceful penetration of society with the message of Christ.

Toward the close of the seventh decade the situation began to change. The Christians had separated from Judaism and were recognized as a different group. Their firm adherence to belief in an invisible God and a risen Christ excited the suspicion and contempt of the public, while their talk of a coming judgment and overthrow of the existing world created misunderstanding and hatred. The reaction against them in Rome under Nero was the product of this popular dislike, activated by Nero's spiteful accusations. The close of the Pastoral Epistles shows that Paul's death marked a turn in the policy of the government from casual tolerance to hostile criticism.

When the churches began to realize this change in attitude, they became apprehensive of what might befall them. They could not organize resistance, for by so doing they would violate their own principle of peaceful obedience to the government, and would only give occasion for further charges against them. Were they faced with extinction? What would the outcome be? Would the brutalities of Nero be duplicated in the provinces? They looked to their leaders to answer their questions for them.

First Peter was written in reply to this situation as it affected the churches of northern Asia Minor in the provinces of Pontus, Galatia, Cappadocia, Asia, and Bithynia. Two of these provinces, Pontus and Cappadocia, are not mentioned in Acts among those evangelized by Paul; Bithynia he attempted to reach, but was forbidden to do so (Acts 16:7). Galatia and Asia he did evangelize, but the way in which these provinces are listed gives the impression that Peter was addressing only those Christians living in the northern sections.

The origin and constituency of these churches are not well known. Men from Cappadocia and Pontus were present on the day of Pentecost (Acts 2:9) and may have returned to their homes with the news of the coming of the Messiah and of the outpouring of the Holy Spirit. It is possible that Peter had preached in these regions, for he had worked with the church at Antioch (Gal. 2:11), and had traveled in the Mediterranean world while Paul was preaching during the European campaign (I Cor. 9:5). While there is no statement on record that Peter founded or even visited these churches, nothing precludes his doing so. Perhaps Paul re-

The ancient amphitheater of Epidauros, Greece.

frained from undertaking a mission in these provinces because he knew
that somebody else had already been there.

The epistle is addressed to "the elect who are sojourners of the Dispersion . . ." (I Pet. 1:1). This salutation, together with the references to the
Gentiles (2:12; 4:3), conveys the impression that the "elect" were converts
from the Dispersion and that these groups were predominantly Jewish in
character. The question may legitimately be raised whether these terms are
literal or figurative. "Gentile" had come to mean non-Jewish not only in
the racial sense, but also in the spiritual sense. To a Jew, a Gentile was a
man who did not know the true God. When the Christians took over
Jewish phraseology, "Gentile" thus became the equivalent of the modern
term "heathen." This use of the word in I Peter is confirmed by one or two
other passages. I Peter 1:14 commands the hearers to set their hope on

Christ "as children of obedience, not fashioning yourselves according to your former lusts in *the time of* your ignorance." Those who had been brought up as Jews with the knowledge of the Scriptures could hardly have been called ignorant. Again Peter spoke of the "vain manner of life handed down from your fathers" (1:18). He said that they were "called . . . out of darkness" (2:9), and in the second passage where the Gentiles are mentioned, he told them that "the time past may suffice to have wrought the desire of the Gentiles, and to have walked in lasciviousness, lusts, winebibbings, revellings, carousings, and abominable idolatries" (4:3). While these churches, like those that Paul established, may have contained a large nucleus of Jews of the Dispersion and of proselytes, there seems to be no doubt that they also included Gentiles. The language of Peter may for the most part apply to either, but the allusion to "abominable idolatries" (4:3) demands some Gentile background.

The ominous shadow of persecution was the occasion for this letter. Suffering is one of the keynotes of the epistle, being mentioned no less than sixteen times. The churches have "been put to grief in manifold trials" (1:6); some of their members were "suffering wrongfully" (2:19); there was a possibility that they might have to "suffer for righteousness' sake" (3:14), even for doing what is right (3:17). Darker days might be ahead, for a "fiery trial" was coming on them in which they would be classed with murderers, thieves, and evildoers. Peter urged them not to be ashamed if they "suffer as Christians" (4:12–16). These sufferings were not to be exclusively their misfortune, for Christians in the whole world would be affected (5:9). All must bear these trials as bravely as they can. The letter was a warning and an encouragement preparatory to the coming emergency.

AUTHOR

Simon Peter, the author of the epistle, is the best known of the apostles of Christ. Like most of his comrades, he was a Galilean, a fisherman by trade, who was brought to Christ early in his ministry (John 1:41–42). Simon was his given name; Peter (Rock) was a nickname conferred on him by Jesus, who predicted that his impulsive and vacillating nature would become as stable and reliable as a rock. Simon left the fishing boats at Jesus' summons (Mark 1:16–20) and joined his company as he toured Galilee. He was a natural leader (10:28) and often was spokesman for the Twelve (8:29; John 6:67–68; Matt. 19:27). Jesus placed him in the inner circle of the disciples (Mark 5:37; 9:2; 14:33) and gave him special attention on several occasions (Luke 5:10; Matt. 16:17; Luke 22:31–32; John 13:6–10). He was impulsive, vacillating, and selfish, hasty in action and quick in recoil. His denial of Jesus was not the result of premeditated malice but of sudden panic, of which he later repented bitterly (Matt. 26:69–75). Nevertheless

THE PROVINCES OF ASIA MINOR
and the
SEVEN CHURCHES
OF
ASIA

BLACK SEA

BYZANTIUM

PONTUS

BITHYNIA

GALATIA

ASIA

CAPPADOCIA

CILICIA

THYATIRA
SARDIS
PERGAMUM
PHILADELPHIA
SMYRNA
LAODICEA
EPHESUS

PAMPHYLIA

LYCIA

ATHENS

MEDITERRANEAN SEA

JERUSALEM

Lake

there was in his soul a deep undercurrent of loyalty (John 13:36–38; 18:10, 15). He was deeply concerned over the disappearance of Jesus' body from the tomb (20:2–6), and rejoiced to see the risen Lord (21:7, 15–21).

On the day of Pentecost Peter, in company with the others who shared in the prayer meeting, was filled with the Holy Spirit. Instantly he became the leader of the group. His sermon set the tone for the new enterprise, and his preaching, healings, and discipline dominate the first five chapters of Acts. With the outbreak of persecution by the Sanhedrin he went farther afield into the coastal plain of Palestine and to Samaria and Antioch. With the passage of the years he traveled widely in an itinerant ministry much like Paul's. Tradition says that he was crucified head downward in Rome during the persecution under Nero, not later than A.D. 68.

First Peter states that it was written from "Babylon" (5:13). There are three possible interpretations of this location: (1) the historic Babylon in Mesopotamia, where there was a Jewish settlement until much later in the Christian era, and where Peter could well have founded a church; (2) a town in Egypt; and (3) a mystic name for Rome, by which Christians applied to it all the evil connotations that had been historically associated with the Babylon on the Euphrates, and by which they could vent their feelings without being detected.

There is no tradition that Peter had ever been in Babylon in Egypt, nor was it a place of sufficient importance to warrant his attention. Babylon on the Euphrates is a better possibility, since it was the home of many Jewish people from the captivity until the times of the Talmud. There is, however, no evidence that Peter was ever in this region, and though a number of commentators have favored his residence in the region of Babylon, their reasons are not very cogent.

Several facts seemingly lend support to the idea that "Babylon" meant Rome. John Mark, who was with Peter at the writing of the epistle, was in Rome at the time of Paul's imprisonment (Col. 4:10). The provinces are named in an order that hints that the messenger bearing the letter would make a circuit terminating in the west rather than in the east. If he were making his way back toward the source of the letter, Rome rather than Babylon would be a more logical end for his travels. Uniform patristic evidence places Peter in Rome at the end of his life. For these reasons, it seems wisest to conclude that the epistle was composed in Rome.

KEY TO MAP:

▬▬▬▬ = *main eastern trade route from the Euphrates River to Ephesus.*
_____ = *main road from Lystra going west meeting eastern trade route at Apameia.*
▬▬▬▬ = *road from the Mediterranean Sea (at Korykos) through Derbe and Ico-nium, meeting eastern trade route at Galatian Laodicea; road from Asian Laodicea to Smyrna; road from Sardis to Pergamum (the old Roman capital of Asia).*

If this conclusion is correct, it does not imply that Peter had founded the church at Rome or that he had ministered there for any great length of time. Neither Acts nor Romans gives any hint that Peter had been in Rome prior to A.D. 60. If he did write from Rome, he was probably paying the city a casual visit in much the same way that he had called at Corinth at an earlier date.[1]

First Peter is much like the epistles of Paul in its general style, and resembles Romans and Ephesians in its language and structure. A Pauline influence on Peter would not be surprising, since the two men had been acquainted with each other for years, and since Paul's influence on the thinking of Peter is affirmed in Galatians 2:11–21. Peter was familiar with Paul's epistles (II Pet. 3:15–16). Furthermore, if Silvanus, Peter's aman-uensis (I Pet. 5:12), is identical with Silas, Paul's associate and helper, Peter could easily have learned much about Paul's teaching from him.

In addition to the theme of suffering that pervades the epistle is the countertheme of "the true grace of God" (5:12). Suffering should be met with grace and should develop grace in the individual. The term appears in the greeting (1:2), as the summary of the message of the prophets (1:10), as the expectation of the future (1:13), as the pattern for conduct under abuse (2:19–20, Greek text), as the fullness of the blessings that come in answer to prayer (3:7), as the equipment for spiritual service (4:10), and as the favor that God shows to those who wait humbly on him (5:5).

OUTLINE

---

1. For a thorough discussion of this question, see Paton J. Gloag, *Introduction to the Catholic Epistles* (Edinburgh: T. & T. Clark, 1887), pp. 144–160, and Elmer T. Merrill, *Essays in Early Christian History* (London: Macmillan & Company, Ltd., 1924), pp. 275–353.

CONTENT

The personal experience of Peter with Christ is reflected in this epistle to his friends who were imperiled by impending persecutions. He had known the feeling of helplessness when he realized that Jesus was dead, but his hope had become living when Jesus rose (1:3). His reference to love for Christ (1:8) recalls Jesus' challenge to him, "Lovest thou me more than these?" (John 21:15ff.), and his exhortation to "tend the flock of God" (I Pet. 5:2) is an echo of Jesus' injunction to him to do the same thing (John 21:15–17). The command, "gird yourselves with humility" (I Pet. 5:5),

Tombs of early Christians in an ancient cemetery at Salona in present-day Yugoslavia.

means "to put on a slave's apron," which recalls Jesus' girding himself with a towel to wash the feet of the disciples (John 13:4). Five times he speaks of the sufferings of Christ (I Pet. 2:23; 3:18; 4:1, 13; 5:1) as if the scene of Gethsemane and the crucifixion left an indelible impression on him.[2]

One notable feature of the structure of the epistle is its use of imperatives. Beginning with 1:13, which follows the opening paragraph of thanksgiving, a continuous chain of commands runs all the way to the end of the book.

1. Be sober	1:13
2. Set your hope . . . on grace	1:13
3. Be holy	1:15
4. Pass the time . . . in fear	1:17
5. Love one another	1:23
6. Long for the spiritual milk	2:2
7. Be subject to every ordinance of man	2:13
8. Honor all men	
9. Love the brotherhood	
10. Fear God	2:17
11. Honor the king	
12. Servants, be in subjection	2:18
13. Wives, be in subjection	3:1
14. Ye husbands, dwell with your wives . . .	3:7
15. Finally *be* ye all . . .	3:8
16. Fear not	3:14
17. Neither be ye troubled	3:14
18. Sanctify in your hearts	3:15
19. Arm yourselves	4:1
20. Be of sound mind	4:7
21. Be sober . . .	4:7
22. Think it not strange	4:12
23. Rejoice	4:13
24. Let none of you suffer	4:15
25. Let him not be ashamed	4:16
26. Let him glorify God	4:16
27. Let them . . . commit their souls	4:19
28. Tend the flock of God	5:2
29. Be subject unto the elders	5:5
30. Gird yourselves with humility	5:5

---

2. These references may have been drawn from Peter's personal reminiscences, or from an acquaintance with the author of the Fourth Gospel, or from common Christian tradition. See M. C. Tenney, "Some Possible Parallels Between 1 Peter and John," in *New Dimensions in New Testament Study*, ed. R. N. Longenecker and M. C. Tenney (Grand Rapids, Mich.: Zondervan Publishing House, 1974), pp. 370–377.

31. Humble yourselves	5:6
32. Be sober	5:8
33. Be watchful	5:8
34. Withstand the devil	5:9

These numerous imperatives give the epistle a directness and informality that resemble a preaching style. Peter was speaking from his heart, not writing a formal essay. All of the stronger and better qualities of his nature, the result of being born "again unto a living hope by the resurrection of Jesus Christ from the dead" (1:3), appear in this work. It is Peter at his regenerate best.

EVALUATION

The chief value of the epistle is that it shows Christians how to live out their redemption in a hostile world. Salvation may involve suffering, but it also brings hope, as the grace of God is amplified in the individual life.[3]

The paragraph 3:18–22 has always been a difficult passage to interpret. Does it mean that Christ preached in the unseen world of spirits between his death and resurrection? If so, did he offer them a "second chance," or did he simply announce to them the results of his Passion? Does this passage mean that these "spirits in prison" were the disembodied persons who died in the Flood? Does it mean that baptism in itself can bring salvation? The passage bristles with questions to which innumerable answers have been given. Every commentator has his own solution.

Peter's language does not necessitate the doctrine of a "second chance." The word "preach" (Gk. *kēryssein*) is a term meaning "to announce" or "to proclaim." Yet in the New Testament it usually carries the sense of "to preach the gospel" (except, e.g., in Luke 12:3; Rom. 2:21; Rev. 5:2). While some commentators prefer to retain a "neutral" sense of the word, and see it as referring to Christ's proclamation of his triumph over the wicked spirits (cf. I Pet. 3:22), others see it as a gospel proclamation, yet with the issue of the actual repentance and salvation of these spirit beings left open.[4]

As to baptism, Noah and his sons were not saved *because* of the water, but *through* it. The water itself was their greatest peril, but in obedience to God they were carried through it. The water of baptism does not save men.

---

3. More references to suffering occur in I Peter than in any other New Testament writing: the suffering of Christ is referred to in 1:11; 2:21, 23; 3:18(?); 4:1, 13; 5:1; and the suffering of believers in 2:19–20; 3:14, 17; 4:1, 15, 19; 5:9–10.

4. For the former view, see J. N. D. Kelly, *A Commentary on the Epistles of Peter and Jude* (London: A. & C. Black, 1969), p. 156; for the latter, see E. Best, *I Peter* (Grand Rapids, Mich.: Wm. B. Eerdmans Publishing Company, 1982), p. 144.

Rather, by passing through the water as emblematic of death and of resurrection the believer enters into a life of glory. As Peter states in 2:24, baptism recalls the atonement of Christ, "who his own self bare our sins in his body upon the tree, that we, having died unto sins, might live unto righteousness." The passage is really a parallel of Paul's figure in Romans 6.

FOR FURTHER READING

Best, Ernest. *I Peter* in *The New Century Bible Commentary*. Grand Rapids, Mich.: Wm. B. Eerdmans Publishing Company, 1982. Pp. 188.

Elliott, J. H. *A Home for the Homeless: A Sociological Exegesis of I Peter, Its Situation and Strategy*. Philadelphia: Fortress Press, 1981.

Gloag, Paton J. *Introduction to the Catholic Epistles*. Edinburgh: T. & T. Clark, 1887. Pp. xvi, 416.

Hayes, Doremus A. *New Testament Epistles*. New York and Cincinnati: The Methodist Book Concern, n.d. Pp. 266. This book covers all of the general epistles. For I Peter, see pp. 121–183. Hayes does not accept the Petrine authorship of II Peter.

Mounce, Robert H. *A Living Hope: A Commentary on 1 and 2 Peter*. Grand Rapids, Mich.: Wm. B. Eerdmans Publishing Company, 1982. Pp. vii, 157.

Robertson, A. T. *Epochs in the Life of Simon Peter*. New York: Charles Scribner's Sons, 1933. Pp. xvi, 342. A plain but thorough study of Peter.

Selwyn, E. G. *The First Epistle of Peter*. London: Macmillan & Company, Ltd., 1946. Pp. 517. Thorough Greek commentary.

Stibbs, A. M. *The First Epistle General of Peter* in *The Tyndale New Testament Commentaries*. Grand Rapids, Mich.: Wm. B. Eerdmans Publishing Company, 1959. Pp. 192.

Thomas, W. H. Griffith. *The Apostle Peter*. Grand Rapids, Mich.: Wm. B. Eerdmans Publishing Company, 1946. Pp. 296. Splendid outlines.

CHAPTER 20

THE BREAK FROM JUDAISM:
HEBREWS

BACKGROUND

THE rapid growth of the Gentile church that was independent of Judaism both by heritage and by conviction could only result in a sharp and final separation between the two. The members of the Jewish church still clung to the observances of the law, though they trusted for their salvation in Jesus, the Messiah. The tension between Jews and Gentiles that appeared all through the first thirty years of Christian history became stronger as the church rivaled the synagogue in the number of its adherents and in its growth throughout the world. Jewish rejection of the Christian message finally came to the point where even Paul abandoned any hope of national repentance. Although he had said, "I could wish that I myself were anathema from Christ for my brethren's sake, my kinsmen according to the flesh . . ." (Rom. 9:3), he turned from them and declared, "Be it known therefore unto you, that this salvation of God is sent unto the Gentiles: they will also hear" (Acts 28:28).

This breach was widened by two other factors. From the first, when Peter had said to a Jewish audience in Jerusalem, "To you [Jews] is the promise, and to your children, and to all that are afar off, *even* as many as the Lord our God shall call unto him" (Acts 2:39), the universality of the gospel had been proclaimed. The Jew was exclusive, and the idea of uniting with the Gentiles in a bond of common fellowship that did not involve their becoming complete Jews was repugnant to him (see, e.g., Acts 10:14, 28, where words attributed to Peter show his ancient prejudices). The

second factor that made the breach complete was the fall of Jerusalem in A.D. 70. Judaism as a religion and Judaism as a political system were one; and when the political system fell so that the Jew was without a land, without a temple, and without a government of his own, he lost much of his essential system. When Judaism was forced to relinquish these means of outward expression, it became solely the worship of God through the study of the law, and consequently its legalism was strengthened more than ever.

For Jewish Christians this tension posed some unusual problems. All Christians believed in the divine authority of the Old Testament Scriptures and used them as the basis for their faith and practice. How, now, should those Scriptures be interpreted? Should they follow the rabbis into a static interpretation, or should they, as Christians, view the entire body of writings in the light of the new revelation of Jesus the Messiah?

What stand should they take on the national situation? If they believed the words of Jesus, who said in his Olivet discourse that not one stone of Jerusalem should be left on another (Matt. 24:2; Luke 19:41–44), they could only accept the overthrow of the city as the inevitable judgment of God for the rejecters of the King. If, however, they turned from the law to grace, and from Jerusalem as a center of worship to their own churches, they would be regarded as traitors by their countrymen who were loyal to the law. If they went back to legalism, they would be abandoning Christ and would lose all that he came to bring.

It was not an easy decision to make, and many of them, both in Palestine and in the Dispersion, wavered in their thinking. The decision was important because it affected the fate of the church. Jewish Christians had, on the whole, more solid training than the Gentile Christians and consequently possessed a more intelligent faith, since they already knew the Scriptures. Their loyalty or their defection would have a powerful influence on the outcome of the missionary enterprise. For their own sake and for the sake of the growing church, they must be shown that God was about to do a new thing, and that they must advance with him in faith rather than draw back.

The book of Hebrews was written to meet this dilemma. Its exact destination is unknown, for it contains no formal salutation, and in the oldest manuscripts its title is simply "To the Hebrews." The people to whom it was sent were schooled thoroughly in the Old Testament and its sacrificial system. They had been acquainted with the gospel and had heard it preached by men who were eyewitnesses of Jesus' life and who possessed the gifts of the Spirit (Heb. 2:3–4). They themselves had been staunch

Fragments of the synagogue of Capernaum, showing a Corinthian capital on which is a representation of the seven-branched candelabrum.

believers, enduring emotional and physical persecution for their new faith
(10:32–34). They were not novices.

Their geographical location is a matter of dispute, and depends largely
on the interpretation of one phrase in the thirteenth chapter (13:24):
"They of Italy salute you." Does it mean that the author was *in* Italy,
sending greetings back to these Hebrew Christians, wherever they were?
Or does it mean that they lived in Italy, and that their friends who were
from Italy in the sense of traveling or residing away from home sent greetings to the homeland? The preposition *apo*, translated "from," would
support the latter conclusion.

On this slim basis and because the earliest known quotation of this
epistle occurs in I Clement, which was written from Rome, some scholars
have concluded that it was sent to the Hebrew Christians in Rome who
were uncertain whether to persist in their profession of Christ or to go back
to the synagogue.[1] The older theory is that it was written to the Jewish
Christians of Palestine for the same reason.[2]

AUTHOR

An even greater puzzle is the authorship. The writer does not give his own
name, nor does he refer to any circumstances or connections that would
identify him with absolute certainty. A study of the epistle shows that he
was a man of high literary ability, with a style that approached more nearly
that of classical Greek than that of any other writer of the New Testament.
He was not an immediate disciple of Christ (Heb. 2:3). He was well versed
in the Old Testament, which he quoted from the Septuagint version. He
may have been a Jew, since he frequently used the first person plural in
addressing his Jewish audience. He was a friend of Timothy and probably
belonged to the Pauline circle (13:23). His use of the quotation from
Habakkuk 2:4, "The righteous shall live by his faith" (10:38), accords with
Paul's usage in Romans 1:17 and Galatians 3:11.

Several hypotheses have been advanced concerning his identity,
though none has behind it the same unanimity of tradition that supports
the Lukan authorship of the Third Gospel and Acts. The Eastern church
from early days considered the epistle to be the product of Paul, but
probably indirectly. Eusebius stated that Clement of Alexandria claimed
that Paul wrote it in Hebrew and that Luke translated it into Greek.[3]

---

1. Edgar J. Goodspeed, *An Introduction to the New Testament* (Chicago: University
of Chicago Press, n.d.), pp. 253–259; James Moffatt, *Introduction to the Literature of the
New Testament* (New York: Charles Scribner's Sons, 1910), pp. 446–447.

2. B. F. Westcott, *The Epistle to the Hebrews*, Second Edition (London: Macmillan
& Company, 1892), p. xli.

3. Eusebius *Historia Ecclesiae* VI.14, quoting Clement's *Hypotyposes*.

Origen frequently quoted it as Paul's and admitted that it was generally received as his, but when giving his own opinion said, "If, then, any church considers this epistle as coming from Paul, let it be commended for this, for neither did those ancient men deliver it as such without cause. But who it was that really wrote the epistle, God only knows."[4] The general line of argument and the style and diction of the book are not Pauline.

Many other names have been suggested for the author, chief among whom are Barnabas, to whom Tertullian attributed it,[5] and Apollos, a guess of Martin Luther. In favor of Barnabas are the facts that he was a Jew, a Levite, a friend of Paul whose teaching must have resembled Paul's closely, and one who could minister to Jew and Gentile alike. His long experience at teaching would fit with the character of the epistle, which is didactic. For Apollos there is no early tradition whatsoever. He, too, was a Jew, an Alexandrian, learned in the Scriptures, and singularly successful in his ministry among Jews. He was a friend of Paul and was still active in his ministry toward the end of Paul's life (Titus 3:13).

In no hypotheses do the conclusions amount to final proof. One thing is certain: as Hayes says, "If the authorship of this epistle is uncertain, its inspiration is indisputable."[6]

DATE

The epistle was written during the lifetime of the second generation of Christians (Heb. 2:1–4) and at a considerable interval after the conversion of the recipients (5:12). They had forgotten the "former days" (10:32) and their leaders had died (13:7). Timothy had been imprisoned (13:23), but was still living and had been liberated. The allusions to the priesthood imply that the temple was still standing, but the removal of Jewish institutions was not too far distant (12:27). Persecution was imminent (10:32–36; 12:4). The epistle seems to fit best the situation of the late sixties, when the church at Rome was fearing persecution and when the fall of the Jewish commonwealth was imminent.

OUTLINE

The entire theme of the epistle is built around the word "better," which is used in a series of comparisons to show how God's revelation in Christ is superior to the revelation that came through the law, especially as the law

---

4. Quoted from Origen by Eusebius *ibid.* VI.25.
5. Tertullian *De Pudicitia* XX.
6. D. A. Hayes, *The New Testament Epistles* (New York: The Methodist Book Concern, n.d.), p. 76.

was applied through the Levitical priesthood. The revelational quality and the validity of the law for its own time is not denied; on the other hand, much of the argument of Hebrews is founded on the Old Testament. The new revelation in Christ has superseded the old; the coming of the substance has made the shadow obsolete.

In structure the book consists of the aforesaid series of comparisons, after each of which is a warning and an exhortation, usually contained in a parenthesis. It is like an oration that begins with a proposition, proceeds with an argument applied periodically to the needs of the readers, and ends with a tremendous climax. Except for the thirteenth chapter it is not at all epistolary in style and could better be described as a speech.

Hebrews: The Epistle of Better Things

CONTENT

The foregoing argument was intended to encourage a group of people who were tempted to abandon their faith because of the pressure of persecution and because of their attachment to the older revelation of the law. The writer showed them that the same God who delivered the law to Moses by the hand of angels has since spoken historically in his Son, who has been made temporarily lower than the angels in order that he might enter perfectly into the sphere of human life as a participant in it (2:9–10, 14–18). Because he is both divine and human, he is qualified to serve as a high priest, in which capacity he is superior to the Aaronic priesthood. Death cannot terminate his tenure (7:24), and his sphere of service is in the heavenly sanctuary, the very presence of God (9:11–12). Furthermore, the sacrifice that he offers does not need to be repeated. He himself is the offering as well as the priest, completely acceptable to God, potent to remove the guilt of transgressions under the law and under grace (9:15; 10:10, 19). The eternal salvation that he has thus purchased is attainable by faith, the same kind of faith that was exercised by the men of the Old Testament who were the spiritual leaders of their generation. This faith, applied under the conditions in which the readers were living, would bring them assurance, endurance, and ultimate entrance into the unshakable kingdom.

Progressive warning may be found in the list of perils besetting the believers. Each of them is a more radical step away from faith than the one preceding it. First is the peril of neglect, characterized by the word "drift away" (2:1). It connotes indifference, not opposition. The second, the peril of unbelief, is epitomized in the quotation of Psalm 95, which in turn describes the attitude of the Israelites toward the promise of entrance into Palestine. By exaggerating the opposition before them and by ignoring the manifest power of God in their previous experience they failed to claim their rightful heritage, and so lost the blessing that God had prepared for them. Coupled with unbelief and practically synonymous with it is the peril of disobedience. Unwillingness to obey the new revelation would be fatal to spiritual progress.

The peril of immaturity and the peril of rejection are much alike. Both have occasioned considerable theological controversy. The warnings seemingly indicate that once a man refuses to obey, or abandons his position of faith, he can never be restored (6:6; 10:26). Both passages refer to a deliberate and purposeful rejection of Christ, a willful abandonment of truth, rather than to a sudden lapse or error that the doer himself might lament. Without minimizing the danger of carelessness, one may say that these warnings relate to voluntary apostasy rather than to unconscious decline. The last peril is climactic and involves point-blank refusal to heed God's revelation in the Son. "See that ye refuse not him that speaketh" (12:25). The reference is to the blood of Jesus, "which speaketh better things than that of Abel" (12:24) because it invites to salvation rather than invoking vengeance. If that voice is refused, doom is final.

Parallel with the warnings that appear periodically in the text are exhortations that add a positive quality to the argument. In the Greek text they are clearly marked by the use of the first person plural hortatory subjunctive, which is consistently translated in English "Let us . . ." The list below will show how these exhortations are distributed in the book.

1. Let us fear . . .	4:1
2. Let us therefore give diligence to enter	4:11
3. Let us hold fast our confession	4:14
4. Let us draw near . . . to the throne of grace	4:16
5. Let us press on unto perfection	6:1
6. Let us draw near	10:22
7. Let us hold fast the confession of our faith	10:23
8. Let us consider one another	10:24
9. Let us . . . lay aside every weight	12:1
10. Let us run the race	12:1
11. Let us have grace	12:28
12. Let us therefore go forth unto him	13:13
13. Let us offer up sacrifice of praise	13:15

With the exception of the first, which describes fear, a negative emotion, every one of these exhortations summons the believer to a higher stage of spiritual perfection, culminating in "Let us therefore go forth unto him without the camp, bearing his reproach," the final test of allegiance to Christ and his cross. Eight out of thirteen of these occur in the last four chapters, for with the conclusion of the argument the application is strengthened. The other five are connected with the severer warnings to offer a word of encouragement to what would otherwise be only a negative deterrent.

EVALUATION

The greatest single value of the book of Hebrews is its teaching on the present ministry and priesthood of Christ. There are many references in the New Testament to his ascension and his place at the right hand of the Father, but with the exception of Romans 8:34 none of these explains what he is now doing. Hebrews, by its interpretation of the Messianic reference in Psalm 110:4, "Jehovah hath sworn, and will not repent: Thou art a priest forever, after the order of Melchizedek," has given a whole new ground of assurance to the believer in Christ. As the Aaronic priesthood by its sacrifices and intercession ministered to the Old Testament believer who obeyed the law, so Christ, in a fuller measure, though invisible, ministers now to those under grace. Those who witnessed the passing of the Jewish priesthood and felt that with it a divinely ordained system of salvation had vanished, must have been greatly reassured by the teaching that this man "for ever hath his priesthood unchangeable" (Heb. 7:24).

Hebrews is an excellent specimen of teaching in the early church. Unlike many of Paul's epistles, it was not taken up with a variety of questions that had no particular relation to each other, nor was it an evangelistic sermon addressed to a promiscuous audience. It is an exposition of one theme, the new revelation of God, based on the passages in the Old Testament that contain the latent truth, and developed in orderly rhetorical fashion to a climax. Its use of quotations gives a good idea of the passages and the methods of interpretation that were used by the Christian teachers of the first century.

Doctrinally Hebrews accords with the Pauline epistles, although it is not patterned according to their phraseology. Its theme, like that of Romans and Galatians, is salvation by faith in the sacrifice of Christ. The illustration of Abraham's faith is given more space in Hebrews than any other instance, thus bringing it into line with Paul's use of it. In the few casual references to the earthly life of Christ there are some resemblances to Luke (2:3, Luke 1:2; 2:18, Luke 4:13; 5:7, Luke 22:44; 12:2, Luke 9:51; 12:24, Luke 22:20), although they are not close enough to prove anything with regard to authorship. Hebrews is a good witness to the growing independence of the Gentile church and to the enlargement of universal revelation that came through Christ.

In its Christology, Hebrews adds much to the doctrine of the atonement, which it places in a covenantal relationship. This book explains the meaning of the new covenant more fully than did Jeremiah, whom it quotes (Heb. 8:8–12; Jer. 31:31–34), or than did Jesus himself. Hebrews connects the incarnation with the atonement (Heb. 2:14–17).

In the study of the Old Testament Hebrews is an excellent guide to the meaning of typology and to an understanding of the lasting significance of the Levitical ritual. It does not purport to give a detailed exposition of all the features of the offerings and feasts, but its confirmation of their prophetic function in pointing forward to Christ is a valuable key for unlocking the treasures of the Old Testament. It is the best commentary available on these subjects.

The most familiar passage in Hebrews is, of course, the eleventh chapter; it sketches the progress of faith by the use of Old Testament illustrations. Romans, taking the text from Habakkuk, explains the meaning of *just* and shows who is justified and how he is justified. Galatians shows what the life under grace really is, an exercise of spiritual liberty, and so expounds the idea of *live*. Hebrews demonstrates the meaning and progress of *faith*. By its warnings, by its exhortations, and by its gallery of examples it seeks to show what faith is, how it functions, and what results it achieves. These three books, Romans, Galatians, and Hebrews, form a trilogy explaining the heart and essence of the Christian life of faith.

FOR FURTHER READING

Bruce, F. F. *The Epistle to the Hebrews: The English Text with Introduction, Exposition, and Notes* in *The New International Commentary on the New Testament*. Grand Rapids, Mich.: Wm. B. Eerdmans Publishing Company, 1964. Pp. xliv, 447.

Davidson, A. B. *Hebrews*. Edinburgh: T. & T. Clark, 1950. Pp. 260.

Delitzsch, Franz. *Commentary on the Epistle to the Hebrews*. Two volumes. Grand Rapids, Mich.: Wm. B. Eerdmans Publishing Company, 1952. Pp. xii, 893.

Hughes, Philip E. *A Commentary on the Epistle to the Hebrews*. Grand Rapids, Mich.: Wm. B. Eerdmans Publishing Company, 1977. Pp. xv, 623.

Lenski, R. C. H. *The Interpretation of the Epistle to the Hebrews and of the Epistle of James*. Columbus, Ohio: The Wartburg Press, 1956. Pp. 673.

Moule, H. C. G. *Messages from the Epistle to the Hebrews*. London: Chas. J. Thynne & Jarvis, Ltd., 1930. Pp. 120.

Murray, Andrew. *The Holiest of All*. New York: A. D. F. Randolph & Company, Inc., n.d. Pp. xv, 552. Unusually helpful outlining of Hebrews, with commentary of high spiritual quality.

Thomas, W. H. Griffith. *Hebrews*. Grand Rapids, Mich.: Wm. B. Eerdmans Publishing Company, repr. 1961. Pp. 186. Bibliography.

Westcott, B. F. *The Epistle to the Hebrews*. Second Edition. Grand Rapids, Mich.: Wm. B. Eerdmans Publishing Company, 1950. Pp. lxxxiv, 504. Greek text.

CHAPTER 21

THE PERIL OF HERESIES: II PETER; JUDE; I, II, III JOHN

BACKGROUND

SUCH evidence as survives from the last four decades of the first century reveals that the churches were "by heresies distressed" as well as "by schisms rent asunder." Digressions from truth occurred in every direction and constant vigilance was necessary if the Christians were to keep their faith pure.

The rise of false doctrines was neither new nor unanticipated. The Judaizing controversy that began at Antioch and that plagued Paul throughout his ministry was a harbinger of many other errors that have existed in the church ever since. Among the Corinthians were those who said that there was no resurrection of the dead (I Cor. 15:12). Perhaps the errorists still claimed to be Christians and felt that their denial of the physical resurrection was of minor importance. Paul, however, showed that it struck at the very heart of all Christian faith. When he made his farewell address at Miletus, he told the Ephesian elders that after his departure grievous wolves would enter in, not sparing the flock; and from among their own number men would arise, speaking perverse things, to draw away the disciples after them (Acts 20:29–30). In the epistles to Timothy and Titus he laid great stress on doctrinal correctness, and he predicted that in later times some would fall away from the faith, listening to seducing spirits and to demoniacal doctrines (I Tim. 4:1). Furthermore, he predicted that the churches themselves would degenerate to the point where they would not endure sound doctrine but, having itching ears, would turn away from the truth to fables (II Tim. 4:4). Although the complete demonstration of this tendency may still await fulfillment in the culmination of this age, the trend became apparent within the first century.

Five short epistles, II Peter, Jude, I, II, and III John, were written to cope with these trends toward false doctrines within the church. Controversy was not their sole aim, nor was their subject matter devoted entirely to attacking heresy. Their approach was positive rather than negative, as their outlines will show. They were, however, all colored by the dangers of the times, in which the church was threatened quite as much by the subtle infiltration of paganism into its thinking as by the frontal attacks of persecution from without.

Whether the errors that these epistles sought to combat can be identified with those that appear in the works of the church fathers may be debatable. Some, for instance, have seen in the Johannine writings the reflection of Docetism, a heresy that held that Christ was not historically real but a phantom that appeared in human guise and then vanished. Perhaps the full-blown heresies of the second century are not historically identical with those intimated in the strictures of the later New Testament books, but the trends are the same and the essential errors are the same. Error, like human nature, does not vary greatly through the centuries. The labels change; the delusions are persistent.

Individually, then, each of these books must be considered in its own setting. Their dates are somewhat uncertain, but unquestionably they all belong to the period after A.D. 60.

II PETER

Background

There is less external evidence for the Petrine authorship of this epistle than there is for the traditional authorship of any other book of the New Testament. None of the early Fathers quotes it definitely, although there are occasional points of similarity to it in Hermas, I Clement, the pseudo-II Clement, and the Didache. Eusebius quotes Origen (c. A.D. 220) as saying that "Peter . . . has left one epistle undisputed. Suppose also the second one left by him, for on this there is some doubt."[1] Unquestionably Origen knew of its existence, and his statement does not necessarily imply that he rejected its genuineness. The fullest conclusion that could legitimately be drawn from his statement is that II Peter was not generally received by all the church.

Such a situation, however, is not unique to II Peter. In the same

---

1. Eusebius *Historia Ecclesiae* VI.xxv.8.

context Origen affirmed that II and III John were not accepted by all the churches, but he dismissed the debate as inconsequential because of the brevity of these epistles. This brevity, and the fact that they had been sent to an obscure destination, possibly prevented wide circulation at first, and may have caused some of the churches to question their validity when they appeared before the public at a later time.

Assuredly II Peter is not anonymous and the biographical touches that it contains accord with Peter's known life. He spoke with feeling of being cleansed from old sins (1:9). There is a clear allusion to his approaching death (1:13), which was predicted by Christ himself (1:14; cf. John 21:18–19). The transfiguration was cited as a landmark in the life of the author and his colleagues (II Pet. 1:16–18). A previous epistle sent to the same destination is mentioned (3:1). The recipients had also received letters from Paul, which Peter had found puzzling, but which he acknowledged to be "scriptures" (3:15–16). This last allusion might require a late date for the epistle, since it presupposes the writing and the circulation of the Pauline letters, were it not for the intimate phrase "our beloved brother, Paul" (3:15). The writer treats Paul as a respected equal and contemporary, not as a canonized saint of a bygone day.

There is a decided difference in vocabulary and style between I and II Peter. The second epistle is written in a more labored and awkward Greek. Perhaps a different amanuensis was employed, or possibly Peter transcribed it himself.

While the external evidence for the genuineness of II Peter is not so clear and convincing as it is for other books of the New Testament, the internal evidence creates at least a presumption of authenticity. The epistle bears no traces of heresy; there is nothing in it that Peter could not have written; and it is not embellished with biographical details that are obviously imaginative, as so many apocryphal works are. Since conclusive proof of spuriousness is lacking, it will be treated here as genuine.[2]

If it was written by Peter, the internal allusions to his career fit into the background of his life. It was his last extant work, sent shortly before his death to the churches with which he had communicated in his first epistle. The threat of persecution seems to have passed away, for the suffering of Christians is not stressed. If the epistle was dispatched from Rome about A.D. 65 to 67, Peter realized that the disturbance that originally

---

2. Modern scholars are quite divided on the question of genuineness. The following are representative: positive, E. M. B. Green, *2 Peter Reconsidered* (London: Tyndale Press, 1960); cautiously positive, D. Guthrie, *New Testament Introduction* (Downers Grove, Ill.: Inter-Varsity Press, 1971), who sees "strong arguments on both sides"; negative, yet affirming its apostolic truth, R. P. Martin, *New Testament Foundations* (Grand Rapids, Mich.: William B. Eerdmans Publishing Company, 1978), II, 383–388; negative, W. G. Kümmel, *Introduction to the New Testament* (Nashville: Abingdon Press, 1975), pp. 430–434.

threatened to affect the provinces had proved to be only local in its scope. New problems had arisen that demanded attention; the danger to his churches was now less from without than it was from within.

The peril confronting the churches was that of doubt and error arising from the false teachings of those who professed to be leaders. "There shall be false teachers, who shall privily bring in destructive heresies, denying even the Master that bought them" (2:1). The nature of this departure from the norm of faith was not outlined completely. It seems to have involved a denial of the redemption and lordship of Christ (2:1), adding a complete abandonment of all moral standards and a bold self-assertiveness that was the accompaniment of spiritual ignorance (2:10–12).

The full manifestation of these conditions was still future to Peter (2:1), although he saw the danger of the existing ignorance and uncertainty in the minds of the people of the church. Twice he asserted that they needed to be reminded of the truths that had been taught them (1:12; 3:1–2); first, that in the Scriptures, which were not the product of human ingenuity or opinion, there was an authoritative revelation by the Holy Spirit (1:19–21); and second, that the coming of the Lord, which had begun to seem vague and distant, would be "as a thief" (3:10). II Peter was designed as a stimulus to loyal faith and as an encouragement to those Christians whose expectation of the Lord's coming was failing because of its apparently unreasonable delay.

Content

As the central theme of I Peter was *suffering*, so that of II Peter is *knowledge*. If the errorists were magnifying their knowledge as the basis of their superiority, Peter wanted to show that the answer to false knowledge is true knowledge. The words *know* and *knowledge* appear sixteen times, six of which refer to the knowledge of Christ. The recurring theme unifies the epistle and lends progression to its thought.

As the following outline shows, it can be divided into three main sections. The first discusses the nature of true knowledge, which is bestowed as a gift of God through his power (1:3) and through his promises (1:4). This makes the believer a partaker of the divine nature, and the ensuing growth prepares him for the fuller experience of the heavenly kingdom yet to come. The basis of this knowledge is to be found in the personal testimony of those who know Christ and in the revelation of the Scriptures that came through the direct impartation and control of the Holy Spirit.

The second section is prophetic denunciation of errorists whose advent in the church is expected. Their divisive mistakes have in common the denial of the lordship and redemptive work of Christ, and are accompanied by moral looseness. Historic precedent is cited to show how God has judged such perversions in the past, and the pictorial language in 2:10b through 19 describes vividly their activities and false premises. Their ultimate doom—"it were better for them not to have known the way of righteousness than, after knowing it, to turn back" (2:21)—recalls the words of the Lord Jesus concerning Judas: "Good were it for that man if he had not been born" (Matt. 26:24).

The prevailingly eschatological character of II Peter appears most clearly in the last chapter. The references to death in chapter 1 indicate that Peter had an eternal perspective, and the allusion to prophecy (II Pet. 1:21) implies a relation to the future. The second section speaks explicitly of error and declension to come. The third chapter points out that the only hope for the future lies in the true knowledge of God's program, and in patience while it is being carried out. Mockers will deny the truth of the Lord's coming, of which the prophets and the apostles, among whom the writer classed himself (1:1), had spoken with assurance. The precedent of the past has shown that absolute uniformity in nature does not prevail and that catastrophic judgments have occurred. In like manner, the day of the Lord will come as a thief in the night—the same phraseology that Paul used (I Thess. 5:2)—and the ensuing dissolution of the existing order will usher in "new heavens and a new earth, wherein dwelleth righteousness" (II Pet. 3:13).

Outline

II PETER: THE TRUE KNOWLEDGE OF GOD

Evaluation

The chief contribution of II Peter to the teaching of the New Testament is its statement concerning the Scriptures: "No prophecy of scripture is of private interpretation. For no prophecy ever came by the will of man: but men spake from God, being moved by the Holy Spirit" (1:20–21). The crucial words in the passage are "private," "interpretation," and "moved." "Private" (*idias*) may be translated as "its own," "belonging peculiarly to itself." "Interpretation" (*epilyseōs*) contains the idea of explanation or illumination. This does not mean that an individual may not attempt to interpret the Scripture, but it is a warning that no single text can be taken by itself, or out of its spiritual context, because the Holy Spirit is the real author and only he is capable of being the final interpreter. The word "moved" (*pheromenoi*) means "borne along," carried as a ship is carried on a tide, the full power of its propulsion being utilized within the larger realm of the resistless ocean current. The allusion to Paul's epistles as "scriptures" in 3:16 indicates the beginning of the canon of the New Testament, though Peter claims no more for Paul's writings than Paul did for his own (I Thess. 2:13). II Peter unites with II Timothy 2:15 and 3:16 to show that the written revelation of the Old Testament was the disclosure of God's mind and will, and that in a day of theological controversy and moral decline it was the accepted standard of faith and practice.

JUDE

Background

The literary relation of Jude to II Peter is an important factor in determining the background. There can be no doubt that the two are separate epistles, and yet the similarities of occasion, thought, and vocabulary between them can hardly be accidental. A comparison of the Epistle of Jude with the second chapter of II Peter will convince any reader of the English or Greek text that some connection exists between them. What is the relationship?

Four different answers have been proposed:

1. II Peter and Jude have no relationship except as they are addressed to people who are facing the same situation. This solution does not explain adequately the minute verbal similarities.

2. II Peter and Jude were paraphrased from some common source. This solution is improbable, for both authors were capable of originating the content of their epistles, and predicating a third unknown epistle only adds to the confusion.

3. II Peter took much of the data from Jude. Jude's references to history are more exact and circumstantial, and his organization is clearer. It

would seem that the shorter epistle would be quoted by the longer, rather than that the shorter should be condensed from the larger.

4. Jude was stimulated to write his epistle by seeing Peter's, but organized his independently.

The last of these views seems most reasonable and has the eminent support of Zahn.[3] The epistle states explicitly that its author intended to write to his constituency concerning "our common salvation" when his purpose was suddenly changed by some new stimulus that prompted an apologetic rather than a theological or a devotional work (Jude 3). He said that "certain men crept in privily," who had already been described, and that they were running rampant in the church. In verses 17 and 18 he quoted verbatim from II Peter 3:3, which he attributed to "the apostles of our Lord Jesus Christ." From these passages it would be reasonable to conclude that the second epistle of Peter had fallen into Jude's hands and that he had written to his hearers concerning the apostasy that Peter had predicted and that was already beginning in the church.

The greater explicitness of references and the closer organization of structure are part of Jude's independent style.

The author was doubtless the brother of James, the moderator of the church of Jerusalem, and the half brother of Jesus who is mentioned in Mark 6:3. Like James he must have believed on Jesus as the Messiah after the resurrection and was numbered among the waiting group on the day of Pentecost. He seems to have taken no prominent part in the affairs of the apostolic church. In style and vocabulary the Epistle of Jude bears a resemblance to that of James. Both are terse and graphic in expression. Both depend largely on figures of speech taken from outdoor life. Both are characterized by a certain ethical sternness. The writer did not class himself among the apostles (17).

Place and Date

No clear indication is afforded by the epistle as to where or when it was written. If Jude ministered to the Jewish churches of Palestine, it may well have been sent to them in the period just prior to the fall of Jerusalem. One might guess that what Peter had predicted for the part of the church to which he wrote had already begun to take place in the church for which Jude was responsible. If Peter's epistle had just been circulated, Jude's may well be dated around A.D. 67 or 68. If, on the other hand, Jude's appeal to the memory of the people (17) means that the text of II Peter had been long in circulation, the obvious conclusion is that Jude may have been issued as

---

3. Theodor Zahn, *Introduction to the New Testament* (translated from the third German edition; New York: Charles Scribner's Sons, 1909), II, 262–270. Most modern scholars argue for view 3, while D. Guthrie, *New Testament Introduction*, p. 248, concludes: "The verdict must remain open."

late as A.D. 80. Jerusalem could not have been the destination at this later date.

Content

Jude announced that his purpose was to urge his readers to "contend earnestly for the faith which was once for all delivered unto the saints" (3). The necessity for this emergency was the infiltration into the Christian ranks of men who were "turning the grace of our God into lasciviousness, and denying our only Master and Lord, Jesus Christ" (4). The phraseology defining the heresy accords with that of Peter, but it is more specific. It sounds as if the error was a type of antinomianism, which made license out of liberty and repudiated the lordship of Christ. So far had the heresy swung away from legalism that it observed no restraints and it possessed no fixed moral standards. It was idle intellectual speculation accompanied by fancy oratory, with no duties attached.

In his general argument Jude follows the order of II Peter, but his pictures are sharper and more cameo-like. Three historic examples of judgment are cited: the destruction of the unbelieving group who came out of Egypt but who would not enter the land of Canaan; the angels "who kept not their own principality"; and the cities of Sodom and Gomorrah. In each case the irrevocable judgment of God fell on those who had sinned blatantly and inexcusably. To these three groups of egregious sinners are likened the apostates, marked out in Jude by the pronoun *these* (8, 10, 12, 14, 16, 19). Their irreverence, ignorance, treachery, emptiness, and egotism are pilloried in Jude's vigorous language. The nature of their error is described by their likeness to the three great rebels of the Pentateuch: the way of bloodless sacrifice—Cain; the error of thinking that God is the minister of man's convenience rather than the Lord of his destinies—Balaam; and the arrogance of a self-devised faith—Korah.

With the last section of Jude the pronoun changes from *these* to *ye*, and the antidote to apostasy is presented to the readers. First, *remember* the words of Christ given by his apostles, echoing Peter's statement that he felt he ought to "put them in remembrance" of the truth that he possessed. Second, Jude commanded them to *keep* themselves in the love of God by prayer and constructive action (20–21). Last of all, preservation from apostasy includes the *rescue* of others from the errors that surround them, so that their doubt may not lead them ultimately to disaster (22–23).

Outline

JUDE: A WARNING AGAINST APOSTASY

Evaluation

One of the curiosities of this small epistle is its fondness for triads of thought. It has six main sections, which are arranged in three pairs: the first two introduce the thought, the second two discuss the apostasy, and the last two state the conclusion. The author described himself in three ways: his proper name, Jude; his function, a servant of Jesus Christ; his relation to the Christian community, the brother of James. He salutes his readers as "called," "beloved," and "kept," and in his greeting he wishes them mercy, peace, and love. There are many other "threes" employed by the author that the student can find for himself. Probably they have no special significance beyond marking a mental trait of the author.

The use of apocryphal literature has occasioned some questioning of this epistle. The reference to Enoch in verse 14 agrees verbatim with a passage in the book of Enoch, and the reference to the dispute between Michael and the devil for the body of Moses appears in The Assumption of Moses. Both of these writings were produced early in the first century by Jewish writers, who sought to advance the teachings of their sect or party by appeal to the authority of Old Testament leaders. The quotations pose a dilemma, for if Jude was inspired, did his quotations of these works give authority to them? If, on the other hand, they were random quotations that carried no authority, why should he quote them at all? There is a fair analogy in Paul's address at Athens when he quoted the Greek poet Aratus (Acts 17:28) to substantiate a point of his address because he knew that it would carry weight with his audience, not because he regarded the Greek poet as inspired or authoritative in the realm of theology. In like manner the apocryphal works were sometimes used to illustrate certain principles for those who regarded them with reverence. In the early Christian church some of these were highly esteemed and were deemed profitable reading. Jude's audience must have been familiar with this literature, for he made extensive allusions to it even apart from the express quotations.[4]

The epistle shows that by the time it was written, quite certainly no later than A.D. 85, there was a recognized body of belief that could be

---

4. For a good discussion of the quotations and allusions, see M. R. James, *The Second Epistle General of Peter and the General Epistle of Jude* in *Cambridge Greek Testament* (Cambridge: University Press, 1912), pp. xl–xlviii.

called Christianity. Doctrinal formulation is a slow process, and the history of Christianity for the last nineteen hundred years is the history of the rise and fall of doctrinal patterns and emphases, some of which were extreme, others of which were erroneous, but all of which belonged to the general stream of thought that is called Christian. One would be tempted to think that these variations might be inconsequential were it not for the fact that the New Testament sets certain rigorous doctrinal standards. Some leeway may be allowed for human ignorance and for intellectual and spiritual limitations, for "now we see in a mirror, darkly," and "we know in part, and we prophesy in part" (I Cor. 13:12, 9). In these epistles, however, which were written when error was prevalent and controversy was beginning, there is a frank insistence on "the pattern of sound words," and Jude speaks with finality of "the once-for-all-delivered-to-the-saints faith" (Jude 3, literal translation), which was to be kept as an inviolate standard.

The proper method of treating those who deviate from this standard is also given in Jude. Nowhere does the New Testament recommend persecution or burning at the stake for heretics. The heretics draw their own lines. "These," says Jude, "are they who make separations . . ." (19). The epistle, instead, counsels mercy and an attempt to rescue those who are deluded and bewildered, though no tolerance is to be shown to the falsehood itself.

The book closes with one of the great benedictions of the New Testament. Its emphasis on the lordship of Christ and his ability to keep his servants from falling into error is singularly appropriate to the theme of Jude.

I, II, III JOHN

BACKGROUND

If the criteria of vocabulary and style are ever adequate for pronouncing judgment on authorship, these three short letters must be attributed to one author who is also the author of the Fourth Gospel. All four of these writings were probably produced about the same time and at the same place. The first epistle opens by summarizing, "That which was from the beginning, that which we have heard, that which we have seen with our eyes, that which we beheld, and our hands handled, concerning the Word of life" (I John 1:1) as the foundation for its application of truth. This summary presupposes the Fourth Gospel both by its content and by its vocabulary, and the similarities persist all through the epistle. The stated purpose of the First Epistle, "These things have I written unto you, that ye may know that ye have eternal life . . ." (5:13), carries the reader one step beyond the Gospel, which says, "These are written, that ye may believe that Jesus is the Christ, the Son of God; and that believing ye may have life in his name" (John 20:31). The Gospel was written to arouse faith; the First Epistle was written to establish certainty.

The Second and Third Epistles, as Goodspeed suggests, may have been written as "covering letters," one to the church, addressed under the figure of the "elect lady" (II John 1), and the other to Gaius, the pastor (III John 1).[5] They were intended to be private notes of counsel and greeting, whereas the main body of teaching was contained in the Gospel and in the First Epistle.

The exact time and place of writing are indeterminate, but the most acceptable view is that these documents were written by John for the Asian churches in the middle of the last third of the first century. By that time the separation between church and synagogue was complete. The controversy over justification by faith versus works had largely died out, and the influx of Gentiles into the church with their heritage of philosophical thought was beginning to affect doctrinal teaching. They were interested in the person of Christ. Who was he? If he was God, how could he die? If he died, how could he be God? Many solutions were proposed for this dilemma, and the debate over the nature of Christ occupied the thinking of church leaders and the discussions of councils down to the fifth century. In fact, this debate has not died out even today.

The particular error that I John was intended to combat seems to have been an early form of Gnosticism, a heresy that was the most dangerous enemy of the church up to the close of the second century. Gnosticism was a philosophy of religion rather than a single system. It was built on the premise that spirit is good, that matter is evil, and that the two can have no enduring relation with each other. Salvation consists of escape from the realm of matter into the realm of the spirit. The means of this escape are numerous. Chief among them is knowledge, by which man can rise above the earthbound chains of matter into the heavenly apprehension of truth. This knowledge, or *gnōsis,* to use the Greek term that gave the philosophy its name, could be attained only by those who were initiated into the inner secrets of the group. The teaching of the Gnostics was to form an unorganized but cohesive cult, bound together by common rites and common thinking rather than by officers and societies.

The conflict of this type of philosophy with Christianity was most acute at the point of the person of Christ. How, asked the Gnostics, could the infinite, pure spirit called God have anything to do with a material body? A complete union would, on their premises, be unthinkable. They

---

5. Edgar J. Goodspeed, *An Introduction to the New Testament* (Chicago: University of Chicago Press, n.d.), pp. 319–320.

proposed two solutions: either Christ was not really human but only apparently so, or else the Christ-spirit did not actually inhabit the human Jesus until the baptism, and left him before his death on the cross. The former theory was called Docetism, from the verb *dokeō*, meaning "to seem"; the latter was called Cerinthianism, from Cerinthus, its chief advocate in the first century.

Either of these proposals would have been fatal to the gospel had it become the standard interpretation of Christianity. Docetism made the human Jesus simply a ghost, an illusion that seemed to appear to man but that had no real existence. Cerinthianism would make a strange contradiction out of the personality of Jesus: one would never know whether the human Jesus or the divine Christ-spirit was speaking and acting. Under Cerinthianism the person of Christ could be a sort of Dr. Jekyll and Mr. Hyde. Probably these two views had not been fully defined and amplified in the time of John, but the language of the First Epistle implies that something like Gnosticism was prevalent when he wrote.

John insists that the Christ whom he preached was audible, visible, and tangible (I John 1:1). He says that whosoever denies the Father and the Son is antichrist (2:22), and he declares that "every spirit that confesseth not Jesus [that he has come in the flesh] is not of God" (4:2–3). Evidently his opponents took a position that approximated closely that of Docetic Gnosticism.

The smaller epistles deal with the same problem from the standpoint of church polity and discipline. I John says that "they," meaning the adherents of the false doctrine, "went out from us, but they were not of us; for if they had been of us, they would have continued with us" (2:19). There had been a schism in some of the churches in which the errorists had withdrawn to form their own group. Some of these, however, had become itinerant teachers, who sought to gain entrance into the smaller churches that were immature and weak. The Second Epistle contains warnings against them:

> For many deceivers are gone forth into the world, even they that confess not that Jesus Christ cometh in the flesh.
>
> (II John 7)

The church is warned that any such teacher is not to be welcomed, "for he that giveth him greeting partaketh in his evil works" (II John 10–11).

The Third Epistle affords one or two interesting insights into church life in this period. Apparently much of the ministry was carried on by itinerant preachers who made periodic rounds, staying a little while with each group and holding "protracted meetings" in private homes. Such a procedure was easily susceptible of abuse by religious racketeers, who would use their privileges to obtain a free living from the people. John commended Gaius for his gracious support of them, since they received no contributions from the Gentiles to whom they ministered (III John 5, 8).

The rise of "church czars" is reflected in the comment on Diotrephes. He was unwilling to receive visitors, but consistently ejected from the church those who were ready to entertain them. John's protest and his promise that when he came he would test the power of Diotrephes show that there were governmental difficulties even within the church of the first century.

The Johannine epistles, then, were written for a church that confronted new philosophies that sought to conquer Christianity by absorbing it, and that was struggling to maintain its distinctive message against perversion by error.

I JOHN

Content

The peculiar style of John appears at its best in I John because the epistle is short enough to show clearly its type of structure. I John is symphonic rather than logical in its plan; it is constructed like a piece of music rather than like a brief for a debate. Instead of proceeding step by step in unfolding a subject, as Paul does in Romans, John selects a theme, maintains it throughout the book, and introduces a series of variations, any one of which may be a theme in itself. For this reason one can follow only with difficulty the single line of thought in the Gospel or in the epistle, and the composition of a progressive outline is even more trying.

Furthermore, the First Epistle is keyed to personal experience. It seeks to inculcate certainty of the possession of eternal life (5:13), and proposes certain tests whereby that certainty can be attained. The phrase "we know," translating two different verbs (*oidamen* and *ginōskomen*), is used thirteen times to signify the certainty that is achieved through experience, or that is a part of normal spiritual consciousness (2:3, 5, 29; 3:14, 16, 19, 24; 4:13, 16; 5:15, 18, 19, 20).

Light and *love*, two peculiarly Johannine words, are prominent in this epistle. Both are used as descriptive of deity (1:5; 4:8), and the development of these two themes comprises a major part of the epistle. They elaborate the abstract ideas that are presented in the Gospel and make them practical for personal application.

Outline

II JOHN

Background

The background of II John is much the same as that of the First Epistle. This letter is more personal, for it is directed to "the elect lady and her children." The translation of this salutation is ambiguous, for it can be rendered "the lady Electa," "the elect Cyria," or, as usual, the "elect lady," depending on whether one sees a proper name in the greeting or not. The interpretation is even more ambiguous than the translation. Was the addressee an individual, or does the term "lady" denote figuratively a church, whose members are her "children"? Or if an individual was intended, did she own a home where a group of believers met, so that they were called her "children"? There is a parallelism in the Jewish feeling for Zion, which Paul called "our mother" (Gal. 4:26). Westcott says that "the problem of the address is insoluble with our present knowledge,"[6] and more recent commentators have shed no additional light on the subject. The main point is that the group for whose benefit the epistle was written was being imperiled by false teachers. John wanted them to cultivate vigilance lest they be led astray.

Content and Outline

The doctrinal content of the Second Epistle differs little from that of the First. The same danger of ignoring the humanity of Christ and the same necessity of abiding in the truth are pressed on the readers.

---

6. B. F. Westcott, *The Epistle of John* (Second Edition; Cambridge and London: Macmillan & Company, 1886), p. 224.

III JOHN

Content and Outline

Addressed primarily to Gaius, a pastor or leader in the church, III John is concerned less with theological truth and more with administrative matters than the other two epistles. It deals with the entertainment of missionary brethren who should be encouraged as they visit the church en route to their work, and with the unkind attitude of Diotrephes, who deserves a reprimand.

Evaluation

The Johannine Epistles, particularly the First, are invaluable as an index of personal spiritual achievement. They are almost purely declarative and hortatory; exposition and theological argumentation are not found in their pages. The historical truth that is embodied in the Gospel is applied in I John to the individual believer, and the proofs of his possession of eternal life are outlined plainly so that he can know certainly whether or not he has really believed. The mellowness of the teaching in them is not to be confused with vagueness of belief or with theological indecision. All of these epistles draw a sharp line between truth and falsehood, between righteousness and unrighteousness, between light and darkness, and between love and hatred. They demand that the Christian place himself on one side of the line or on the other. "He that hath the Son hath the life; he that hath not the Son of God hath not the life" (I John 5:12). They presuppose a clear and perfected revelation of eternal life in Christ that constitutes the standard of truth and that must be accepted or rejected. The obligations and consequences of its acceptance are sketched so that believers may be able to say, "We have passed from death unto life."

Against the rise of heresies and errors these later epistles present a solid front. They are not solely polemic, however, but they are constructive in their presentation of the teaching of the gospel. Maturity of thought and holiness of life are their objectives, not simply argument over a point of tradition. They were written not just to win a debate, but to aid and develop the Christian so that he might keep himself, and that the evil one might not lay hold of him (5:18).

FOR FURTHER READING

II Peter and Jude

See also the literature under I Peter.

Green, Michael. *The Second Epistle of Peter and the Epistle of Jude* in *The Tyndale New Testament Commentaries*. Grand Rapids, Mich.: Wm. B. Eerdmans Publishing Company, 1968. Pp. 192.

Kelly, John Norman Davidson. *A Commentary on the Epistles of Peter and Jude*. London: A. & C. Black, 1969.

Mayor, Joseph B. *The Epistle of Jude and the Second Epistle of Peter*. London: Macmillan & Company, Ltd., 1907. Pp. 239.

Wand, John W. C. *The General Epistles of St. Peter and St. Jude*. London: Methuen & Company, 1934. Pp. 234.

I, II, III John

There are very few separate commentaries on the Johannine Epistles. Consult the volumes in the standard sets that deal with these epistles, and also the general works on John such as those of A. T. Robertson and W. H. Griffith Thomas.

Bruce, F. F. *The Epistles of John: Introduction, Exposition, and Notes*. Grand Rapids, Mich.: Wm. B. Eerdmans Publishing Company, 1979.

Candlish, R. S. *The First Epistle of John*. Grand Rapids, Mich.: Zondervan Publishing House, 1952. Pp. 577.

Marshall, I. Howard. *The Epistles of John* in *The New International Commentary on the New Testament*. Grand Rapids, Mich.: Wm. B. Eerdmans Publishing Company, 1978. Pp. xvii, 274.

Westcott, B. F. *The Epistles of John*. Third Edition. Grand Rapids, Mich.: Wm. B. Eerdmans Publishing Company, 1950. Pp. lvi, 378. Greek text.

CHAPTER 22

THE EXPECTANT CHURCH:
REVELATION

BACKGROUND

THE book of Revelation closes the canon and the history of the New Testament. Irrespective of whether or not it was the last in order to be written, it is final in its thought, for it embodies the expectation of a church that had been launched in the world as an institution, and that was eagerly awaiting the consummation of its mission.

Revelation is unique in many ways. It is the only book of the New Testament that is completely devoted to prophecy. Practically all of its imagery is related to figures that appear in the Old Testament prophetical books, and a large part of its content is predictive, dealing with the future. The author stated explicitly that the messenger who brought him the last vision had come from "the Lord, the God of the spirits of the prophets, [who] sent his angel to show unto his servants the things which must shortly come to pass" (Rev. 22:6), and in the following verse he spoke of "the prophecy of this book."

Revelation belongs to the category of apocalyptic literature. Apocalyptic literature was usually produced in times of persecution and oppression as a means of encouraging those who were suffering for their faith. It was characterized (1) by an intense despair of present circumstances and an equally intense hope of divine intervention in the future; (2) by the use of symbolic language, dreams, and visions; (3) by the introduction of celestial and demonic powers as messengers and agents in the progress of God's purpose; (4) by the prediction of a catastrophic judgment of the wicked and

381

Albrecht Dürer's famous woodcut "The Apocalypse: the Four Horsemen"

of a supernatural deliverance for the righteous; and (5) frequently by the pseudonymous ascription of the writing to a prominent character of biblical history, such as Ezra (II Esdras) or Enoch (The Book of Enoch). The book of Revelation possesses most of these characteristics, except that the author declares his name, and assumes that he is known, not as a past celebrity, but as a present participant in the affairs of those whom he addressed.

The conditions under which the book was written may fairly be deduced from a study of its content. It was addressed to seven churches of the province of Asia, which had been in existence for a considerable period of time, and in which there had been spiritual development and decline. In the letters to these churches are hints either that persecution was imminent, or that it had already begun. The church at Smyrna was "about to suffer," and "have tribulation ten days" (2:10). Antipas had suffered martyrdom at Pergamum (2:13). Philadelphia was to be exempted from "the hour of trial" (3:10). Even if these passages are interpreted in terms of future events, the atmosphere of Revelation bespeaks hostility and oppression. In the main body of the book famine, war, pestilence, economic pressure, and persecution are regarded as the ordinary phenomena of its setting.

There is little doubt that imperial Rome formed the model for the power of the state that Revelation depicted as the enemy of Christianity. The beast that had "authority over every tribe and people and tongue and nation" (13:7) had its counterpart in the universal rule of Rome under the Caesars. The "mark" that men would be compelled to carry in order to buy or sell (13:16–17) was the term used for the imperial seal that was stamped on wills, contracts, bills of sale, and other documents to give them legal standing.[1] The harlot, called Babylon the Great, drunken with the blood of saints and of martyrs, was seated on seven mountains (17:9), the number of hills in Rome. Whether or not the Apocalypse should be finally interpreted in terms of Rome, it was certainly applied to Rome when it was first read by Christians.

Two schools of thought prevail concerning the time and circumstances for which it was written. One group assigns it to the days of Nero, when the burning of Rome evoked persecution of Christians. This opinion is substantiated chiefly by two considerations. If John the son of Zebedee wrote Revelation, as well as the Gospel and epistles that are attributed to him, the radical differences in language and style between the two could be explained better if Revelation was an early effort, written when his command of Greek was still imperfect, while the Gospel and the epistles were written at a later date when he had gained in proficiency. Again, it has been suggested that the mystic number six hundred and sixty-six (13:18) is the sum total of the numerical values of the Hebrew letters that spell *Neron Kesar*, and therefore the personage described in the chapter must be Nero.

---

1. G. A. Deissmann, *Bible Studies*. Authorized Translation by Alexander Grieve (Edinburgh: T. & T. Clark, 1901), pp. 240–247.

This type of reasoning seems too flimsy to warrant any fixed conclusion, especially when it has no support from external tradition.

The second possibility for dating the Apocalypse places it late in the first century in the reign of Domitian, A.D. 81 to 96. This dating has at least the advantage of explicit external evidence. Irenaeus said that John received the vision "no very long time since, but almost in our day, towards the end of Domitian's reign."[2] While there was probably no extended persecution under Domitian, his insistence that he be worshiped as deity and the increasing tyranny of his dictatorship put him in opposition to the growth of Christianity and presaged the growth of social, economic, and religious conditions such as Revelation prophesied.

Revelation, then, is a witness to the growing hostility between the church and the Roman state. It does not necessarily imply that a universal policy of persecuting Christians had been adopted, but it does make clear that there can be no compromise between a pagan state and the Christian church. The logical outcome of paganism is totalitarianism, which involves the worship of the ruler, who controls all political allegiance, all economic resources, all religious observances, and all personal worship. The tolerance that Rome extended to the early church passed into suspicion as Paul and other Christian preachers were brought to trial by the Jewish leaders, and then the suspicion deepened into contempt and hatred. By the end of the first century Christians found themselves on the defensive everywhere. They were realizing the truth of the words of Jesus: "If ye were of the world, the world would love its own: but because ye are not of the world, but I chose you out of the world, therefore the world hateth you" (John 15:19).

Revelation was written as an encouragement for the churches that were feeling this growing hostility and as a warning to the careless and negligent Christians who were tempted to lapse into an easy conformity to the world. It was the last voice of a closing century.

The author, according to his own testimony, was named John, and was an eyewitness of the things that he saw (Rev. 1:1–2). He was on Patmos, a rocky island off the coast of Greece, where he had been incarcerated because of his faith (1:9). While there, he was given the vision that he described, and was ordered to transmit it to the seven churches of Asia (1:10), with which he was familiar.

Some of the Greek in the Apocalypse seems awkward and even ungrammatical. One should remember that the author was attempting to put into human language scenes that could not be described in ordinary terms, and consequently his grammar and vocabulary both proved inadequate.

---

2. Irenaeus *Against Heresies* V.xxx.3.

The island of Patmos

Furthermore, he was probably of Aramaic descent, and may have had difficulty in expressing himself smoothly in Greek. If in writing the Gospel and the epistles he had the aid of a skilled amanuensis, but wrote the Apocalypse himself, some of the differences could easily be explained.

Revelation is interpretative. It contains no less than four hundred allusions to the Old Testament, although no direct citation can be found. Its imagery and its program are related to Old Testament prophecy, and they connect its meaning with the trends of the new dispensation. Revelation gives an estimate of the spiritual temper of church life through the judgment on the seven churches of Asia. The sequence of visions that follows, by whatever system it is interpreted, is a picture of the ultimate consummation of God's purpose. However strange its symbolism may be, it is the one book of the New Testament that gives any organized forecast of the future.

INTERPRETATIONS

There are four main schools of interpretation of the book of Revelation among modern expositors.

The Preterist School

The Preterist school holds that the symbolism of Revelation relates only to the events of the day in which it was written. All the imagery of the seals and trumpets and vials has no bearing on the future. The writer was simply expressing his moral indignation concerning the abuses of his own day when he spoke of future judgment. This is the view of the majority of liberal scholars, such as R. H. Charles and C. C. Torrey. It has the advantage of connecting Revelation with the thought and historical events of the day in which it was written, but it makes no allowance for any element of predictive prophecy.

The Idealist School

The Idealist view, which is often closely allied with the Preterist school, considers Revelation to be only a symbolic picture of the enduring struggle between good and evil, and between Christianity and paganism. It holds that its symbols cannot be identified as historic events either in the past or in the future; they are simply trends or ideals. So Raymond Calkins says:

> We understand now what the word "revelation" means. It does not mean a revelation of the future mysteries of the end of the world, the millennium, or the Day of Judgment. Neither does it mean primarily a revelation of the glories of Heaven or the blessedness of the re-deemed. Rather it means a revelation of the infinite God, mighty to save; an uncovering for the consolation and inspiration of God's people of the all-conquering power of an omnipotent Saviour. . . .[3]

The Idealistic method of interpretation has the advantage of focusing the attention of the reader on the ethical and spiritual truth of Revelation rather than on the debatable aspects of its symbolism. On the other hand, it tends to undervalue that symbolism as a vehicle of predictive prophecy. Its "spiritualization" strips the Apocalypse of all predictive value, and dissociates it from any definite historical consummation. Judgment day, according to this theory, comes whenever a great moral issue is decided; it is not a final climax in which a supernatural Christ ascends a visible throne.

The Historicist School

The Historicist interpretation holds that Revelation outlines in symbolic form the entire course of history of the church from Pentecost to the advent of Christ. The symbols portray in sequence the great events that have taken place—that is, the seals are the breakup of the Roman empire, the eruption of locusts from the bottomless pit is a picture of the Moham-

---

3. Raymond Calkins, *The Social Message of the Book of Revelation* (New York: The Woman's Press, n.d.), p. 13.

The great altar of Zeus at Pergamum as reconstructed by R. Bohn. The temple of Athena Polias and that of Augustus are seen in the background.

medan invasions, etc.[4] Each major event in the history of Christendom was thus broadly foreshadowed, so that Revelation becomes a calendar of events written in advance. Most of the Reformers, insofar as they dealt with Revelation at all, the majority of the older commentaries, and many modern evangelical preachers such as A. J. Gordon and A. B. Simpson, held this view. It has at least ostensible warrant in the phrase of Revelation 4:1: "Come up hither, and I will show thee the things which must come to pass hereafter." The Historicist view is more literal than the Idealist view, but its advocates have never achieved unanimity on what the individual symbols mean. Even among the Historicists there are nearly as many interpretations as there are commentators. Not all of them can be right; and since there is such wide divergence among them, there is at least the possibility that the methods may be wrong.

The Futurist School

The Futurists hold that the first three chapters of Revelation apply either to the day in which the book was written, or else that the seven churches of Asia represent seven eras of church history, bridging the gap from the apostolic age to the return of Christ. To this extent the Futurists are Historicists. Beginning with the phrase in 4:1, "the things which must come to pass hereafter," they contend that the remainder of the book deals

---

4. See the collected comments quoted in John Peter Lange, *The Revelation of John.* Translated from the German by Evalina Moore; enlarged and edited by E. R. Craven (New York: Scribner, Armstrong & Company, 1874), pp. 2, 7, 215.

with events that will take place in a period called the "Great Tribulation," just preceding the return of Christ, and variously estimated from three and a half to seven years in length. The events of the Apocalypse, relegated to this period, are interpreted as literally as possible, and are thus regarded as wholly future to the existing era. Expositors like J. A. Seiss, C. I. Scofield, A. C. Gaebelein, and H. A. Ironside are Futurists.

The Millennial Views

A somewhat different approach to Revelation from the eschatological rather than from the historical standpoint gives three other divisions of thought, based on varying interpretations of the twentieth chapter. The crux of the interpretation is centered in the question as to whether the "thousand years" are to be considered as literal or figurative, and as to whether they precede or follow the second coming of Christ.

The *postmillennial* view regards the thousand years as probably figuratively of a long interval that precedes the coming of Christ. At the beginning of the period the triumph of the gospel over the nations will introduce the reign of peace that will endure until Christ returns in final judgment.

The *amillennial* view holds that the millennium is nonexistent as a literal period, or possibly that it represents the intermediate state of the dead. Christ may return at any time, when he will judge the world and usher in the eternal state of bliss for the righteous, the new heavens and the new earth.

The *premillennial* view holds that Christ will return personally to initiate his kingdom; that the righteous dead will be raised; that they will reign personally with him on the earth for one thousand years; that subsequent to his reign there will be a final rebellion that shall be immediately suppressed, the wicked dead will be judged, and the eternal state will begin.

There is no necessary correlation between these views and the chronological interpretations previously defined. Generally, the millennial question is treated seriously only by Historicists and Futurists, since the Preterists and Idealists would not regard the "thousand years" as anything

Silver denarius of Tiberius. This was a common coin in New Testament times and is referred to as a "penny" (Luke 20:24).

more than another symbol. The following diagram will illustrate the different methods of interpretation:

INTERPRETATIONS OF REVELATION

Revelation	1–3	4–19	20–22
Preterist	Historic Churches	Symbolic of Contemporary Conditions	Symbolic of Heaven and Victory
Idealist	Historic Churches	Symbolic of Conflict of Good and Evil	Victory of Good
Historicist	Literal Historic Churches	Symbolic of Events of History: Fall of Rome, Mohammedanism, Papacy, Reformation	Final Judgment Millennium (?) Eternal State
Futurist	Seven Stages of Church History	Future Tribulation Concentrated Judgments on Apostate Church and on Antichrist Coming of Christ	Millennial Kingdom Judgment of Wicked Dead Eternal State
Postmillennial	Historic Churches	Generally Historicist	Victory of Christianity over the World
Amillennial	Historic Churches	Generally Historicist	Coming of Christ Judgment Eternal State
Premillennial	Historic Churches Representative of Historical Stages	Generally Futurist	Literal Millennial Reign Judgment of Great White Throne New Jerusalem

CONTENT

The real key to the interpretation of Revelation does not lie in any one of these theories, however great its merits, but in the structure of the book itself as it presents the person of Christ. The very title of the book, "The Revelation of Jesus Christ, which God gave him to show unto his servants, even the things which must shortly come to pass. . . ," indicates that the central theme is the person of Christ as he reveals the future. There is some question as to whether "the Revelation of Jesus Christ" means the revelation of his person, or the revelation that he gave, which came from him. If the former interpretation of the title sets the topic, then Revelation is an unfolding of the person of Christ as he is related to the future. If the second interpretation is taken, the main topic is the program of the future as mediated through Christ. Either is grammatically possible,[5] and either makes Christ the central figure of the book. Much controversy might have been averted had expositors approached Revelation from the neutral standpoint of its literary structure, making their eschatology dependent on their Christology.

A second clue to the content of the book appears in the form that the author's own experience has given to it. Obviously the book consists of a series of visions, each of which is a unit in itself. While there are many small units introduced by the phrase "and I saw" (5:1, 11; 6:1, 9; etc.), the four main divisions are introduced by the phrase "in the Spirit" (1:10; 4:2; 17:1–3; 21:9–10). These divisions are of varied content and unequal length, but they give a unitary organization to the book. Together with the opening prologue and the closing epilogue, they divide Revelation into six sections.

Several series of sevens appear throughout the book. There are seven churches (2:1, 8, 12, 18; 3:1, 7, 14), seven spirits of God (4:5), seven seals (6:1, 3, 5, 7, 9, 12; 8:1), seven trumpets (8:6, 7, 8, 10, 12; 9:1, 13; 11:15), seven thunders (10:3), seven bowls (16:1, 2, 4, 8, 10, 12, 17), seven major personages (12:1, 3, 5, 7; 13:1, 11; 14:1), and seven beatitudes (1:3; 14:13; 16:15; 19:9; 20:6; 22:7, 14). Some of these are part of the literary structure of the book and are listed in close sequence, and some are not. The use of the number seven indicates a design of thought that makes Revelation more than a haphazard accumulation of weird symbols.

Other numerical combinations or series appear sporadically. There are twenty-four elders (4:4), four living creatures (4:6), four horsemen (6:1–8), four angels (9:14), one hundred and forty-four thousand in companies of the redeemed (7:4; 14:1), twelve gates of the city of God (21:12), twelve

---

5. The former interprets *hē apokalypsis tou Iēsou Christou* as an objective genitive; the latter, as a subjective genitive.

foundations (21:14), twelve kinds of fruit in the tree of life (22:2), and various others.

One other phrase deserves mention. In 4:5, 8:5, 11:19, and 16:18 "there were lightnings, and voices, and thunders." The last three of these occur respectively at the termini of a series of judgments. Are they repeated, or are they a clue that the three judgments are coterminous, and consequently that each judgment is simply an intensification of its predecessor?

OUTLINE

Using the clues thus provided by the book itself, the following outline is proffered:

THE REVELATION OF JESUS CHRIST
in "the things shortly to come to pass"

I. Prologue: Christ Communicating	1:1–8
Title	1:1
Agent	1:2
Commendation	1:3
Destination	1:4–5a
Dedication	1:5b–6
Motto	1:7
Imprimatur	1:8
II. Vision I: Christ in the Church: The Living One	1:9–3:22
Place: Patmos	
The Portrait	1:9–20
The Messages	2:1–3:22
To Ephesus	2:1–7
To Smyrna	2:8–11
To Pergamum	2:12–17
To Thyatira	2:18–29
To Sardis	3:1–6
To Philadelphia	3:7–13
To Laodicea	3:14–22
III. Vision II: Christ in the Cosmos: The Redeemer	4:1–16:21
Place: Heaven	
The Scene in Heaven	4:1–5:14
The Seven Seals	6:1–8:5
The white horse	6:1–2
The red horse	6:3–4
The black horse	6:5–6
The pale horse	6:7–8

EVALUATION

A final interpretation of Revelation is not within the province of this book, but a few observations may prove helpful to the student.

Revelation is written in the style of apocalyptic literature, but it differs sharply from the general body of such writings in that it has a definite author who names himself and has a definite destination in view. His chief purpose is not to predict in advance all the details of church history, but to show the general trends of the present age and their consummation in the personal return of Christ. The threefold declaration and challenge of the epilogue: "I come quickly" (22:7, 12, 20), reiterates Christ's promise to his churches (2:16; 3:11), and makes the entire book a warning to the world and an encouragement to God's people.

Certain unities pervade the entire book. The person of Christ is dominant, first as the glorified figure with blazing countenance, clothed in white, who inspects, reproves, and counsels the church. As the claimant of the right to administer judgment under the authority of the sealed roll, he is the Lamb, who has acquired this right by his redemptive work (5:4–7). In the execution of judgment he is the Conqueror, riding on a white horse like a Roman general in triumphal procession (19:11), with the title "KING OF KINGS, AND LORD OF LORDS" (19:16). In the consummation of all things he is the Bridegroom of his people (19:7; 21:9), again called the Lamb because of his redemption.

The chronological arrangement of Revelation is disputable. The Historicist sees in it a complete calendar of all major events from the time of its writing until the coming of Christ, the Futurist relegates most of the book to a seven-year period immediately preceding the appearing of the Lord, and the Preterist and the Idealist regard it as independent of all chronology. Certain facts, however, seem plain. The letters in the first three chapters were directed to the existing churches in the cities of Asia so that they relate to a period contemporary with the author. The opening of the vision in the fourth chapter assigned it to "the things which must come to pass hereafter" (4:1), beginning with the writer's day and continuing indefinitely. The last two visions of the book have not yet been fulfilled, and apply to the end time yet to come. Revelation thus belongs partly to the past, partly to the present, and partly to the future.

The last two sections parallel each other. The former, Revelation 17:1 to 21:8, is occupied with the doom of the evil world-system represented by the harlot, Babylon. The second, Revelation 21:9 to 22:5, describes the final appearance of the bride of Christ, the New Jerusalem. The parallelism of these two sections involves both similarity and contrast. Both are introduced by one of "the seven angels that had the seven bowls." The heavenly messenger invited the seer to view the scene with the words, "Come hither." Each represents the terminus of a purpose: one, the end of the trend away from God; the other, the end of redemption.

The parallelism of contrast is equally plain. The former section introduces a harlot; the latter, a bride. The former sets the scene in a wilderness (17:3); the latter, on a mountain (21:10). The former says that on the harlot are written names of blasphemy (17:3); the latter states that the names of the twelve tribes and the twelve apostles are inscribed on the Holy City (21:12, 14). The former presents Babylon, the city of corruption and judgment (17:6); the latter describes the New Jerusalem, which comes down out of heaven pure and chaste (21:10). The former perishes in dire judgment; the latter endures in eternal light. The former is cursed; the latter is blessed.

The book of Revelation gives a divine perspective on history. However its symbols may be interpreted in detail, its overall outlook is that of divine holiness that sees both the virtues and the shortcomings of the churches, and the doom and hope of the world. The message to the churches is sent by the Figure who moves in the midst of the golden lampstands; the scene for the administration of judgment centers around the throne of God (4:2–19:5); and the final judgment is pronounced from the selfsame throne (20:11). In the description of the new heavens and the new earth the throne is still central (22:1) as the source of the river of life. This emphasis on the throne makes clear the concept of the sovereignty of God in Revelation, and his eternal rulership in the affairs of men.

The dominant optimism of the book is countered by its glaring picture of evil. It contains no hint that the world at large will improve with the passing of time, nor that at the end all men will have turned to God in repentance and faith. It depicts the last civilization as highly prosperous, culturally advanced, and utterly godless (18:1–5). The last act of organized humanity is an armed rebellion against God and his Christ (20:7–10). In no other book of the Bible, unless it be in the words of Jesus, is the final doom of sin more terribly drawn (20:15).

To the modern man of the latter part of the twentieth century, the Apocalypse seems less apocalyptic than it did to his father and his grandfather. The mysterious references to images that talked (13:15), to making fire come down out of heaven (13:13), to economic control of large populations (13:16–17), to compulsory obedience to a synthetic religion (13:14), to the wholesale devastation of the earth by elemental changes in the sea and by physical changes in the heat of the sun (16:3, 8), the summoning of all the kings of the earth to do battle (16:14), the leadership of the nations vested in one or two persons (19:19–20), and the complete collapse of the center of civilization in "one hour" (18:18–20) are not outside the reach of possibility at the present time. In many respects, the Apocalypse is the most modern book in existence.

With the final promise, "I come quickly," the New Testament ends. God spoke by the law and the prophets; he has spoken again by his Son, who "now once at the end of the ages hath been manifested to put away sin by the sacrifice of himself" (Heb. 9:26). One greater revelation is yet to come when he "shall appear a second time, apart from sin, to them that wait for him, unto salvation" (9:28). To that revelation and that victory the book of Revelation points.

FOR FURTHER READING

INTRODUCTORY STUDY

Moffatt, James. *The Historical New Testament*. New York: Charles Scribner's Sons, 1901. Pp. xxvii, 726. See especially pp. 459–465.

Orr, James. "Revelation of John," in *International Standard Bible Encyclopedia*, IV, 2582b–2587a. Grand Rapids, Mich.: Wm. B. Eerdmans Publishing Company, 1949.

COMMENTARIES

Blanchard, Charles A. *Light on the Last Days*. Chicago: Bible Institute Colportage Association, 1913. Pp. 149. Simple and clear.

Beckwith, Isbon T. *The Apocalypse of John*. New York: The Macmillan Company, 1919. Pp. xv, 794. Greek text; thorough discussions.

Dean, J. T. *The Book of the Revelation*. Edinburgh: T. & T. Clark, 1915. Pp. 191.

Hendriksen, William. *More than Conquerors: An Interpretation of the Book of Revelation*. Grand Rapids, Mich.: Baker Book House, 1939.

Hengstenberg, Ernest W. *The Revelation of St. John*. Translated by Patrick Fairbairn. Two volumes. Edinburgh: T. & T. Clark, 1851.

Ladd, George E. *A Commentary on the Revelation of John*. Grand Rapids, Mich.: Wm. B. Eerdmans Publishing Company, 1972. Pp. 308.

Lang, G. H. *The Revelation of Jesus Christ: Select Studies*. London: Oliphants, Ltd., 1945. Pp. 420.

Lenski, R. C. H. *The Interpretation of St. John's Revelation*. Columbus, Ohio: The Wartburg Press, 1935. Pp. 686.

Moorehead, Wm. G. *Studies in the Book of Revelation*. New York: Fleming H. Revell Company, 1908. Pp. 153.

Mounce, Robert H. *The Book of Revelation* in *The New International Commentary on the New Testament*. Grand Rapids, Mich.: Wm. B. Eerdmans Publishing Company, 1977. Pp. 426.

Newell, Wm. R. *The Book of the Revelation*. Chicago: Moody Press, n.d. Pp. 404.

Seiss, J. A. *Lectures on the Apocalypse*. Tenth Edition. One volume. Grand Rapids, Mich.: Zondervan Publishing House, 1951.

Swete, Henry B. *The Apocalypse of St. John*. Grand Rapids, Mich.: Wm. B. Eerdmans Publishing Company, 1951. Pp. 338. Advanced commentary with Greek text.

Tenney, Merrill C. *Interpreting Revelation*. Grand Rapids, Mich.: Wm. B. Eerdmans Publishing Company, 1957. Pp. 220.

THE SEVEN CHURCHES

Crosby, Howard. *The Seven Churches of Asia*. New York: Funk and Wagnalls Company, 1890. Pp. 168. Popular devotional work.

Morgan, G. Campbell. *A First Century Message to Twentieth Century Christians*. Third Edition. New York: Fleming H. Revell Company, 1902. Pp. 217.

Ramsay, William. *The Letters to the Seven Churches of Asia and Their Place in the Plan of the Apocalypse*. New York: George H. Doran Company, 1905. Pp. 446. Unexcelled for historical and archaeological background of the seven churches.

Stott, John R. W. *What Christ Thinks of the Church: Insights from Revelation 2–3*. Grand Rapids, Mich.: Wm. B. Eerdmans Publishing Company, 1958. Pp. 128.

Trench, Richard C. *Commentary on the Epistles to the Seven Churches in Asia*. Fourth Edition, Revised. London: Kegan Paul, Trench, & Company, 1886. Pp. 249.

THE MILLENNIUM

The following works represent widely differing viewpoints, and are labeled accordingly.

Boettner, Loraine. *The Millennium*. Philadelphia: The Presbyterian and Reformed Publishing Company, 1958. Pp. 380. Postmillennial position.

Case, Shirley J. *The Millennial Hope*. Chicago: University of Chicago Press, 1918. Pp. ix, 253. Utterly rationalistic; dismisses any possibility of a millennium.

Clouse, R. G., Editor. *The Millennium: Four Views*. Downers Grove, Ill.: Inter-Varsity Press, 1977.

Feinberg, Charles. *Premillennialism or Amillennialism?* Grand Rapids, Mich.: Zondervan Publishing House, 1936. Pp. 250. Premillennial and dispensational.

Hoekema, Anthony A. *The Bible and the Future*, Grand Rapids, Mich.: Wm. B. Eerdmans Publishing Company, 1979. Pp. xi, 343. Amillennial.

Kellogg, Samuel H. *Are Premillennialists Right?* New Edition. New York: Fleming H. Revell Company, 1903. Pp. 128. Premillennial.

Kromminga, D. H. *The Millennium in the Church.* Grand Rapids, Mich.: Wm. B. Eerdmans Publishing Company, 1945. Pp. 359. Historical survey.

_____. *The Millennium.* Grand Rapids, Mich.: Wm. B. Eerdmans Publishing Company, 1948. Pp. 121. Covenantal Premillenarianism.

Walvoord, John F. *The Millennial Kingdom.* Findlay, Ohio: Dunham Publishing Company, 1959. Pp. 373. Premillennial, dispensational.

PART V

THE CANON AND TEXT OF THE NEW TESTAMENT

CHAPTER 23

THE CANON OF THE NEW
TESTAMENT

At the close of the first century the books that made up the New Testament had reached their destinations. Not all of them were known to all Christians at first; on the contrary, it is quite probable that some early Christians did not see all of the Gospels, nor all of Paul's letters, nor all of the other epistles before the end of the century. Furthermore, many of the apocryphal Gospels, Acts, and epistles were circulated during the second century and were accepted by some groups; otherwise they would not have survived at all. By what criteria were some accepted and others rejected? By what principles were the four Gospels, Acts, the thirteen epistles of Paul, the General Epistles, and Revelation brought together to make the New Testament, while others of almost equal age were excluded? These questions constitute the problem of the New Testament canon.

DEFINITION

The word "canon" is derived from the Greek *kanōn*, which meant a "reed," and then a "rod" or "bar," which, because it was used for measuring, came to mean metaphorically "a standard." In grammar it meant a rule of procedure; in chronology, a table of dates; and in literature, a list of works that would correctly be attributed to a given author. Thus "the canon of Plato" refers to the list of treatises that can be ascribed to Plato as genuinely his.

Literary canons are important, because only the genuine works of an author can reveal his thought, and the inclusion of spurious writings in the list would warp or misrepresent the principles that he wished to state. In like fashion, if the canon of the New Testament cannot be established with any degree of accuracy, its authority will be uncertain and there can be no fixed standard for faith and life.

Contrary to the principle used with most literature, the canon of the New Testament cannot be settled solely on the question of authorship. Nine different men wrote the books in it, nor is there any special reason why only those nine should have been chosen. There is no assignable explanation why Philip, for instance, should not have been inspired to write a Gospel as Matthew was. The criterion that makes all of these works canonical is certainly not uniformity of human authorship. Nevertheless, if it could be shown that any of the books of the New Testament was falsely attributed to the person whose name it bears, its place in the canon would be endangered.

The canon cannot be determined wholly by the church's acceptance of the books. Some were widely and readily received, a few were hesitantly accepted by certain churches and not at all by others, and some were not mentioned until a relatively late date, or else their right to be included in the canon was definitely disputed. Local prejudice or individual taste could influence the verdict that had come down from the churches and the writers of antiquity. Notwithstanding this fact, what one person or section of the church rejected another person or section accepted; and it was not true that those who passed judgment were so uncritical as to accept anything that struck their fancy irrespective of its inherent merits. The critique of the ancients was no less fallible than that of modern scholars. On the other hand, they had access to records and traditions that have now perished, and their testimony cannot be set aside simply because it does not belong to the twentieth century. Ecclesiastical assent to canonicity supplies corroborative evidence, though it may not in itself be decisive.

If these foregoing criteria are not sufficient, what is? The true criterion of canonicity is inspiration. "All scripture is given by inspiration of God, and *is* profitable for doctrine, for reproof, for correction, for instruction in righteousness: that the man of God may be perfect, thoroughly furnished unto all good works" (II Tim. 3:16–17, A.V.). In other words, whatever was given by inspiration of God was Scripture, and whatever did not come by inspiration of God was not Scripture, if "scripture" means the written record of the authoritative word of God.

If this criterion is adopted as final, one must answer the next question: "How is inspiration to be demonstrated?" The books of the New Testament do not all begin with the statement that they are inspired of God. Some of them deal with very ordinary affairs; others contain historical, literary, and theological puzzles that can be resolved only with difficulty. Can their inspiration be demonstrated to the satisfaction of all?

The answer to this problem is threefold. First, the inspiration of these documents may be supported by their intrinsic content. Second, their inspiration may be corroborated by their moral effect. Third, the historic testimony of the Christian church will show what value was placed on these books, even though the church did not *cause* them to be inspired or canonical.

With regard to their intrinsic content, they all have for their central subject the person and work of Jesus Christ. The Gospels are biographical, Acts recounts the historic effects of his personality, the epistles are concerned with theological and practical teachings that emanate from a consideration of him, and the Apocalypse is predictive of his relation to the future. The objection that any prominent character of antiquity could be so immortalized by a body of literature is not valid. Outside the New Testament there is no indication that Jesus Christ was considered important by the leaders and teachers of his day, and there was no natural reason why the writings concerning him should survive in the Roman world. The New Testament admits that the message about Christ was "unto Jews a stumbling block, and unto Gentiles foolishness" (I Cor. 1:23). In the eyes of his contemporaries he meant no more than any other aspirant to messiahship who had been suppressed by the government. If the literature regarding him persisted and grew powerful, there must have been something in it to produce that effect.

The message concerning the person of Christ was unique. Cults centering in individuals were not unknown in the first century, but these individuals were mythical, or else, if they were historical, their worship did not endure. This unique message centers in the books that are called "canonical." The apocryphal Gospels and Acts are more concerned with miracle-mongering than they are with teaching, and the few apocryphal epistles are mosaics of pieces taken from the acknowledged canon. In precision of narrative, in depth of teaching, and in concentration on the person of Christ, there is a discernible difference between the canonical and the noncanonical books.

In ethical and spiritual effect the canonical books are different. All literature may record human thought, some may influence it profoundly, but the books of the New Testament transform it. Their power is good proof of their inspiration. Although this test may seem to be highly subjective because it is based on human response to the written word, it is nevertheless valid. The writings of the New Testament are not only profitable reading, they are also a potent dynamic.

Their moral effect is demonstrated by their power within the Christian church. While it cannot be contended that every member of the early church possessed a pocket copy of the New Testament that he studied assiduously, it can be shown that the leaders knew it and used it. Wherever its message was proclaimed and received, the church expanded and brought with it a moral cleansing of society. Not all professing Christians from the first century onward were lily-white in character, nor was the church always free from evil. Notwithstanding these facts, between the moral standards of paganism and those of the New Testament church a great gulf was fixed. Love, purity, meekness, truth, and many other virtues, which scarcely existed in heathenism, came to life. However poorly the Christians may have followed the ideals that they possessed, they were distinct from the pagans around them because of the power of New Testament truth.

The tests of the divine message and of the moral power of these books cannot be applied successfully by a single individual in a limited sphere lest it be argued that the dynamic of the canon was only a chance effect produced by the accidental relation of time and temperament. When the internal testimony of the works themselves and the external testimony of those who knew and used them concur that these works are of God, the criteria of canonicity are made more sure.

INTERNAL TESTIMONY

The New Testament writings themselves testify to the authority of the message. The Old Testament was cited freely as "the word of God," inspired and profitable for both faith and life (e.g., II Tim. 3:15–17; II Pet. 1:20–21; Heb. 8:8; Acts 28:25). Yet along with this there was an appeal to "a word of the Lord," a reference to the teachings of Jesus (e.g., I Cor. 9:9, 13–14; I Thess. 4:15; I Cor. 7:10, 25). These two norms were regarded as divine authority for the teachings of the early church.

In addition, one can observe the appeal to divine revelation to and through commissioned messengers (namely, the apostles). Paul claimed to have been sent "not from men nor by man, but by Jesus Christ and God the Father" (Gal. 1:1), and that his message was not received from man, neither was he taught it, but he "received it by revelation from Jesus Christ" (v. 12). The gospel he preached was accepted by his hearers "not as the word of men, but as it actually is, the word of God, which is at work in you who believe" (I Thess. 2:13). Any other message than this is not from God, and a curse of some sort is called down on any who would proclaim "another gospel" or who would be disobedient to the apostolic instruction (Gal. 1:6–9; II Thess. 3:14).

Before long the authority of Paul's letters was recognized by the church. Thus a move was made toward the idea of a "canon" when it is implied that Paul's epistles were regarded on a par with "the other scriptures" (II Pet. 3:15–16).

So, along with the appeal to the Old Testament, "it may be inferred that a new living norm was shaped in the church which included in the first place the Lord and then the apostles who bore witness to the message of the Lord."[1]

EXTERNAL TESTIMONY

As observed above, the final decision on this question of the canon could not be made arbitrarily by any one person or by any local group. The distinction between canonical and noncanonical books was the product of a growing spiritual consciousness. At an early date, however, lines of discrimination were drawn and these were not merely the result of uncritical personal preference or prejudice. The church did not *determine* the canon; it *recognized* the canon. In the fullest sense no church council could create a canon, if inspiration is the essential quality of canonicity, because no group or council could breathe inspiration into works already existing. All that the councils could do was to give their opinion concerning which books were canonical and which were not, and then to let history justify or reverse their verdict.

The external witness to the existence of a New Testament canon is both informal and formal. The informal witness consists of the casual use made of the books of the New Testament by the early church fathers. Their quotations attest both the existence and the authority of the books, for nonexistent books cannot be quoted, and the manner of quoting will show whether the quotation implies authority or just passing allusion. The formal witness is found in lists or canons that had been purposely compiled as authoritative, or in the records of the councils that dealt with the question.

Quotations, of course, may be disputed since they may be so indirect that their origin is uncertain. In many instances, however, even though the quotation may be inexact, its vocabulary or content will identify it as belonging to some book that the author of the quotation must have known and used, so that it is valid for all practical purposes.

The Informal Witnesses

Probably the earliest document to quote any of the books of the New Testament was I Clement, which was itself considered canonical by some Christians. It is found in Codex Alexandrinus, included with the New Testament books. It was written from Rome to the church in Corinth, and is usually dated about A.D. 95. In it are plain allusions to Hebrews, I Corinthians, Romans, and the Gospel of Matthew.

Ignatius of Syrian Antioch (c. A.D. 116) knew all of Paul's epistles

---

1. W. G. Kümmel, *Introduction to the New Testament* (Nashville: Abingdon Press, 1975), p. 478.

and quoted Matthew, with a possible allusion to John. He considered as authorities "the prophets, but above all the gospel," and he regarded the words of the Lord (probably in oral form) as an authority alongside the Old Testament.

Polycarp of Smyrna (c. A.D. 150) was also familiar with the Pauline epistles and the Gospel of Matthew. He quoted I Peter and I John, and probably knew Acts.

The Didache, produced during the first half of the second century, used Matthew, Luke, and many other New Testament books.

The Epistle of Barnabas (c. A.D. 130) quoted Matthew, using the formal phrase "it is written"[2] to introduce the quotation. This passage "could also be adduced as evidence for the fact that a gospel writing is beginning to be assigned equal value with an OT scripture" (Kümmel).

The Shepherd of Hermas, an allegory of the early second century (c. A.D. 140), alluded to James.

Justin Martyr (c. A.D. 100 to 165), a Syrian Greek, who had been a philosopher, referred to Matthew, Mark, Luke, John, Acts, and many of the Pauline epistles. He stated that the "Memoirs of the Apostles," called Gospels, were read every Sunday in the worship of the church along with the Old Testament.[3] From Justin's statement we see that, alongside the Old Testament, a new norm (i.e., canon) begins to appear with reference to the reading of Scripture in the services of the early church. His pupil, Tatian, composed the first harmony of the Gospels, called the Diatessaron, which became a standard harmony for the church for many years.

With the age of Irenaeus, who flourished about A.D. 170, there was no question that the books of the New Testament were authoritative. The growth of Gnosticism and of kindred errors evoked a flood of apologetic literature that continued to the time of Origen (A.D. 250). The necessity of an authoritative basis for argument became apparent and the apologists turned naturally to the apostolic writings. Irenaeus used and quoted at length all four Gospels, Acts, the epistles of Paul, many of the General Epistles, and Revelation. He said that there could be only four Gospels, and that any attempt to increase or to decrease the number would be heresy. He quoted Paul more than two hundred times. In one passage he criticized Marcion for saying that Luke and the epistles of Paul were alone authentic, by which he implied that he accepted as authoritative not only those writings acknowledged by Marcion, but others as well.[4] He alluded to every book of the New Testament except Philemon and III John.

Tertullian of Carthage (c. A.D. 200) quoted from all of the New

---

2. *Epistle of Barnabas* IV.14.
3. Justin Martyr *Apology* I.66–67.
4. Irenaeus *Against Heresies* III.xii.12.

Testament except Philemon, James, II and III John. Like Irenaeus, he quoted not simply for illustrations, but as proof of truth. By recognizing for the church "the complete instrument of each testament," he made plain that there is "an Old Testament" and "a New Testament."

Origen, the great Alexandrian Father who was contemporary with Tertullian (c. A.D. 185 to 250), not only was acquainted with the church of his own city, but had traveled extensively in Rome, Antioch, Caesarea, and Jerusalem. He divided the sacred books into two classes, the *homologoumena*, which were undoubtedly genuine and which were accepted by all the churches, and the *antilegomena*, which were disputed and not accepted by all the churches. The former included the Gospels, thirteen epistles of Paul, I Peter, I John, Acts, and the Apocalypse. The latter consisted of Hebrews, II Peter, II and III John, James, and Jude. In the same class he placed Barnabas, the Shepherd of Hermas, the Didache, and the Gospel of Hebrews. On some occasions he used many of these as Scripture, so that he did not draw the lines of the canon as closely as they were drawn later.

In the Nicene period, Eusebius of Caesarea (c. A.D. 265 to 340) followed Origen's lead.[5] He placed in the category of accepted books the Gospels, fourteen epistles of Paul (including Hebrews), I Peter, the Acts, I John, and Revelation. Among the disputed books were James, Jude, II Peter, and II and III John. He rejected flatly the Acts of Paul, the Revelation of Peter, the Shepherd of Hermas, and others, and drew a sharp line between the canonical and apocryphal works.

These men who were leaders of the church, and others who are not mentioned here, spoke for the most part for themselves. Their judgment may not have been infallible, but they were by no means uncritical recipients of unreliable rumor. While they did not agree unanimously on the canonicity of all the books of the New Testament, they show very fairly that a canon had begun to be formed in their day, and that some books were accepted without hesitation while others were regarded as dubious.

The Formal Lists or Canons

The list of New Testament books known or accepted by individual churches or leaders may be deduced from the quotations and statements that appear in the works of the early Fathers. Such lists, however, were unofficial, and were not always representative of anything more than private taste or opinion. Sometimes they reflected general practice, but quite often they reflected the canon of one locality, or of one church, or of one man.

The first known canon to be adopted consciously by any sizable unitary

---

5. Eusebius *Historia Ecclesiae* III.iii.25.

group of people was the Canon of Marcion, which appeared about A.D. 140. Marcion was a native of Sinope in Pontus, where his father was a bishop. He was so anti-Judaic that he repudiated the whole Old Testament and sought to establish a canon of the New Testament that would be free from Jewish influences. He selected Luke for his Gospel, though he rejected the first two chapters containing the account of the virgin birth, and used ten epistles of Paul, excluding the Pastorals and Hebrews. His list began with Galatians and was followed by I and II Corinthians, Romans, I and II Thessalonians, Ephesians (which he called Laodiceans), Colossians, Philippians, and Philemon.

The Canon of Marcion produced a violent reaction in the church. The fact that he rejected certain books showed that they had been regarded as authoritative in his day, and his opponents flew to their defense. Irenaeus attacked him, and Tertullian wrote five books against his errors. Marcion's arbitrary organization of a canon showed (1) that the books he included must have been regarded as indisputably authentic, and (2) that those he rejected were accepted as canonical by the masses at large.

A second list of great importance was the Muratorian Canon, named for the Italian historian and librarian who first found it in the Ambrosian Library at Milan. The manuscript itself is not older than the seventh century, but its content probably belongs to the last third of the second century, about A.D. 170.[6] Since the manuscript is only a fragment of a larger work, it is not complete. It begins in the middle of a sentence, and the first book mentioned is Luke, which the fragment calls the third Gospel. Matthew and Mark almost certainly preceded Luke in this list; John follows with an unmistakable reference to the First Epistle. Acts, I and II Corinthians, Ephesians, Philippians, Colossians, Galatians, I and II Thessalonians, Romans, Philemon, Titus, I and II Timothy, Jude, II and III John, and Revelation were also included. The writer of the Muratorian fragment rejected the epistles of Paul to the Laodiceans and to the Alexandrians, and, while he put the Revelation of Peter in the same "acknowledged" class as the Revelation of John, he was dubious about it, for he said, "Some of you do not think that it should be read publicly in the church." He did not mention James or Hebrews, nor the Petrine epistles. Perhaps he was ignorant of them, though it seems hardly possible that he should have overlooked Hebrews when Clement of Rome quoted it freely.

An African list of the fourth century (c. A.D. 360), written by an unknown person, included the four Gospels, thirteen epistles of Paul,

---

6. For a full discussion of the Muratorian Canon, see C. R. Gregory, *Canon and Text of the New Testament* (New York: Charles Scribner's Sons, 1912), pp. 129–133. The Latin text is given in A. Souter's *The Text and Canon of the New Testament* (New York: Charles Scribner's Sons, 1923), pp. 208–211.

Acts, Revelation, three epistles of John, of which the writer acknowledged only one, and two of Peter, of which he allowed only one to be genuine.

The "Festal Letter" of Athanasius (A.D. 367)[7] distinguishes sharply between "God-inspired Scripture . . . handed down to our fathers by those who were eyewitnesses and servants of the word from the beginning" and the "so-called secret writings" of heretics. Athanasius' list comprised the four Gospels, Acts, James, I and II Peter, I, II, and III John, Jude, Romans, I and II Corinthians, Galatians, Ephesians, Philippians, Colossians, I and II Thessalonians, Hebrews, I and II Timothy, Titus, Philemon, and Revelation. "These," said Athanasius, "are springs of salvation . . . let no one add to them or take away from them."

The Church Fathers who were engaged in controversy were more positive about the veracity and reliability of the writings of the New Testament than those who quoted it simply for the edification of the faithful, for the latter accepted them without question, whereas the pagans and heretics did not do so. By the close of the fourth century public opinion had agreed quite thoroughly on the reliability and authenticity of these books.

The Councils

Formal discussion of the canon by delegates of the church meeting in official council did not take place until the close of the fourth century. The first council at which the subject was introduced was the Council of Laodicea in A.D. 363. Apparently it was not a full assembly of all the churches, but represented chiefly the region of Phrygia. The fifty-ninth canon of this council decreed that only canonical books of the New Testament should be read in the church services, but the so-called sixtieth canon, which contained a definitive list, is probably not genuine and cannot be cited as the actual ruling of the council.

The Third Council of Carthage in A.D. 397 issued a decree similar to that of the Synod of Laodicea and submitted a list of writings identical with the twenty-seven books of the present New Testament.

The Council of Hippo in A.D. 419 reiterated the same decision and the same list.

CONCLUSIONS

From the data assembled here it is evident that not all of the present books of the New Testament were known or accepted by all of the churches in the east and west during the first four centuries of the Christian era. Some, like the Gospels, were known from the earliest days; others, like Hebrews, were

---

7. A. Souter, *ibid.*, pp. 213–217.

known but were questioned because their authorship was uncertain; still others, such as II Peter or II and III John, were not mentioned at all, or their right to a place in the canon was disputed. None of these books was accepted by the churches because of ecclesiastical compulsion. The councils that discussed the canon were not held until the fourth century, by which time the New Testament had already become the Scripture of the church.

The seeming reluctance with which certain books like James, II and III John, and Jude were taken into the canon does not mean that they were spurious. Philemon, II and III John, and Jude are all so brief that they would only seldom be quoted, and furthermore they were directed to individuals whose location may have been obscure. Unlike the larger epistles that were sent to sizable churches or that were circulated throughout provinces, the smaller epistles would not come into general notice until there was a demand for them or until the persons or groups to which they belonged called them to public attention.

The variations in the canon, then, were due to local conditions and interest. They showed, however, that in spite of miracle-mongering and superstition, the churches and their leaders did not accept every manuscript that happened to bear the name of an apostle or that professed to relate previously untold history and teaching. The existing canon emerged from a large body of oral and written tradition and speculation and made its way in the churches because of its inherent authenticity and dynamic power. Important to the choices of books were at least two factors: (1) apostolic authorship was required; and (2) a writing was intended for the church as a whole—criteria reflected, for example, in the Muratorian Canon.

Three stages in the early development of the canon have been noted. First, the writings are quoted individually by authors who take the force of their witness for granted rather than making it a point of argument. Second, writers like Irenaeus and Origen, who were engaged in controversy, felt the necessity of defining their authorities, but did not appeal to any single church decision. Last came the verdict of the councils, which followed the judgment of the leaders past and present and drew an official distinction between the canonical and the apocryphal works.

This distinction appeared in the list of books in the various versions and manuscripts used by the churches. The great manuscripts Sinaiticus (Aleph) and Vaticanus (B), dating from the fourth century, originally included all of the New Testament. The Syriac version did not admit II and III John, II Peter, Jude, and Revelation into its canon until the sixth century.

A study of the various quoted books, lists, and canons of the first four centuries will show that the books most generally disputed or omitted were James, Jude, II Peter, II and III John, and Philemon. Several reasons may be advanced for the neglect of these works. James was written to the members of the Jewish Dispersion and contained little of doctrinal interest that would appeal to the speculative mind of Greek Christians. Jude, II and III John, and Philemon were all so brief that they had little content that would be of general appeal. The last three were also private or semiprivate in content, so that they may not have been put in circulation as quickly as the more extensive works of their authors. II Peter was disputed up to the time of Eusebius. It was quoted less and discussed more by the Church Fathers than any other single book of the New Testament. Jerome stated that the Fathers were hesitant to accept this epistle because its style was so different from that of I Peter.[8] Whether or not the seeming disparity between II Peter and I Peter is due wholly to a difference in amanuensis may never be settled. The fact that it was written to a group of people on the outer fringe of the Christian frontier to meet a peculiar emergency may account for the fact that the early churches had so little acquaintance with it, and for its questionable status among biblical students of the first three centuries.

Since the fourth century there have been no material changes in the recognized canon, although from the period of the Reformation to the present many individual viewpoints have been expressed. Luther virtually rejected the Epistle of James, chiefly because it did not seem to accord with the doctrine of justification by faith. Calvin was unsure of II Peter. In more recent days the pursuit of historical criticism has almost dissolved the idea of any canon by making the difference between the literature of the New Testament and the apocryphal books, and the writings of the Fathers, a difference of degree or time rather than of kind or quality. Such a conclusion would strip the New Testament of any objective authority and make any general application of its truth impossible.

The canon, then, is not the product of any one person's arbitrary judgment, nor was it set by conciliar vote. It was the outcome of the use of various writings that proved their merits and their unity by their inward dynamic. Some were recognized more slowly than others because of the smallness of their size, their remote or private destination or anonymity of authorship, or their seeming lack of applicability to the immediate ecclesiastical need. None of these factors mitigates against the inspiration of any one of these books, or against its right to its place in the authoritative word of God.

---

8. Jerome *Epistle to Hedibia* 120, Quaest. xi.

FOR FURTHER READING

Aland, Kurt. *The Problem of the New Testament Canon.* London: A. R. Mowbray, 1962.

Gregory, Caspar R. *Canon and Text of the New Testament* in *International Theological Library.* New York: Charles Scribner's Sons, 1907. Pp. vii, 509.

Riggs, J. S. "The Canon of the New Testament," in *International Standard Bible Encyclopaedia,* I, 563a–566a. Grand Rapids, Mich.: Wm. B. Eerdmans Publishing Company, 1949. See also R. P. Meye, "Canon of the New Testament," in *The International Standard Bible Encyclopedia, Fully Revised,* I, 601–606. Grand Rapids, Mich.: Wm. B. Eerdmans Publishing Company, 1979.

Souter, Alexander. *The Text and Canon of the New Testament.* New York: Charles Scribner's Sons, 1923. Pp. x, 254. For the canon, see pp. 146–254. Bibliography.

Stanton, V. H. "New Testament Canon," in Hastings' *Dictionary of the Bible,* III, 529b–542b. New York: Charles Scribner's Sons, 1902. Good bibliography.

von Campenhausen, Hans. *The Formation of the Christian Bible.* Philadelphia: Fortress Press, 1972.

Westcott, B. F. *General Survey of the History of the Canon of the New Testament.* Seventh Edition. London: Macmillan & Company, Ltd., 1896. Pp. lvi, 605.

CHAPTER 24

THE TEXT AND TRANSMISSION OF THE NEW TESTAMENT

Collecting the books of the New Testament was a slow process, of which few traces remain. The Gospels and epistles were written at different times and places, and were sent to widely separated destinations. The originals were probably written on papyrus, a thin and fragile kind of paper made from the reeds of the papyrus plant, which grew in the marshes of Egypt and the Middle East. They were inscribed by hand with pen and ink (III John 13), and were usually transmitted by messengers to the persons or churches for whom they were intended (Rom. 16:1; Eph. 6:21–22; Col. 4:7–9, 16).

It is impossible to determine when the first collections of New Testament writings were created. Copies of the Gospels and epistles must have been made and circulated at an early date. There are traces of the utterances of Jesus in the Pauline writings, though these may have been taken from oral tradition rather than from written accounts. "All [Paul's] epistles" are mentioned in II Peter (3:15–16) before the end of the first century, and they must have been published as a group, since they never appear singly in manuscript form. By the middle of the second century the Gospel of Luke had been separated from Acts and had been combined with Matthew, Mark, and John to make a fourfold life of Christ. Justin Martyr (c. 140) alluded to the "memoirs of the apostles,"[1] and Irenaeus (c. 180)

---

1. Justin Martyr *I Apology* LXVII.

ΟΤΙΟΥΚΟΙΔΑϹΙΤΩ
ΑΛΛΟΤΡΙΩΝΤΗΝ
ΦΩΝΗΝΤΑΥΤΗΝ
ΤΗΝΠΑΡΟΙΜΙΑΝ
ΕΙΠΕΝΑΥΤΟΙϹΟΙϹ ΕΚΙΝΟΙ
ΚΑΙΟΥΚΕΓΝΩϹΑΝ ΔΕ
ΤΙΝΑΛΙΝΔΕΛΑΛΕΙ
ΑΥΤΟΙϹ· ΕΙΠΕΝΟ Ι̅Ϲ̅
ΤΟΙϹΠΑΛΙΝΟϹΑΜΗ
ΑΜΗΝΛΕΓΩΥΜΙΝ
ΟΤΙΕΓΩΕΙΜΙΗΟΥ
ΡΑΤΩΝΠΡΟΒΑΤΩ
ΠΑΝΤΕϹΟϹΟΙΗΛ
ΚΛΕΠΤΑΙΕΙϹΙΝΚΑ
ΛΗϹΤΑΙΑΛΛΟΥΚΗ
ΚΟΥϹΑΝΑΥΤΩΝ
ΤΑΠΡΟΒΑΤΑΕΓΩΗ
ΕΙΜΙΗΟΥΡΑΛΙΕΜ
ΕΑΝΤΙϹΕΙϹΕΛΘΗ
ϹΩΘΗϹΕΤΑΙΚΑΙΕΙ
ϹΕΛΕΥϹΕΤΑΙΚΑΙ
ΕΞΕΛΕΥϹΕΤΑΙΚΑΙ
ΝΟΜΗΝΕΥΡΗϹΕΙ
ΟΚΛΕΠΤΗϹΟΥΚΕΡ
ΧΕΤΑΙΕΙΜΗΙΝΑ
ΚΛΕΨΗΚΑΙΘΥϹΗ
ΚΑΙΑΠΟΛΕϹΗΕΓ
ΗΛΘΟΝΙΝΑΖΩΗ
ΑΙΩΝΙΟΝΕΧΩϹΙ
ΚΑΙΠΕΡΙϹϹΟΝΕ
ΧΩϹΙΝΕΓΩΕΙΜΙ·
ΠΟΙΜΗΝΟΚΑΛΟ
ΟΠΟΙΜΗΝΟΚΑΛ
ΤΗΝΨΥΧΗΝΑΥΤΟ
ΔΙΔΩϹΙΝΥΠΕΡΤΩ
ΠΡΟΒΑΤΩΝ·ΟΛΕΜΙ
ϹΘΩΤΟϹΚΑΙΟΥΚ
ΠΟΙΜΗΝΟΥΟΥΚ
ΕϹΤΙΝΤΑΠΡΟΒΑΤΑ
ΔΙΑΘΕΩΡΙΤΟΝΛΥ
ΚΟΝΕΡΧΟΜΕΝΟΝ
ΚΑΙΑΦΙΗϹΙΝΤΑΠΡ
ΒΑΤΑΚΑΙΦΕΥΓΕΙ·
ΚΑΙΟΛΥΚΟϹΑΡΠΑ
ΖΕΙΑΥΤΑΚΑΙϹΚΟΡ
ΠΙΖΕΙΟΤΙΜΙϹΘΩ
ΤΟϹΕϹΤΙΝΚΑΙΟΥ
ΜΕΛΕΙΑΥΤΩΠΕΡΙ

ΤΩΝΠΡΟΒΑΤΩΝ·
ΕΓΩΕΙΜΙΟΠΟΙΜ
ΟΚΑΛΟϹΚΑΙΓΕΙ
ΝΩϹΚΩΤΑΕΜΑΚ
ΓΕΙΝΩϹΚΟΥϹΙΜ
ΤΑΕΜΑΚΑΘΩϹΤΙ
ΝΩϹΚΙΜΕΟΠΑΤΗΡ
ΚΑΓΩΓΙΝΩϹΚΩ
ΤΟΝΠΑΤΕΡΑΚΑΙΤΗ
ΨΥΧΗΝΜΟΥΔΙΔΩ
ΜΙΥΠΕΡΤΩΝΠΡ
ΒΑΤΩΝ·ΚΑΙΑΛΛΑ
ΠΡΟΒΑΤΑΕΧΩΑ
ΟΥΚΕϹΤΙΝΕΚΤΗ
ΑΥΛΗϹΤΑΥΤΗϹΚΑ
ΚΕΙΝΑΔΕΙΜΕΝΑ
ΓΙΝΚΑΙΤΗϹΦΩ
ΝΗϹΜΟΥΑΚΟΥϹ
ϹΙΝΚΑΙΓΕΝΗϹΕ
ΤΑΙΜΙΑΠΟΙΜΝΗ
ΕΙϹΠΟΙΜΗΝΔΙΑ
ΤΟΥΤΟΜΕΟΠΑΤΗΡ
ΑΓΑΠΑΟΤΙΕΓΩΤΙ
ΘΗΜΙΤΗΝΨΥΧΙΝ
ΜΟΥΙΝΑΠΑΛΙΝ
ΛΑΒΩΑΥΤΗΝΟΥ
ΛΙϹΗΡΕΙΑΥΤΗΝ
ΑΠΕΜΟΥΑΛΛΕΓ
ΤΙΘΗΜΙΑΥΤΗΝΑ
ΠΕΜΑΥΤΟΥ·ΕΞΟΤ
ϹΙΑΝΕΧΩΘΕΙΝΑ
ΑΥΤΗΝ·ΚΑΙΕΞΟΤ
ΑΝΕΧΩΠΑΛΙΝΛΑ
ΒΙΝΑΥΤΗΝΤΑΥΤΗ
ΤΗΝΕΝΤΟΛΗΝΕΜ
ΒΟΝΠΑΡΑΤΟΥΠΑ
ΤΡΟϹΜΟΥ·ϹΧΙϹΜΑ
ΠΑΛΙΝΕΓΕΝΕΤΟ
ΕΝΤΟΙϹΙΟΥΔΑΙΟΙ·
ΔΙΑΤΟΥϹΛΟΓΟΥϹ
ΤΟΥϹΕΛΕΓΟΝΟΥΝ
ΠΟΛΛΟΙΕΞΑΥΤΩ
ΔΑΙΜΟΝΙΟΝΕΧΕΙ
ΚΑΙΜΑΙΝΕΤΑΙΤΙ
ΑΥΤΟΥΑΚΟΥΕΤΑΙ·
ΑΛΛΟΙΔΕΕΛΕΓΟΝ·
ΤΑΥΤΑΤΑΡΗΜΑΤΑΟΥ
ΚΕϹΤΙΝΔΑΙΜΟΝΙ

mentioned the four by name.[2] Tatian (c. 170) combined them into the first harmony, the Diatessaron, which had wide vogue in the eastern church and was generally used for public reading until the beginning of the fifth century.

The remaining writings of the New Testament, commonly known as the General Epistles and Revelation, did not initially constitute a fixed group, for they do not appear in any uniform sequence in the works of the earliest Church Fathers. Gradually they were drawn into the larger collection with the others, until the New Testament as it now exists emerged in the early third century.

THE TRANSMISSION OF THE TEXT

The books of the New Testament were first reproduced either by private individuals for their own use or by professional scribes for churches and monasteries. Usually copies were made one at a time, but as the demand increased, it is likely that trained slaves transcribed a number of copies simultaneously from dictation. In the process of transcription errors crept into the manuscripts that were perpetuated by later copyists, so that a large number of variants appeared. As the copies multiplied, the variants tended to increase, but the very multiplicity of the documents enhanced the probability that the original text would be preserved in at least a few of them.

From the beginning of the second century to the close of the third the church suffered intermittent persecution from the Roman government. Christians were arrested, tried before the local judges, and condemned to death. Frequently their Scriptures were confiscated, with the result that many manuscripts were destroyed and others were damaged, making survival precarious. One Gospel manuscript of the fifth century, Codex Washingtoniensis (W), shows traces of having been copied from several different sources that may have been earlier fragments left from the devastation accompanying the persecution of Diocletian (A.D. 302–311). During this period the production of manuscripts must have been irregular, and probably many copies were made by persons who had little learning or skill in writing. The major divergences in the readings of the New Testament text date from the period before Constantine, and may reflect the stress and confusion prevailing in the Christian world.

With the cessation of persecution after the victory of Constantine and the virtual adoption of Christianity as the state religion in A.D. 313,

---

2. Irenaeus *Against Heresies* III.xi.7.

Section of the Gospel of John (10:5b–21a) from the Codex Sinaiticus.

Christians began to prepare the scriptural text for public use. Constantine himself ordered that fifty copies of the Bible be made and distributed to the larger churches in the cities of the empire. These "authorized editions" doubtlessly became the archetypes for many lesser manuscripts, while others that may have been even more ancient were reproduced in monasteries and in smaller communities. From the fourth to the twelfth century the New Testament was published either in portions such as the Gospels or Pauline epistles, or occasionally in complete volumes called *pandects*.

In this process new materials were employed for writing. Papyrus was too frail for use in public services or in monastery libraries. The scribes generally used *vellum*, thin sheets of calfskin, or *parchment*, manufactured from sheepskin. From the time of Constantine almost to the age of printing these materials prevailed; paper was unknown until a relatively late date.

Despite the mediocre ability and limited knowledge of many scribes, the text that they produced was surprisingly accurate. Available manuscripts for copying were often defective. Carelessness and prejudice occasionally affected a scribe's judgment in altering or "correcting" the original. On the other hand, some of the scribes whose names are known from their signatures were phenomenally accurate, and show by their painstaking exactness that they endeavored to follow faithfully their archetype. While none of them was infallible, few deliberately altered or falsified the text.

THE SOURCES OF THE TEXT

In spite of the numerous possibilities for error, the New Testament is probably the most trustworthy piece of writing that has survived from antiquity. There are greater resources for reconstructing its text than for any document of the classic age. One small piece of papyrus, the Rylands Fragment of John, may have been written within fifty years of the lifetime of the Gospel's author, while the Chester Beatty papyri, originally containing a large part of the New Testament, were produced about A.D. 250. By contrast, the dialogues of Plato, the works of the Greek dramatists, and the poems of Virgil have come down through copies that are very few in number, and that may be separated from their originals by as many as 1400 years. It is not unlikely that a first-century papyrus of some Gospel or epistle may yet be discovered that will carry the written text back to the second generation of the Christian church.

For the purpose of reconstructing the text of the New Testament, five different types of sources are presently available. The first and most important of these comprises the manuscripts, which are the Greek texts that have been preserved from remote antiquity. The Rylands Fragment mentioned above, a single piece of papyrus about an inch and a half square, the Chester Beatty papyri, containing portions of the Gospels, Acts, the epistles of Paul, and Revelation, and the Bodmer Papyrus of John date from the third century or earlier. The most ancient extensive manuscripts are Aleph, or Codex Sinaiticus, now in the British Museum, and B, or Codex Vaticanus, belonging to the Vatican Library in Rome. Both were written in the fourth century and may have been among the copies that Constantine ordered for the churches. Originally they contained the entire New Testament, though both have suffered the loss of some pages.

The foregoing manuscripts belong to the class known as "uncials," so named because they were written in large printed letters that seemed an inch in height. They were evidently made for public reading, and were copied quite carefully. For this reason the uncial text is generally the most reliable.

A second type of text, called "cursive," was written in a flowing hand. The letters, instead of being printed separately as in the uncial manuscripts, were connected by ligatures. Many of the cursives were used privately; others were made for public reading. Generally they belong to a later date than the uncials, beginning with the tenth century and passing out of existence in the fifteenth century, after printing was introduced into Europe. In some instances they seem to have preserved a text that parallels that of the uncial manuscripts; the majority represent the popular text of the Byzantine church.

Another source of information is provided by the numerous "versions" or translations that were made during the missionary expansion of the church. As the gospel spread westward into the Latin-speaking portion of the Roman empire, and eastward into the Aramaic settlements of the Middle East, the Scriptures were translated into Latin and Syriac. These two versions may have been produced as early as the latter half of the second century, and were consequently based on Greek manuscripts older than any that now survive. Although it is not always possible to ascertain by a translation the precise word used in the original writing, the versions afford fairly exact knowledge of the general order and content of their underlying text.

A large number of Old Latin manuscripts date from the fourth to the seventh centuries, and a few even later. There is little uniformity among them; there were almost as many versions as there were copies. Either they were produced independently of each other, or else the first translation was so freely altered and so carelessly copied that the variants multiplied rapidly. The former alternative seems more probable, for the early leaders of the western church spoke both Latin and Greek, and used their Greek Testament to a great degree for much of their studying and teaching. Some of the early manuscripts, like Codex D (Bezae) of the fifth century, were bilingual, and show that the persons who used them were more familiar with Latin than with Greek.

The proliferation of Latin translations became so confusing that Pope Damasus in A.D. 384 commissioned Jerome to produce a new standard Latin version. By means of the oldest Greek manuscripts that he could find he corrected the Latin text, and produced the Vulgate (common) version, which is still the standard Bible of the Roman church.

The Old Syriac version is represented chiefly by two manuscripts of the Gospels: the Curetonian Syriac, discovered by William Cureton in the British Museum among some manuscripts brought from a monastery in the Nitrian desert of Egypt, and the Sinaitic Syriac, which was found in 1892 by two sisters, Mrs. Agnes Lewis and Mrs. Margaret Gibson, in the monastery of St. Catherine on Mt. Sinai. The latter was a palimpsest, a manuscript that had been partially erased and rewritten. Both of these dated from the fifth century, and many of their readings resembled closely those of the Old Latin.

Along with these should be noted the Diatessaron of Tatian, the first attempted harmony of the four Gospels, dating from the late second century. A recently discovered fragment shows that it existed in Greek as well as in Syriac, and that the Syrian harmony was a translation. It was the popular version of the Eastern church until the beginning of the fifth century when Rabbula, bishop of Edessa (A.D. 411), decreed that the churches must use the four independent Gospels, known as "the Separated Ones." He sponsored the Peshitta, the Syriac Vulgate, which is the present official version of the Syrian church.

In later centuries other versions were produced, some directly from the Greek text, some from the Latin and Syriac. The Old Armenian, now known only through occasional readings appearing in the newer Armenian version, the Georgian, the Coptic, Ethiopic, and Gothic, were produced before the beginning of the seventh century. They have preserved some ancient witness to the early text, but are less valuable for purposes of study than the Latin and the Syriac. Today there are more than one thousand versions of the New Testament or parts of it, but they do not affect the essential character of the text, which has already been well settled.

A third important source for knowledge of the primitive text is the writings of the early Church Fathers, the leaders and teachers of Christianity during the first six centuries, who used the language of the New Testament freely in their sermons and books. In many cases the references were mere allusions; a large number are seemingly inexact, but identifiable; and in some instances a sufficient number of consecutive verses were quoted to show plainly what was the original text. Despite the fact that many of these "quotations" were loose, so much of the New Testament appears in the patristic writings that if the existing copies were lost, all but a few verses could be reconstructed from these works. The accord between these allusions or quotations and the readings of various manuscripts affords valuable clues for establishing the date, place of origin, and types of the text that they reproduce.

By way of example, Cyprian, a Christian preacher who lived in North Africa about A.D. 250, quoted extensively from a Latin version. His quotations agree closely with the readings of k, an Old Latin manuscript of the fourth or fifth century. The agreement shows that k contains a type of text that must have been current in North Africa in the middle of the third century, and that consequently antedated the Vulgate of Jerome.

The "lectionaries," or collections of readings used in the liturgical worship of the church, preserve some passages from the Gospels and epistles. They are of much lesser importance than the sources previously mentioned, since they are manifestly incomplete and date mostly from the ninth century or later. Because they were used for public reading of the Scriptures their uniformity was carefully guarded, and they are useful in checking the type of text the medieval church officially sanctioned.

A few scattered texts have been found written on *ostraca*, the broken pieces of pottery that served very poor people as memorandum pads. Because of their nature an extensive amount of writing could not be inscribed on them; certainly nobody could keep an entire Gospel or epistle on ostraca, to say nothing of the New Testament. They do afford an insight into the way in which popular quotations were made, and while they are more open to error than carefully prepared manuscripts, they may occasionally preserve genuine readings of contemporary texts.

During the first fourteen centuries of the present era the New Testament was kept alive by the manuscript tradition. Most of these documents were in the possession of the great central churches and monasteries or in the libraries of the wealthy men, though it is not impossible that individuals may have owned copies of the Gospels or epistles. In the fifteenth century two events occurred that greatly affected the distribution of the New Testament: the invention of printing by Johannes Gutenberg in 1437, and the capture of Constantinople by the Turks in 1453.

The fall of Constantinople brought the dissolution of the Byzantine empire, which was the last direct heir of Graeco-Roman culture. Its court had been a center of Greek learning, and its library contained the finest existing collection of classical and biblical manuscripts in the civilized world. Many of these were lost, but a large number were transferred to monasteries scattered throughout Asia Minor; others were taken by scholars who fled westward into Europe, where they reintroduced Greek learning in the schools of the western church. The resulting revival of interest in classical Greek brought with it a new familiarity with the Greek Testament, which in the West had been almost completely supplanted by the Latin version. Scholars began to collect and study these manuscripts, which had been neglected for years, and to discuss their merits.

The first book issued by Johannes Gutenberg from his press in Mainz, Germany, was the now famous Mazarin or Gutenberg Latin Bible, which appeared in 1456. The mechanical reproduction of printed text guaranteed uniformity, eliminating the possibility of widespread errors, and reduced the cost of production so that persons of ordinary means could possess copies of the Scriptures. Whereas the manuscript copies of the Greek text or of the earlier translations had been circulated by dozens, the printed copies could be distributed by hundreds. The new interest in Bible study that followed the wider dissemination of the Bible promoted the Protestant Reformation under Luther, Calvin, and their associates in the sixteenth century. Luther's German Bible was a powerful agent in awakening and enlightening his countrymen.

MODERN TRANSLATIONS

Translations of the Bible into English began before the Reformation. John Wycliffe, in 1382, published an English Bible based on the Latin text. The Old Testament was largely the work of his friend Nicholas of Hereford; the New Testament was Wycliffe's. After his death John Purvey revised it, and published it in 1388. It was circulated widely in manuscript form, but did not have the wide distribution that printed books enjoyed later.

William Tyndale, a graduate of Oxford, had probably seen Erasmus' Greek Testament, which was published in 1516. Realizing that the laity could be established in the faith only if they possessed the Scriptures in their own tongue, he undertook to make a new translation. He began his task in London, but finding too great opposition in England, he went to the Continent and finished his work abroad.

The first edition of his New Testament was published at Worms in 1525. When it was brought to England the bishops confiscated all available copies and burned them publicly. So thoroughly did they do their work that only two or three copies of the early editions have survived. A revised edition followed later in 1534; it was more widely distributed. Tyndale was burned at the stake in 1536 for heresy, but his influence has lived on. His phraseology has colored every major English translation since his day. In quick succession a number of English versions appeared. Coverdale's was based on the Latin Vulgate, compared with Tyndale's translation and that of Luther in German. "Matthew's Bible" (1537) was really the work of John Rogers, a friend of Tyndale, who used both Tyndale's and Coverdale's work. It became popular and quickly went through five editions. In 1539 it was revised by Richard Taverner.

Coverdale's Bible, or "The Great Bible," as it was called, was begun about 1536, and production was started in 1538 by Regnault, a French printer. During the Inquisition attempts were made to confiscate the sheets, but most of them were rescued, and printing was completed in London in 1539. It was authorized for use in the churches, and was so eagerly welcomed that seven printings were exhausted in three years. The Anglican prayer book still contains the Psalms according to Coverdale's translation.

The Geneva Bible of 1560 was produced through the efforts of English Protestants who were leaving to escape the rigors of repression at home. It became the Bible of the Puritans, and was the means whereby the English population came to understand the meaning of biblical doctrine.

The first of the English versions still in active use is the King James, so called because it was finished in the reign of James I of England. A number of Oxford and Cambridge scholars collaborated, using the preceding English versions as models. In 1611 the new version was presented to the public, and in half a century it became the standard Bible of England. For nearly three hundred years it has been the most popular of all English translations.

From the Greek manuscripts to the King James, Revised, American Revised, and Revised Standard Versions of the present day there is an unbroken line of descent. To be sure, there are some errors in transmission, and some uncertainties of rendering. There are not enough, however, to warrant a charge of wholesale corruption of the text, nor can it be said that the New Testament of today is far different from that of the early church. The very multiplicity of manuscripts provides checks by which errors may be detected, and the numerous versions demonstrate by their ancestry that there was a common origin. The modern English Bible is a faithful reproduction of the apostolic teachings in which the essence of the gospel was first expressed in written form.

By the mid-nineteenth century the discovery of new manuscript sources affecting the Greek text of the New Testament, and the progressive changes in English speech from the usages of the Elizabethan period called for a revision of the King James Version. In 1870 a committee including almost all of the contemporary biblical scholars in Britain and many of those in America was organized by the Anglican church. The American and British revisers worked cooperatively, though there were differences between them. The English revision was published in 1881, the American Revised Version in 1901. The differences between the two lie chiefly in the use of Jehovah for LORD, and in the elimination of some Anglicisms that would seem strange to American ears. Basically, the two versions are alike, giving as literal a rendering of their underlying text as possible. Numerous archaisms were purposely retained if in the opinion of the revisers they were intelligible to literate readers. The American revision preserved fewer of these renderings than did the English revision. Both attempted "to give to modern [1885] readers a faithful representation of the meaning of the original documents."[3]

The twentieth century has brought several more editions, undertaken for the express purpose of bringing the translation of the King James up to date. The first of these, the Revised Standard Version, was begun in 1937 by the International Council of Religious Education,[4] which included forty denominations in the United States and Canada. The version was an attempt to carry further the work of the American Revised Version, and to prepare for public and private worship a Bible that would preserve the literary values of the King James Version, incorporating at the same time whatever advances had been made in scholarship since 1900. The Revised Standard Version of the New Testament appeared in 1946; the entire Bible in 1952. Not all of its renderings have been acceptable, and in a few instances its choice of readings in the Greek text seems definitely erroneous.[5] The work purports to be a revision of the American Standard Version, and preserves much of the phraseology of its predecessors.

The second translation, the New English Bible, planned and directed by representatives of the major denominations in the British Isles, was published jointly by the Oxford and Cambridge Presses in 1961. It is not a revision of the former versions, but is a totally new production in modern English. The result of the Committee's labors is a work that is eminently readable and generally faithful to the original, though it is not absolutely literal, and occasionally resembles a paraphrase more than a translation. For purposes of study and theological discussion it is less satisfying than the other standard versions, which are more literal.

A number of other committee translations have appeared in recent years, aside from many individual translations and paraphrases. The New American Standard Bible (1963) is a more literal rendering of the Greek text, accurate in most respects, and well suited for a study text. In 1974, the New Testament segment of the New International Version was published (and the Old Testament in 1978). It is a new and fresh translation, acclaimed by many for use in both private and public reading. One of the most widely heralded efforts has been Today's English Version/Good News for Modern Man (1966, 1976), prepared and distributed by the American

---

3. Revised Version; Preface to the Edition of 1885.
4. Now known as The Division of Christian Education of the National Council of the Churches of Christ in the United States of America.
5. See Matthew 1:16, where the unique reading of the Old Syriac text was adopted as the base for translation against the almost unanimous testimony of the manuscript tradition. (Note: This reading has been replaced in the Second Edition [1971] by the reading of the best Greek texts. For discussion of this passage, see B. M. Metzger, A Textual Commentary on the Greek New Testament [United Bible Societies, 1971], pp. 2–7.)

Bible Society. It is based on the principle of translation called "dynamic-equivalence," one giving much attention to the receptor language and thus benefitting the modern reader. Most recent has been the New King James Bible (1982), an effort to conserve the essential style and content of the 1611 edition, while bringing the language up to date.

FOR FURTHER READING

Carson, D. A. *The King James Debate.* Grand Rapids: Baker Book House, 1979.

Finegan, Jack. *Encountering New Testament Manuscripts: A Working Introduction to Textual Criticism.* Grand Rapids, Mich.: Wm. B. Eerdmans Publishing Company, 1974. Pp. 203.

Greenlee, J. H. *Introduction to New Testament Textual Criticism.* Grand Rapids, Mich.: Wm. B. Eerdmans Publishing Company, 1964. Pp. 160.

Kenyon, F. G. *Handbook to the Textual Criticism of the New Testament.* London: Macmillan and Company, 1901.

Lake, Kirsopp. *The Text of the New Testament.* Sixth Edition, revised by Silva New, A. B. London: Rivingtons, 1933. Pp. 104.

Metzger, B. M. *Chapters in the History of New Testament Textual Criticism.* Grand Rapids, Mich.: Wm. B. Eerdmans Publishing Company, 1963.

———. *The Text of the New Testament: Its Transmission, Corruption and Restoration.* Second Edition. New York: Oxford University Press, 1968.

Robertson, A. T. *An Introduction to the Textual Criticism of the New Testament.* New York: Doubleday, Doran & Company, 1928.

Taylor, Vincent. *The Text of the New Testament: A Short Introduction.* London: Macmillan and Company, 1961.

APPENDIXES

THE ROMAN EMPERORS OF THE FIRST CENTURY

YEARS	NAMES	EVENTS	REFERENCES
30 B.C.– A.D. 14	Augustus	Birth of Christ	Luke 2:1
A.D. 14–37	Tiberius	Ministry and death of Jesus Christ	Luke 3:1
A.D. 37–41	Caligula		
A.D. 41–54	Claudius	Famine	Acts 11:28
		Expulsion of Jews from Rome	Acts 18:2
A.D. 54–68	Nero	Trial of Paul	Acts 25:10–12
		Persecution at Rome	Acts 27:24 II Tim. 4:16–17
A.D. 68	Galba		
A.D. 69	Otho		
A.D. 69	Vitellius		
A.D. 69–79	Vespasian	Destruction of Jerusalem	
A.D. 79–81	Titus		
A.D. 81–96	Domitian	Persecution (?)	
A.D. 96–98	Nerva		
A.D. 98–117	Trajan		

THE ROMAN PROCURATORS OF JUDEA

Years	Procurators	Relation to New Testament
5		
A.D. 6	Coponius	
10 — A.D. 10	M. Ambivius	
A.D. 13		
15 — A.D. 15	Annius Rufus	
20	Valerius Gratus	
25		
A.D. 26	*Pontius Pilate*	Crucifixion of Jesus
30		
35		
A.D. 36		
A.D. 37	Marcellus	
40	Maryllus	
A.D. 41		
45 — A.D. 44	Cuspius Fadus	
A.D. 46		
A.D. 48	Tiberius Alexander	
50	Ventidius Cumanus	
A.D. 52		
55	*M. Antonius Felix*	Trial of Paul: Acts 23–24
A.D. 59		
60	*Porcius Festus*	Trial of Paul: Acts 25–26
A.D. 61	Albinus	
65 — A.D. 65	Gessius Florus	
70	*Siege of Jerusalem*	
	Vettulenus Cerialis	
	Lucilius Bassus	
75		
80	M. Salvienus	
	Flavius Silva	
85		
A.D. 86	Pompeius Longinus	
90		

428

THE HERODIAN FAMILY

GENERATION I	GENERATION II	GENERATION III	GENERATION IV
	Son of *Doris* Antipater		
	Sons of *Mariamne* Aristobulus Alexander	Herod of Chalcis	Bernice became consort of her brother Acts 25:13
		HEROD AGRIPPA I —— King of Judea A.D. 37–44 Acts 12:1–24	HEROD AGRIPPA II Tetrarch of Chalcis and of northern territory A.D. 48–70 Acts 25:13–26:32
	Son of *Mariamne* of Simon Herod Philip (First husband of Herodias—Mark 6:17)		Drusilla married FELIX procurator of Judea A.D. 52(?)–59(?)
HEROD THE GREAT King of Judea 37–4 B.C. Matt. 2:1–19 Luke 1:5	Sons of *Malthace* HEROD ANTIPAS Tetrarch of Galilee 4 B.C.–A.D. 39 Luke 3:1; Mark 6:14ff. Luke 13:31ff.; 23:7–12	Herodias Consort of Herod Antipas Mark 6:17	Salome Matt. 14:6–11
	ARCHELAUS Ethnarch of Judea 4 B.C.–A.D. 6 Matt. 2:22		
	Son of *Cleopatra* HEROD PHILIP Tetrarch of Iturea and Trachonitis 4 B.C.–A.D. 34 Luke 3:1		

Reigning kings of New Testament note are in CAPITALS, wives and relatives by marriage are in *italics*. Other members of the house are in small letters.

429

A CHART OF THE CANONS OF THE FIRST FOUR CENTURIES

	INDIVIDUALS											CANONS				COUNCILS	
Date	95	150	150 (?)	c. 130	c. 140	c. 140	c. 170	c. 200	c. 200	c. 250	c. 315	c. 140	c. 170	c. 360	367	397	419
Source	Clement (Rome)	Polycarp	Didache	Barnabas	Hermas	Justin Martyr	Irenaeus	Clement (Alex.)	Tertullian	Origen	Eusebius	Marcion	Muratorian	Cheltenham	Athanasius	Carthage	Hippo
Matthew	O	O	O	O		O	X	O	O	O	O		X	X	X	X	X
Mark						O	X	O	O	O	X		X	X	X	X	X
Luke			O			O	X	O	O	O	X	X	X	X	X	X	X
John						X	X	O	O	O	X		X	X	X	X	X
Acts						O	X	O	O	O	X		X	X	X	X	X
Romans	O	O				O	X	X	O	O	X	X	X	X	X	X	X
I Corinthians	X	O				O	X	X	O	O	X	X	X	X	X	X	X
II Corinthians		O				O	X	X	O	O	X	X	X	X	X	X	X
Galatians		O				O	X	X	O	O	X	X	X	X	X	X	X
Ephesians		O				O	X	O	O	O	X	X	X	X	X	X	X
Philippians		O					X	X	O	O	X	X	X	X	X	X	X

	1	2	3	4	5	6	7	8	9	10	11	12	13	14
Colossians	o	o	o				o	x	x	x	x	x	x	x
I Thess.	o	o	o				o	x	x	x	x	x	x	x
II Thess.	o	o	o					x	x	x	x	x	x	x
I Timothy	o							x	x	x	x	x	x	x
II Timothy								x	?	x	?	?		x
Titus								x	x	x	x			x
Philemon								x		x				x
Hebrews	o		o		o	o	o	x	?	x	?	x	x	x
James		o	o						?					x
I Peter				x			x	x	x	x	?	x	x	x
II Peter				x			x	?	?		?	x	?	x
I John				x			x	x	x	x	?	x		x
II John				o			o		?					o
III John									?					o
Jude								o	x	o	x	x	o	x
Revelation								x	x	x	o	x	x	o

SIGNS: o denotes quotation or allusion; ? denotes that the book is mentioned as doubtful; x means that it is mentioned by name and considered authentic.

A TABLE OF ENGLISH TRANSLATIONS
OF THE NEW TESTAMENT

TRANSLATION OR EDITOR	DATE	REMARKS
Wycliffe and Purvey	1382–88	Printed in 1848.
Tyndale	1525	
Coverdale	1535	
Matthew's Bible	1537	
Taverner's Bible	1539	Revision of Matthew.
Cranmer-Coverdale	1539	"The Great Bible."
"Geneva Bible"	1557	Used by Puritans.
"Bishops' Bible"	1568	Revision of "Great Bible."
Douay, or Rheims	1582	Catholic translation.
King James Version	1611	Sometimes called "Authorized Version." Produced by committee.
Revised King James	1769	
Whitton	1745	
Wesley	1755	New Testament with Notes.
Newcome	1796	
Kneeland	1823	
Palfrey	1830	
Alford	1870	Private revision of King James by a noted English scholar.
Revised Version	1881–1885	Revision of King James Version by a company of English and American scholars.
Fenton, Farrar	1895	
Spencer	1898	Catholic.
Ballentine	1899	American vernacular.
Twentieth Century	1899–1900	Translated by about twenty anonymous scholars.
American Revised Version	1901	Similar to English Revision of 1881, with some modifications representing dissenting judgment of American Committee.
Weymouth	1903	
Moffatt	1913	
Ballantyne	1923	"Riverside New Testament."
Goodspeed	1923	Part of "American Translation of the Bible."
Montgomery	1923	"Centenary Translation."
Way	1926	Translation of Paul's Epistles and Hebrews. Sixth Edition.

Challoner-Rheims	1941	Revision of Douay Version.
Verkuyl	1945	Berkeley Version.
Revised Standard Version	1946	Produced by Committee.
Williams	1950	
Wuest: Expanded Translation of Greek New Testament	1956–1959	Explanatory paraphrase.
Amplified New Testament	1958	Explanatory paraphrase.
Phillips: The New Testament in Modern English	1958	A free paraphrase.
The New English Bible	1961	A fresh translation produced by Joint Committee.
The New American Standard Bible	1963	Revision of ARV (1901).
Good News for Modern Man	1966	American Bible Society Edition.
Jerusalem Bible	1966	Based on French translation.
The Living Bible Paraphrased	1972	Done initially for children.
New International Version	1978	New translation.
New King James Bible	1982	Modernizing of 1611 version.

GENERAL BIBLIOGRAPHY

This bibliography contains only works of general scope that can be used as primary texts; reading lists on the subjects treated in the individual chapters are found in the sections For Further Reading at the end of each chapter. Brief comments are added to some of the titles to assist the reader in his selection. Periodical literature has generally been omitted because it is not readily available in the average school library.

The Text

Aland, K., Black, M., Martini, C. M., Metzger, B. M., and Wikgren, A., Editors. *The Greek New Testament.* New York: United Bible Societies, 1975.

Aland, Kurt. *Synopsis of the Four Gospels.* New York: United Bible Societies, 1970.

————. *Synopsis Quattuor Evangeliorum: Locis parallelis evangeliorum apocryphorum et patrum adhibitis edidit.* Editio decima et recognita. Stuttgart: Deutsche Bibelstiftung, 1978.

Hodges, Z. and Farstad, A., Editors. *The Greek New Testament According to the Majority Text.* Nashville: Thomas Nelson, 1982.

Nestle, E. and Aland, K. *Novum Testamentum Graece.* Twenty-sixth Edition. New York: United Bible Societies, 1979.

Burton, E. D. and Goodspeed, E. J. *A Harmony of the Synoptic Gospels.* New York, etc.: Charles Scribner's Sons, n.d. Pp. xv, 279. Uses text of the American Standard Version.

————. *A Harmony of the Synoptic Gospels in Greek.* Chicago: University of Chicago Press, 1920.

Burton, E. D. and Stevens, W. A. *A Harmony of the Gospels for Historical Study.* Third Edition, Revised. New York: Charles Scribner's Sons, 1904. Pp. xv, 275.

Gospel Parallels: A Synopsis of the First Three Gospels. Burton H. Throckmorton, Jr., Editor. New York: Thomas Nelson and Sons, 1949.

Huck, Albert. *A Synopsis of the First Three Gospels.* Ninth Edition. Edited by Hans Lietzmann. English Edition by Frank Leslie Cross. New York: American Bible Society, 1954.

Robertson, A. T. *A Harmony of the Gospels for Students of the Life of Christ.* New York: Harper & Brothers, Publishers, 1922. Pp. xxxvii, 305.

Sparks, H. F. D. *The Johannine Synopsis of the Gospels.* New York: Harper & Row, 1974.

Thomas, R. L. and Gundry, S. N., eds. *A Harmony of the Gospels with Explanations and Essays.* New American Standard Bible text. Chicago: Moody Press, 1978.

Wieand, Albert Cassel. *A New Harmony of the Gospels—The Gospel Records of the Message and Mission of Jesus Christ.* Grand Rapids, Mich.: Wm. B. Eerdmans Publishing Company, 1953. Pp. 268. Text of Revised Standard Version. Contains many useful diagrams and maps.

COMMENTARIES

Albright, W. F. and Freedman, D. N., Editors. *The Anchor Bible.* Garden City, N.Y.: Doubleday, 1970–. Volumes 26–38 on the New Testament.

Alford, Henry. *The Greek New Testament.* New Edition. Four volumes. Boston: Lee & Shepard, 1878.

An American Commentary on the New Testament. Alvah Hovey, Editor. Philadelphia: American Baptist Publications Society, 1881–1890. Complete on the New Testament. Broadus on Matthew is exceptionally good.

The Cambridge Bible for Schools and Colleges. J. J. S. Perowne, General Editor. Cambridge: University Press, 1886–.

The Cambridge Greek Testament. J. J. S. Perowne, General Editor. Cambridge: University Press, 1894–1927. Passed through several editors after Perowne; some volumes rewritten.

Clements, R. and Black, M., Editors. *The New Century Bible.* Grand Rapids, Mich.: Wm. B. Eerdmans Publishing Company, 1980–.

Ellicott's Commentary on the Whole Bible. Ellicott, Charles J., Editor. Twelve volumes. Grand Rapids, Mich.: Zondervan Publishing House. For New Testament see Vols. VI–VIII.

The Expositor's Greek Testament. W. Robertson Nicoll, Editor. Five volumes. Grand Rapids, Mich.: Wm. B. Eerdmans Publishing Company, 1952.

The Evangelical Bible Commentary. George Allen Turner, Chairman of the Editorial Board. Grand Rapids, Mich.: Zondervan Publishing House, 1957.

Gaebelein, F., Editor. *Expositor's Bible Commentary on the New International Version.* Grand Rapids: Zondervan Publishing House, 1976–1984. Volumes 8–12 on the New Testament.

Hendriksen, William. *New Testament Commentary.* (Currently being completed by Simon Kistemaker.) Grand Rapids: Baker Book House, 1953–.

Howley, G. C. D., Editor. *The New Layman's Bible Commentary in One Volume.* Grand Rapids: Zondervan Publishing House, 1979.

Hubbard, D. and Barker, G. W., General Editors. *The Word Bible Commentaries.* Waco, Tex.: Word Books, 1982–. Volumes 33–52 on the New Testament.

The International Critical Commentary. Edited by C. A. Briggs, S. R. Driver, and A. Plummer. New York: Charles Scribner's Sons, 1896–1929. Covers all of the New Testament except Acts. Based on Greek text; critical and grammatical. Theological and critical viewpoints vary.

The Interpreter's Bible. Editors: G. A. Buttrick, W. R. Bowie, John Knox, Paul Scherer, Samuel Terrien, Nolan B. Harmon. Twelve volumes. New York and Nashville: Abingdon-Cokesbury Press, 1951. For New Testament see Vols.

VII–XII. Now fully published. An extensive recent commentary. Viewpoint of neo-orthodox theology.

Laymon, Charles, Editor. *The Interpreter's One Volume Commentary on the Bible.* Nashville: Abingdon Press, 1971.

Lenski, Richard Charles Henry. *Interpretation of St. Matthew's Gospel* [and the other books of the New Testament]. Columbus, Ohio: Lutheran Book Concern, 1932–1946. Lutheran viewpoint; strongly conservative.

Marshall, I. H., Editor. *The New International Greek Testament Commentary.* Grand Rapids, Mich: Wm. B. Eerdmans Publishing Company, 1978–.

Meyer, H. A. W. *Critical and Exegetical Commentary on the New Testament.* Translation revised and edited by Wm. P. Dickson and Frederick Crombie. Edinburgh: T. & T. Clark, 1877. Detailed comment on Greek text; exhaustive in scope.

The New Bible Commentary, Francis Davidson, Editor. Grand Rapids, Mich.: Wm. B. Eerdmans Publishing Company, 1953. Pp. 1199. For New Testament see pp. 771–1189.

The New Bible Commentary, revised. D. Guthrie and J. A. Motyer, Editors. Third edition, completely revised and reset. Grand Rapids, Mich.: Wm. B. Eerdmans Publishing Company, 1970.

The New International Commentary on the New Testament. F. F. Bruce, General Editor. Grand Rapids, Mich.: Wm. B. Eerdmans Publishing Company, 1951–. An expository commentary; viewpoint of conservative theology.

Robertson, A. T. *Word Pictures in the New Testament.* Six volumes. New York: Harper & Brothers, Publishers, 1933.

Smith, David. *The Disciple's Commentary on the New Testament.* Five volumes. London: Hodder & Stoughton, Ltd., 1928–32.

The Tyndale New Testament Commentaries. R. V. G. Tasker, General Editor. Grand Rapids, Mich.: Wm. B. Eerdmans Publishing Company, 1956–. Good quality throughout.

Vincent, Marvin R. *Word Studies in the New Testament.* Second Edition. Four volumes. Grand Rapids: Wm. B. Eerdmans Publishing Company, 1918, 1919. Old, but still useful. Does not include discoveries in the papyri.

CONCORDANCES

Englishman's Greek Concordance of the New Testament. Ninth Edition. London: Samuel Bagster and Sons, Ltd., 1903. Pp. 1020, 14, 71.

Moulton, W. F. and Geden, A. S. *A Concordance to the Greek New Testament.* Second Edition. Edinburgh: T. & T. Clark, 1899. Pp. xi, 1033.

Strong, James. *The Exhaustive Concordance of the Bible.* New York: Abingdon-Cokesbury Press, 1947.

Walker, J. B. R. *The Comprehensive Concordance to the Holy Scriptures.* New York: The Macmillan Company, 1948. Pp. vi, 957.

Young, Robert. *Analytical Concordance to the Bible.* Twenty-first American Edition. Edited by Wm. B. Stevenson. New York: Funk and Wagnalls, n.d. Grand Rapids, Mich.: Wm. B. Eerdmans Publishing Company, 1951.

DICTIONARIES AND ENCYCLOPEDIAS

Dictionary of the Bible. James Hastings, Editor. Five volumes. New York: Charles Scribner's Sons, 1902. Complete and scholarly.

Dictionary of Christ and the Gospels. James Hastings, Editor. Two volumes. New York: Charles Scribner's Sons, 1908.

Dictionary of the Apostolic Church. James Hastings, Editor. Two volumes. New York: Charles Scribner's Sons, 1915.

The International Standard Bible Encyclopedia. James Orr, General Editor. Five volumes. Grand Rapids, Mich.: Wm. B. Eerdmans Publishing Company, 1952. Predominantly conservative.

The International Standard Bible Encyclopedia, Fully Revised. Geoffrey Bromiley, General Editor. Four volumes. Grand Rapids, Mich.: Wm. B. Eerdmans Publishing Company, 1979–.

The Interpreter's Bible Dictionary. G. A. Buttrick, Editor. Four volumes and Supplement. Nashville: Abingdon Press, 1962, 1976.

Kittel, G. and Friedrich, G., Editors, *Theological Dictionary of the New Testament.* Translated by G. W. Bromiley. Ten volumes. Grand Rapids, Mich.: Wm. B. Eerdmans Publishing Company, 1964–1976.

Kittel, G. and Friedrich, G., Editors. *Theological Dictionary of the New Testament, Abridged in One Volume.* Abridged by G. W. Bromiley. Grand Rapids, Mich.: Wm. B. Eerdmans Publishing Company, 1985.

The New Bible Dictionary. J. D. Douglas, Editor. Second Revised Edition. Wheaton: Tyndale House, 1982.

The New International Dictionary of New Testament Theology. Colin Brown, General Editor. Three volumes. Grand Rapids, Mich.: Zondervan Publishing House, 1975–1978.

Unger's Bible Dictionary. Merrill F. Unger, Editor. Chicago: Moody Press, 1957.

The Westminster Dictionary of the Bible. John D. Davis, Editor. Fifth Edition Revised and Rewritten by Henry S. Gehman. Philadelphia: The Westminster Press, 1944. Inclines toward liberal critical views of the authorship of the Old Testament.

The Wycliffe Bible Encyclopedia. C. F. Pfeiffer, Vos, H. F., and Rea, J., Editors. Two volumes. Chicago: Moody Press, 1976.

The Zondervan Pictorial Bible Encyclopedia. M. C. Tenney, Editor. Five volumes. Grand Rapids, Mich.: Zondervan Publishing House, 1976.

HANDBOOKS

Alexander, David and Pat. *Eerdmans' Handbook to the Bible.* Grand Rapids, Mich.: Wm. B. Eerdmans Publishing Company, 1973; Revised Edition 1983. Pp. 680.

Arnold, Arthur O. and Hall, G. F. *A New Testament Handbook.* St. Peter, Minn.: Gustavus Adolphus College Press, 1948. Pp. 208.

Blair, E. P. *The Abingdon Bible Handbook.* Nashville: Abingdon Press, 1975.

Bruce, F. F. *New Testament History.* Garden City, N.Y.: Doubleday, 1969.

Heim, Ralph D. *Workbook for New Testament Study.* New York: The Ronald Press, 1948. Pp. 124.

Lohse, E. *The New Testament Environment.* Translated by J. E. Steely. Nashville: Abingdon Press, 1976.

Manley, G. T. *The New Bible Handbook.* London: Inter-Varsity Fellowship, 1948. Pp. xii, 433. For New Testament, see pp. 300–433.

Manson, T. W. *A Companion to the Bible.* Edinburgh: T. & T. Clark, 1942. Pp. xii, 515.

Marshall, I. Howard, Editor. *New Testament Interpretation: Essays on Principles and Methods.* Grand Rapids, Mich.: Wm. B. Eerdmans Publishing Company, 1977.

Reicke, Bo. *The New Testament Era: The World of the Bible from 500 B.C. to A.D. 100.* Translated by D. E. Green. Philadelphia: Fortress Press, 1968.

Robertson, A. T. *Syllabus for New Testament Study.* Fourth Revised and Enlarged Edition. Louisville, Ky.: Baptist World Publishing Company, 1923. Pp. 207. Contains full bibliography.

Scroggie, W. Graham. *Know Your Bible.* Vol. II: Analytical. *The New Testament.* London: Pickering & Inglis, Ltd., n.d. A systematic study of the New Testament with excellent analytical outlines.

_____. *The Unfolding Drama of Redemption.* Vols. II, III: Synthetic. London: Pickering and Inglis, Ltd., n.d. Pp. 494. Covers the Inter-Testamental Period, the Gospels, and Acts.

Tenney, M. C. *New Testament Times.* Grand Rapids, Mich.: Wm. B. Eerdmans Publishing Company, 1965. Pp. xv, 396.

Wade, G. W. *New Testament History.* Second Edition, Revised. London: Methuen & Company, Ltd., 1932. Pp. xi, 690. Liberal in viewpoint; contains large bulk of critical material. Good treatment of historical backgrounds. See pp. 1–105.

INTRODUCTION

Batey, Richard A., Editor. *New Testament Issues.* New York: Harper & Row, 1970.

Goodspeed, Edgar J. *An Introduction to the New Testament.* Chicago: The University of Chicago Press, 1937. Pp. xiii, 362. Modern critical viewpoint.

Guthrie, Donald. *New Testament Introduction.* Downers Grove, Ill.: Inter-Varsity Press, 1979. Third Edition.

Harrison, Everett F. *Introduction to the New Testament.* Second Edition. Grand Rapids, Mich.: Wm. B. Eerdmans Publishing Company, 1971. Pp. xiv, 508.

Hiebert, D. E. *An Introduction to the New Testament.* Three volumes. Revised Edition. Chicago: Moody Press, 1975–1977.

Kümmel, Werner Georg. *Introduction to the New Testament.* Translated by Howard Clark Kee. Revised Edition. Nashville: Abingdon Press, 1975.

_____. *The New Testament: The History of the Investigation of Its Problems.* Translated by S. M. Gilmour and H. C. Kee. Nashville: Abingdon Press, 1972.

Lake, Kirsopp and Silva. *An Introduction to the New Testament.* New York and London: Harper & Brothers, Publishers, 1937. Pp. x, 302.

Miller, H. S. *General Biblical Introduction.* Houghton, N.Y.: The Word-Bearer Press, 1937. Excellent, thorough treatment of the origins of the Bible.

Neill, Stephen C. *The Interpretation of the New Testament, 1861–1961.* London/New York: Oxford University Press, 1964.

Pullan, Leighton. *The Books of the New Testament.* London: Rivingtons, 1901. Pp. 300.

Salmon, George. *A Historical Introduction to the Books of the New Testament.* Ninth Edition. London: J. Murray, 1899. Pp. xxxi, 643.

Scott, Ernest Findlay. *The Literature of the New Testament.* New York: Columbia University Press, 1932. Pp. xiii, 312. A liberal introduction to the New Testament.

Thiessen, Henry C. *Introduction to the New Testament.* Grand Rapids, Mich.: Wm. B. Eerdmans Publishing Company, 1951; Revised Edition 1979. Pp. xx, 347. A consistently conservative introduction.

Zahn, Theodor B. *Introduction to the New Testament.* Translated from the third German edition; ed. by J. M. Trout, W. A. Mather, and others. Three volumes. Edinburgh: T. & T. Clark, 1909. Grand Rapids, Mich.: Kregel Publications, 1953.

ARCHAEOLOGY

Blaiklock, E. M. *Out of the Earth*. Revised and Enlarged Edition. Grand Rapids, Mich.: Wm. B. Eerdmans Publishing Company, 1961. Pp. 92.

Cobern, Camden A. *The New Archaeological Discoveries and Their Bearing upon the New Testament and upon the Life and Times of the Primitive Church*. Ninth Edition. New York: Funk and Wagnalls Company, 1929. Pp. xxxiv, 748.

Ewert, David. *From Ancient Tablets to Modern Translations: A General Introduction to the Bible*. Grand Rapids, Mich.: Zondervan Publishing House, 1983.

Finegan, Jack. *The Archaeology of the New Testament: the Life of Jesus and the Beginning of the Early Church*. Princeton: University Press, 1969.

_____. *The Archaeology of the New Testament: The Mediterranean World of the Early Christian Apostles*. Boulder, Col.: West View Press, 1981.

Finegan, J. *Discovering Israel*. Grand Rapids, Mich.: Wm. B. Eerdmans Publishing Company, 1981.

Free, J. P. *Archaeology and Bible History*. Fifth Edition, Revised. Wheaton, Ill.: Scripture Press, 1956. Pp. xviii, 398.

Milligan, George. *The New Testament Documents: Their Origin and Early History*. London: Macmillan & Company, Ltd., 1913. Pp. xvi, 322.

Moule, C. F. D. *The Birth of the New Testament*. New and Revised Edition. New York: Harper & Row, 1981.

National Geographical Society. *Everyday Life in Bible Times*. National Geographic Society, 1967.

Thompson, J. A. *The Bible and Archeology*. Grand Rapids, Mich.: Wm. B. Eerdmans Publishing Company, 1962; Third Edition, Fully Revised, 1982.

Twilley, L. D. *The Origin and Transmission of the New Testament*. Grand Rapids, Mich.: Wm. B. Eerdmans Publishing Company, 1957. Pp. 69. Excellent, brief survey of development and transmission of text.

Vos, H. F. *Archaeology of Bible Lands*. Chicago: Moody Press, 1977.

Wilkinson, J. *Jerusalem as Jesus Knew It*. London: Thames and Hudson, 1978.

Yamauchi, Edward. *The Archaeology of New Testament Cities in Western Asia Minor*. Grand Rapids, Mich.: Baker Book House, 1980.

GEOGRAPHY

Aharoni, Y. and Avi-Yonah, M. *The Macmillan Bible Atlas*. New York: Macmillan, 1977.

Baly, D. *The Geography of the Bible*. New and Revised Edition. New York: Harper & Row, 1974.

Blaiklock, E. M., Editor. *The Zondervan Pictorial Bible Atlas*. Grand Rapids, Mich.: Zondervan Publishing House, 1972.

May, H. G. *Oxford Bible Atlas*. Third Edition. New York: Oxford University Press, 1984.

Pfeiffer, C. F. and Vos, H. F. *The Wycliffe Historical Geography of Bible Lands*. Chicago: Moody Press, 1967.

Smith, George Adam. *The Historical Geography of the Holy Land*. New York: Armstrong, 1895. Pp. xxv, 692. Still a standard work.

Wright, G. E. and Filson, F. V. *The Westminster Historical Atlas to the Bible*, Philadelphia: The Westminster Press. Revised Edition 1956. Pp. 114. Archaeological and geographical data fully up to date. For the New Testament see pp. 79–117. Follows liberal critical position.

INDEX OF PERSONS

441

INDEX OF SUBJECTS

443

INDEX OF PLACES

INDEX OF TEXTS

CHRISTIANITY AT THE END OF THE 1ST CENTURY

THE TRAVELS OF ST. PAUL

FIRST MISSIONARY JOURNEY ——·——·
SECOND MISSIONARY JOURNEY ——————
THIRD MISSIONARY JOURNEY ·················
JOURNEY TO ROME – – – – –

ITALY

SALONA

DURAZZO

THESSA

BEROEA

NICOPOLIS

ROME
APPII FORUM
PUTEOLI

SYRACUSE

MELITA

HIPPO REGIUS   CARTHAGE

HADRUMITUM

M E D I T E R R A N